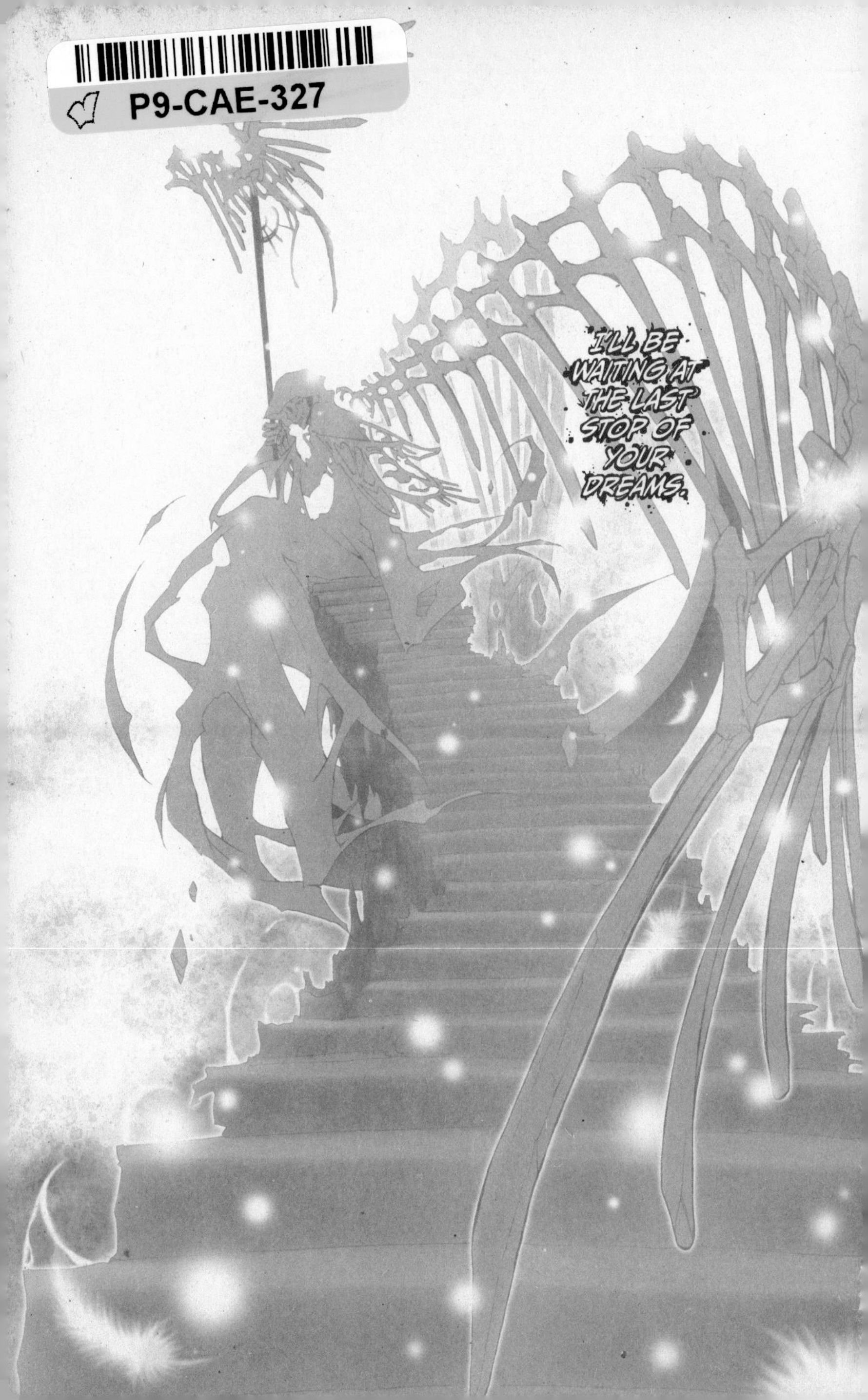
I'LL BE WAITING AT THE LAST STOP OF YOUR DREAMS.

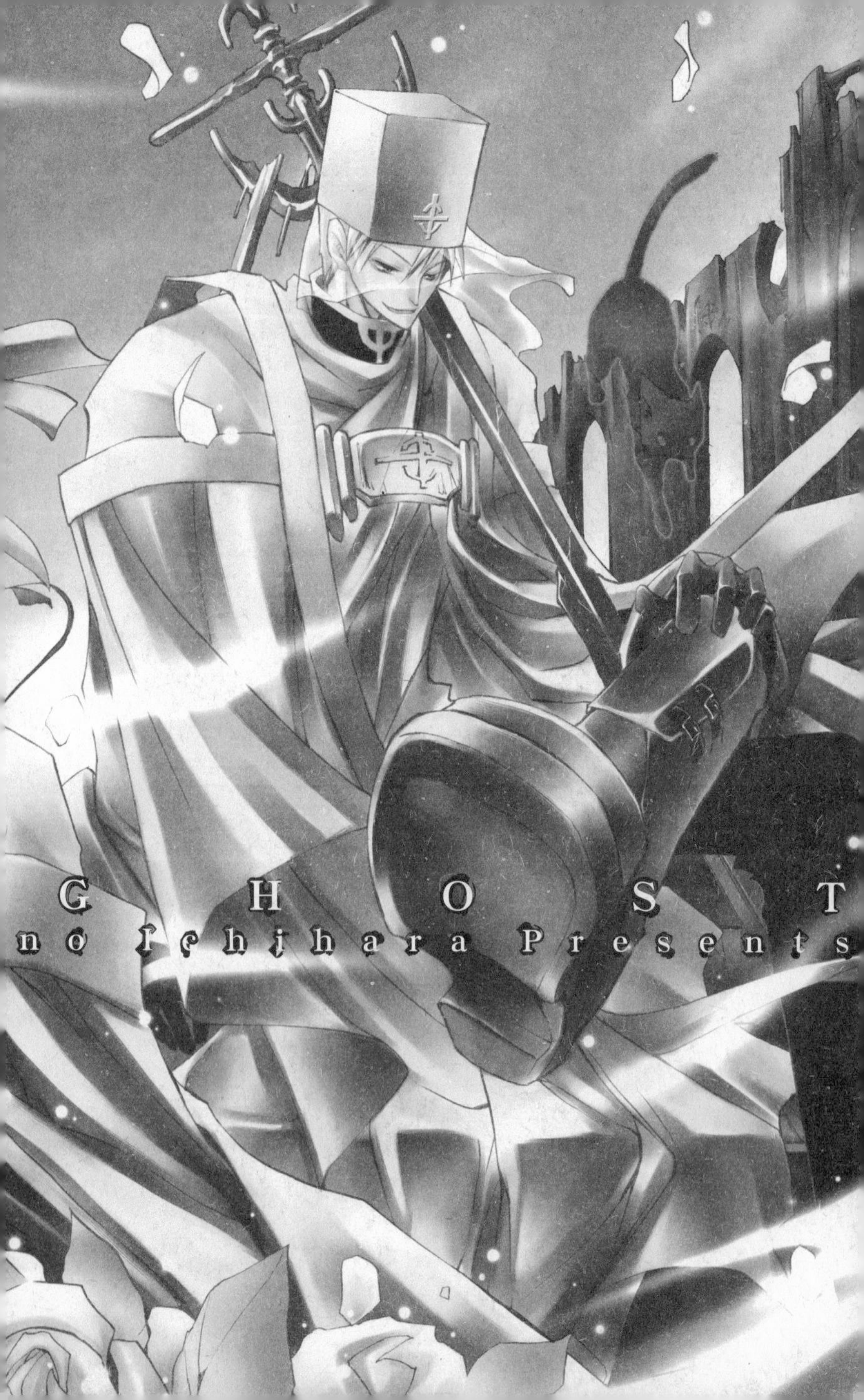
G H O S T
no Ichihara Presents

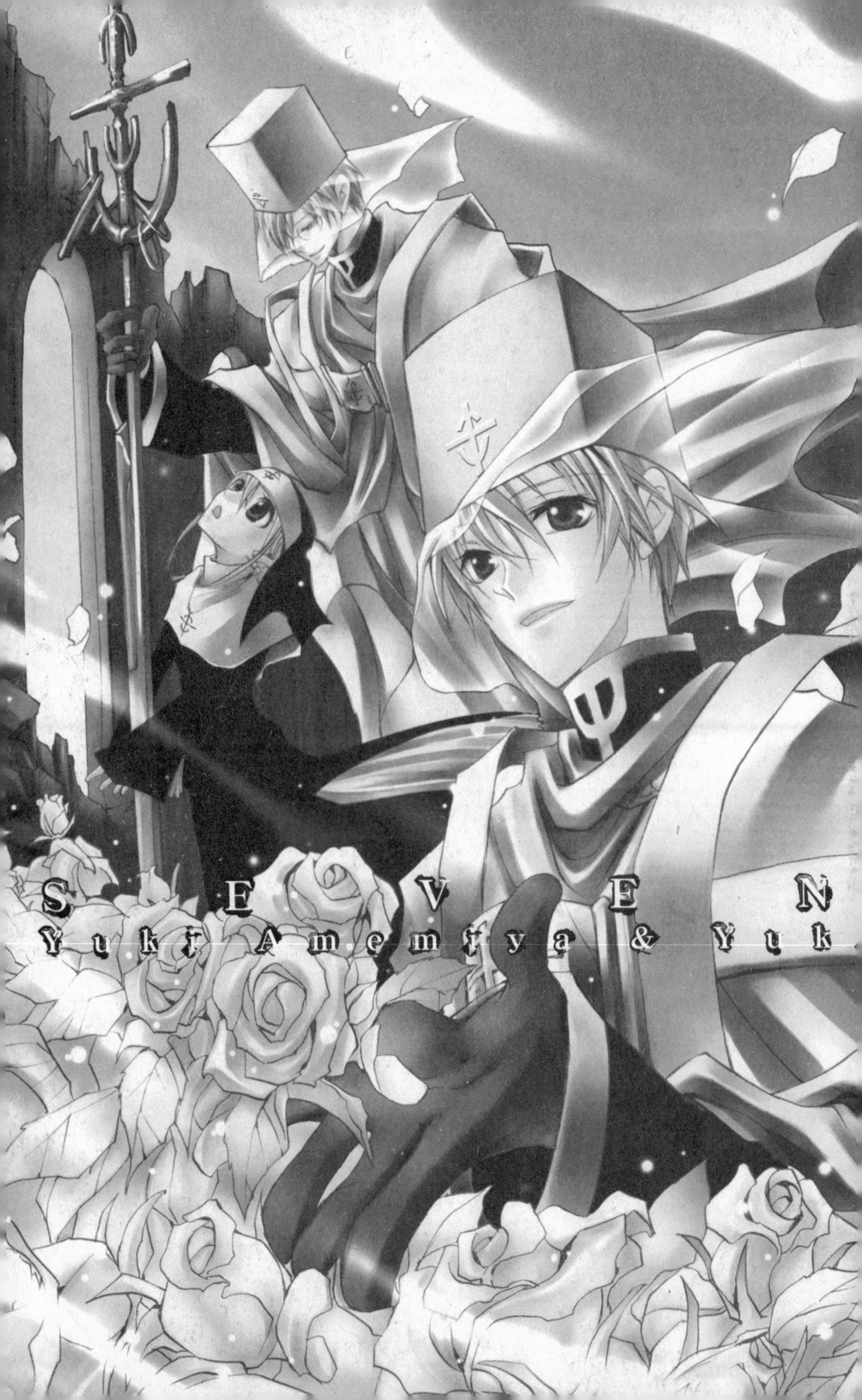
SEVEN
Yuki Amemiya & Yuk

C O N T E N T S

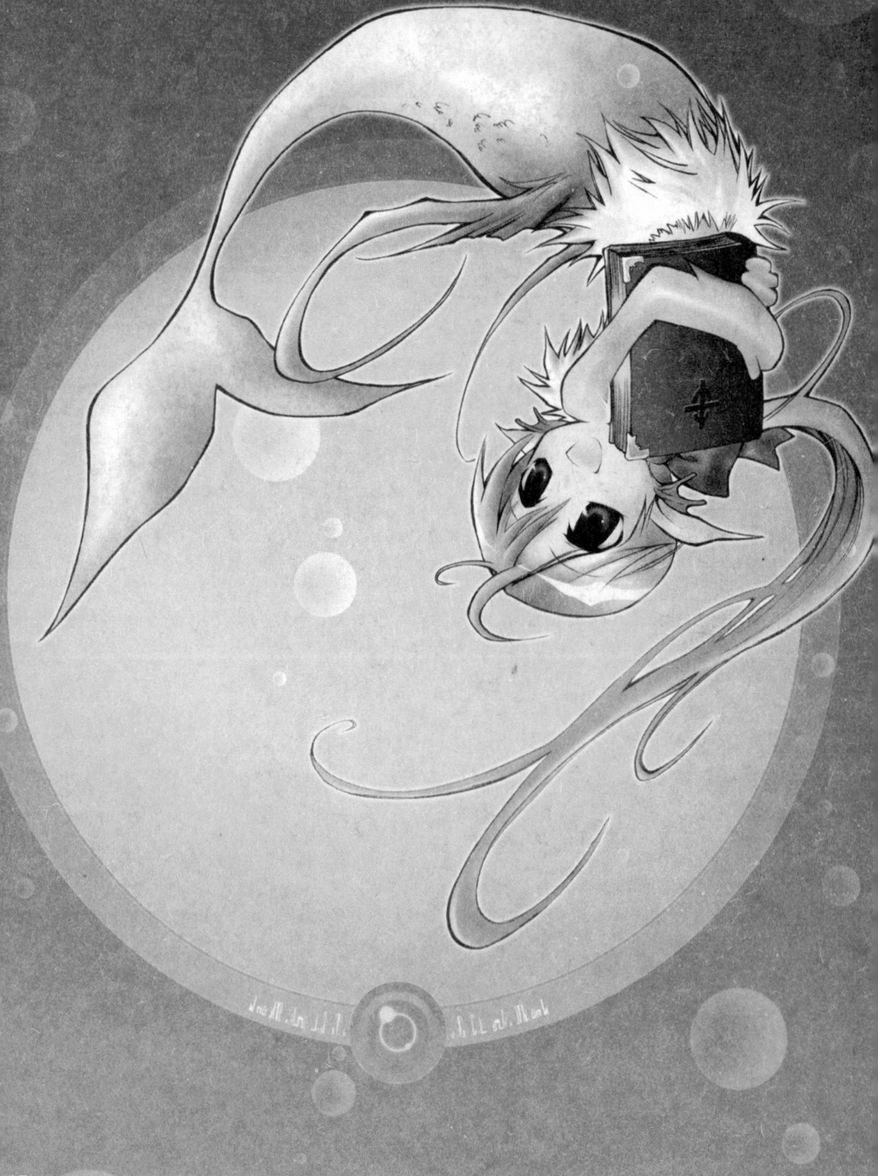

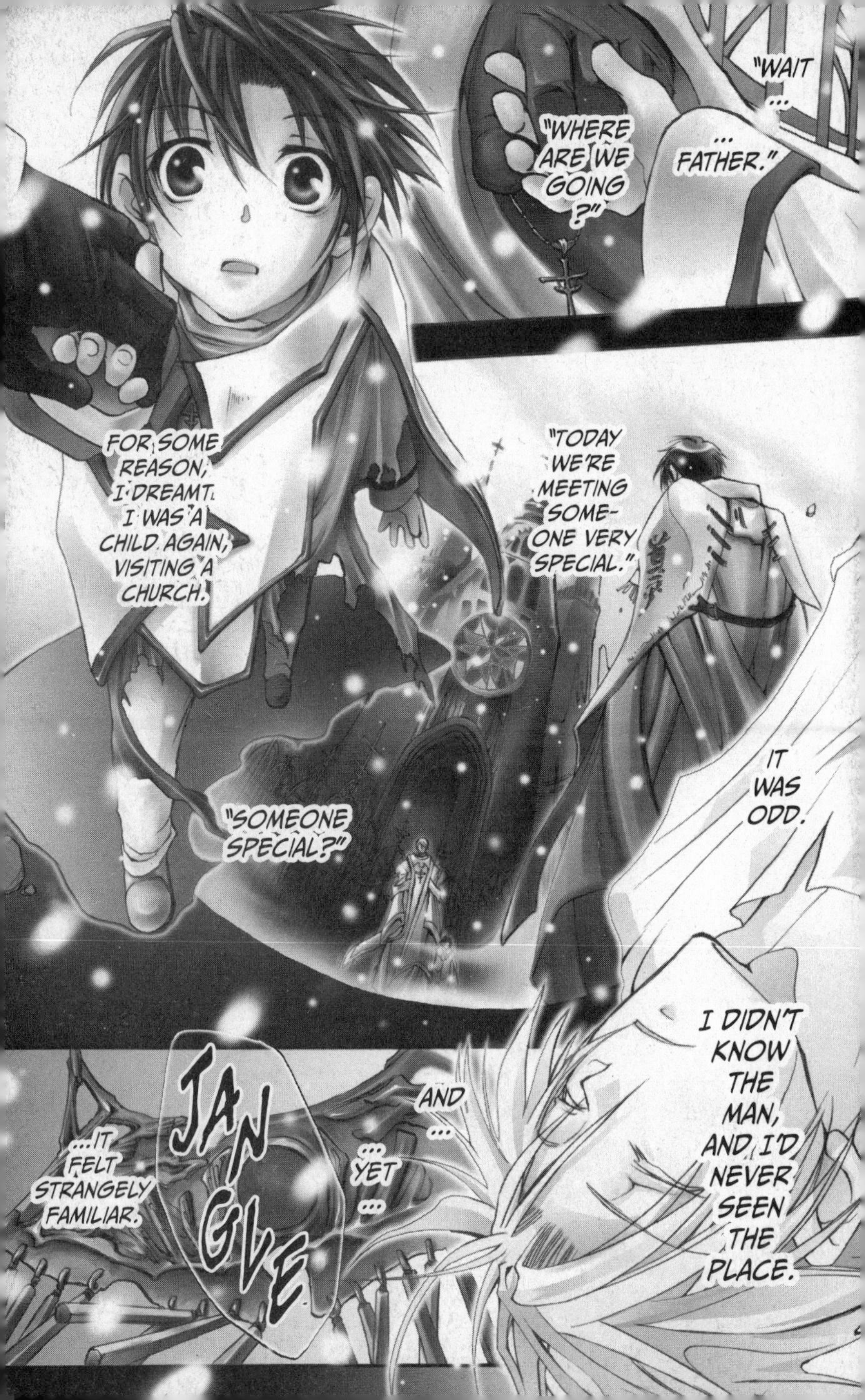

"WAIT ...
... FATHER."
"WHERE ARE WE GOING ?"
FOR SOME REASON, I DREAMT I WAS A CHILD AGAIN, VISITING A CHURCH.
"TODAY WE'RE MEETING SOME-ONE VERY SPECIAL."
"SOMEONE SPECIAL?"
IT WAS ODD.
I DIDN'T KNOW THE MAN, AND I'D NEVER SEEN THE PLACE.
AND ...
... YET ...
...IT FELT STRANGELY FAMILIAR.
JAN GLE

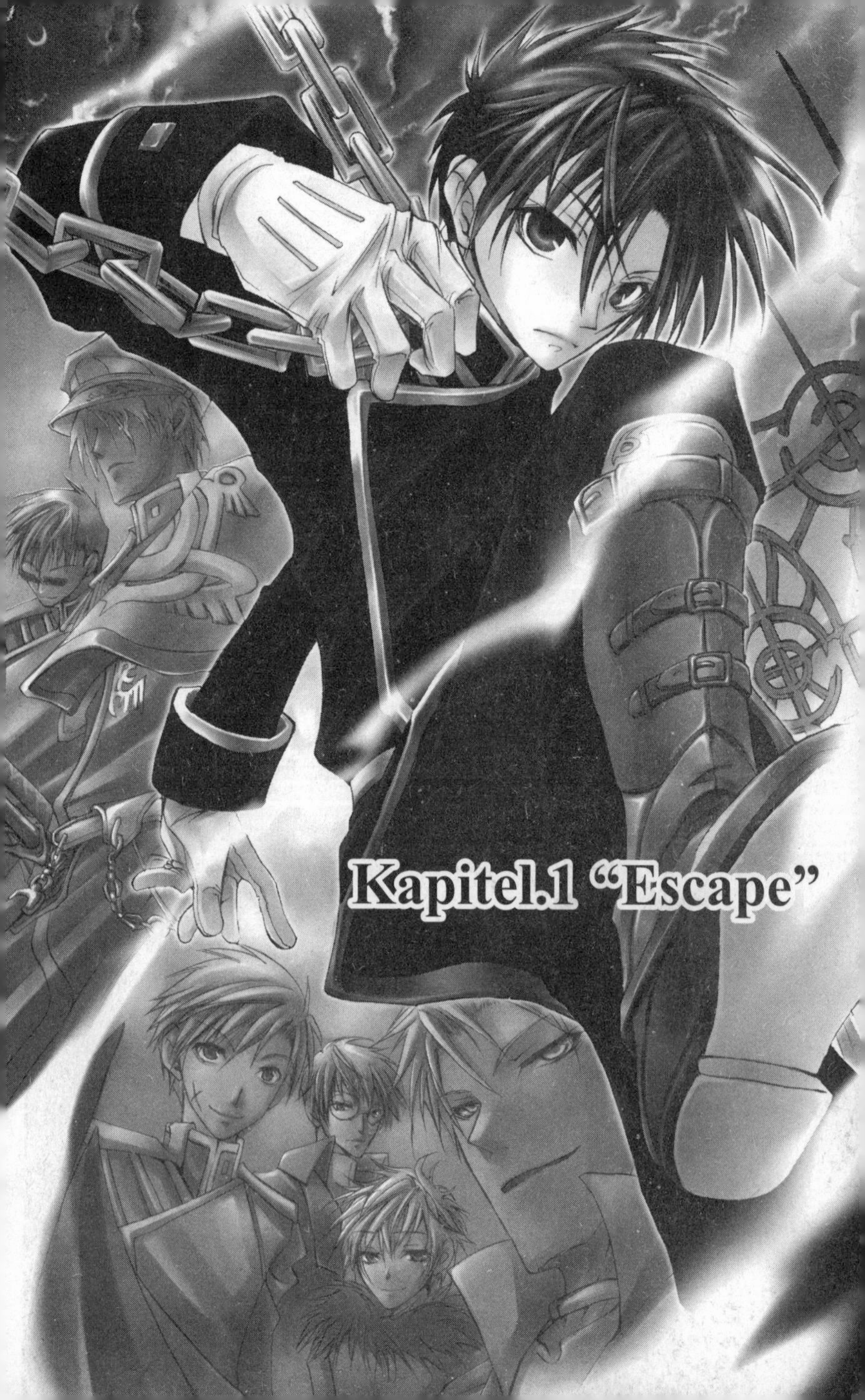
Kapitel.1 “Escape”

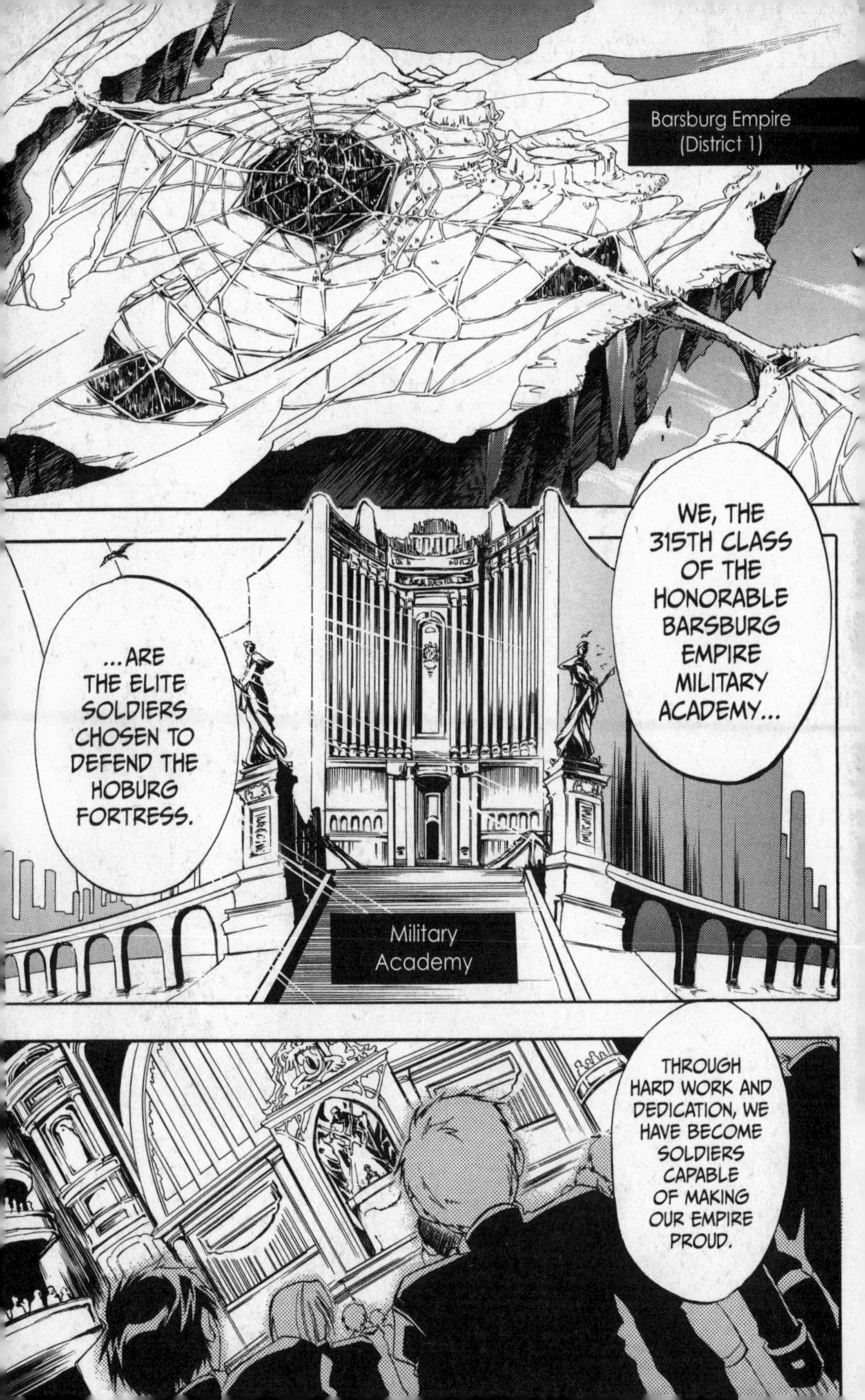
Barsburg Empire (District 1)
WE, THE 315TH CLASS OF THE HONORABLE BARSBURG EMPIRE MILITARY ACADEMY...
...ARE THE ELITE SOLDIERS CHOSEN TO DEFEND THE HOBURG FORTRESS.
Military Academy
THROUGH HARD WORK AND DEDICATION, WE HAVE BECOME SOLDIERS CAPABLE OF MAKING OUR EMPIRE PROUD.

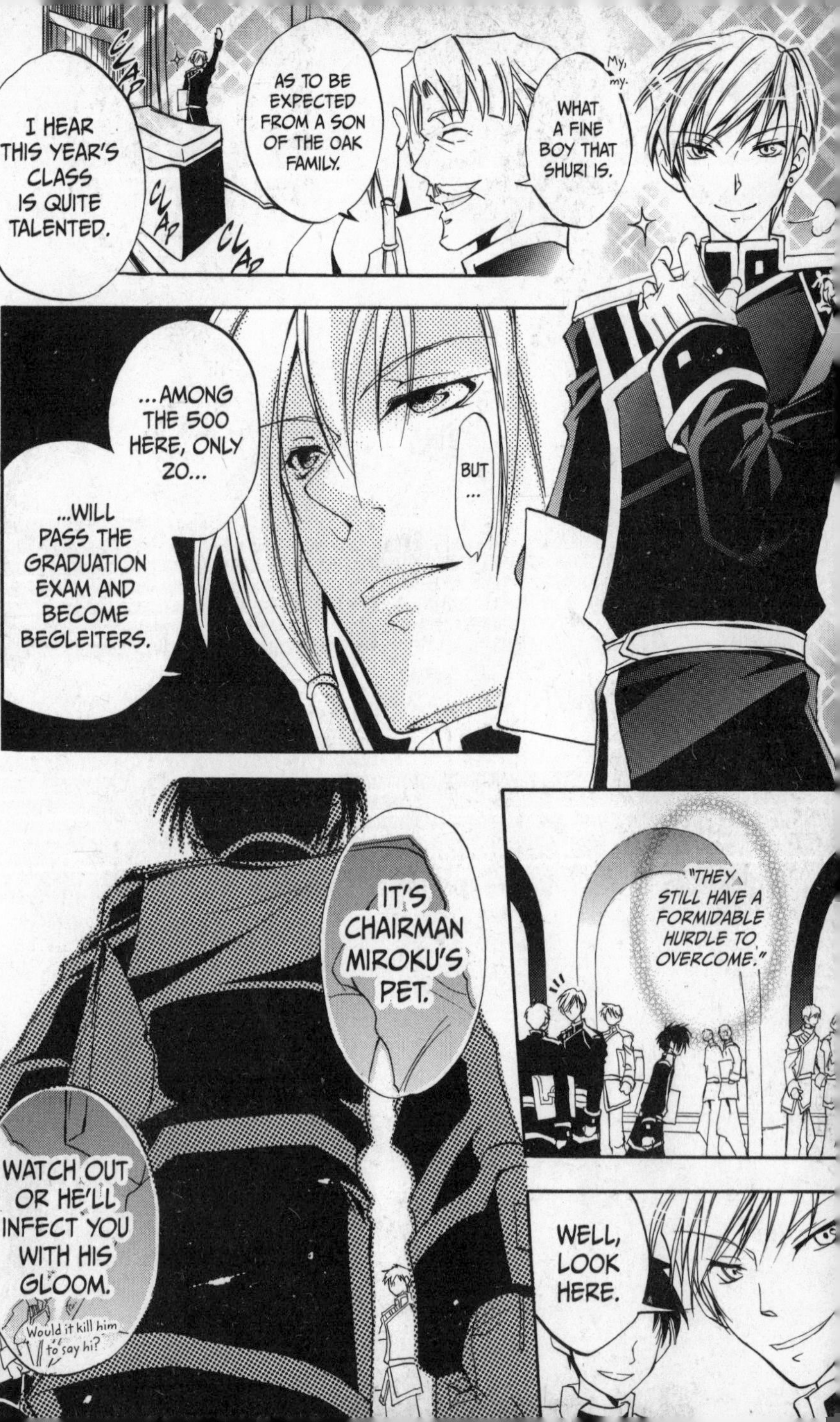
My, my.
WHAT A FINE BOY THAT SHURI IS.
AS TO BE EXPECTED FROM A SON OF THE OAK FAMILY.
I HEAR THIS YEAR'S CLASS IS QUITE TALENTED.
CLAP
CLAP
CLAP
CLAP
BUT ...
...AMONG THE 500 HERE, ONLY 20...
...WILL PASS THE GRADUATION EXAM AND BECOME BEGLEITERS.
"THEY STILL HAVE A FORMIDABLE HURDLE TO OVERCOME."
WELL, LOOK HERE.
IT'S CHAIRMAN MIROKU'S PET.
WATCH OUT OR HE'LL INFECT YOU WITH HIS GLOOM.
Would it kill him to say hi?

Begleiter = Assistant to an officer of high military rank

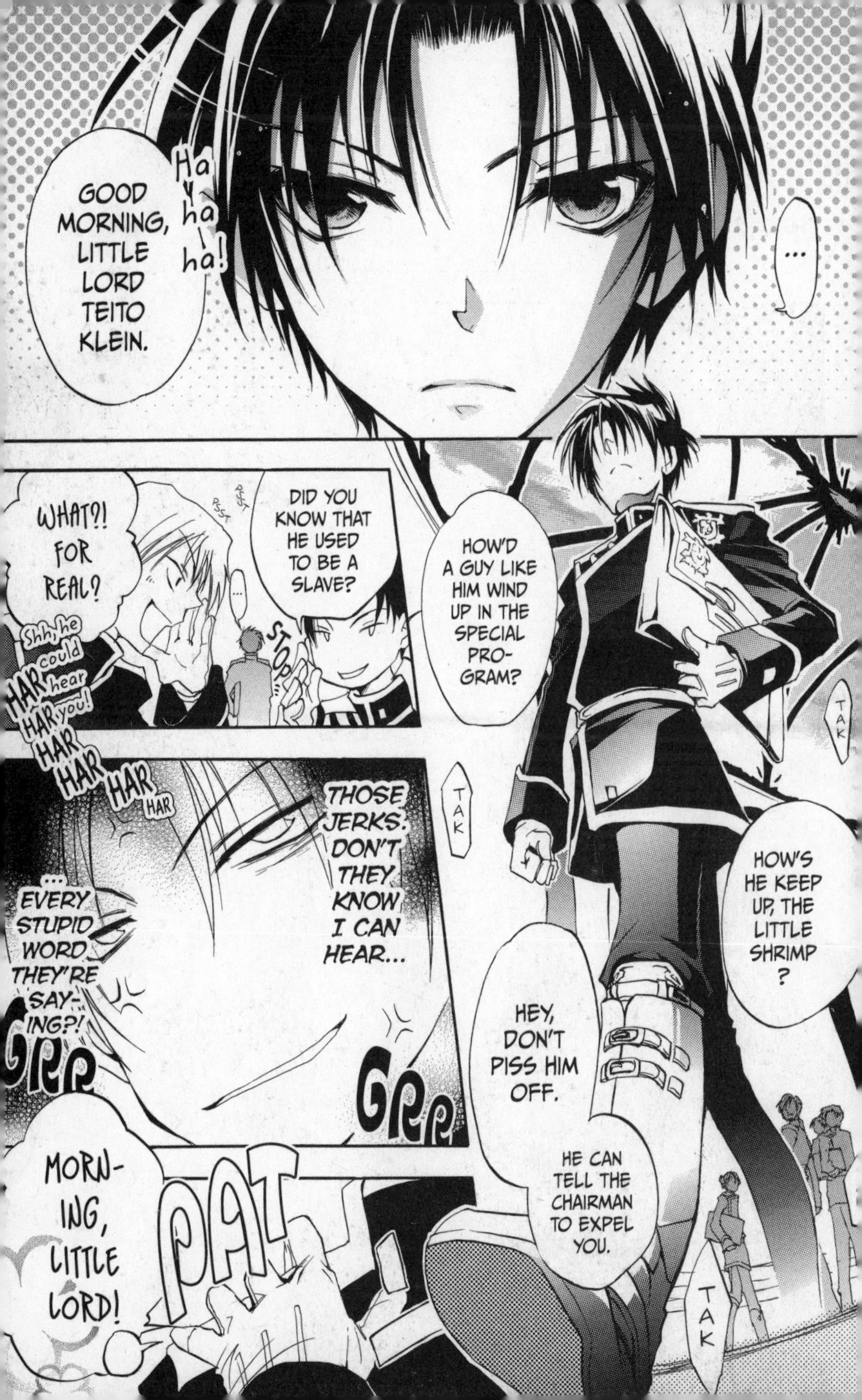
GOOD MORNING, LITTLE LORD TEITO KLEIN.
Ha ha ha!
...
HOW'D A GUY LIKE HIM WIND UP IN THE SPECIAL PRO-GRAM?
TAK
TAK
HOW'S HE KEEP UP, THE LITTLE SHRIMP?
HEY, DON'T PISS HIM OFF.
HE CAN TELL THE CHAIRMAN TO EXPEL YOU.
TAK
DID YOU KNOW THAT HE USED TO BE A SLAVE?
PSST PSST
WHAT?! FOR REAL?
...
STOP...
Shh, he could hear you!
HAR HAR HAR HAR HAR HAR
THOSE JERKS. DON'T THEY KNOW I CAN HEAR...
...EVERY STUPID WORD THEY'RE SAYING?!
GRR
GRR
MORN-ING, LITTLE LORD!
PAT

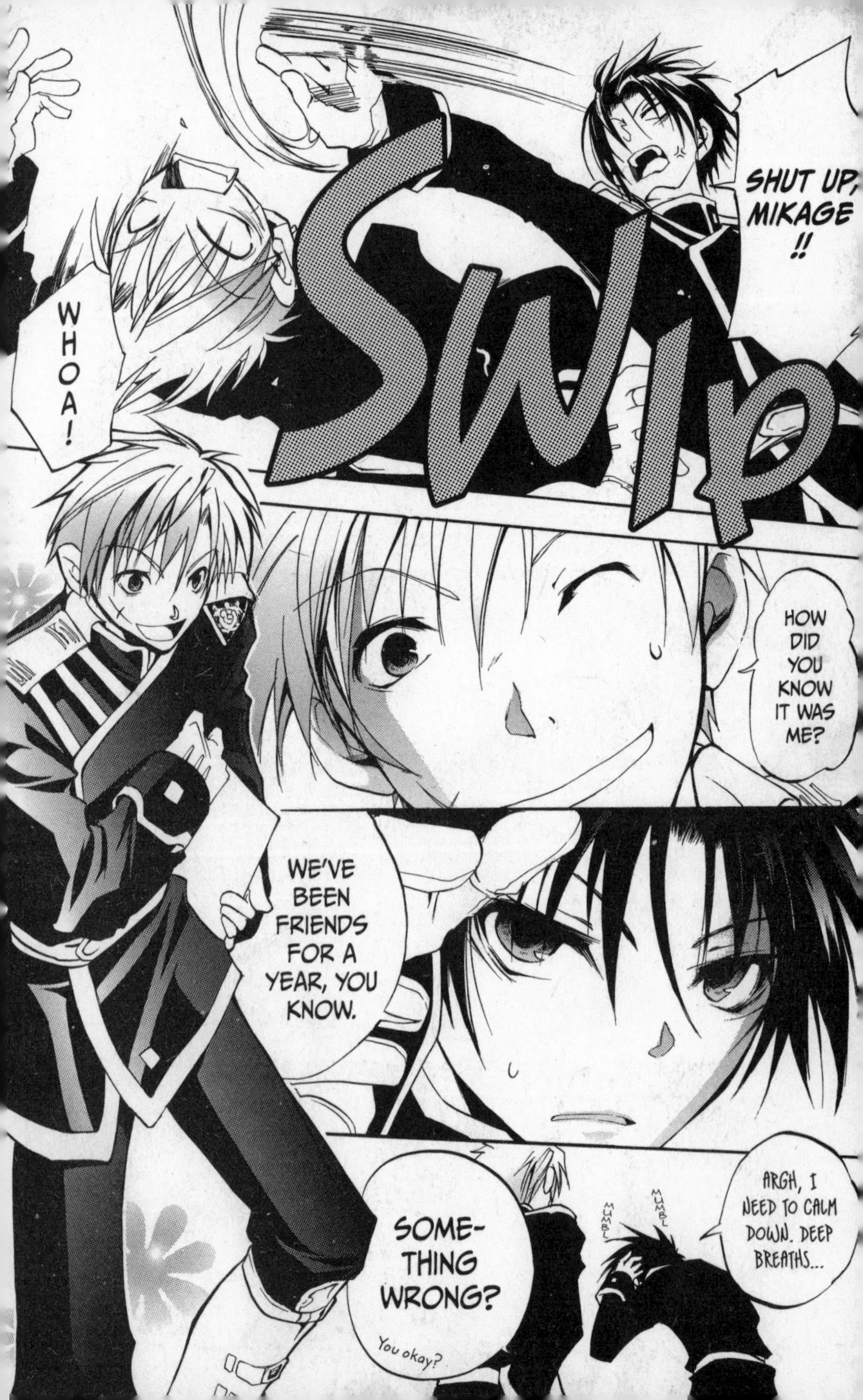
SHUT UP, MIKAGE !!
SWIP
WHOA!
HOW DID YOU KNOW IT WAS ME?
WE'VE BEEN FRIENDS FOR A YEAR, YOU KNOW.
ARGH, I NEED TO CALM DOWN. DEEP BREATHS...
MUMBL
MUMBL
SOME-THING WRONG?
You okay?

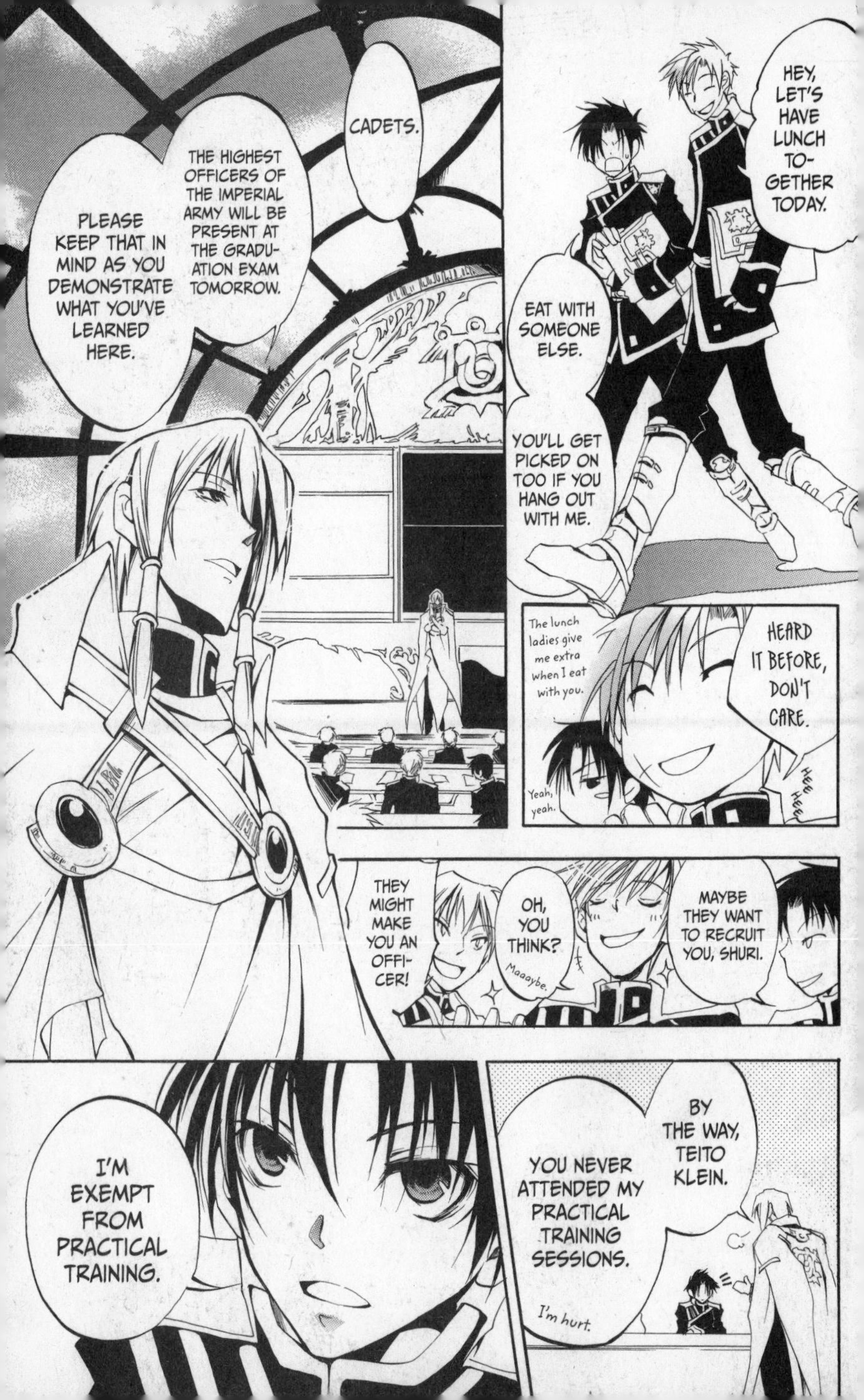
HEY, LET'S HAVE LUNCH TO-GETHER TODAY.
EAT WITH SOMEONE ELSE.
YOU'LL GET PICKED ON TOO IF YOU HANG OUT WITH ME.
HEARD IT BEFORE, DON'T CARE.
HEE HEE
The lunch ladies give me extra when I eat with you.
Yeah, yeah.
CADETS.
THE HIGHEST OFFICERS OF THE IMPERIAL ARMY WILL BE PRESENT AT THE GRADU-ATION EXAM TOMORROW.
PLEASE KEEP THAT IN MIND AS YOU DEMONSTRATE WHAT YOU'VE LEARNED HERE.
MAYBE THEY WANT TO RECRUIT YOU, SHURI.
OH, YOU THINK?
Maaaybe.
THEY MIGHT MAKE YOU AN OFFI-CER!
BY THE WAY, TEITO KLEIN.
YOU NEVER ATTENDED MY PRACTICAL TRAINING SESSIONS.
I'm hurt.
I'M EXEMPT FROM PRACTICAL TRAINING.

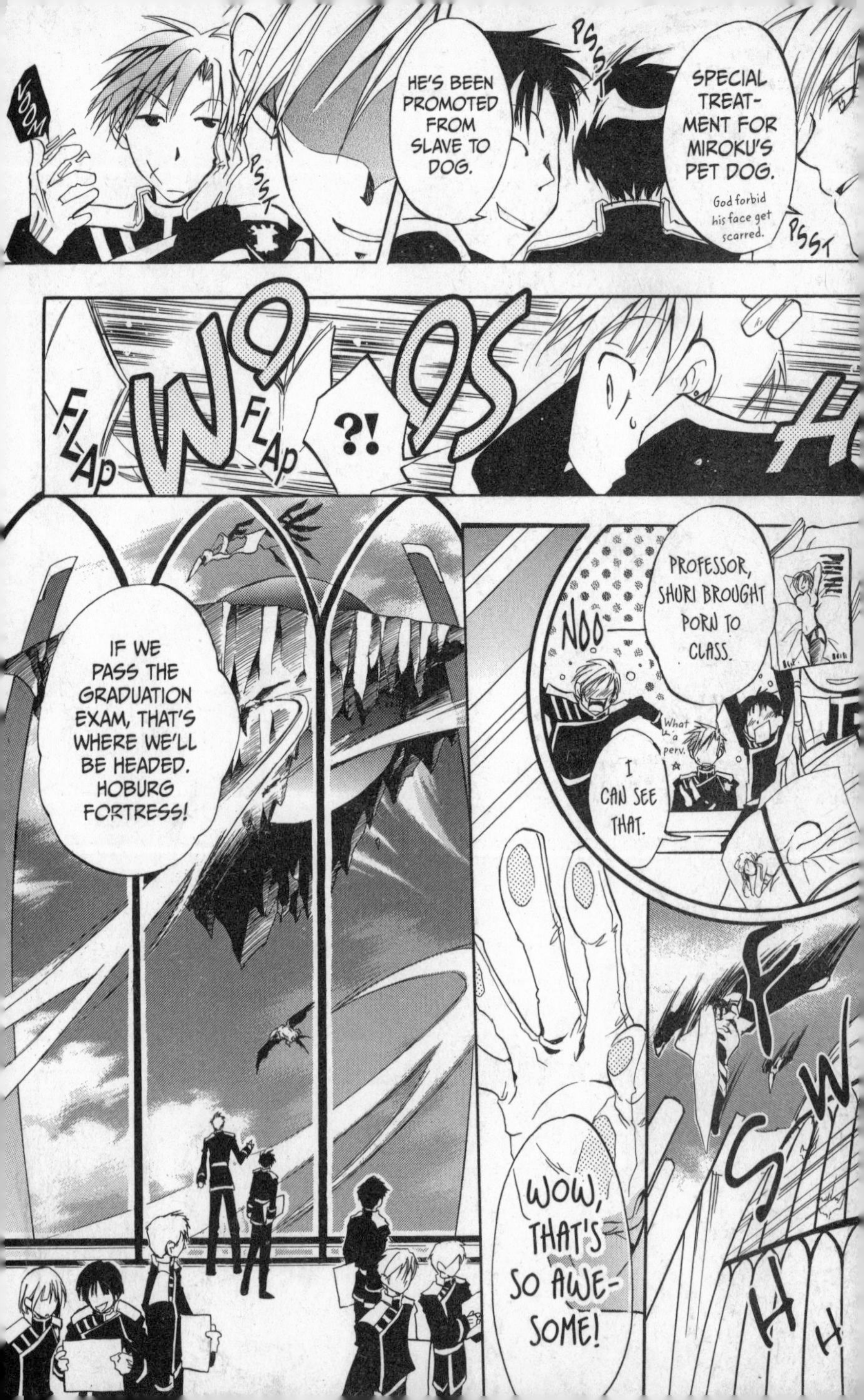
SPECIAL TREAT-MENT FOR MIROKU'S PET DOG.
God forbid his face get scarred.
PSST
PSSS
HE'S BEEN PROMOTED FROM SLAVE TO DOG.
PSSK
VOOM
?!
FLAP
FLAP
PROFESSOR, SHURI BROUGHT PORN TO CLASS.
NOO
What a perv.
I CAN SEE THAT.
WOW, THAT'S SO AWE-SOME!
IF WE PASS THE GRADUATION EXAM, THAT'S WHERE WE'LL BE HEADED. HOBURG FORTRESS!

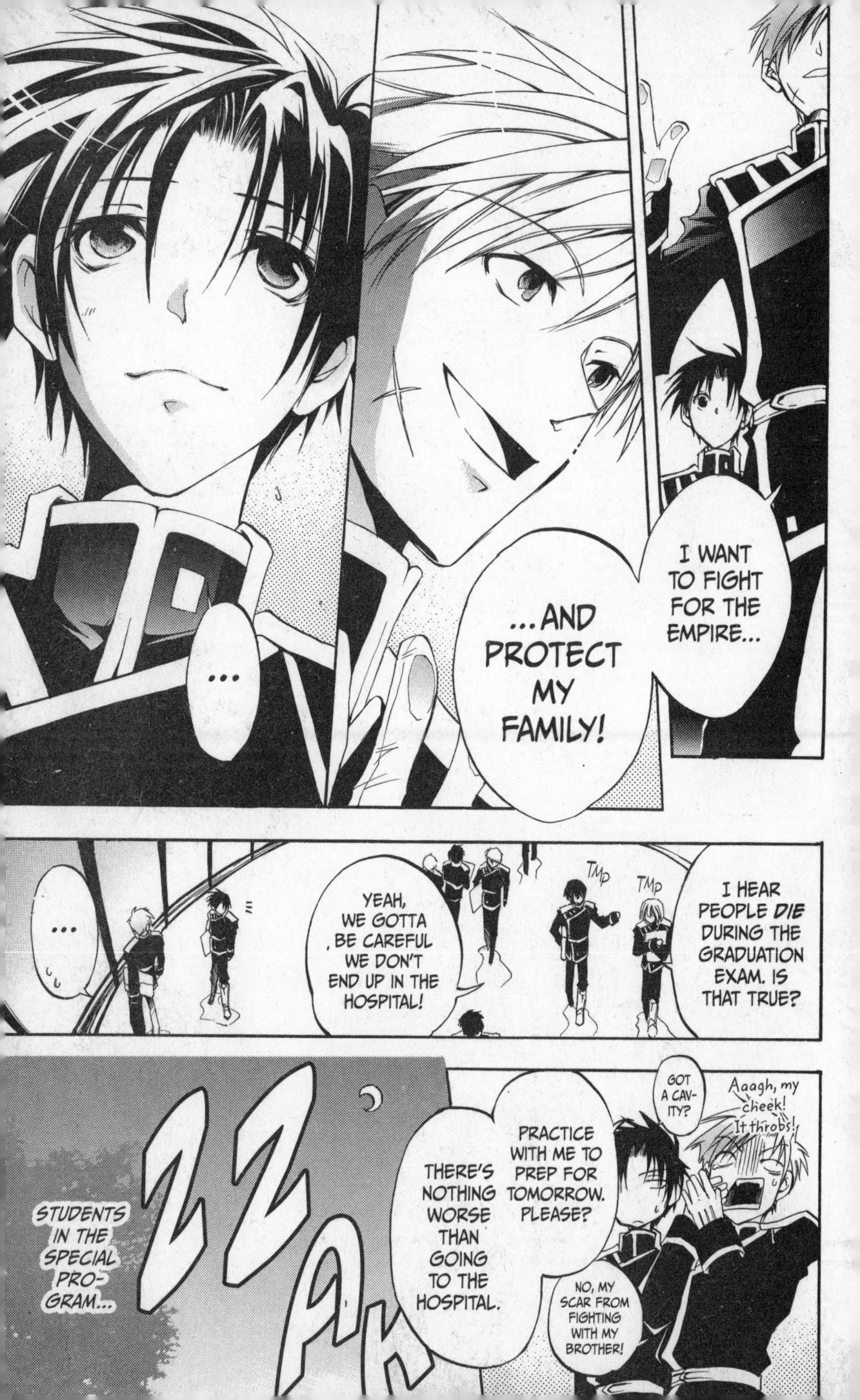
I WANT TO FIGHT FOR THE EMPIRE...
...AND PROTECT MY FAMILY!
...
I HEAR PEOPLE *DIE* DURING THE GRADUATION EXAM. IS THAT TRUE?
TMP
TMP
YEAH, WE GOTTA BE CAREFUL WE DON'T END UP IN THE HOSPITAL!
...
Aaagh, my cheek! It throbs!
GOT A CAVITY?
PRACTICE WITH ME TO PREP FOR TOMORROW. PLEASE?
THERE'S NOTHING WORSE THAN GOING TO THE HOSPITAL.
NO, MY SCAR FROM FIGHTING WITH MY BROTHER!
STUDENTS IN THE SPECIAL PRO-GRAM...

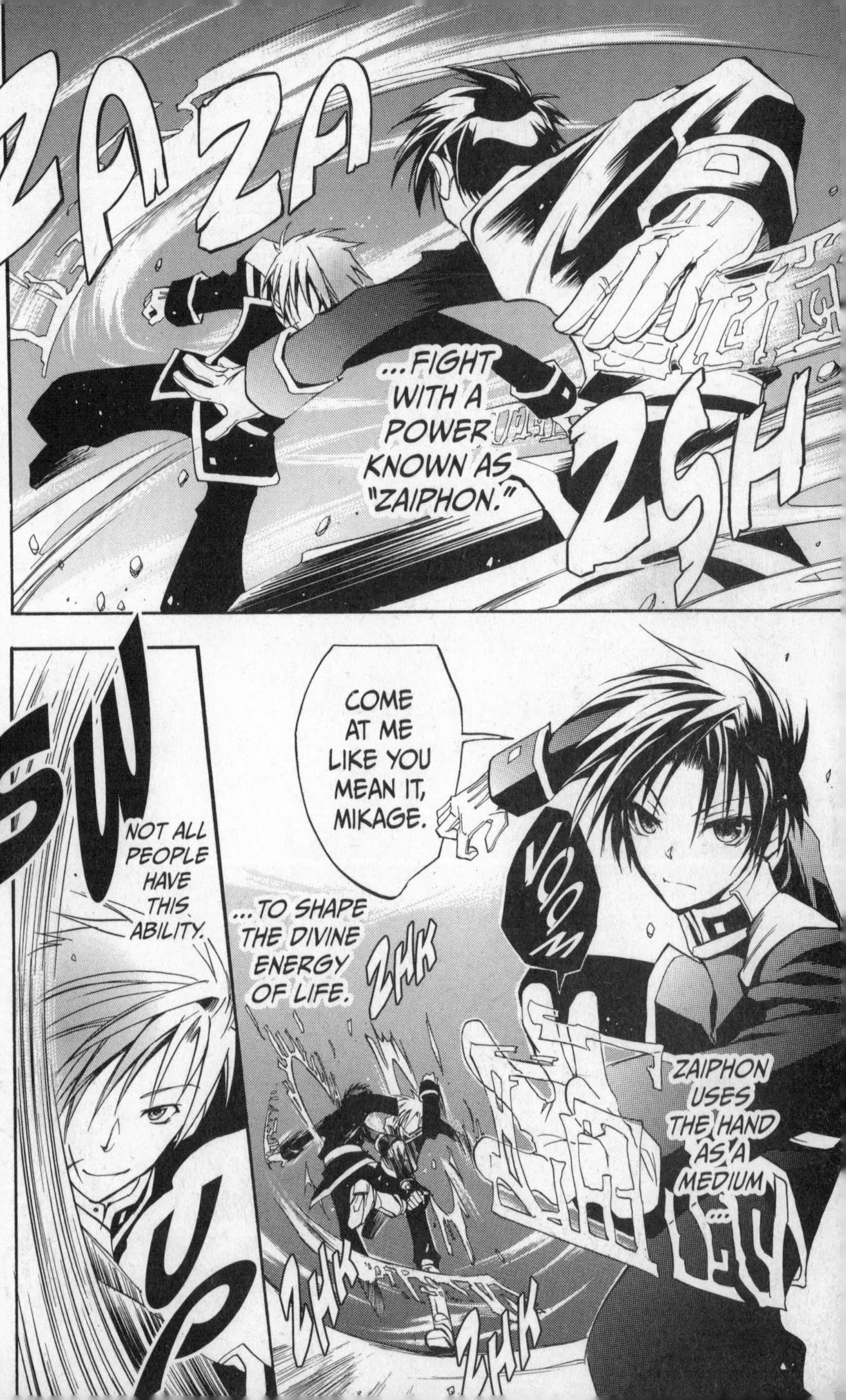
ZA ZA
...FIGHT WITH A POWER KNOWN AS "ZAIPHON."
ZSH
COME AT ME LIKE YOU MEAN IT, MIKAGE.
VOOM
ZAIPHON USES THE HAND AS A MEDIUM...
...TO SHAPE THE DIVINE ENERGY OF LIFE.
ZHK
NOT ALL PEOPLE HAVE THIS ABILITY.
SW
ZHK
ZHK

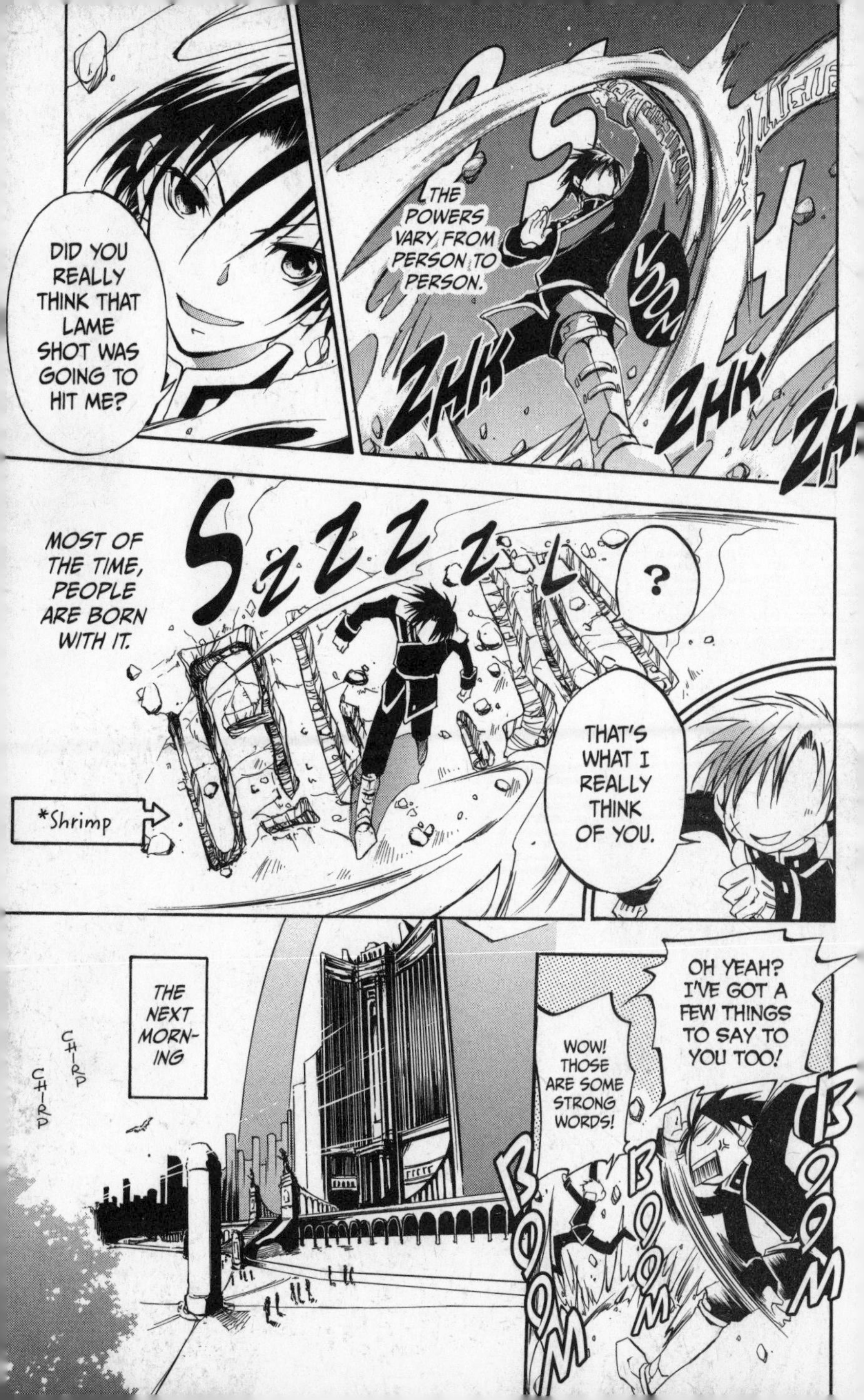

THE POWERS VARY FROM PERSON TO PERSON.
VOON
ZHK ZHK ZH
DID YOU REALLY THINK THAT LAME SHOT WAS GOING TO HIT ME?
?
THAT'S WHAT I REALLY THINK OF YOU.
SZZZZZL
MOST OF THE TIME, PEOPLE ARE BORN WITH IT.
*Shrimp
OH YEAH? I'VE GOT A FEW THINGS TO SAY TO YOU TOO!
WOW! THOSE ARE SOME STRONG WORDS!
BOOOM BOOOM BOOOM
THE NEXT MORNING
CHIRP CHIRP

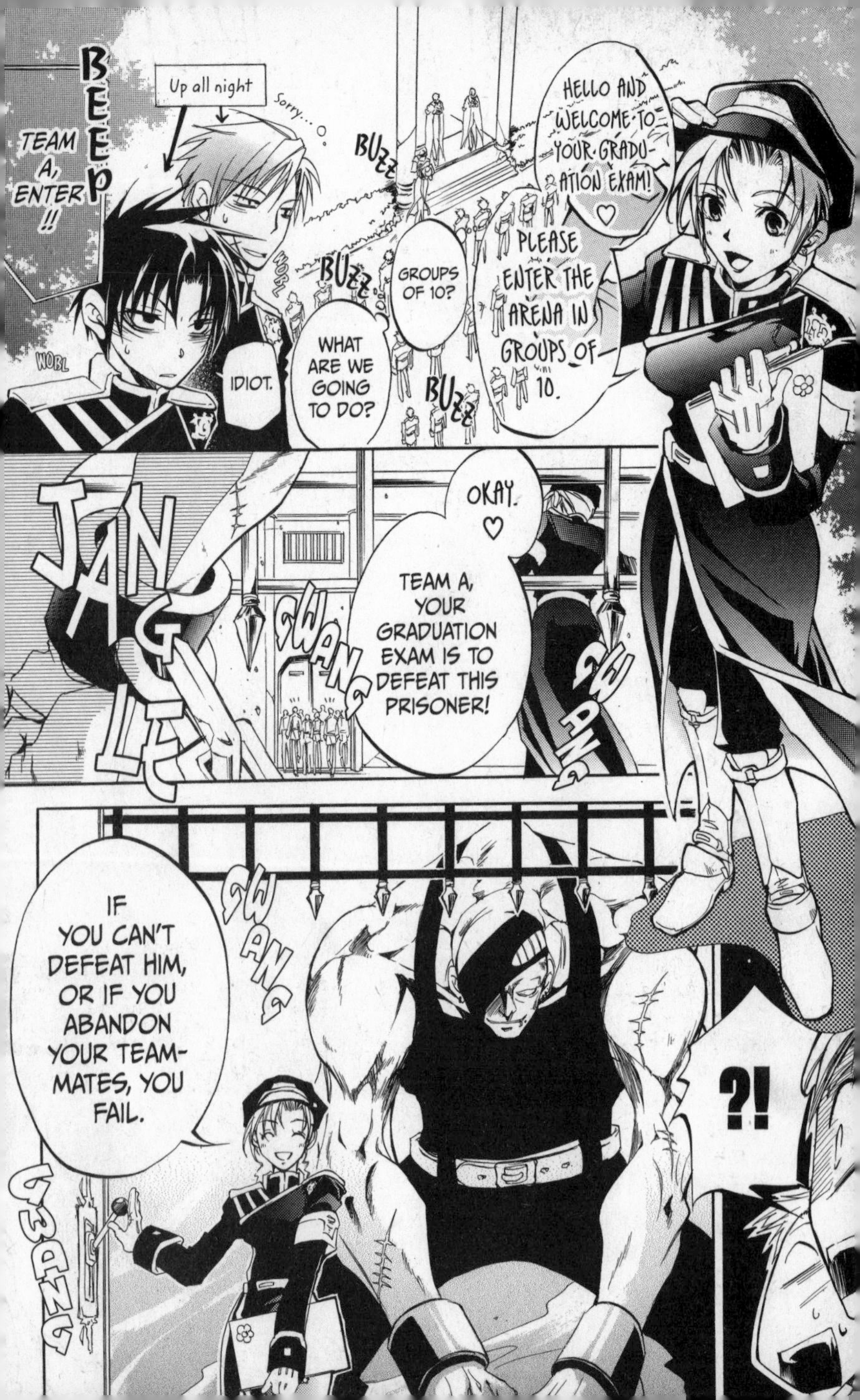
HELLO AND WELCOME TO YOUR GRADUATION EXAM! ♡
PLEASE ENTER THE ARENA IN GROUPS OF 10.
BUZZ
GROUPS OF 10?
BUZZ
WHAT ARE WE GOING TO DO?
BUZZ
BEEP
TEAM A, ENTER!!
Up all night
Sorry...
WOBL
IDIOT.
WOBL
OKAY. ♡
TEAM A, YOUR GRADUATION EXAM IS TO DEFEAT THIS PRISONER!
GWANG
GWANG
JANGLE
?!
GWANG
IF YOU CAN'T DEFEAT HIM, OR IF YOU ABANDON YOUR TEAM-MATES, YOU FAIL.
GWANG

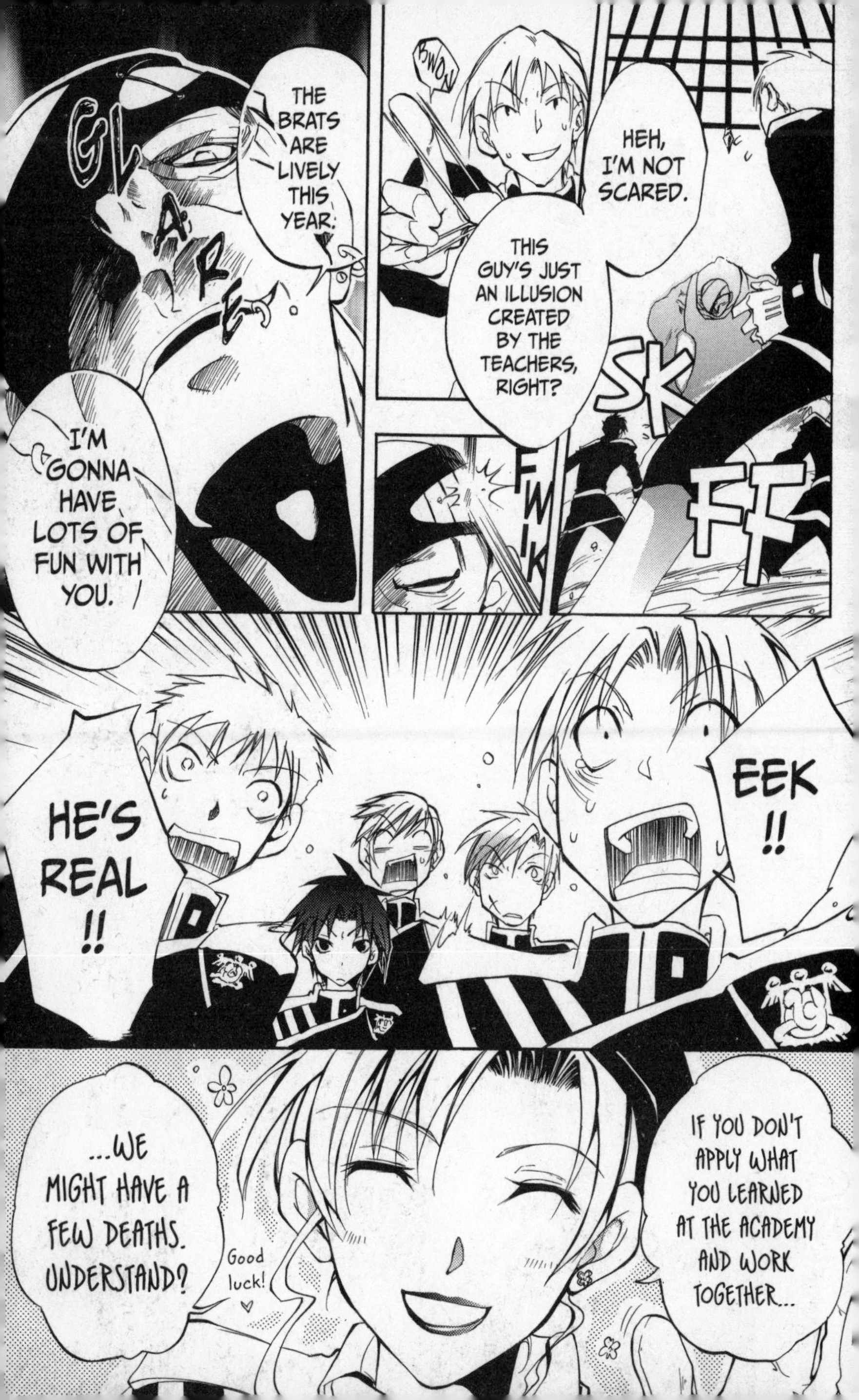
BWON
HEH, I'M NOT SCARED.
THIS GUY'S JUST AN ILLUSION CREATED BY THE TEACHERS, RIGHT?
SK
FF
FWIK
GLARE
THE BRATS ARE LIVELY THIS YEAR.
I'M GONNA HAVE LOTS OF FUN WITH YOU.
EEK!!
HE'S REAL!!
IF YOU DON'T APPLY WHAT YOU LEARNED AT THE ACADEMY AND WORK TOGETHER...
...WE MIGHT HAVE A FEW DEATHS. UNDERSTAND?
Good luck!

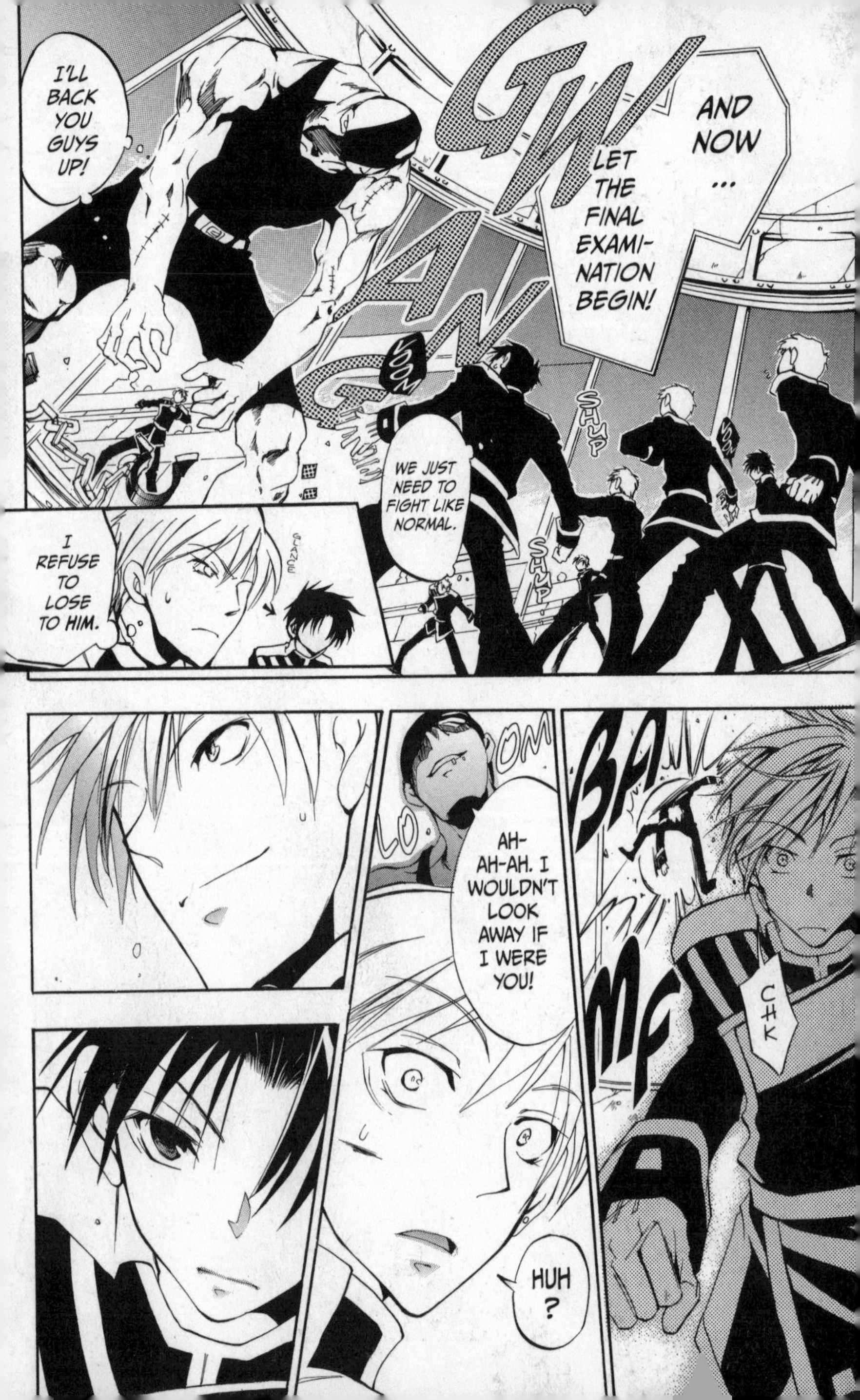
AND NOW ...
LET THE FINAL EXAMI-NATION BEGIN!
GWANG
I'LL BACK YOU GUYS UP!
SHUP
WE JUST NEED TO FIGHT LIKE NORMAL.
SHUP
GLANCE
I REFUSE TO LOSE TO HIM.
BAM
CHK
LOOM
AH-AH-AH. I WOULDN'T LOOK AWAY IF I WERE YOU!
HUH?

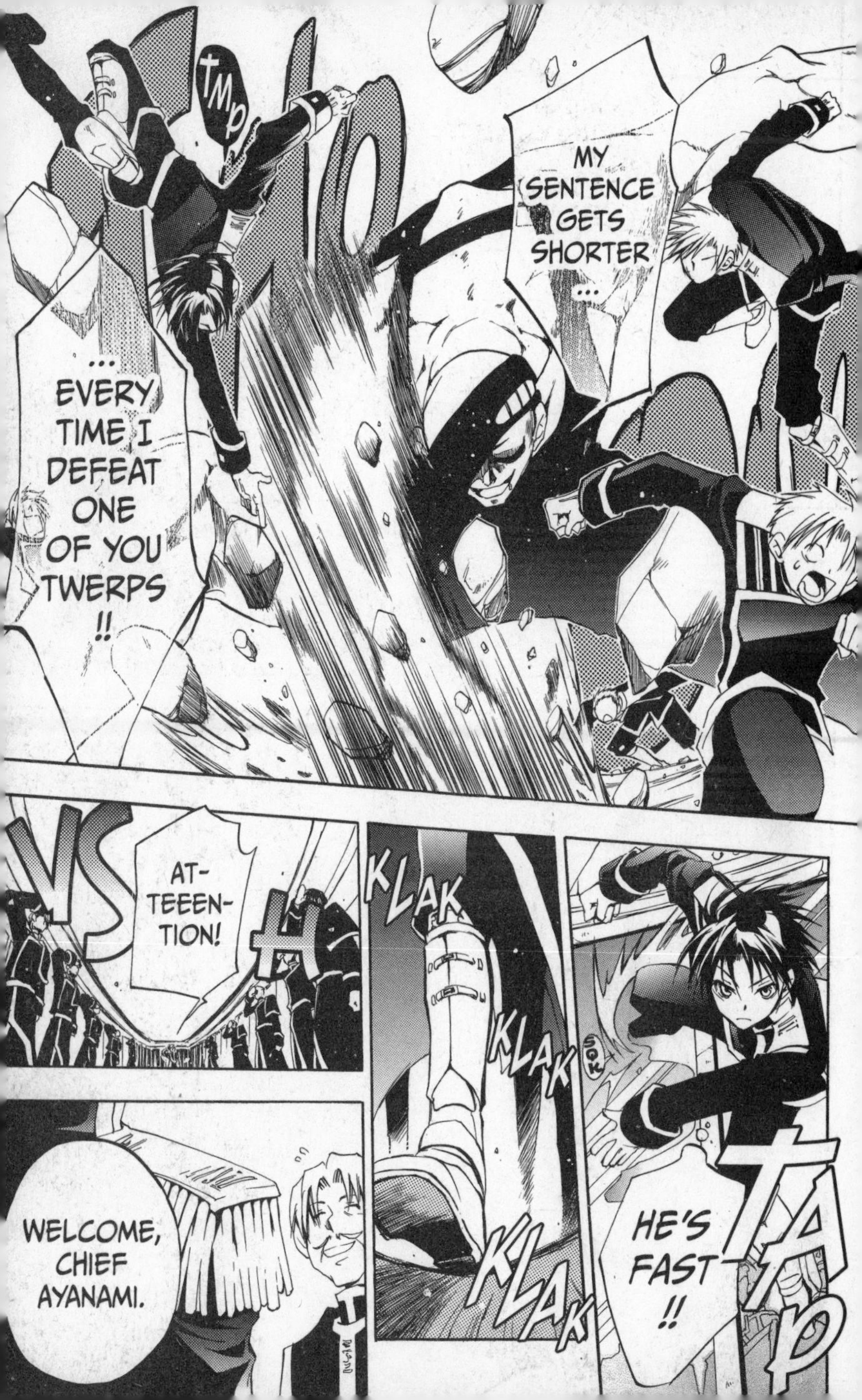
MY SENTENCE GETS SHORTER ...
TMP
... EVERY TIME I DEFEAT ONE OF YOU TWERPS !!
SOK
HE'S FAST !!
TAP
KLAK
KLAK
KLAK
AT-TEEEN-TION!
WELCOME, CHIEF AYANAMI.

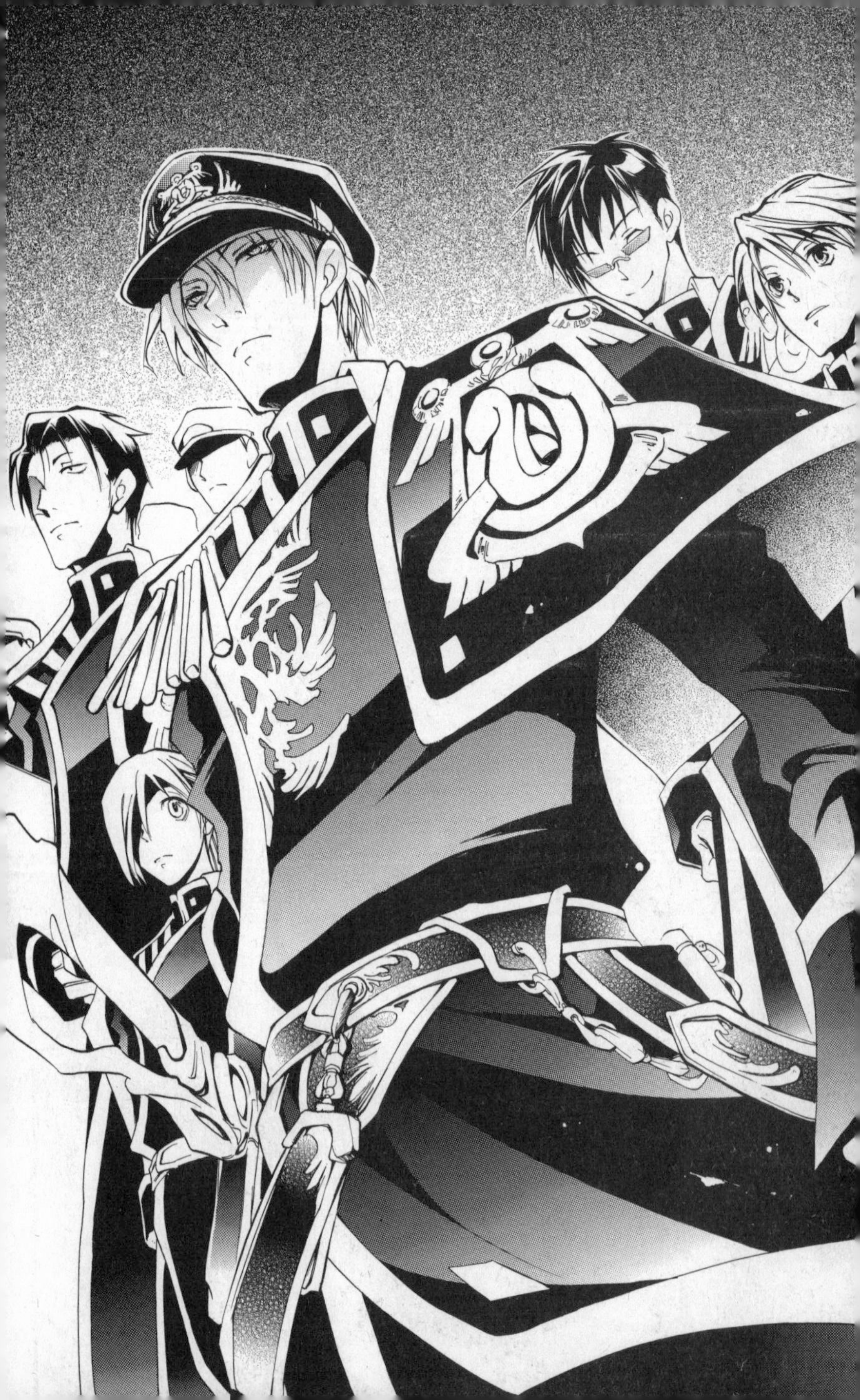

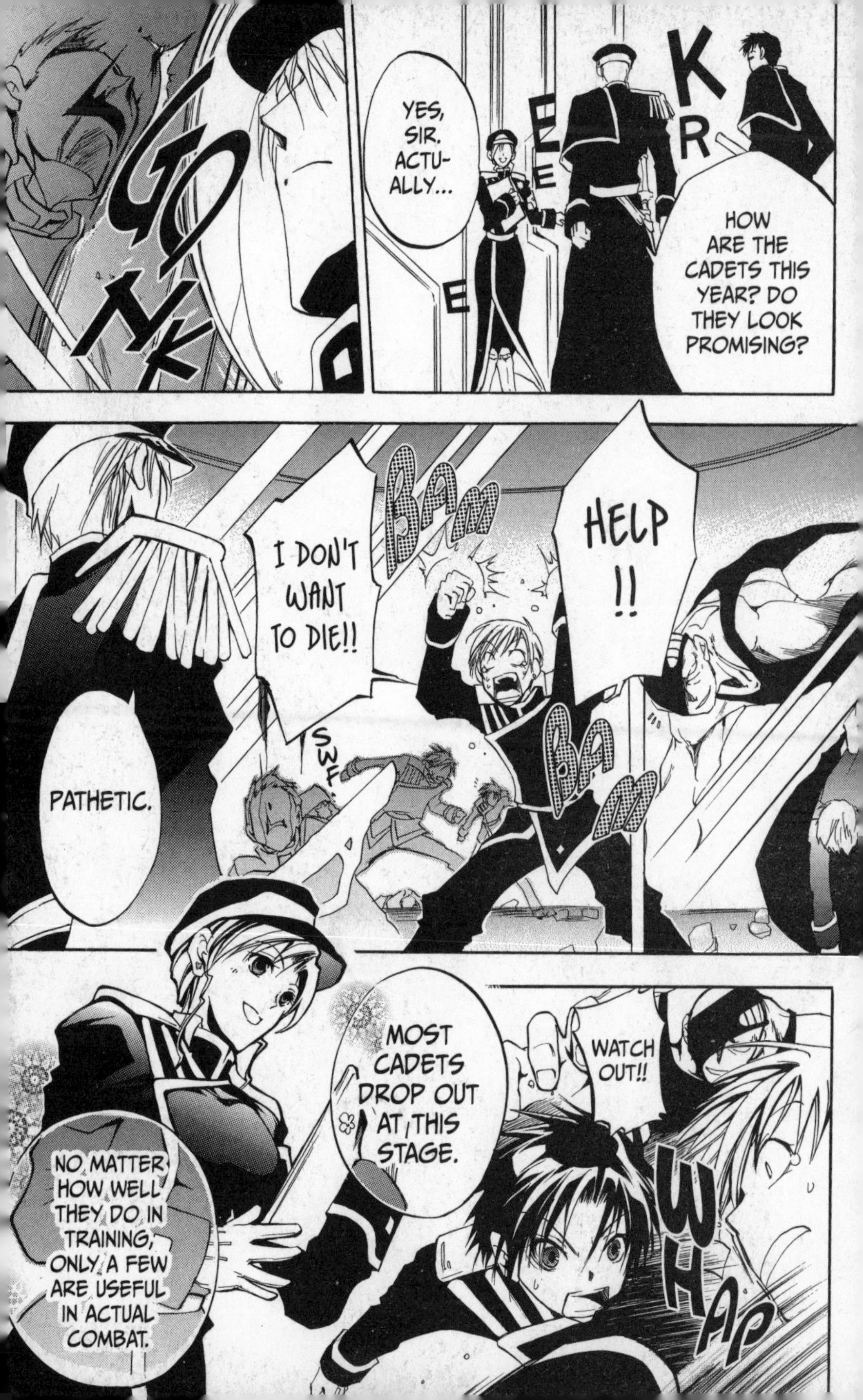
HOW ARE THE CADETS THIS YEAR? DO THEY LOOK PROMISING?
KREEE
YES, SIR. ACTU-ALLY...
HELP!!
I DON'T WANT TO DIE!!
BAM
BAM
SWF
PATHETIC.
WATCH OUT!!
WHAP
MOST CADETS DROP OUT AT THIS STAGE.
NO MATTER HOW WELL THEY DO IN TRAINING, ONLY A FEW ARE USEFUL IN ACTUAL COMBAT.

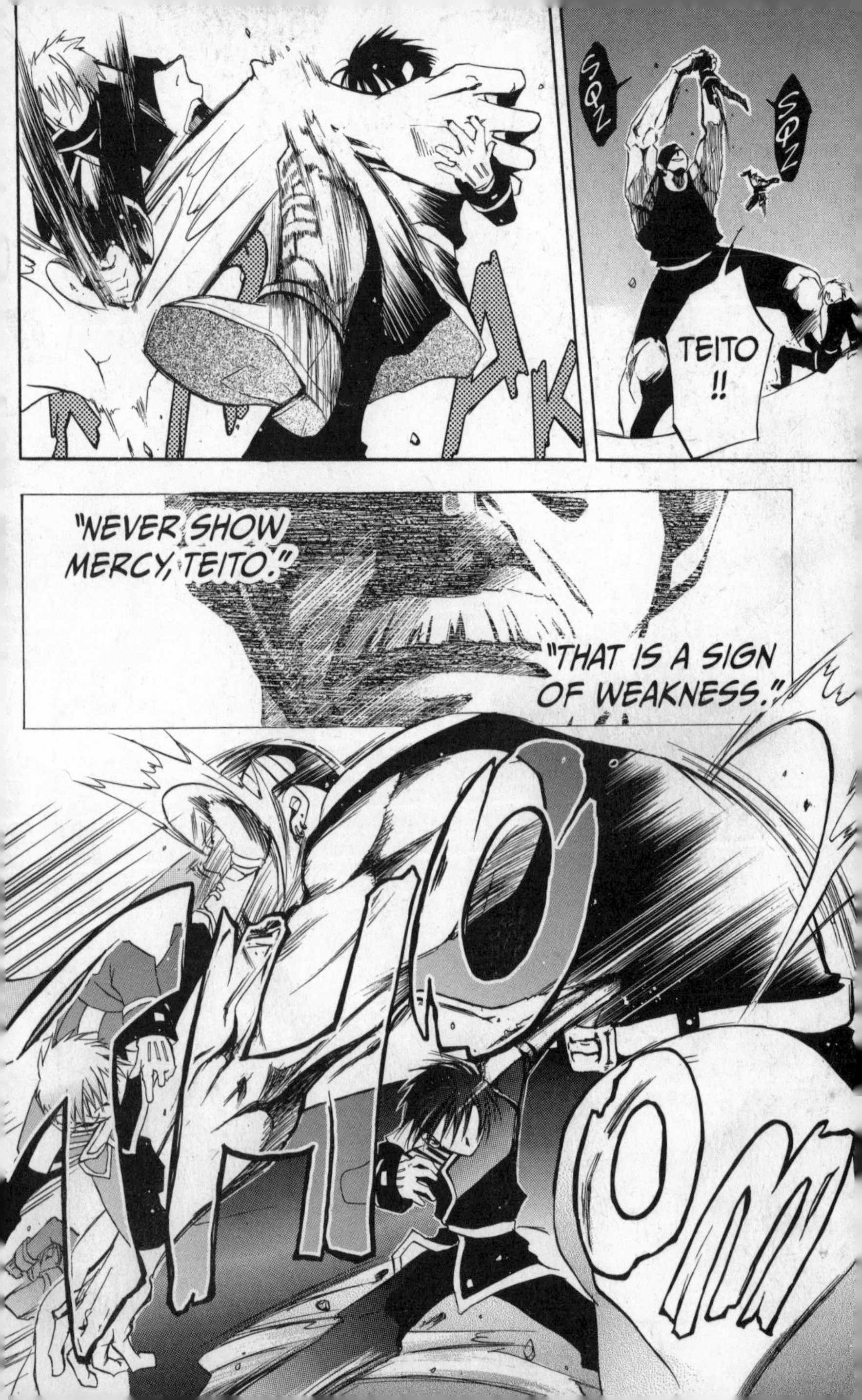
SQZ
SQZ
TEITO !!
"NEVER SHOW MERCY, TEITO."
"THAT IS A SIGN OF WEAKNESS."

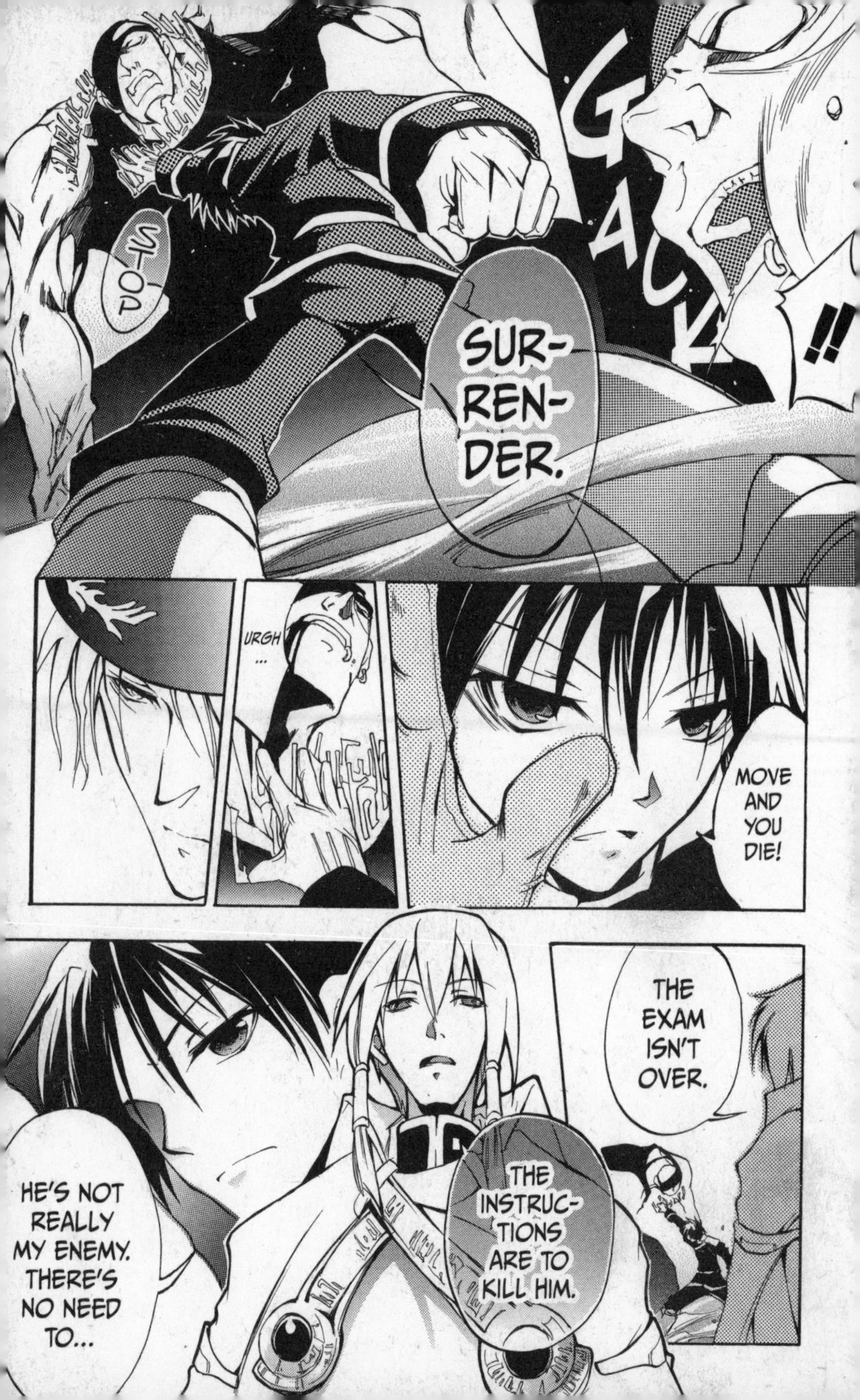
GACK!!
SUR-REN-DER.
STOP
MOVE AND YOU DIE!
URGH...
THE EXAM ISN'T OVER.
THE INSTRUC-TIONS ARE TO KILL HIM.
HE'S NOT REALLY MY ENEMY. THERE'S NO NEED TO...

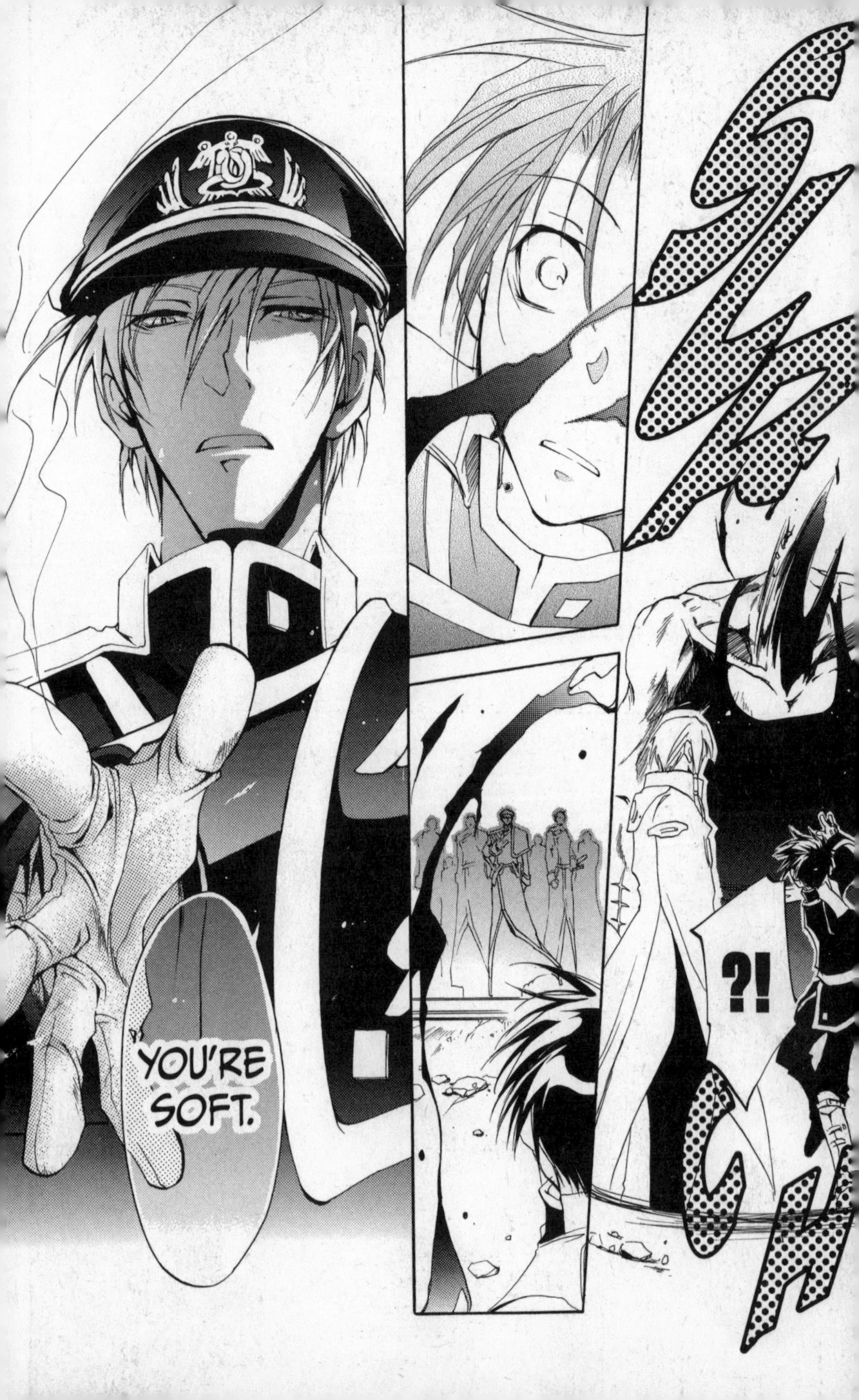
?!
YOU'RE SOFT.

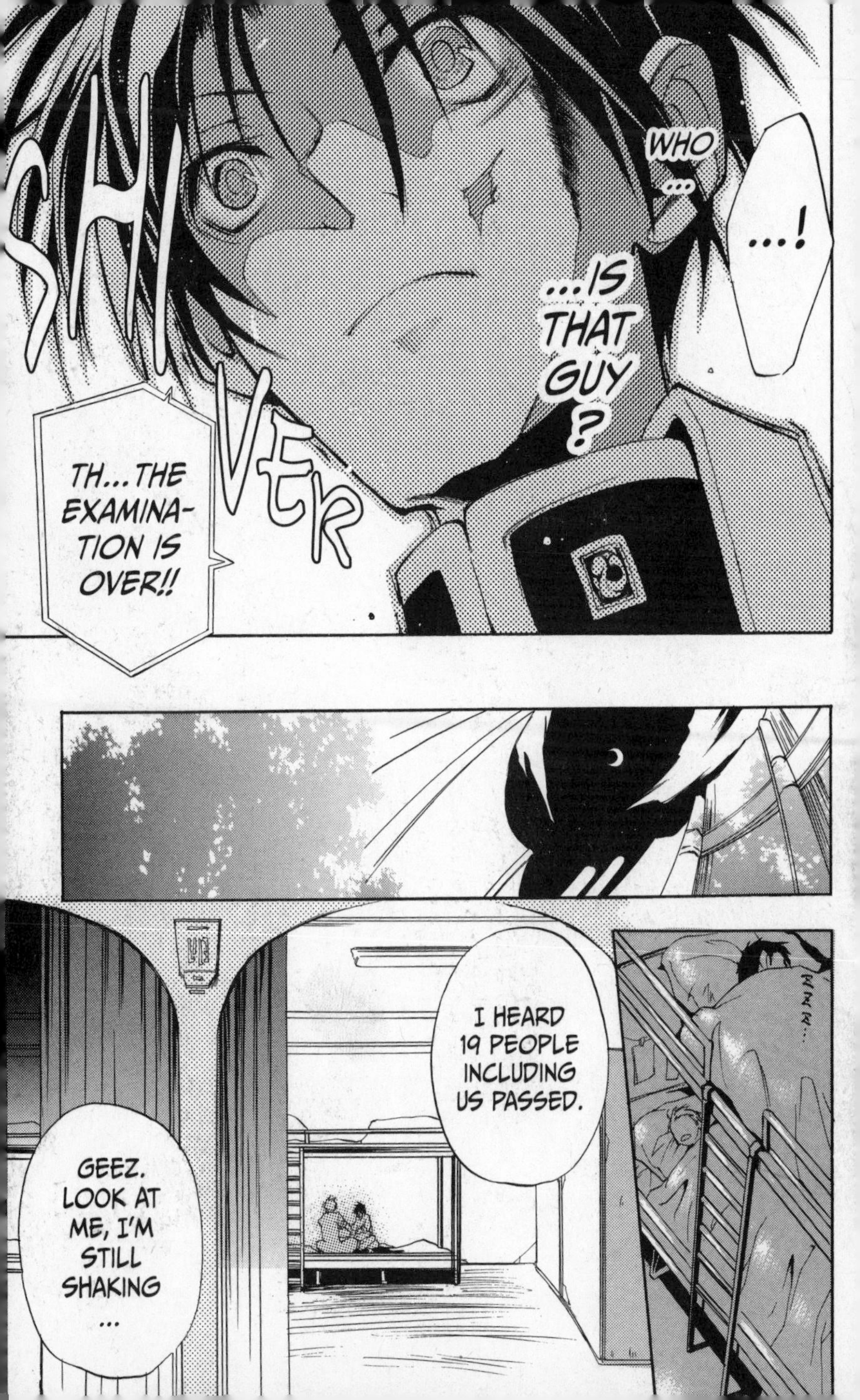
...!
WHO... ...IS THAT GUY?
SHIVER
TH...THE EXAMINATION IS OVER!!
I HEARD 19 PEOPLE INCLUDING US PASSED.
GEEZ. LOOK AT ME, I'M STILL SHAKING...

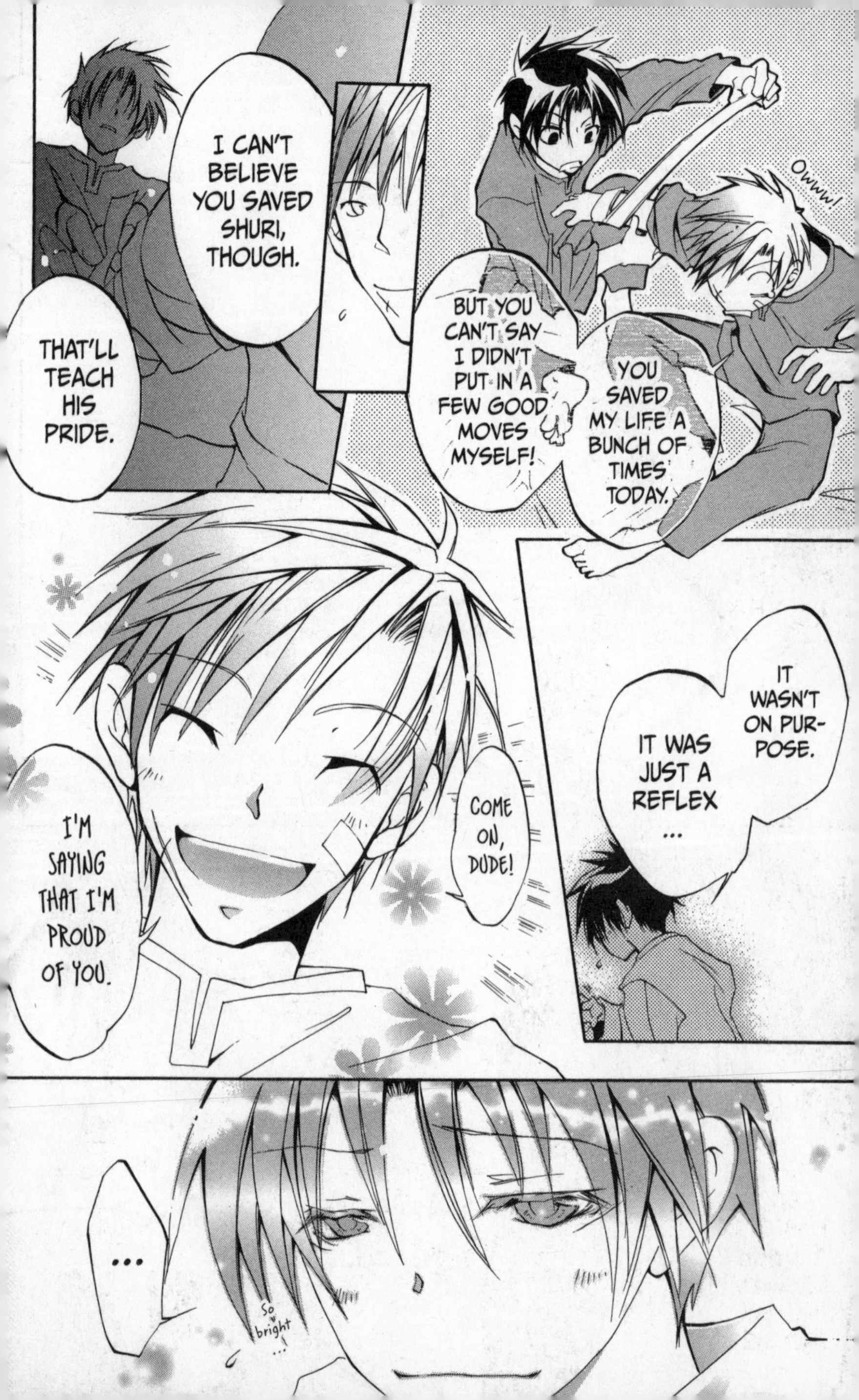
Owww!
YOU SAVED MY LIFE A BUNCH OF TIMES TODAY.
BUT YOU CAN'T SAY I DIDN'T PUT IN A FEW GOOD MOVES MYSELF!
I CAN'T BELIEVE YOU SAVED SHURI, THOUGH.
THAT'LL TEACH HIS PRIDE.
IT WASN'T ON PURPOSE.
IT WAS JUST A REFLEX ...
COME ON, DUDE!
I'M SAYING THAT I'M PROUD OF YOU.
...
So bright ...

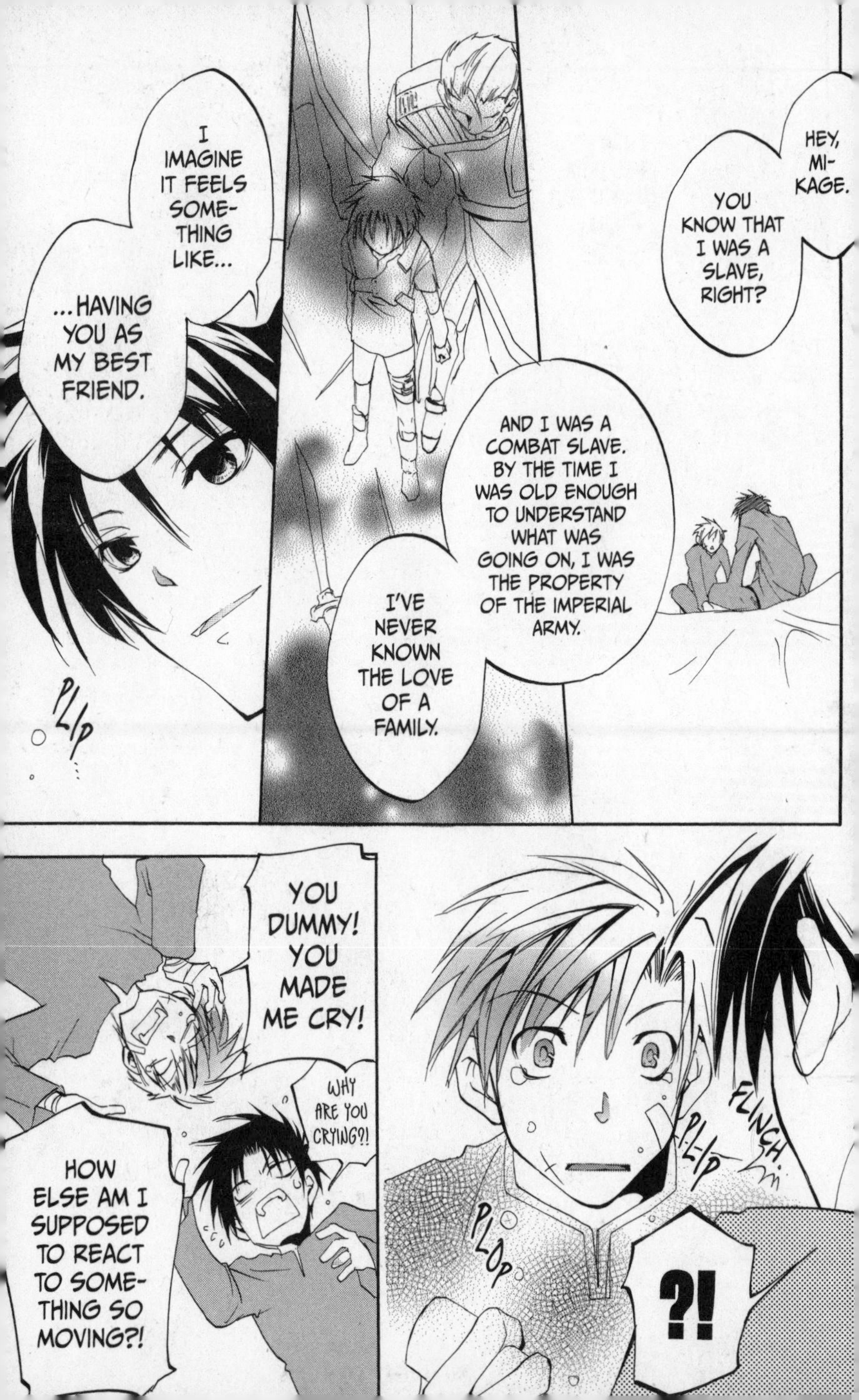
HEY, MI-KAGE.
YOU KNOW THAT I WAS A SLAVE, RIGHT?
AND I WAS A COMBAT SLAVE. BY THE TIME I WAS OLD ENOUGH TO UNDERSTAND WHAT WAS GOING ON, I WAS THE PROPERTY OF THE IMPERIAL ARMY.
I'VE NEVER KNOWN THE LOVE OF A FAMILY.
I IMAGINE IT FEELS SOMETHING LIKE...
...HAVING YOU AS MY BEST FRIEND.
PLIP...
FLINCH...
PL-L-IP
PLOP
?!
YOU DUMMY! YOU MADE ME CRY!
WHY ARE YOU CRYING?!
HOW ELSE AM I SUPPOSED TO REACT TO SOMETHING SO MOVING?!

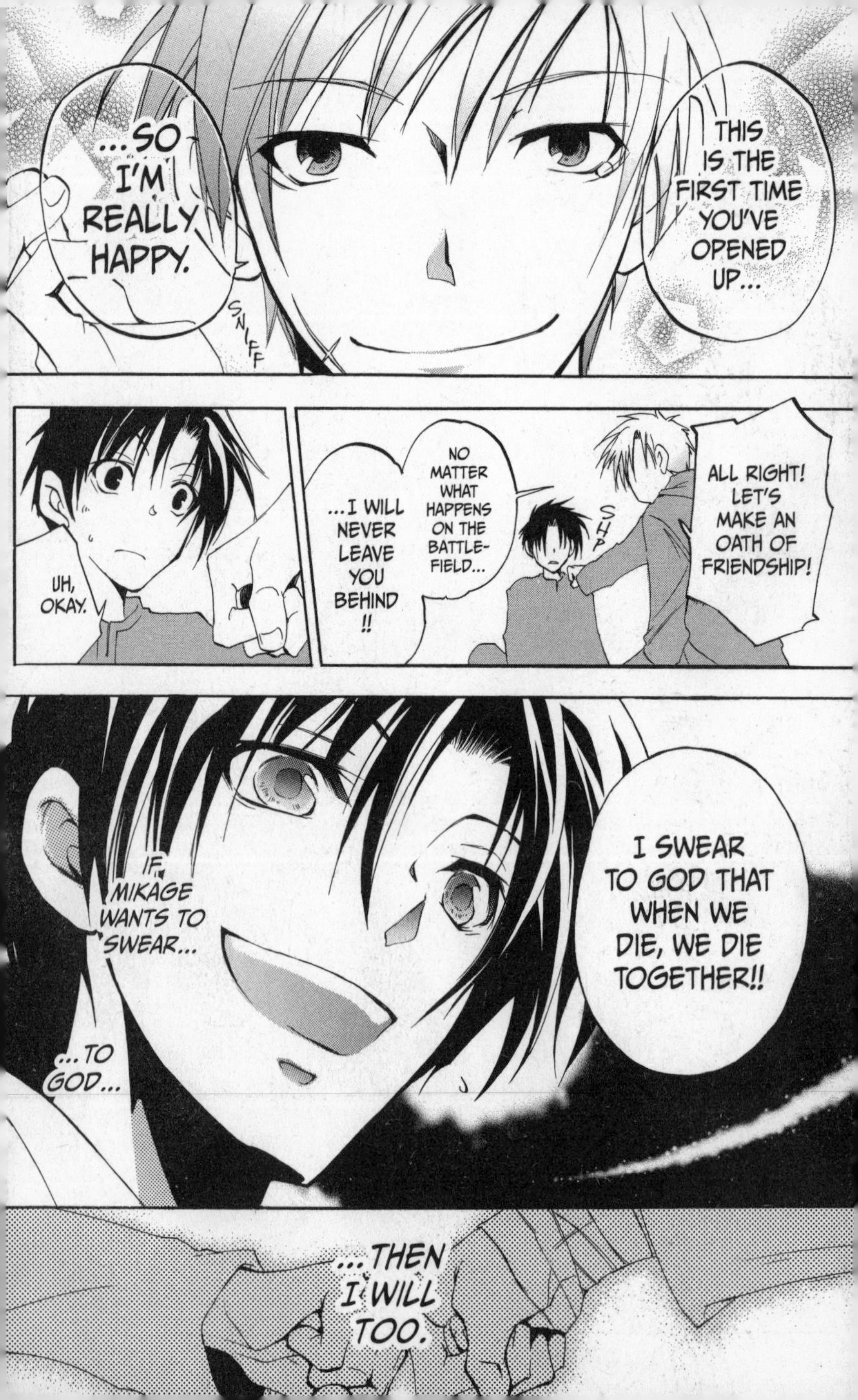
THIS IS THE FIRST TIME YOU'VE OPENED UP...
...SO I'M REALLY HAPPY.
SNIFF
ALL RIGHT! LET'S MAKE AN OATH OF FRIENDSHIP!
SHP
NO MATTER WHAT HAPPENS ON THE BATTLE-FIELD...
...I WILL NEVER LEAVE YOU BEHIND !!
UH, OKAY.
I SWEAR TO GOD THAT WHEN WE DIE, WE DIE TOGETHER!!
IF MIKAGE WANTS TO SWEAR...
...TO GOD...
...THEN I WILL TOO.

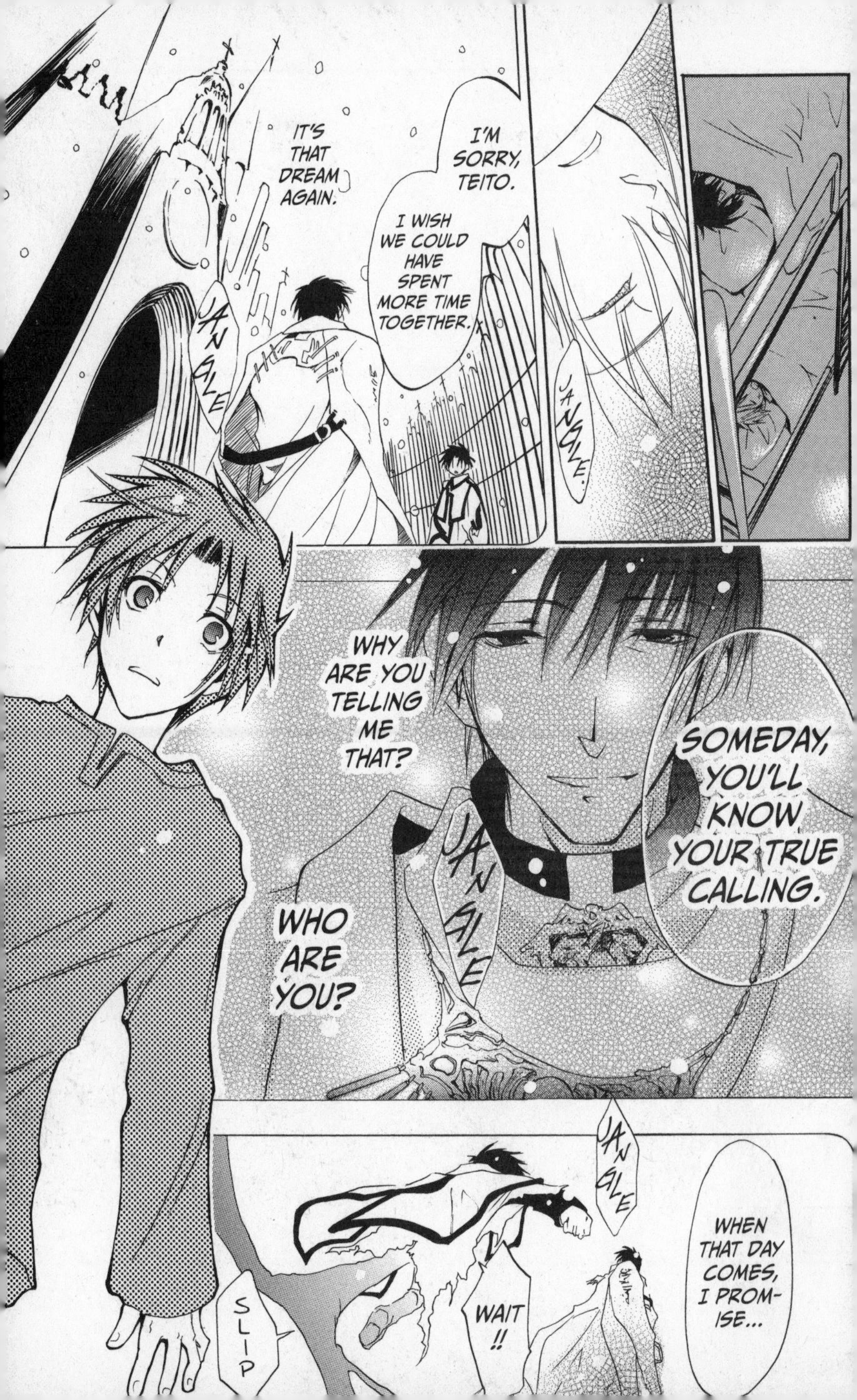
JANGLE
I'M SORRY, TEITO.
I WISH WE COULD HAVE SPENT MORE TIME TOGETHER.
IT'S THAT DREAM AGAIN.
JANGLE
SOMEDAY, YOU'LL KNOW YOUR TRUE CALLING.
WHY ARE YOU TELLING ME THAT?
JANGLE
WHO ARE YOU?
JANGLE
WHEN THAT DAY COMES, I PROMISE...
WAIT!!
SLIP

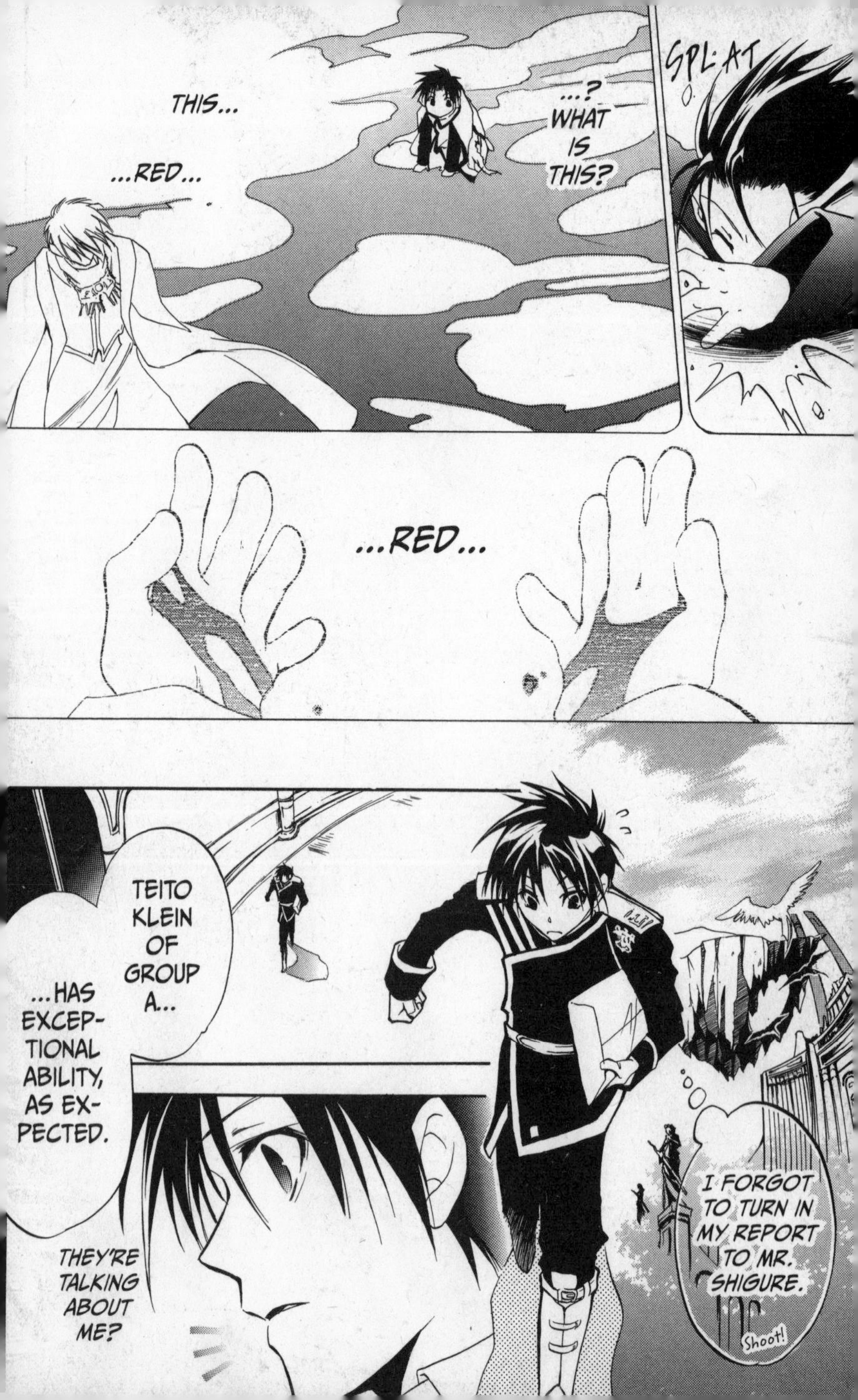
SPLAT
...? WHAT IS THIS?
THIS...
...RED...
...RED...
I FORGOT TO TURN IN MY REPORT TO MR. SHIGURE.
Shoot!
TEITO KLEIN OF GROUP A...
...HAS EXCEPTIONAL ABILITY, AS EXPECTED.
THEY'RE TALKING ABOUT ME?

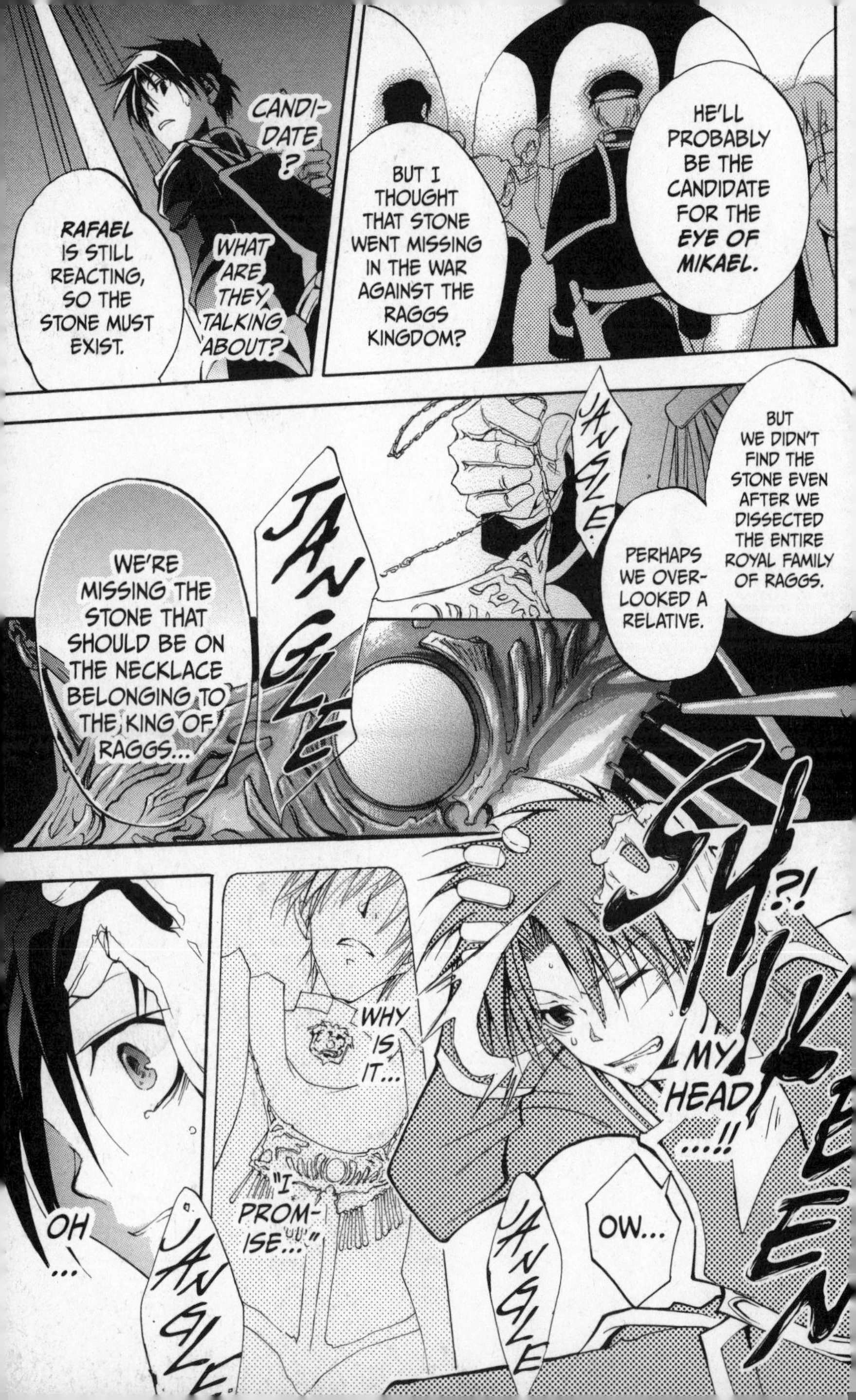
HE'LL PROBABLY BE THE CANDIDATE FOR THE EYE OF MIKAEL.
BUT I THOUGHT THAT STONE WENT MISSING IN THE WAR AGAINST THE RAGGS KINGDOM?
CANDI-DATE?
WHAT ARE THEY TALKING ABOUT?
RAFAEL IS STILL REACTING, SO THE STONE MUST EXIST.
BUT WE DIDN'T FIND THE STONE EVEN AFTER WE DISSECTED THE ENTIRE ROYAL FAMILY OF RAGGS.
PERHAPS WE OVER-LOOKED A RELATIVE.
JANGLE.
JANGLE
WE'RE MISSING THE STONE THAT SHOULD BE ON THE NECKLACE BELONGING TO THE KING OF RAGGS...
?!
MY HEAD...!!
OW...
JANGLE
WHY IS IT...
"I PROMISE..."
OH...
JANGLE

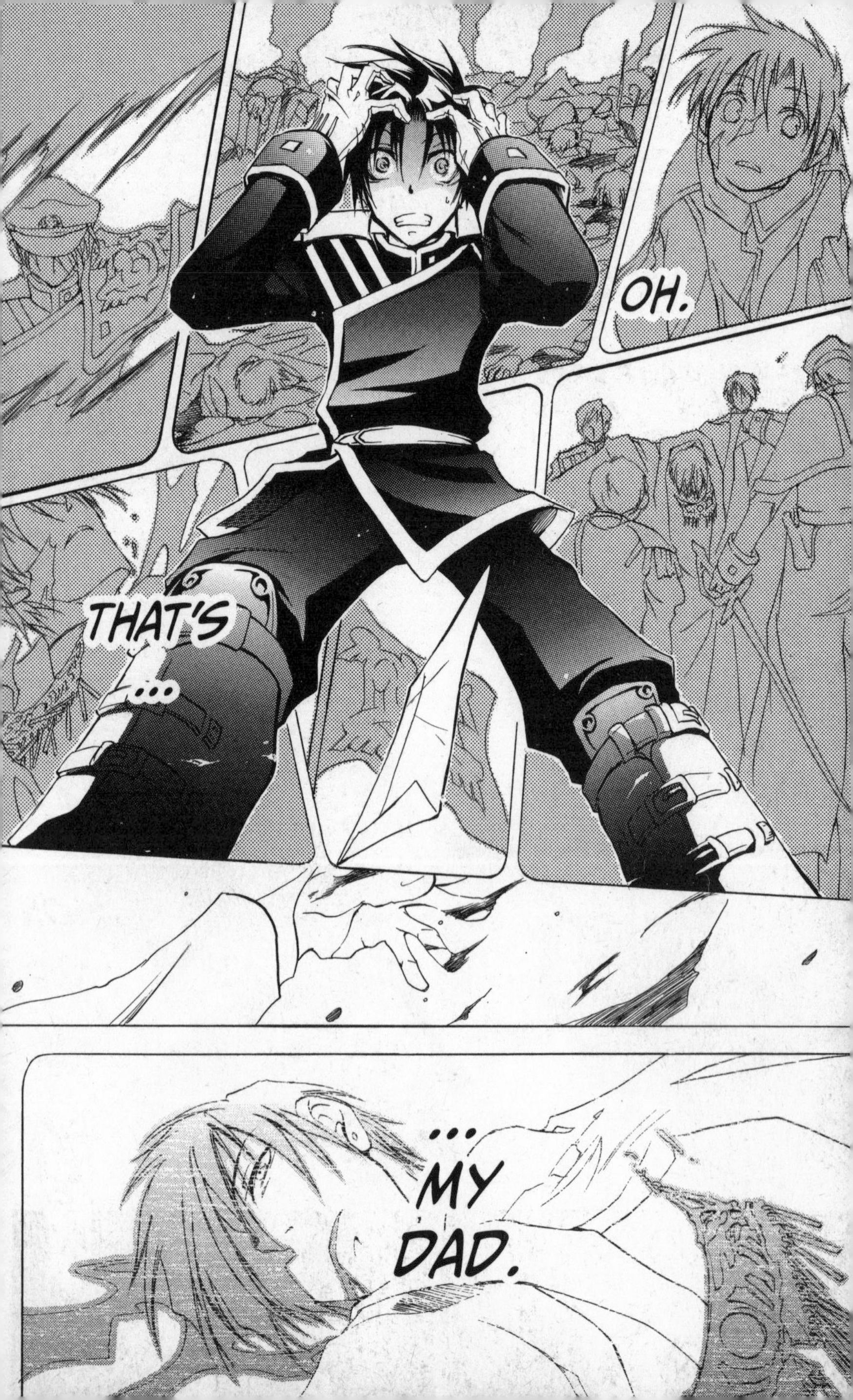
OH.
THAT'S ...
... MY DAD.

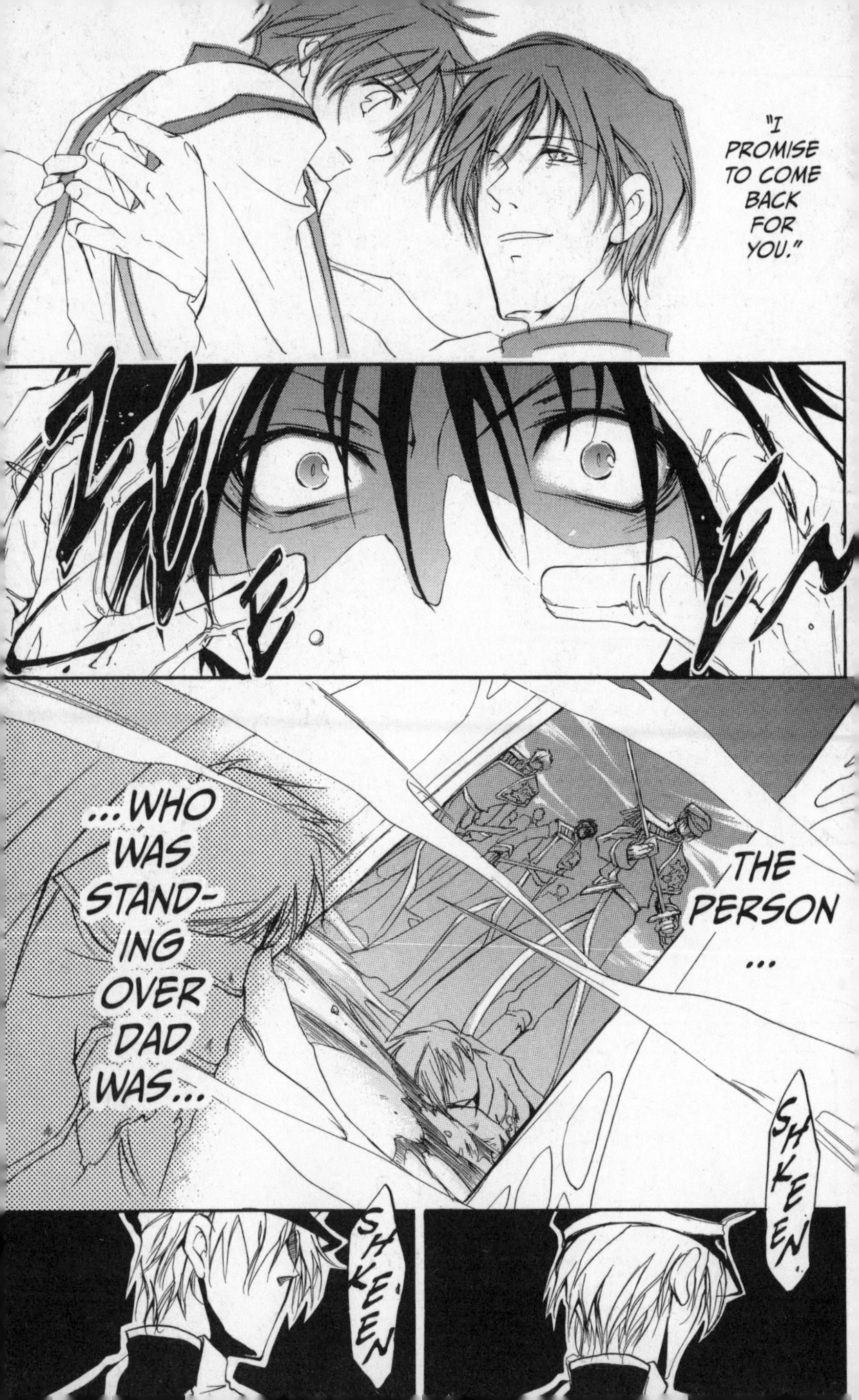
"I PROMISE TO COME BACK FOR YOU."
THE PERSON...
...WHO WAS STAND-ING OVER DAD WAS...
SHKEEN.
SHKEEN

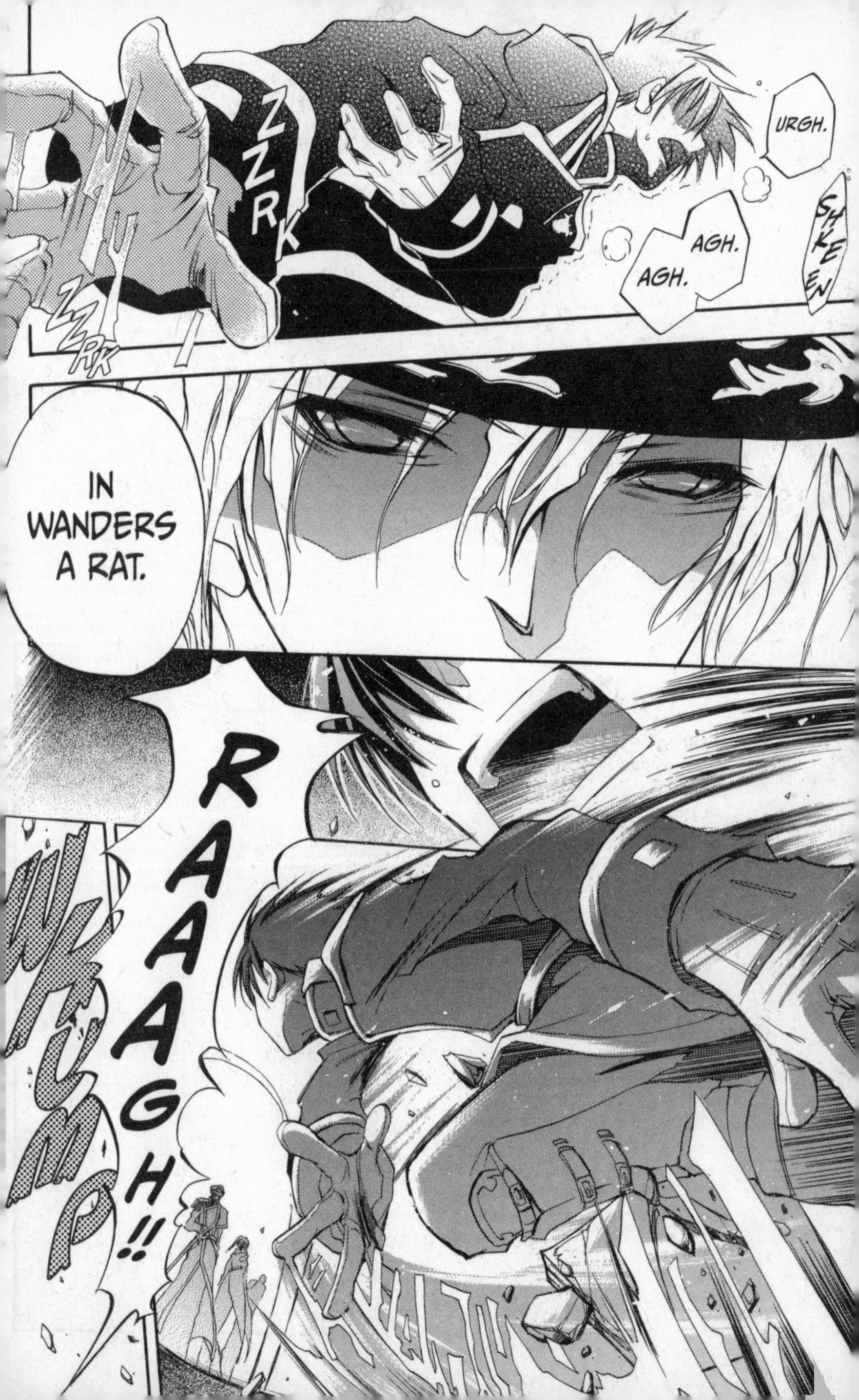
SHKEEN
URGH.
AGH.
AGH.
ZZRK
ZZRK
IN WANDERS A RAT.
RAAAAGH!!
WHUMP

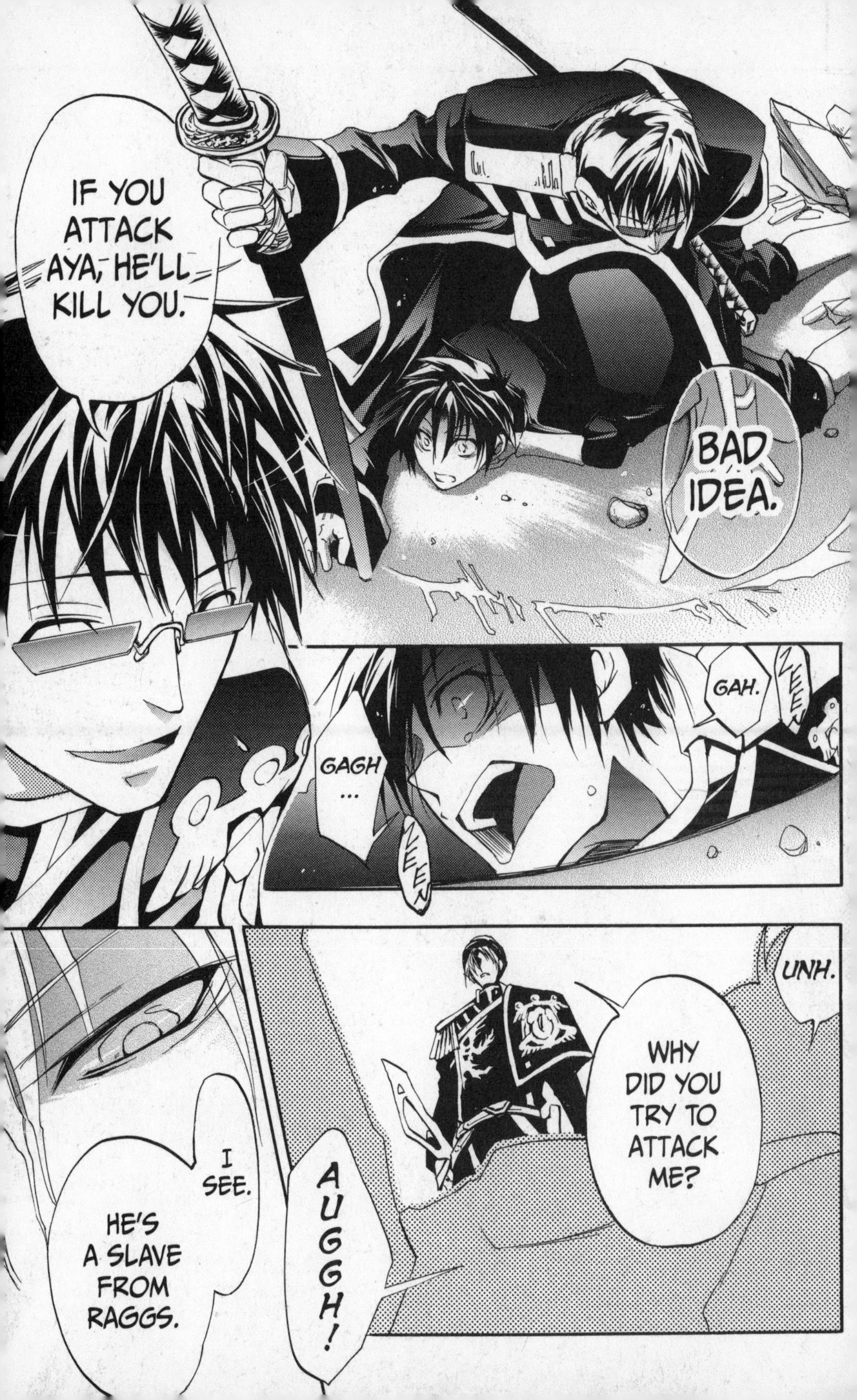
BAD IDEA.
IF YOU ATTACK AYA, HE'LL KILL YOU.
GAH.
ZEEN
GAGH ...
ZEEN
UNH.
WHY DID YOU TRY TO ATTACK ME?
AUGGH!
I SEE.
HE'S A SLAVE FROM RAGGS.

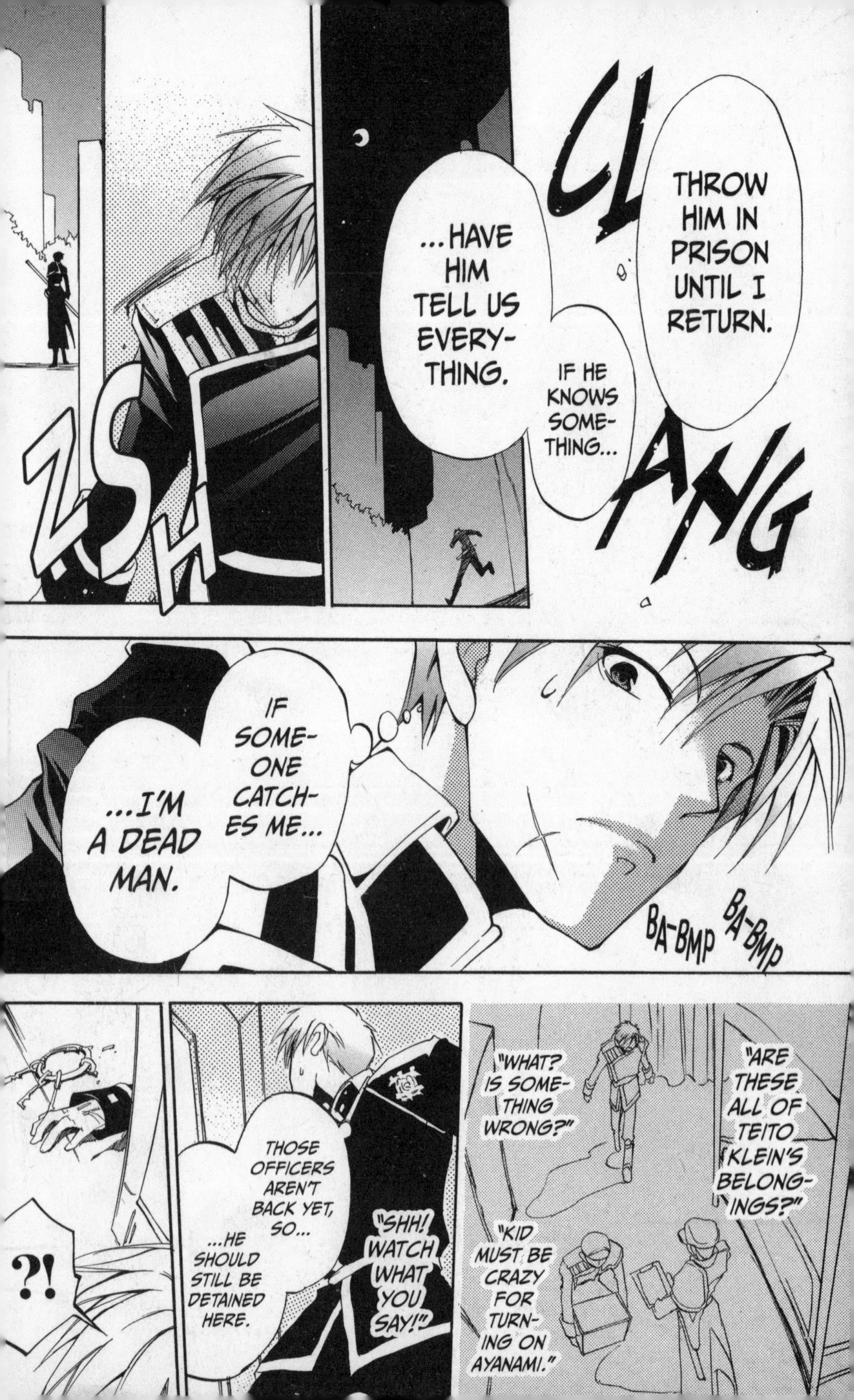
CLANG
THROW HIM IN PRISON UNTIL I RETURN.
IF HE KNOWS SOMETHING...
...HAVE HIM TELL US EVERYTHING.
ZSH
IF SOMEONE CATCHES ME...
...I'M A DEAD MAN.
BA-BMP
BA-BMP
"ARE THESE ALL OF TEITO KLEIN'S BELONGINGS?"
"WHAT? IS SOMETHING WRONG?"
"KID MUST BE CRAZY FOR TURNING ON AYANAMI."
"SHH! WATCH WHAT YOU SAY!"
THOSE OFFICERS AREN'T BACK YET, SO...
...HE SHOULD STILL BE DETAINED HERE.
?!

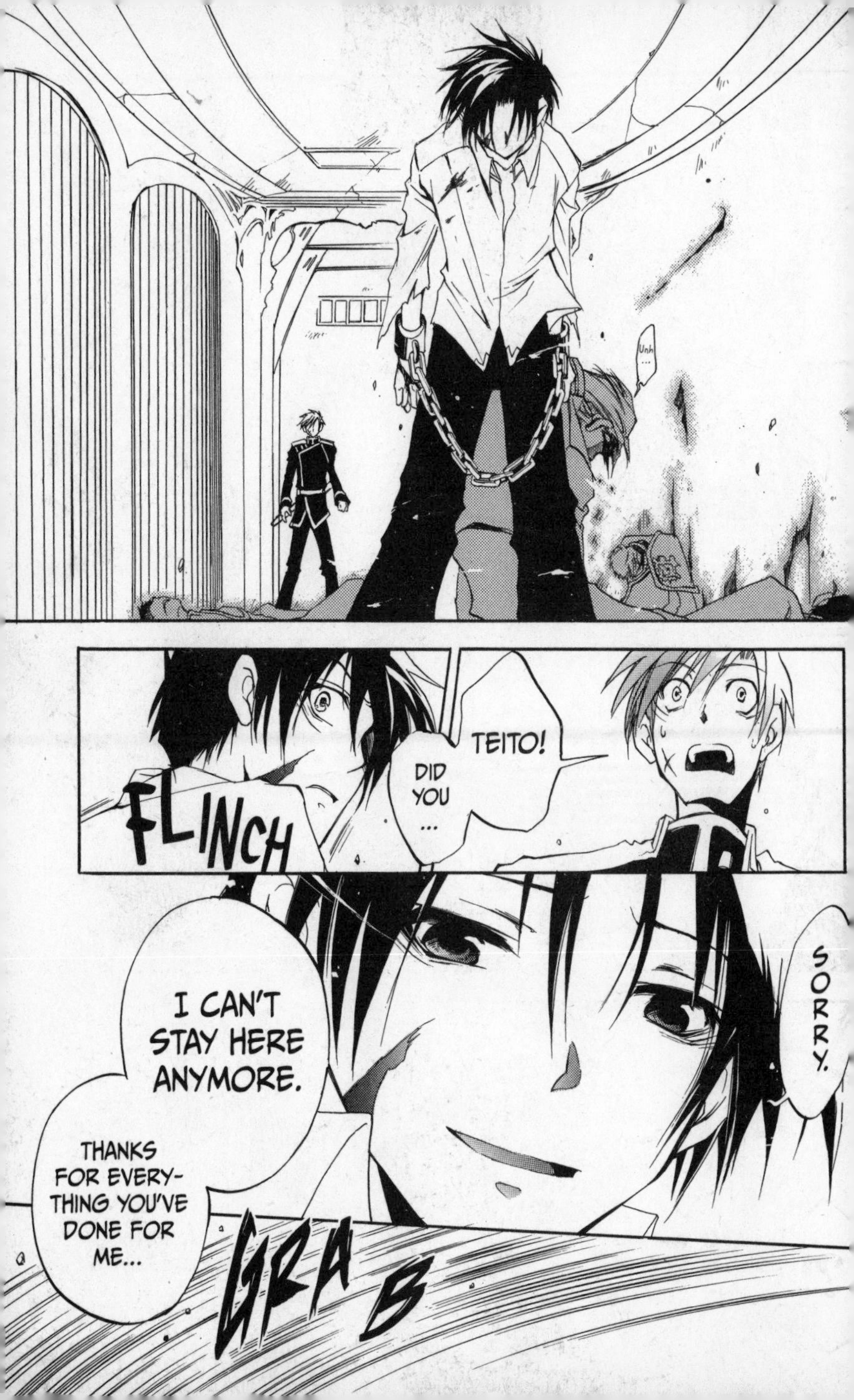
Unh...
TEITO!
DID YOU...
FLINCH
SORRY.
I CAN'T STAY HERE ANYMORE.
THANKS FOR EVERYTHING YOU'VE DONE FOR ME...
GRAB

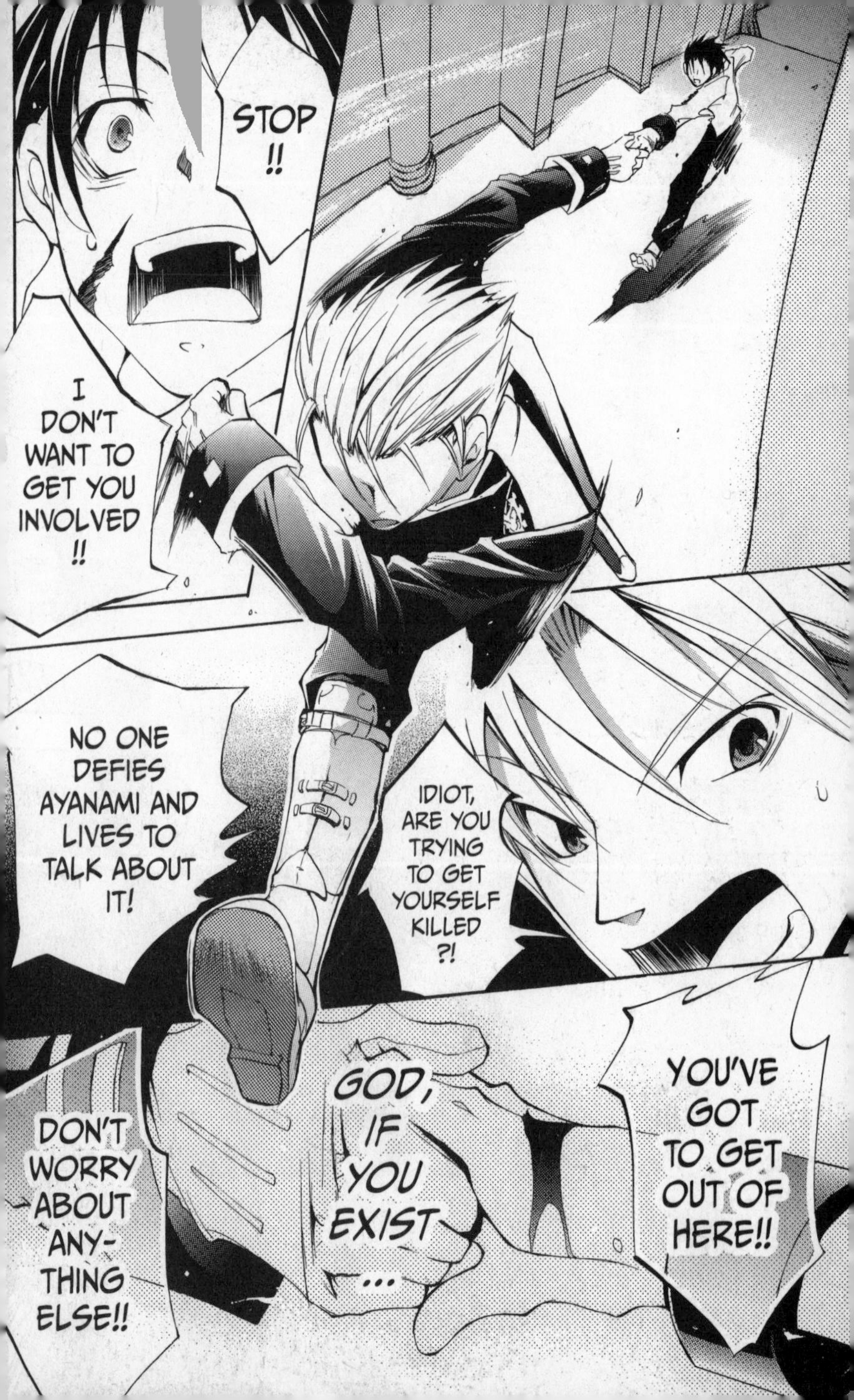
STOP!!
I DON'T WANT TO GET YOU INVOLVED!!
IDIOT, ARE YOU TRYING TO GET YOURSELF KILLED?!
NO ONE DEFIES AYANAMI AND LIVES TO TALK ABOUT IT!
YOU'VE GOT TO GET OUT OF HERE!!
GOD, IF YOU EXIST...
DON'T WORRY ABOUT ANY-THING ELSE!!

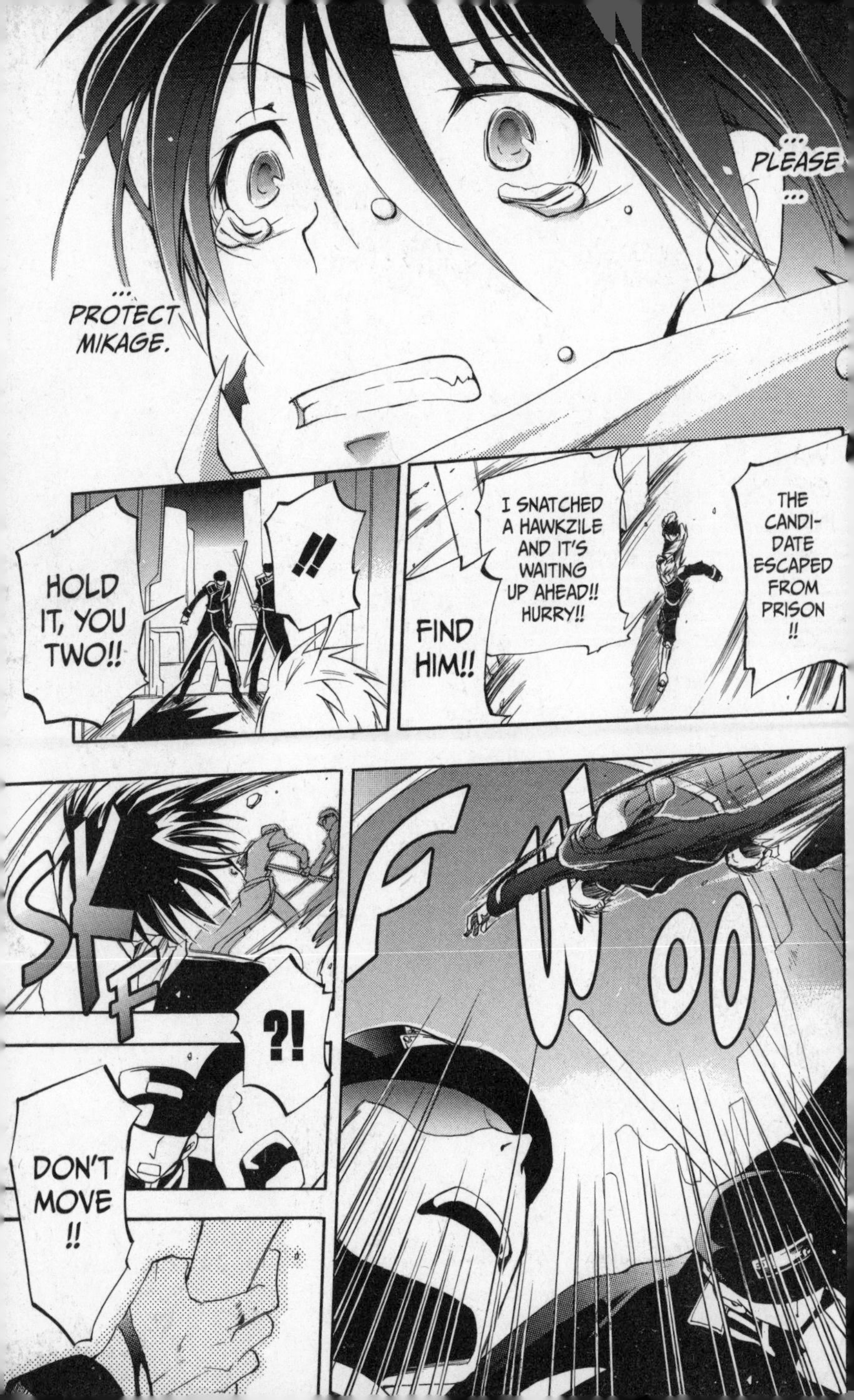
...PLEASE...
...PROTECT MIKAGE.
THE CANDIDATE ESCAPED FROM PRISON!!
I SNATCHED A HAWKZILE AND IT'S WAITING UP AHEAD!! HURRY!!
FIND HIM!!
!!
HOLD IT, YOU TWO!!
FWOO
?!
DON'T MOVE!!

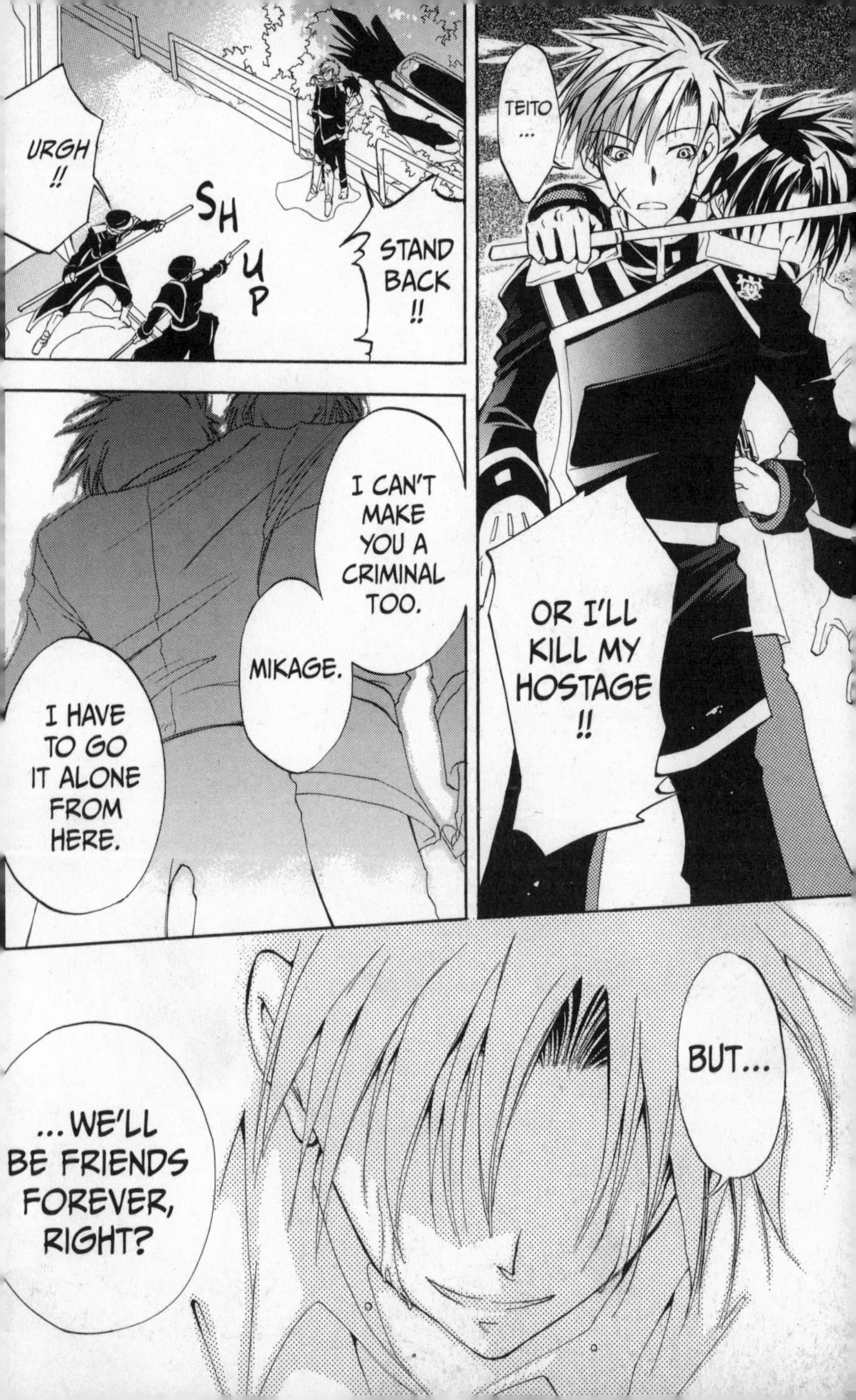
TEITO...
OR I'LL KILL MY HOSTAGE!!
STAND BACK!!
SHUP
URGH!!
I CAN'T MAKE YOU A CRIMINAL TOO.
MIKAGE.
I HAVE TO GO IT ALONE FROM HERE.
BUT...
...WE'LL BE FRIENDS FOREVER, RIGHT?

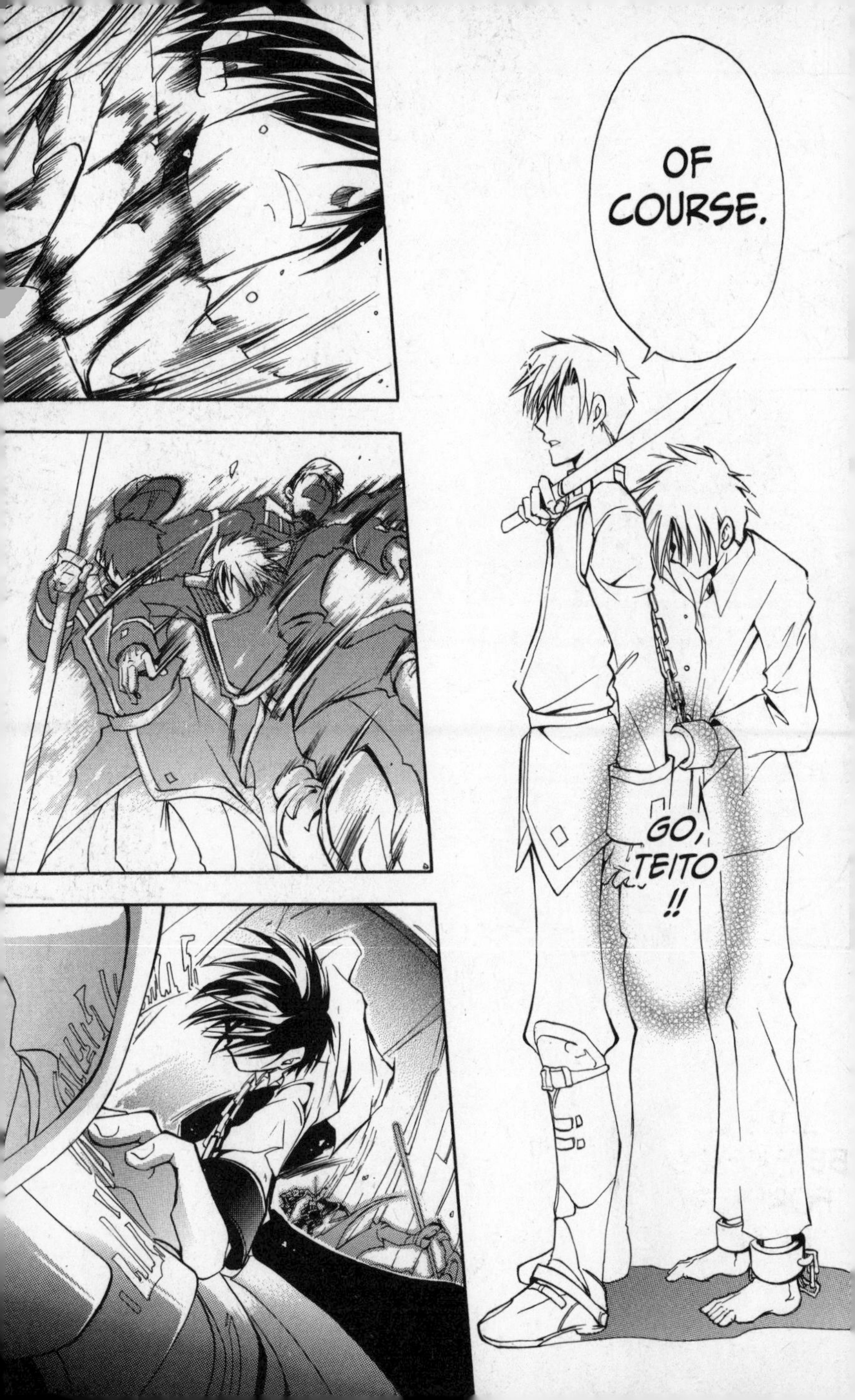

OF COURSE.
GO, TEITO !!

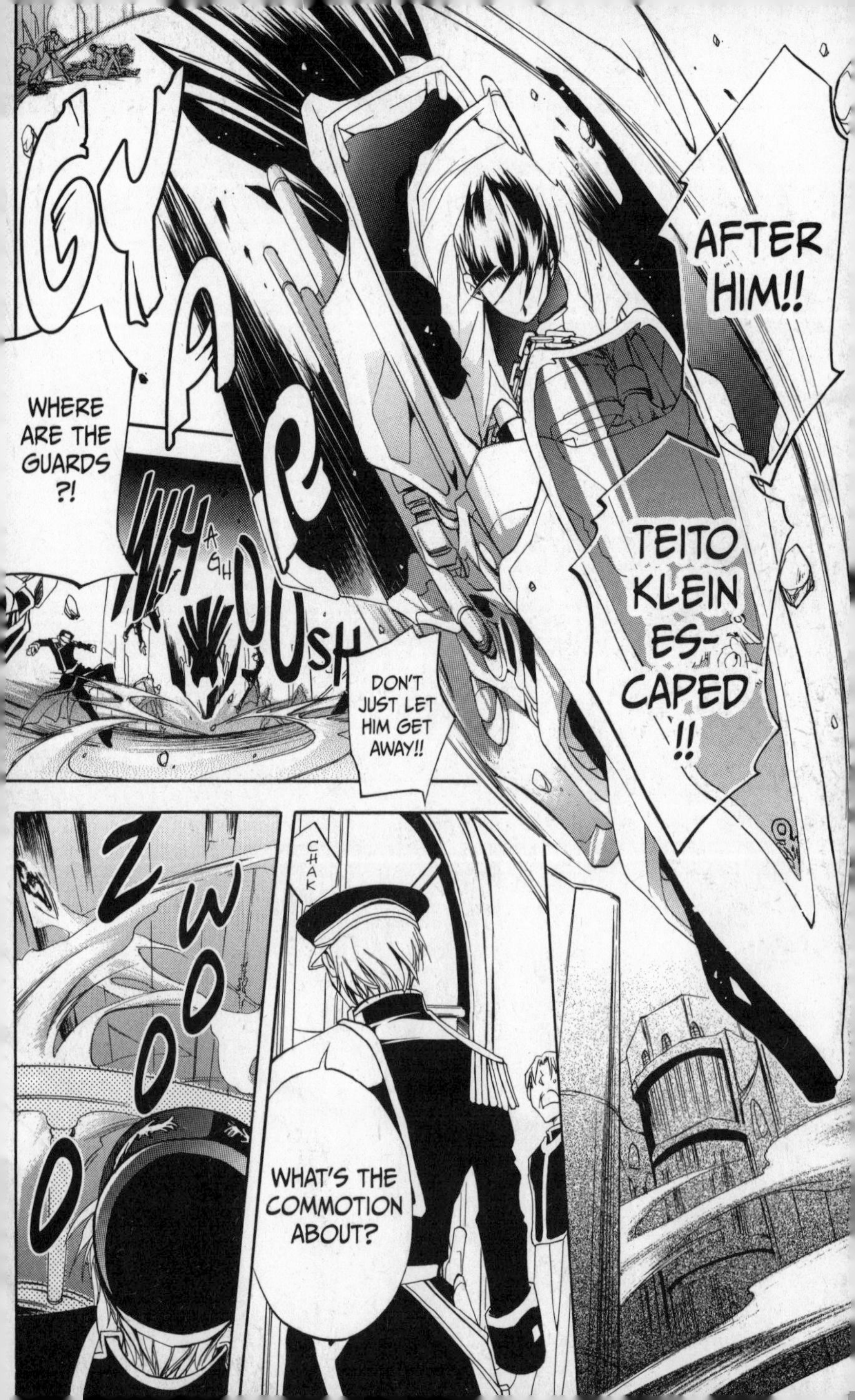
AFTER HIM!!
TEITO KLEIN ES-CAPED!!
DON'T JUST LET HIM GET AWAY!!
WHERE ARE THE GUARDS?!
AGH
CHAK
WHAT'S THE COMMOTION ABOUT?

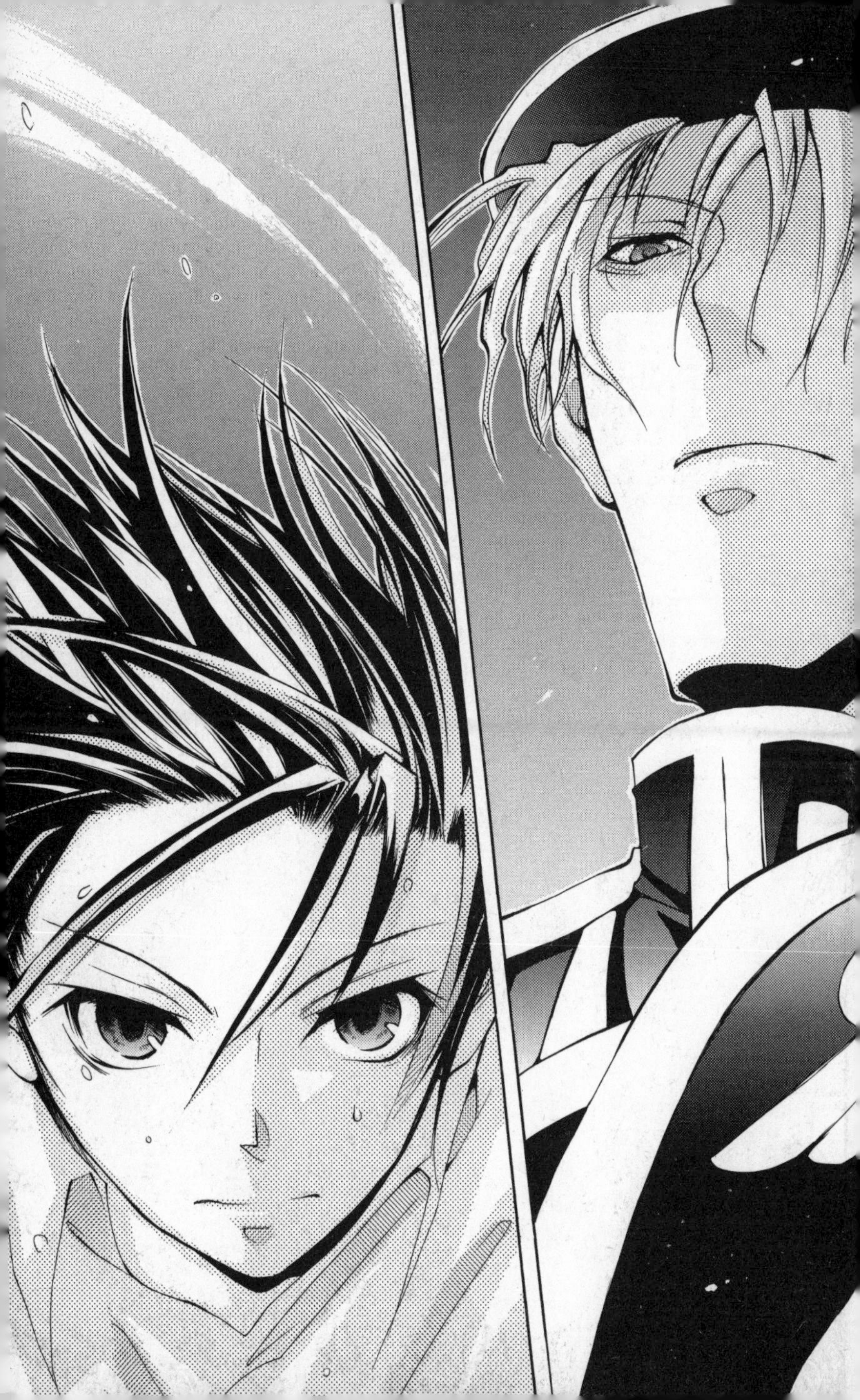

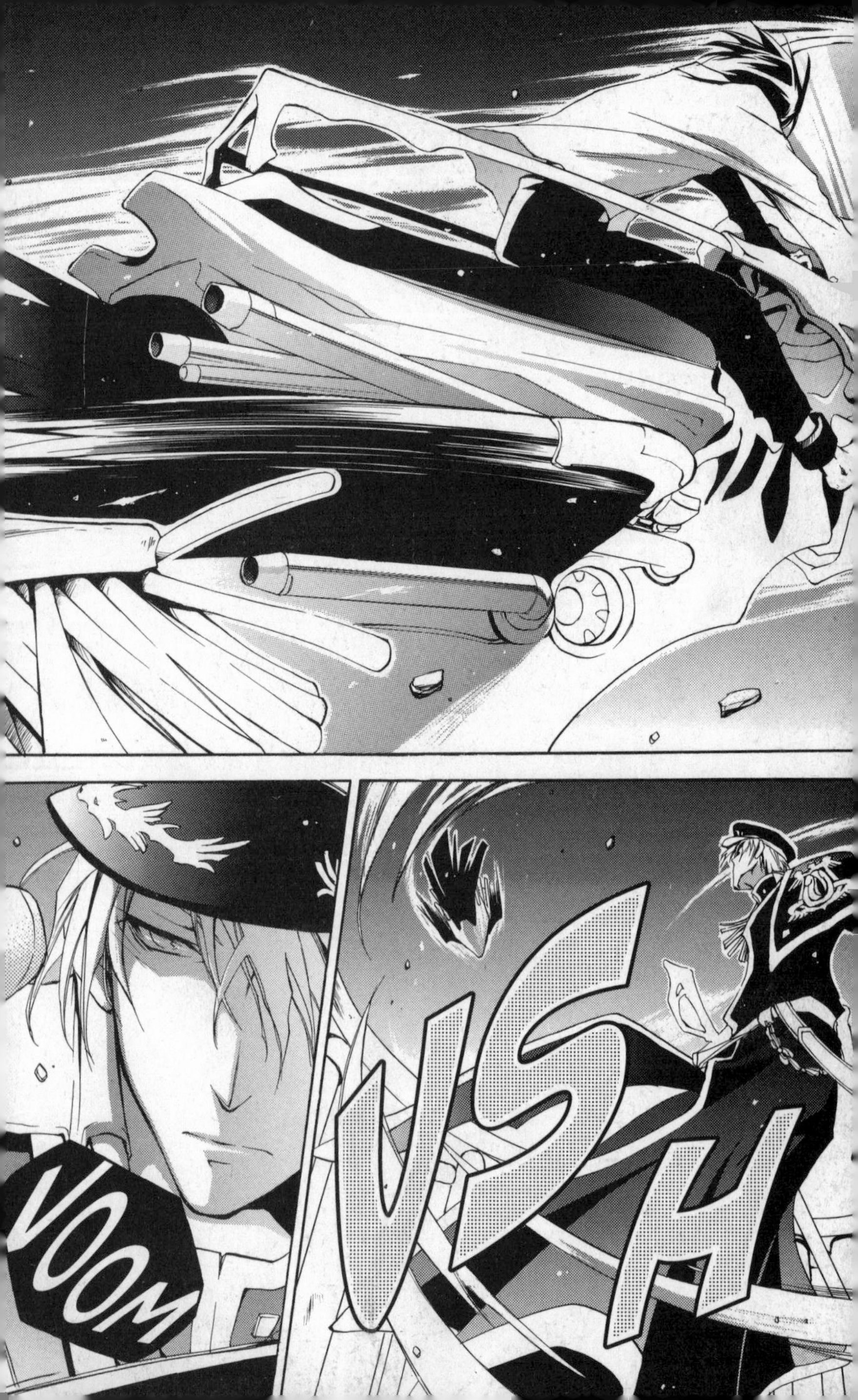
VSH
VOOM

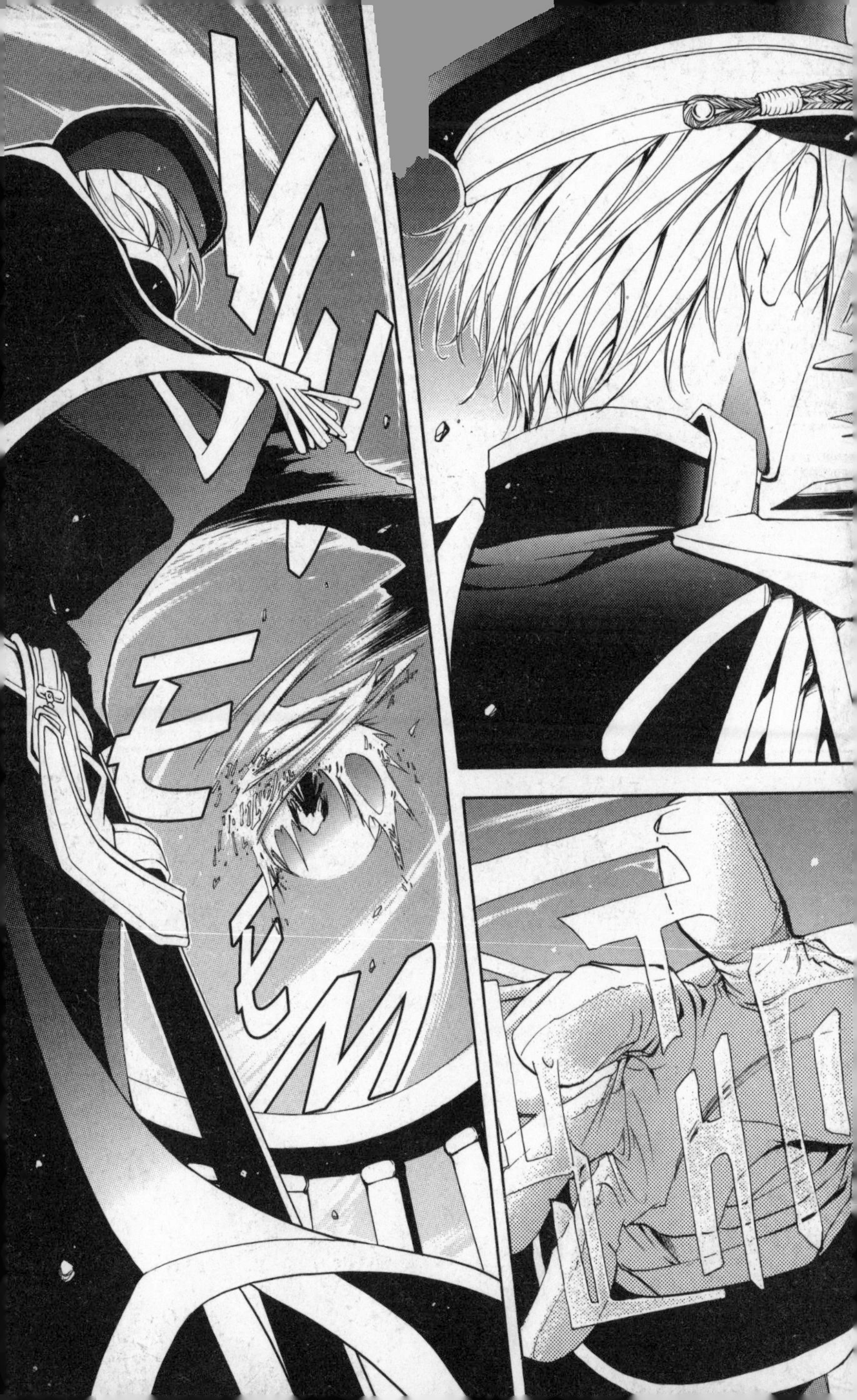

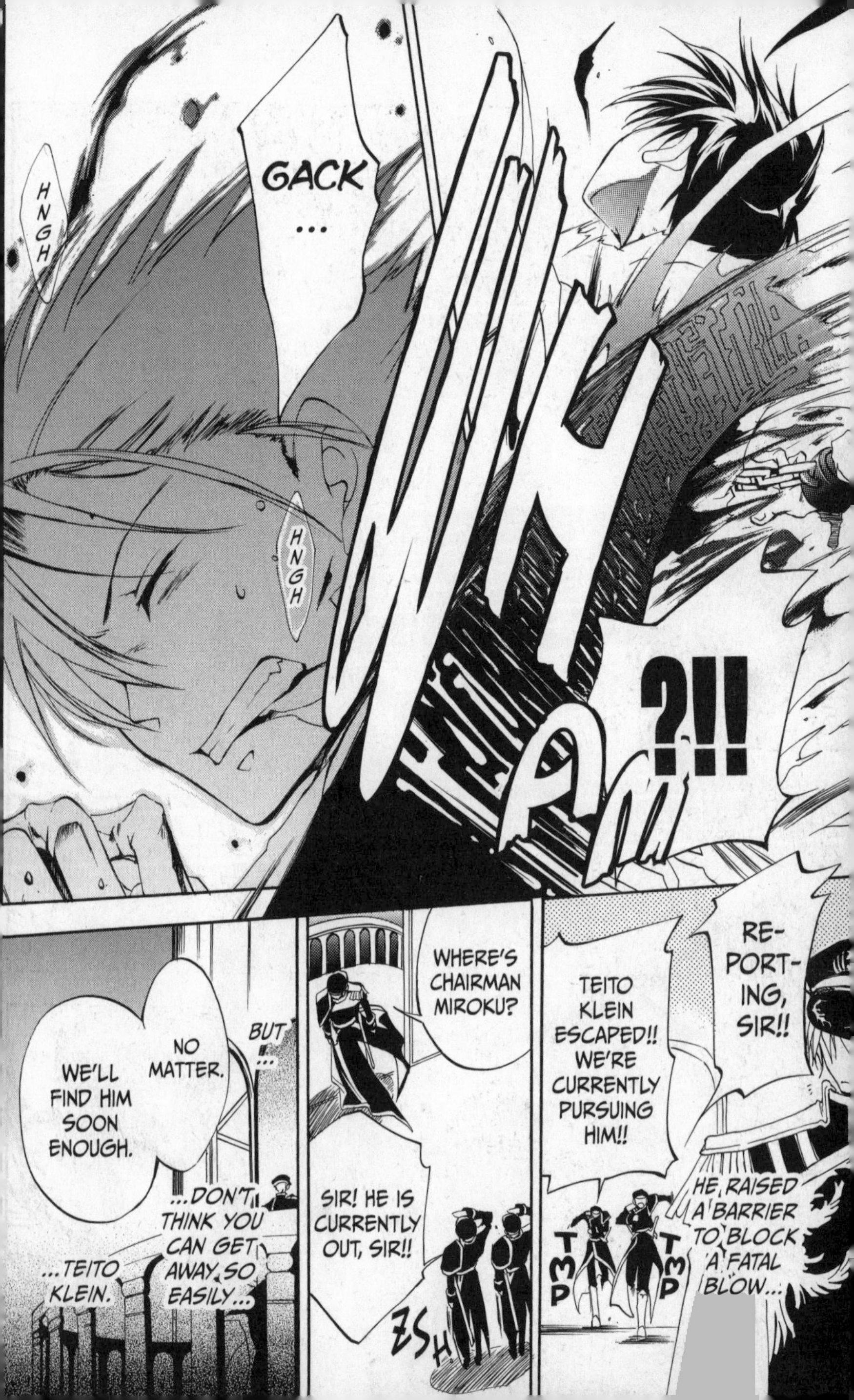
GACK ...
HNGH
HNGH
?!!
RE-PORT-ING, SIR!!
TEITO KLEIN ESCAPED!! WE'RE CURRENTLY PURSUING HIM!!
HE RAISED A BARRIER TO BLOCK A FATAL BLOW...
TMP
TMP
WHERE'S CHAIRMAN MIROKU?
SIR! HE IS CURRENTLY OUT, SIR!!
ZSH
BUT ...
NO MATTER.
WE'LL FIND HIM SOON ENOUGH.
...DON'T THINK YOU CAN GET AWAY SO EASILY...
...TEITO KLEIN.

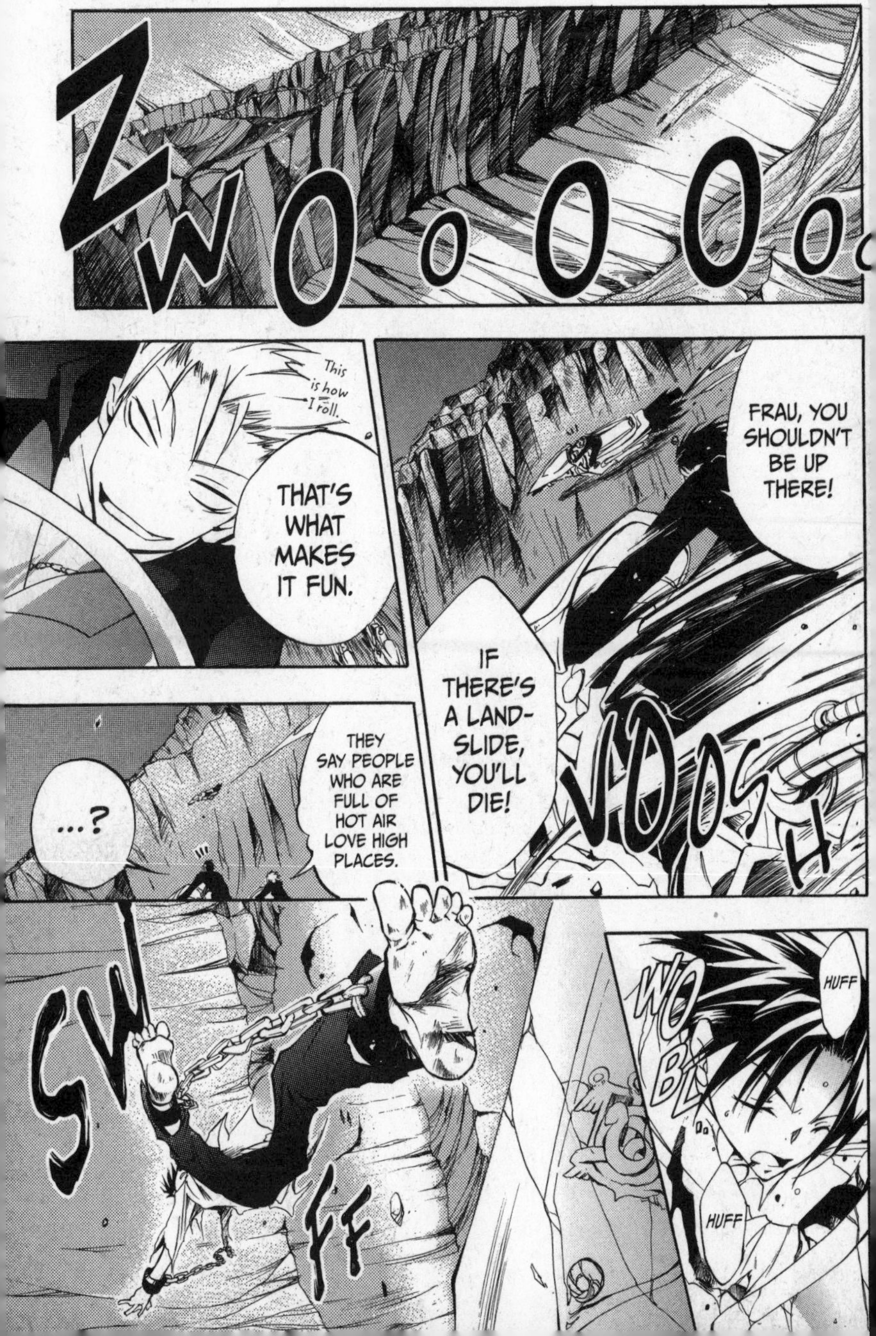
ZWOOOOO
FRAU, YOU SHOULDN'T BE UP THERE!
IF THERE'S A LAND-SLIDE, YOU'LL DIE!
VOOSH
THAT'S WHAT MAKES IT FUN.
This is how I roll.
THEY SAY PEOPLE WHO ARE FULL OF HOT AIR LOVE HIGH PLACES.
...?
WOBBL
HUFF
HUFF
SWFF

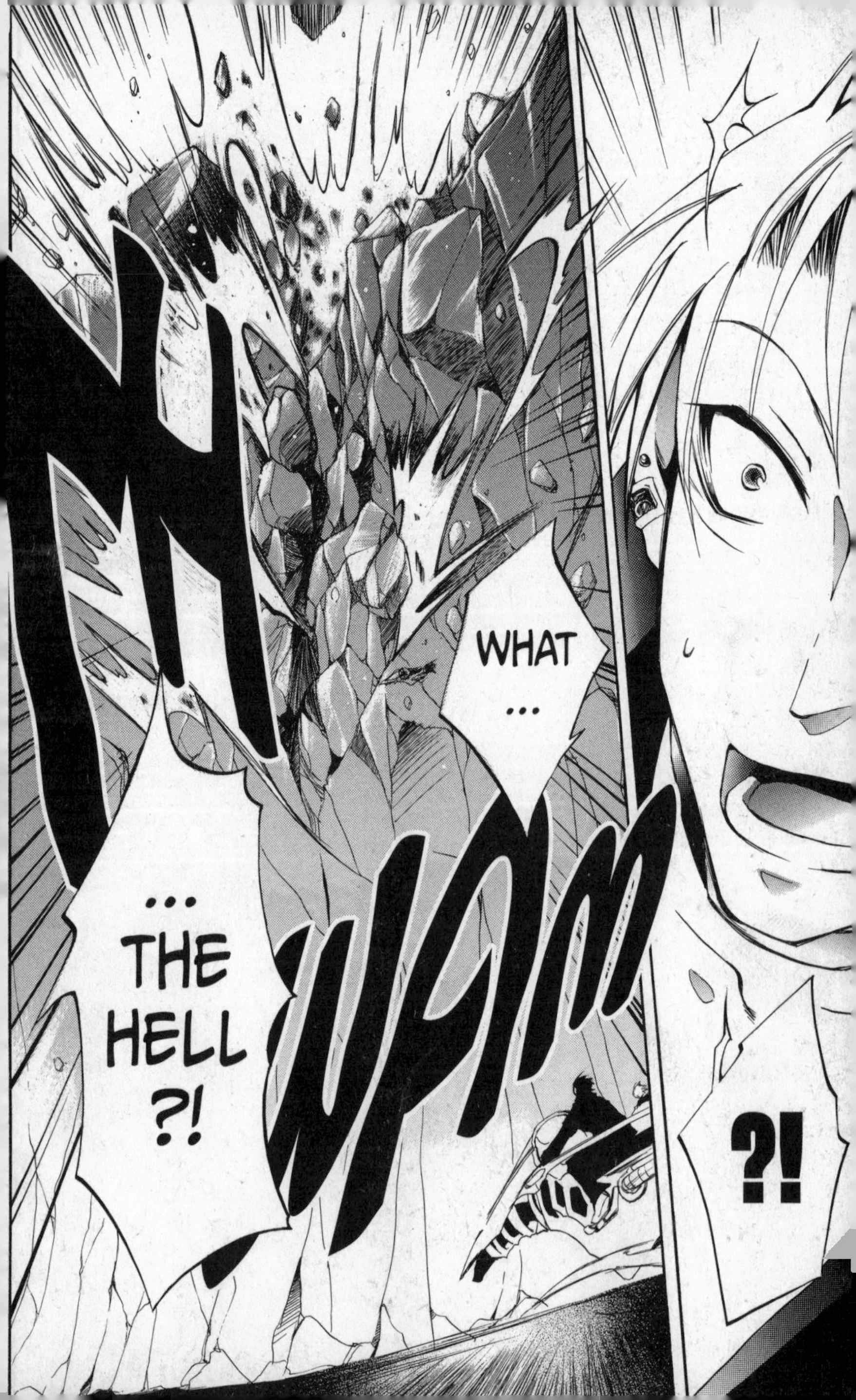
WHAT ...
?!
... THE HELL ?!

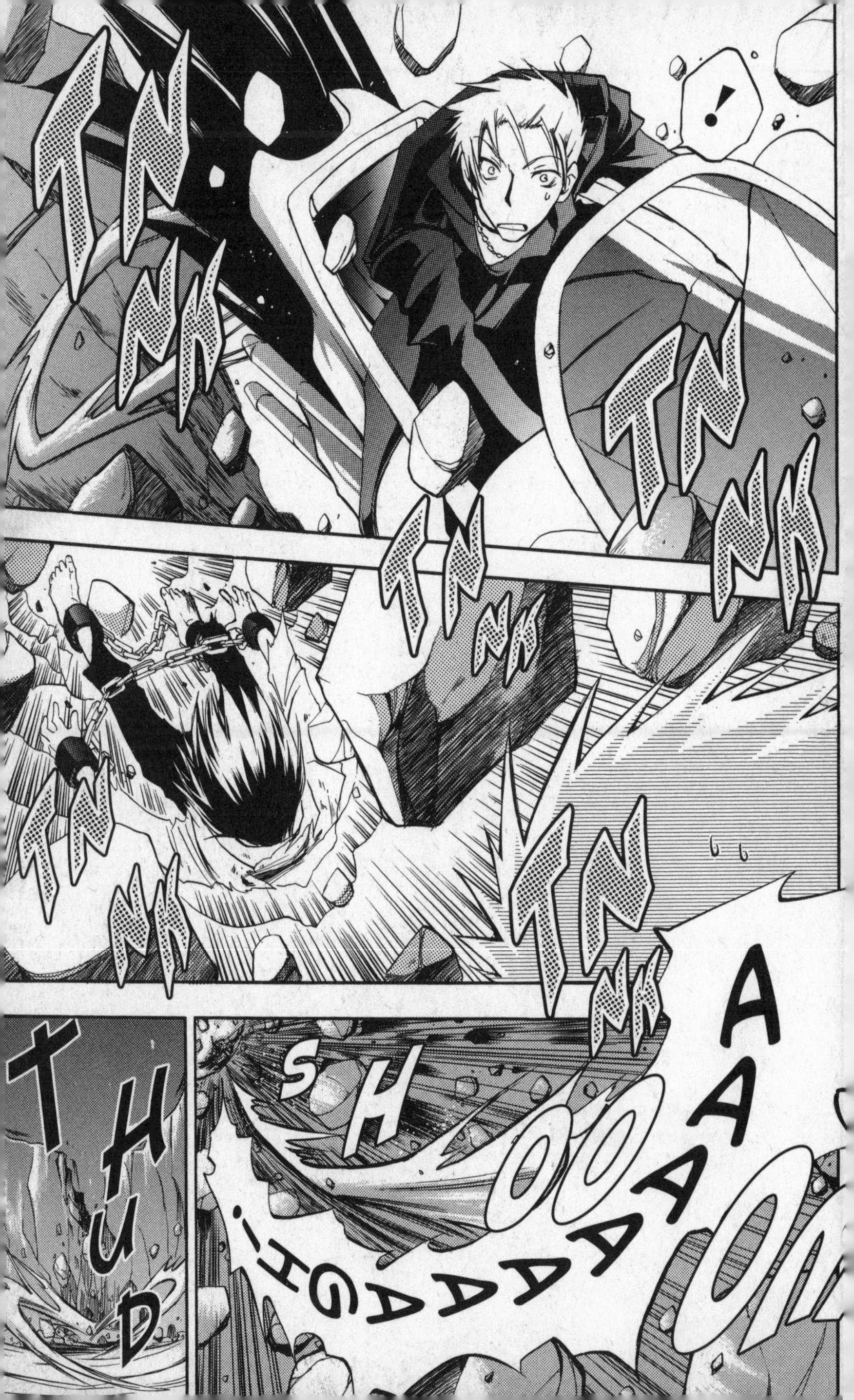
!
TNNK
TNNK
TNNK
TNNK
TNNK
TNNK
SH
AAAAAAGH!!
THUD

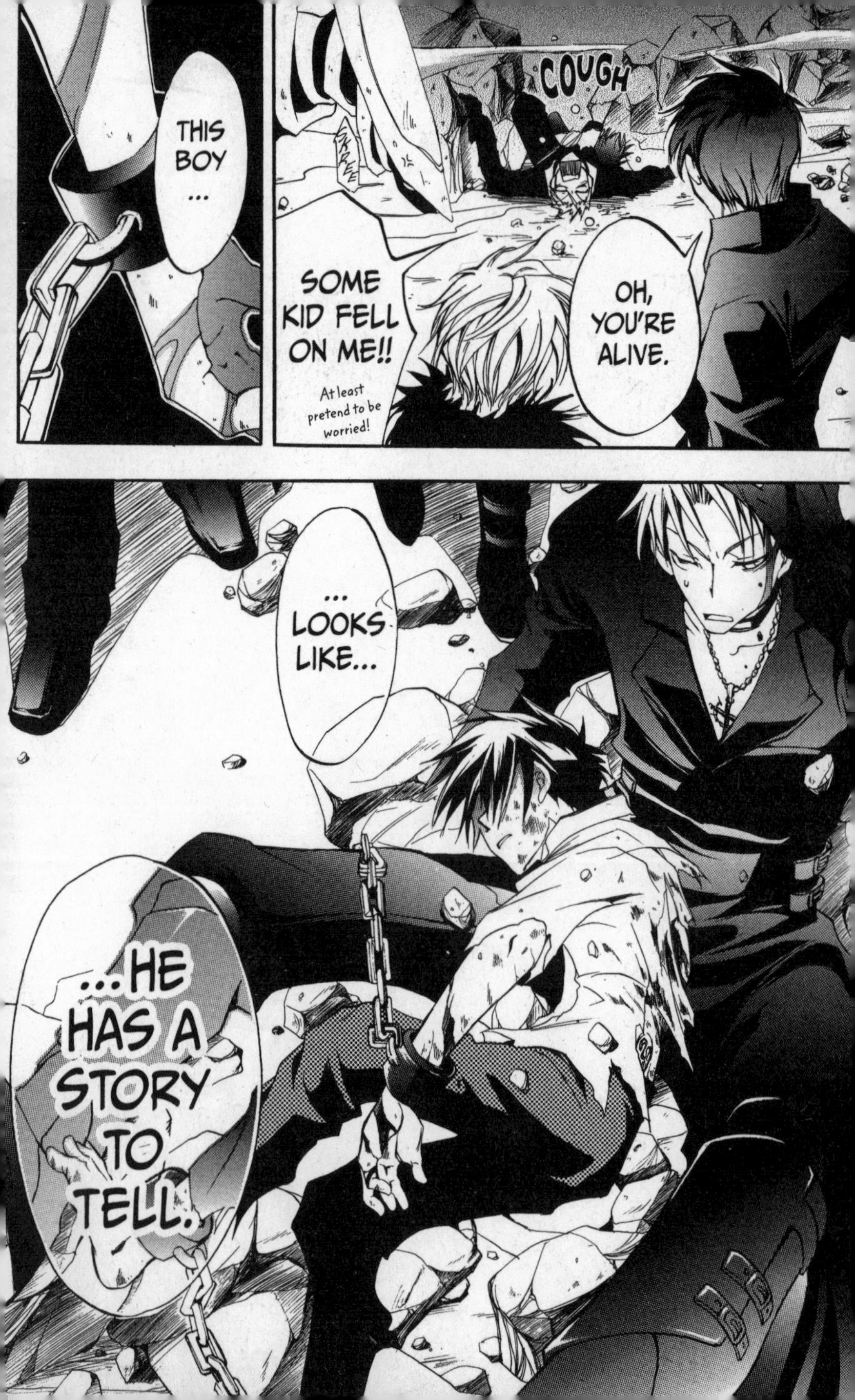
COUGH
OH, YOU'RE ALIVE.
SKREE
SOME KID FELL ON ME!!
At least pretend to be worried!
THIS BOY ...
... LOOKS LIKE...
...HE HAS A STORY TO TELL.

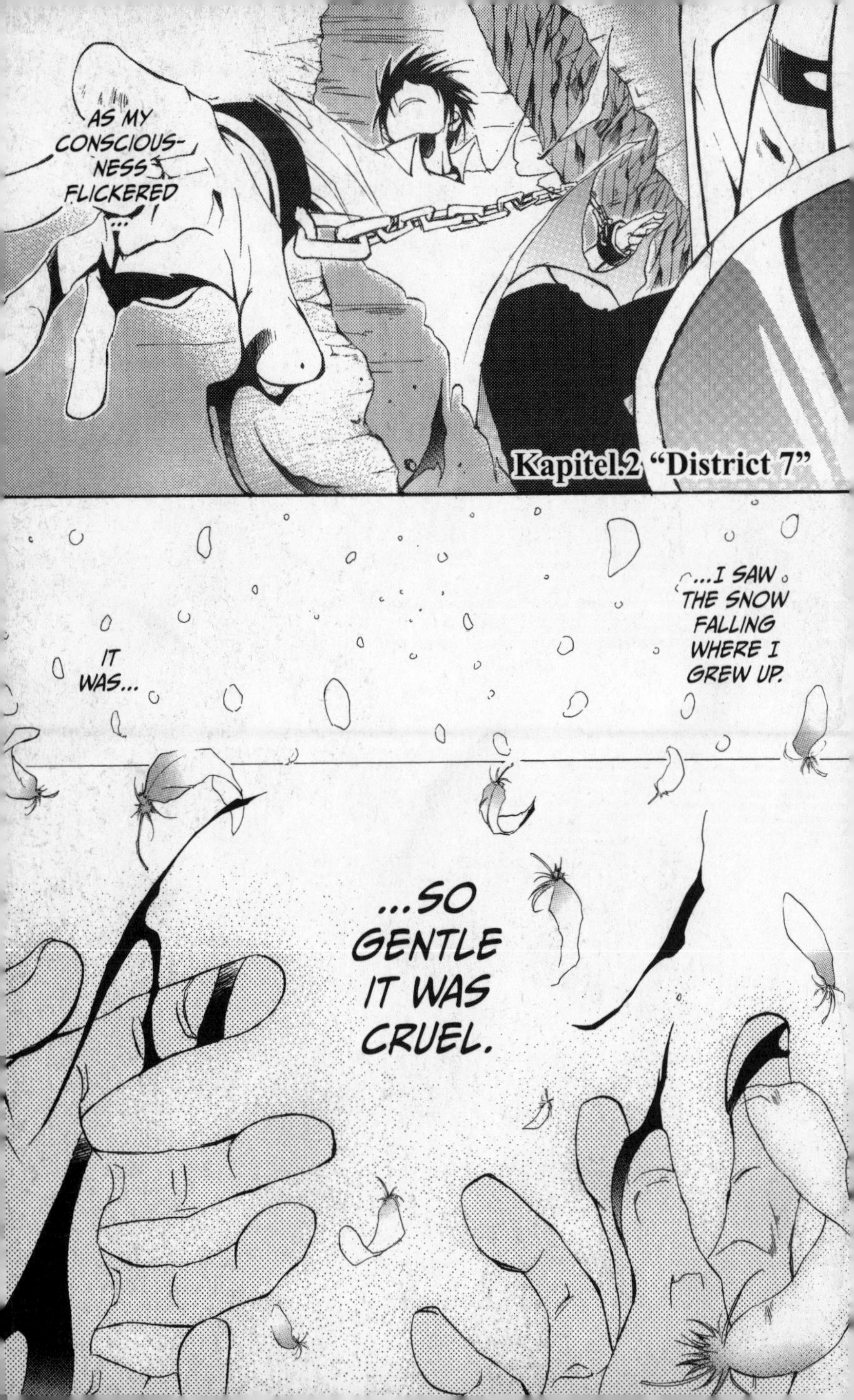
AS MY CONSCIOUS-NESS FLICKERED ...
Kapitel.2 "District 7"
...I SAW THE SNOW FALLING WHERE I GREW UP.
IT WAS...
...SO GENTLE IT WAS CRUEL.

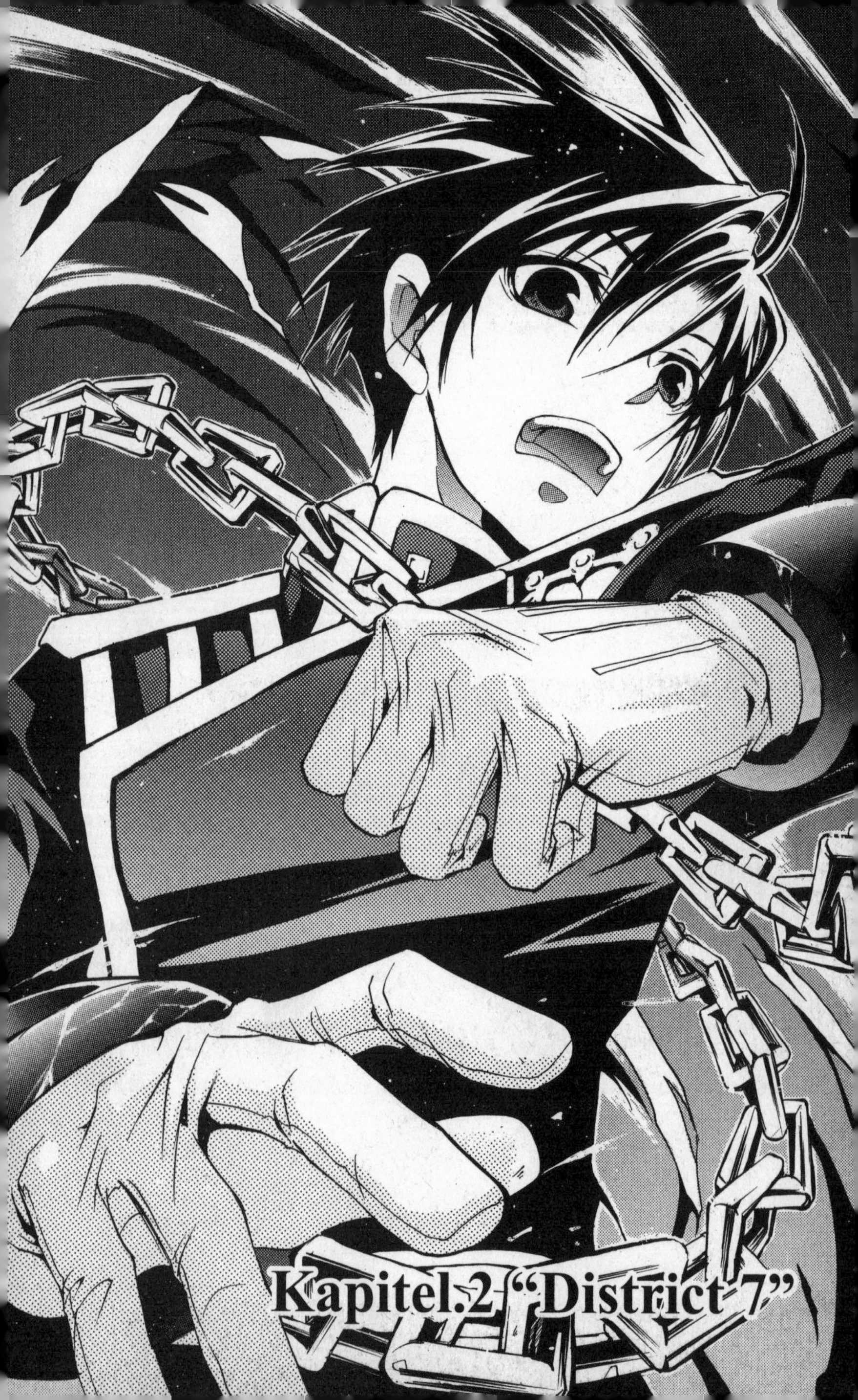
Kapitel.2 "District 7"

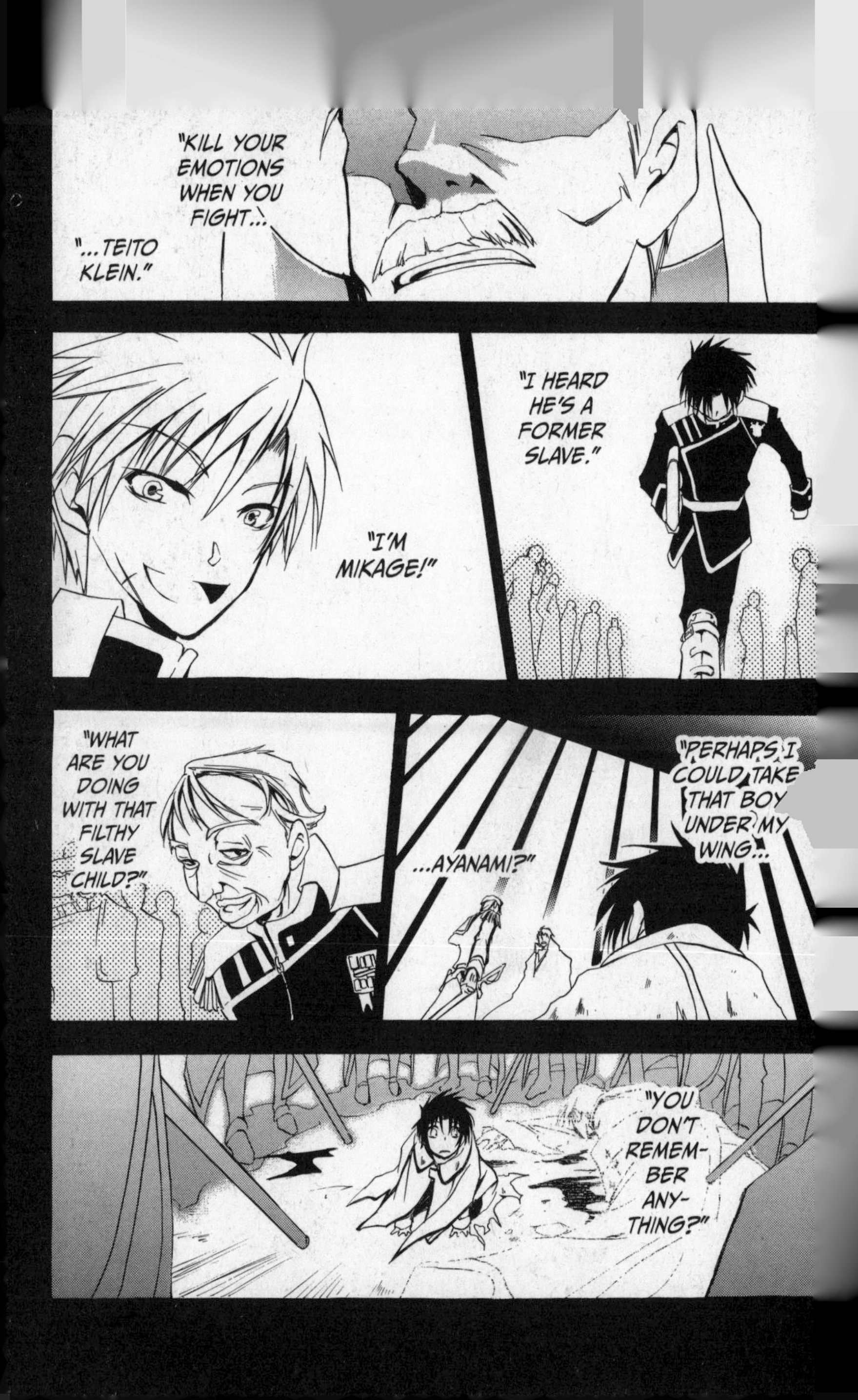
"KILL YOUR EMOTIONS WHEN YOU FIGHT...
"...TEITO KLEIN."
"I HEARD HE'S A FORMER SLAVE."
"I'M MIKAGE!"
"PERHAPS I COULD TAKE THAT BOY UNDER MY WING...
...AYANAMI?"
"WHAT ARE YOU DOING WITH THAT FILTHY SLAVE CHILD?"
"YOU DON'T REMEMBER ANYTHING?"

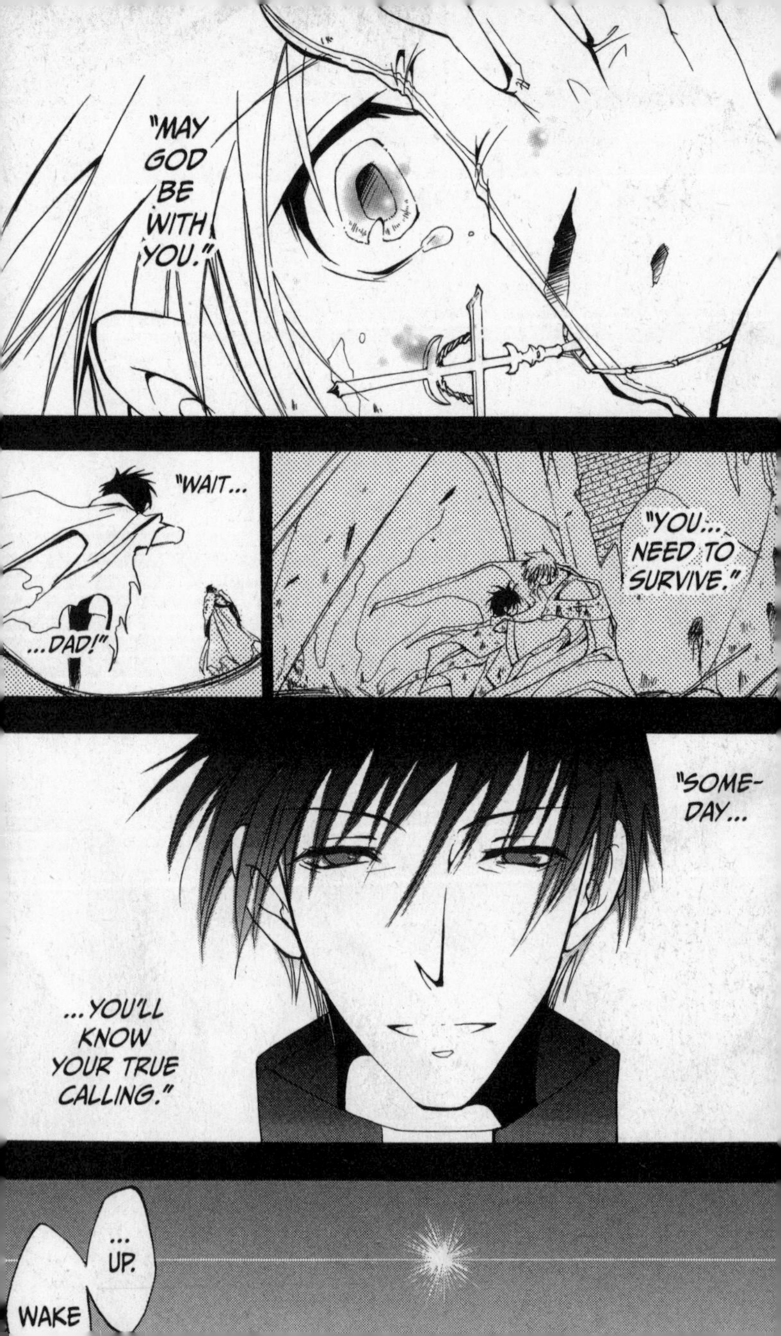
"MAY GOD BE WITH YOU."
"YOU... NEED TO SURVIVE."
"WAIT...
...DAD!"
"SOME-DAY...
...YOU'LL KNOW YOUR TRUE CALLING."
... UP.
WAKE

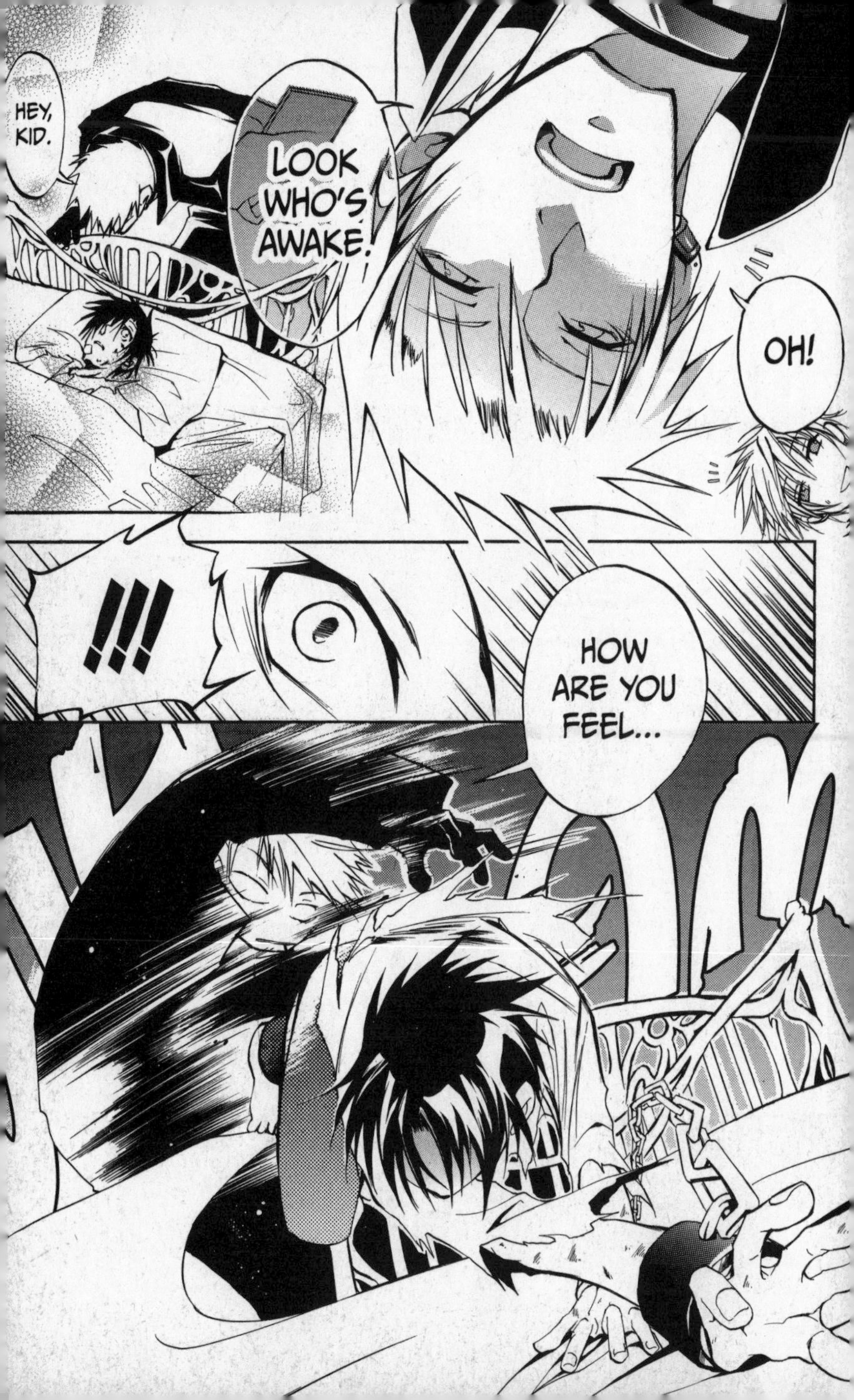
OH!
LOOK WHO'S AWAKE!
HEY, KID.
HOW ARE YOU FEEL...
!!!

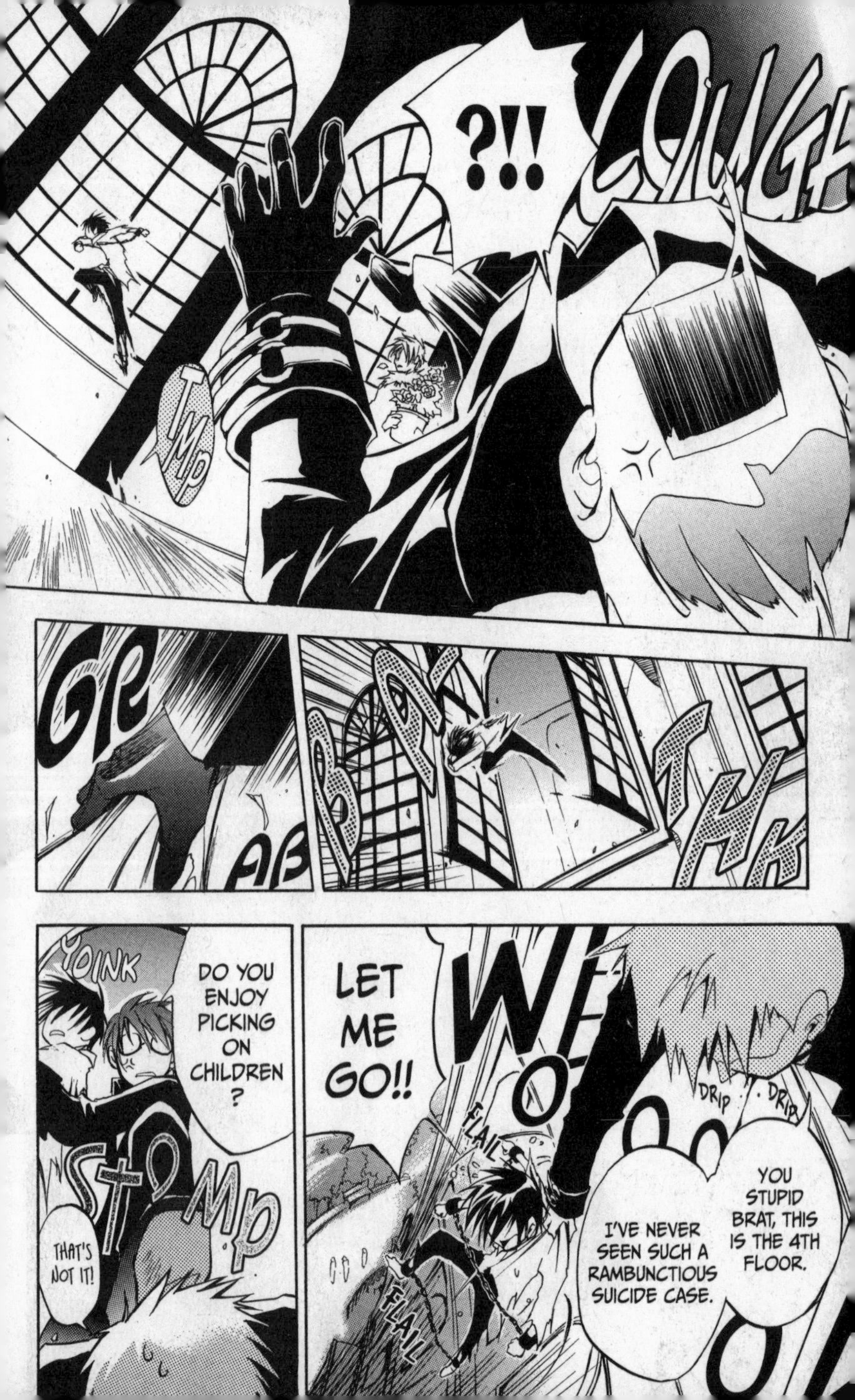
COUGH
?!!
TMP
THK
DRIP DRIP
YOU STUPID BRAT, THIS IS THE 4TH FLOOR.
I'VE NEVER SEEN SUCH A RAMBUNCTIOUS SUICIDE CASE.
LET ME GO!!
FLAIL
FLAIL
DO YOU ENJOY PICKING ON CHILDREN?
YOINK
STOMP
THAT'S NOT IT!

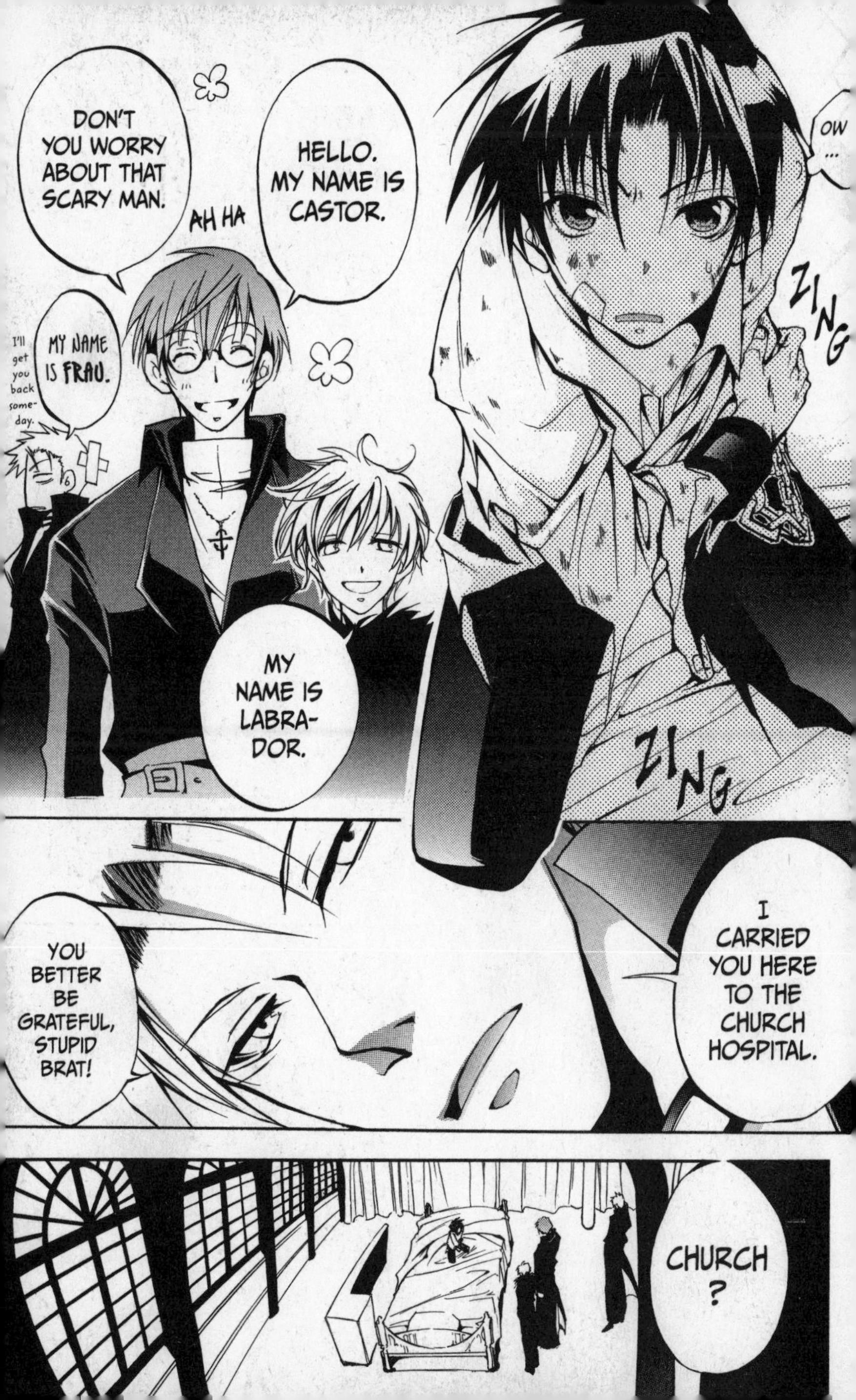
OW ...
ZING
ZING
HELLO. MY NAME IS CASTOR.
AH HA
DON'T YOU WORRY ABOUT THAT SCARY MAN.
MY NAME IS FRAU.
I'll get you back someday.
MY NAME IS LABRADOR.
I CARRIED YOU HERE TO THE CHURCH HOSPITAL.
YOU BETTER BE GRATEFUL, STUPID BRAT!
CHURCH ?

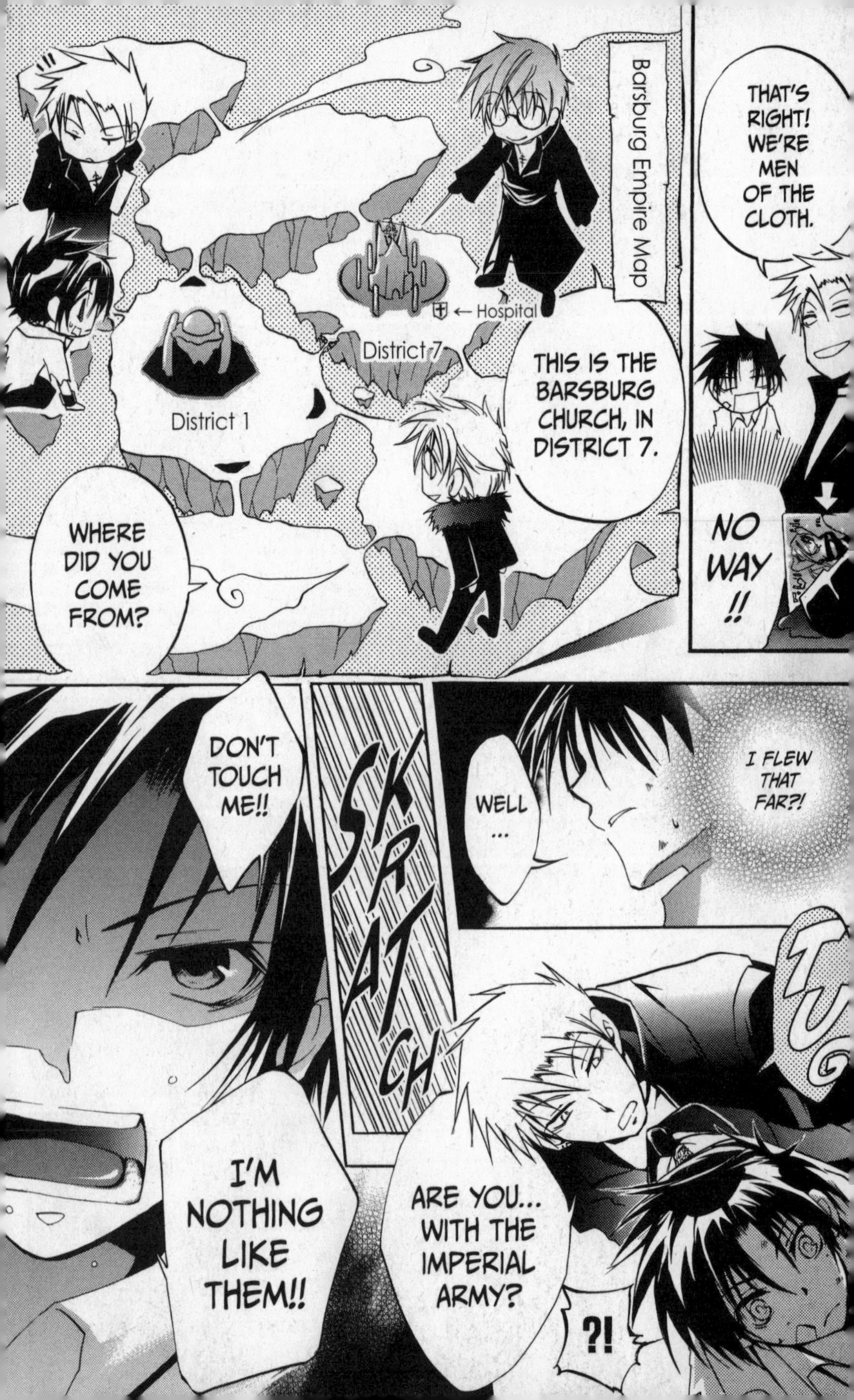
THAT'S RIGHT! WE'RE MEN OF THE CLOTH.
NO WAY!!
Barsburg Empire Map
← Hospital
District 7
THIS IS THE BARSBURG CHURCH, IN DISTRICT 7.
District 1
WHERE DID YOU COME FROM?
I FLEW THAT FAR?!
WELL...
TUG
ARE YOU... WITH THE IMPERIAL ARMY?
?!
SKRATCH
DON'T TOUCH ME!!
I'M NOTHING LIKE THEM!!

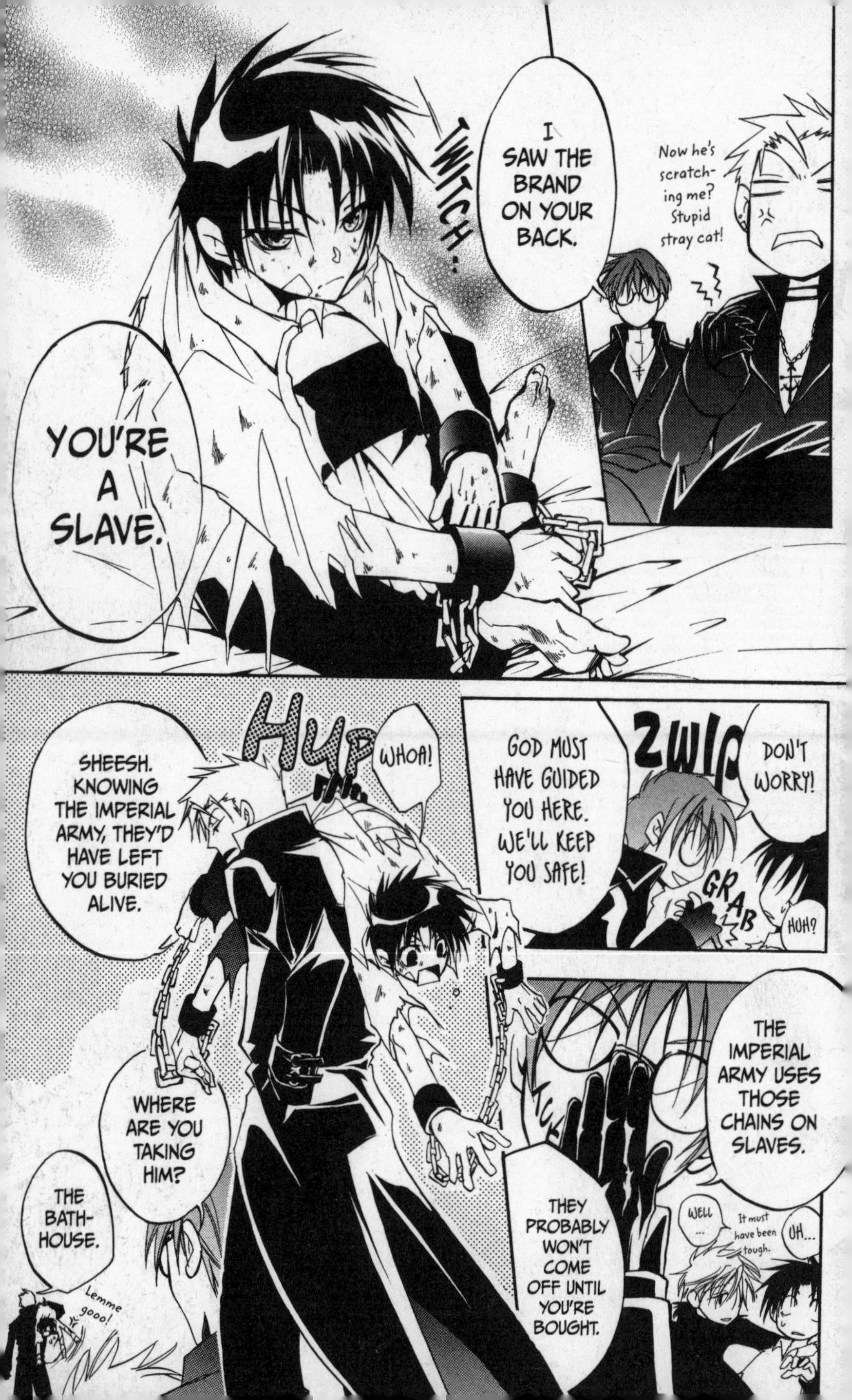
Now he's scratch-ing me? Stupid stray cat!
I SAW THE BRAND ON YOUR BACK.
TWITCH..
YOU'RE A SLAVE.
DON'T WORRY!
ZWIP
GOD MUST HAVE GUIDED YOU HERE. WE'LL KEEP YOU SAFE!
GRAB
HUH?
THE IMPERIAL ARMY USES THOSE CHAINS ON SLAVES.
UH...
It must have been tough.
WELL ...
THEY PROBABLY WON'T COME OFF UNTIL YOU'RE BOUGHT.
HUP
WHOA!
SHEESH. KNOWING THE IMPERIAL ARMY, THEY'D HAVE LEFT YOU BURIED ALIVE.
WHERE ARE YOU TAKING HIM?
THE BATH-HOUSE.
Lemme gooo!

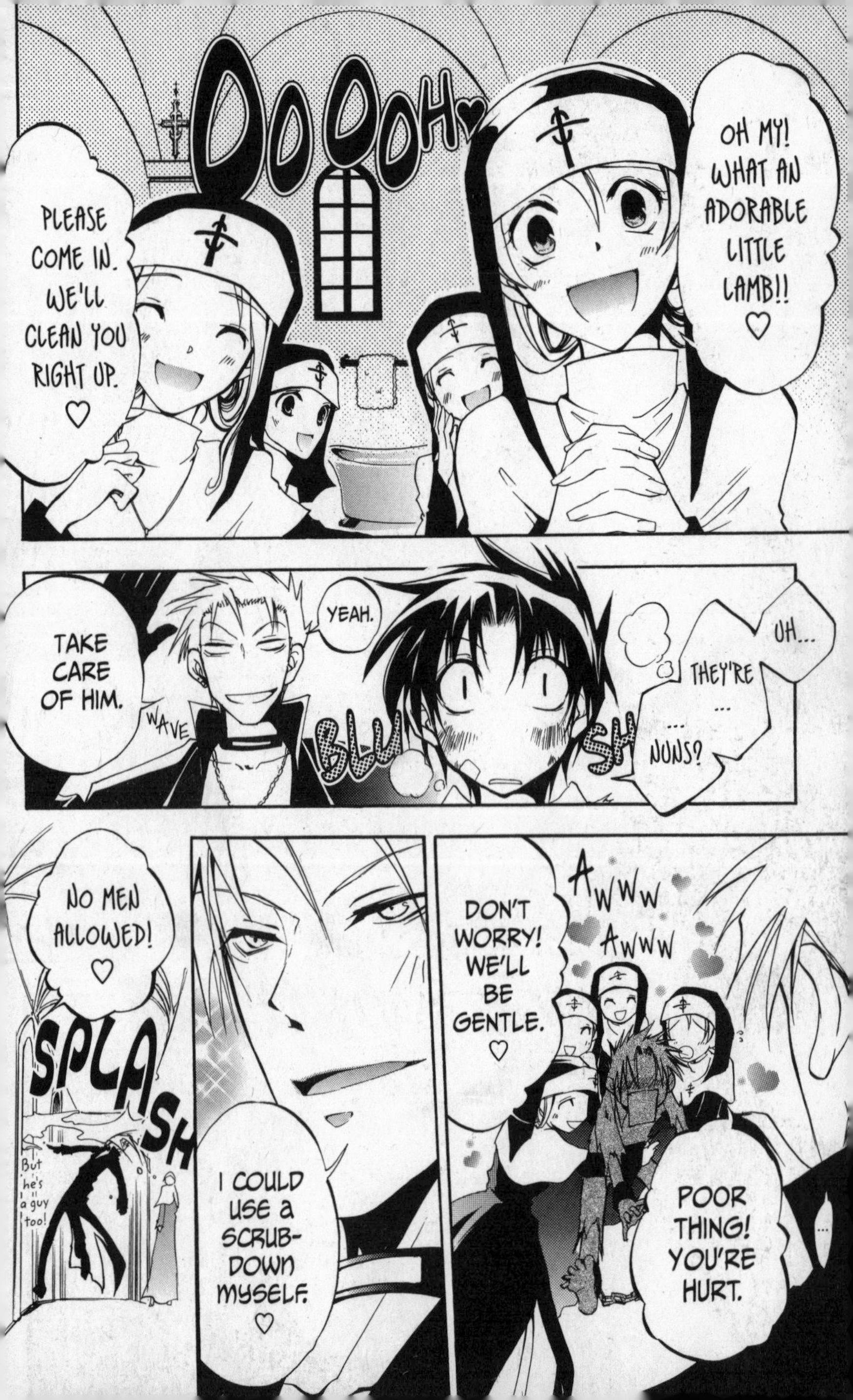
OH MY! WHAT AN ADORABLE LITTLE LAMB!! ♡
OOOOH♥
PLEASE COME IN. WE'LL CLEAN YOU RIGHT UP. ♡
UH...
THEY'RE ... ... NUNS?
BLUSH
YEAH.
TAKE CARE OF HIM.
WAVE
AWWW AWWW
DON'T WORRY! WE'LL BE GENTLE. ♡
...
POOR THING! YOU'RE HURT.
I COULD USE A SCRUB-DOWN MYSELF. ♡
NO MEN ALLOWED! ♡
SPLASH
But he's a guy too!

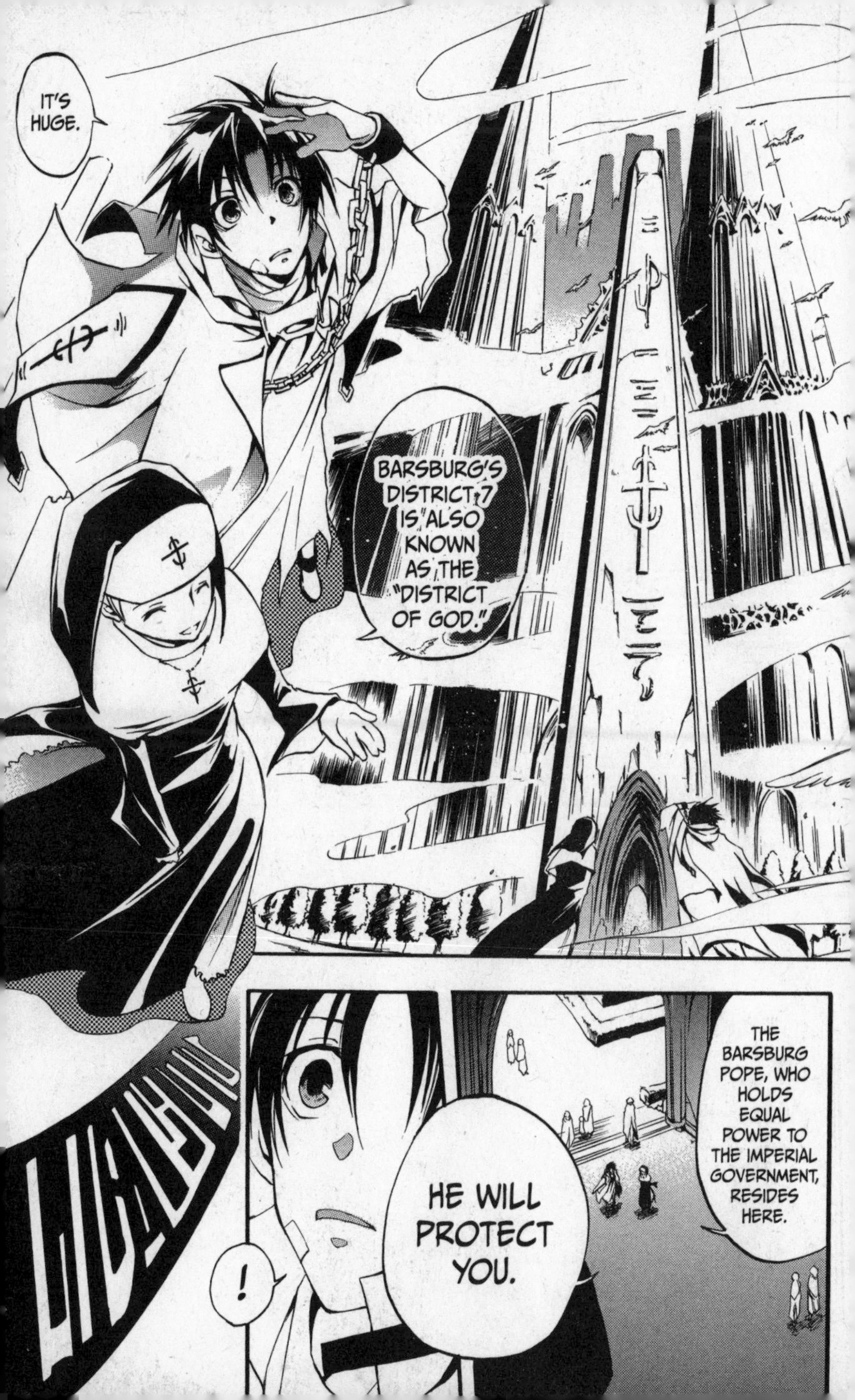
IT'S HUGE.
BARSBURG'S DISTRICT 7 IS ALSO KNOWN AS THE "DISTRICT OF GOD."
THE BARSBURG POPE, WHO HOLDS EQUAL POWER TO THE IMPERIAL GOVERNMENT, RESIDES HERE.
HE WILL PROTECT YOU.
!

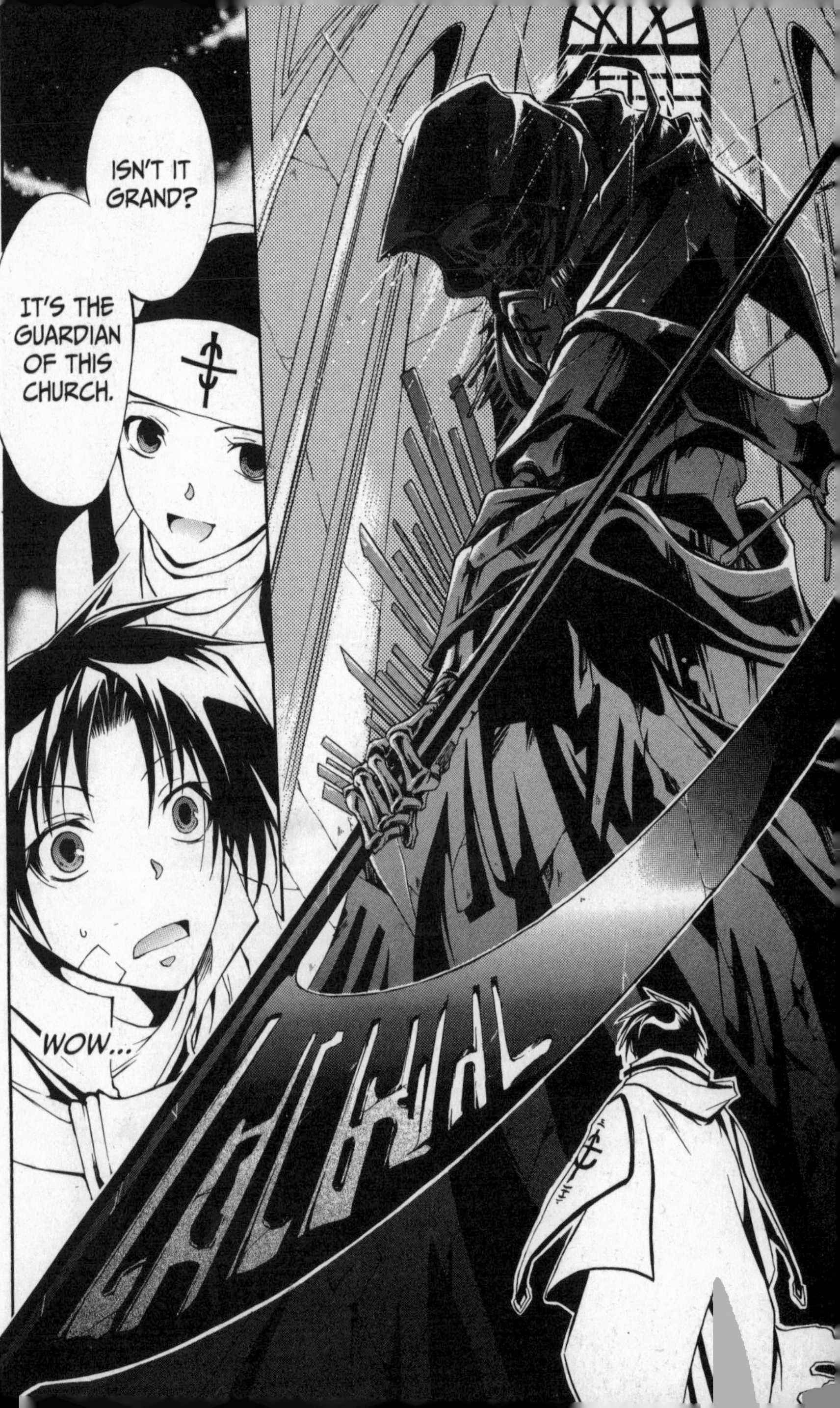
ISN'T IT GRAND?
IT'S THE GUARDIAN OF THIS CHURCH.
WOW...

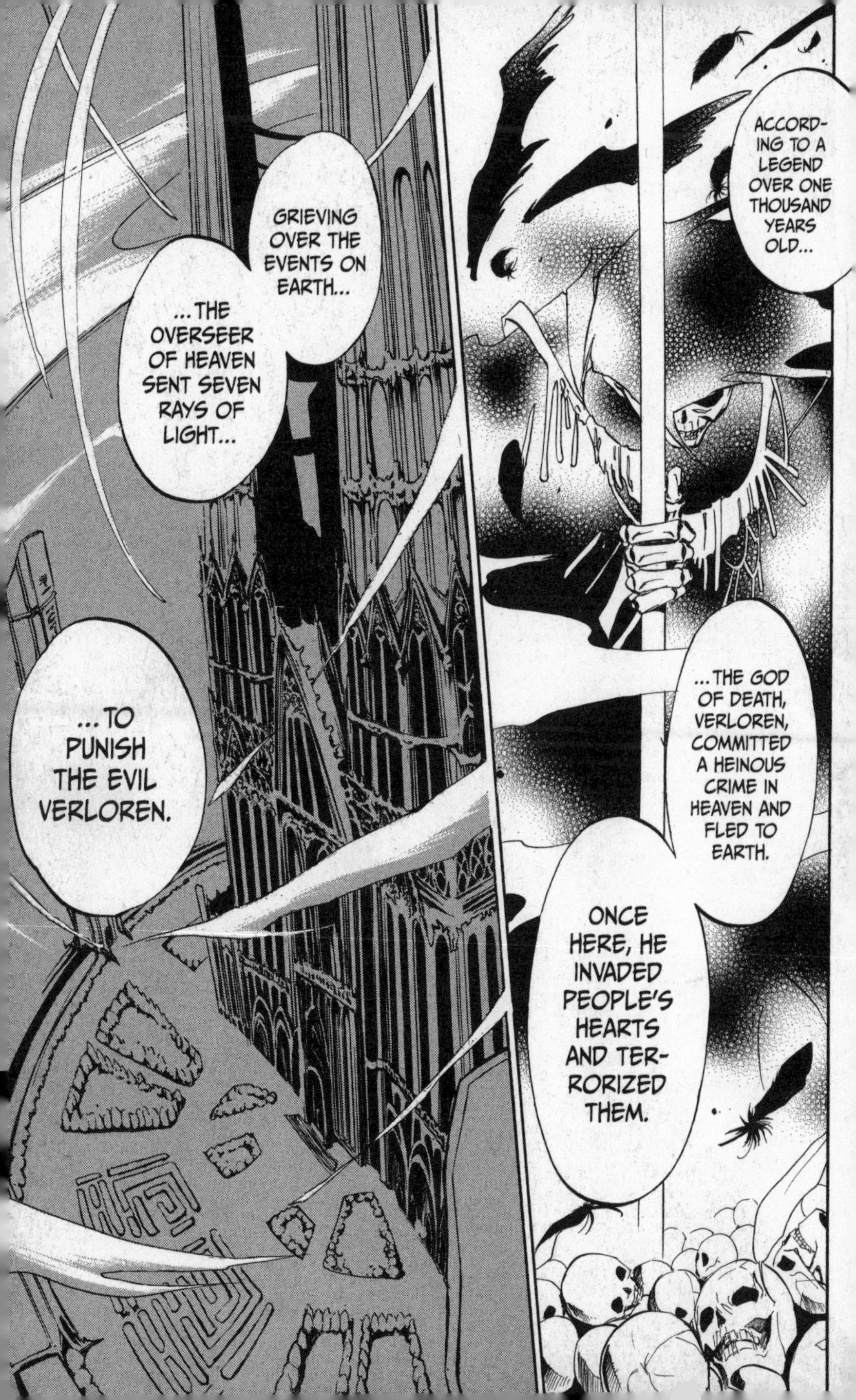
ACCORDING TO A LEGEND OVER ONE THOUSAND YEARS OLD...
...THE GOD OF DEATH, VERLOREN, COMMITTED A HEINOUS CRIME IN HEAVEN AND FLED TO EARTH.
ONCE HERE, HE INVADED PEOPLE'S HEARTS AND TERRORIZED THEM.
GRIEVING OVER THE EVENTS ON EARTH...
...THE OVERSEER OF HEAVEN SENT SEVEN RAYS OF LIGHT...
...TO PUNISH THE EVIL VERLOREN.

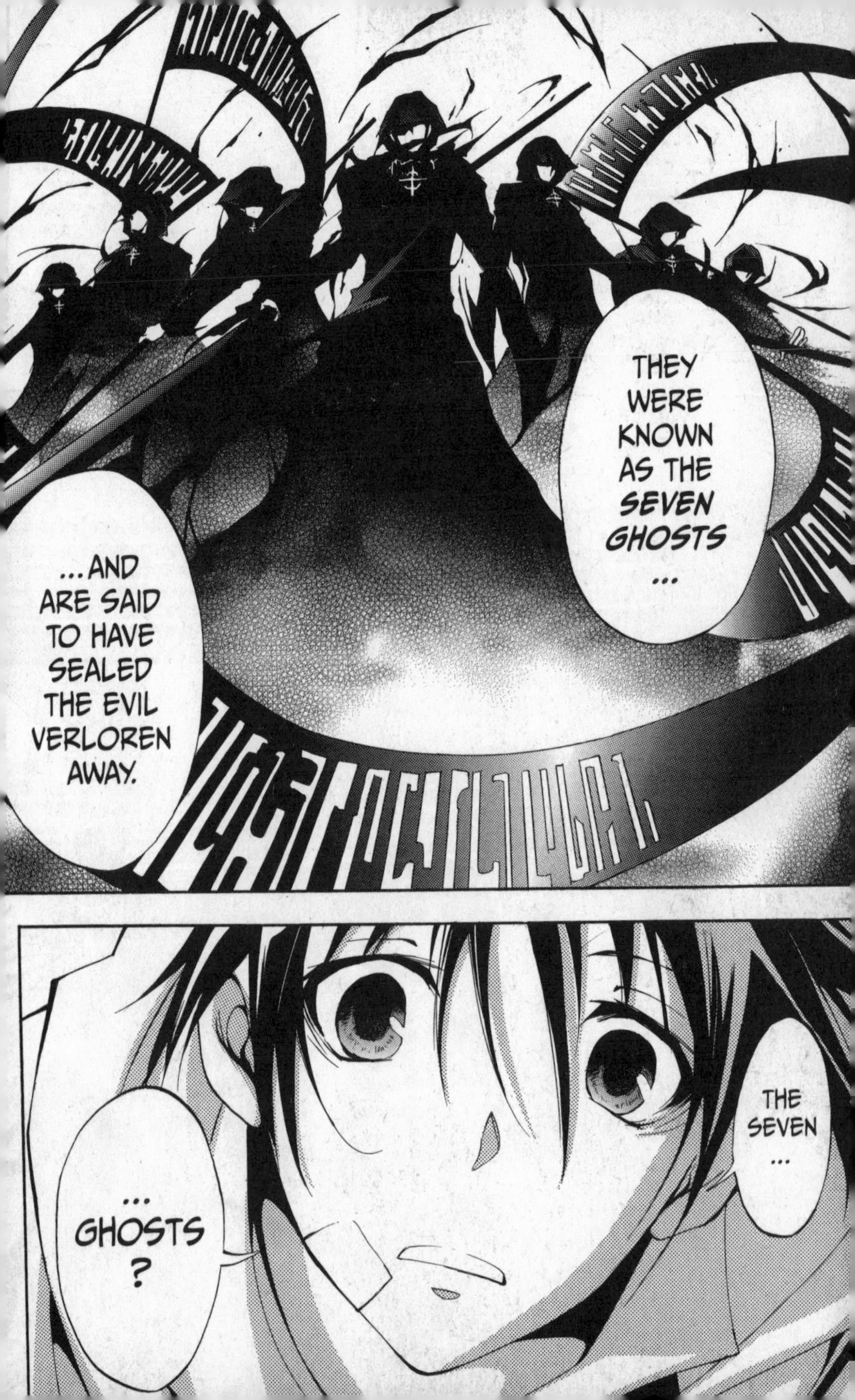
THEY WERE KNOWN AS THE SEVEN GHOSTS...
...AND ARE SAID TO HAVE SEALED THE EVIL VERLOREN AWAY.
THE SEVEN...
...GHOSTS?

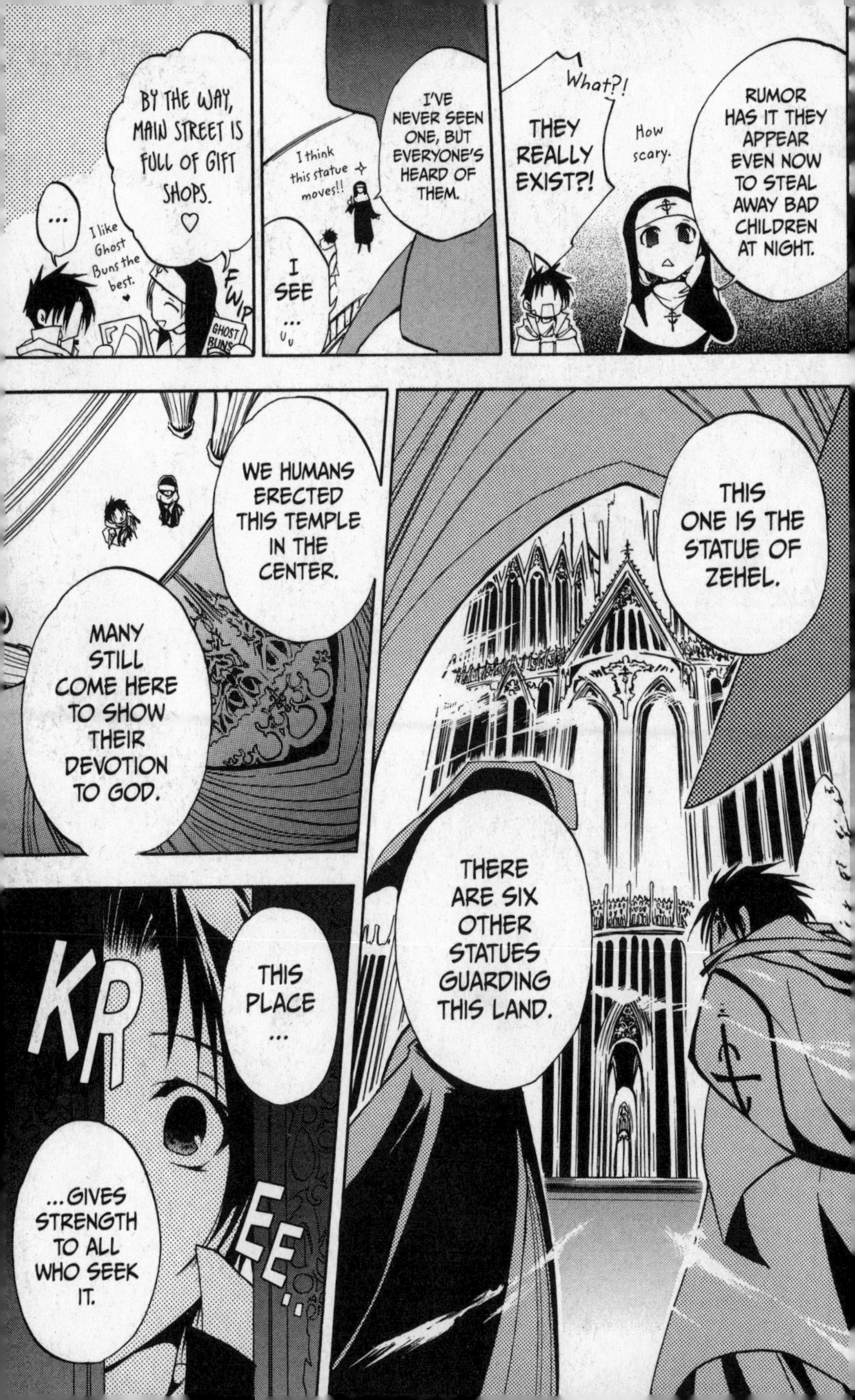
RUMOR HAS IT THEY APPEAR EVEN NOW TO STEAL AWAY BAD CHILDREN AT NIGHT.
How scary.
What?!
THEY REALLY EXIST?!
I'VE NEVER SEEN ONE, BUT EVERYONE'S HEARD OF THEM.
I think this statue moves!!
I SEE...
BY THE WAY, MAIN STREET IS FULL OF GIFT SHOPS. ♡
...
I like Ghost Buns the best. ♥
FWIP
GHOST BUNS
THIS ONE IS THE STATUE OF ZEHEL.
THERE ARE SIX OTHER STATUES GUARDING THIS LAND.
WE HUMANS ERECTED THIS TEMPLE IN THE CENTER.
MANY STILL COME HERE TO SHOW THEIR DEVOTION TO GOD.
THIS PLACE...
KREE..
...GIVES STRENGTH TO ALL WHO SEEK IT.

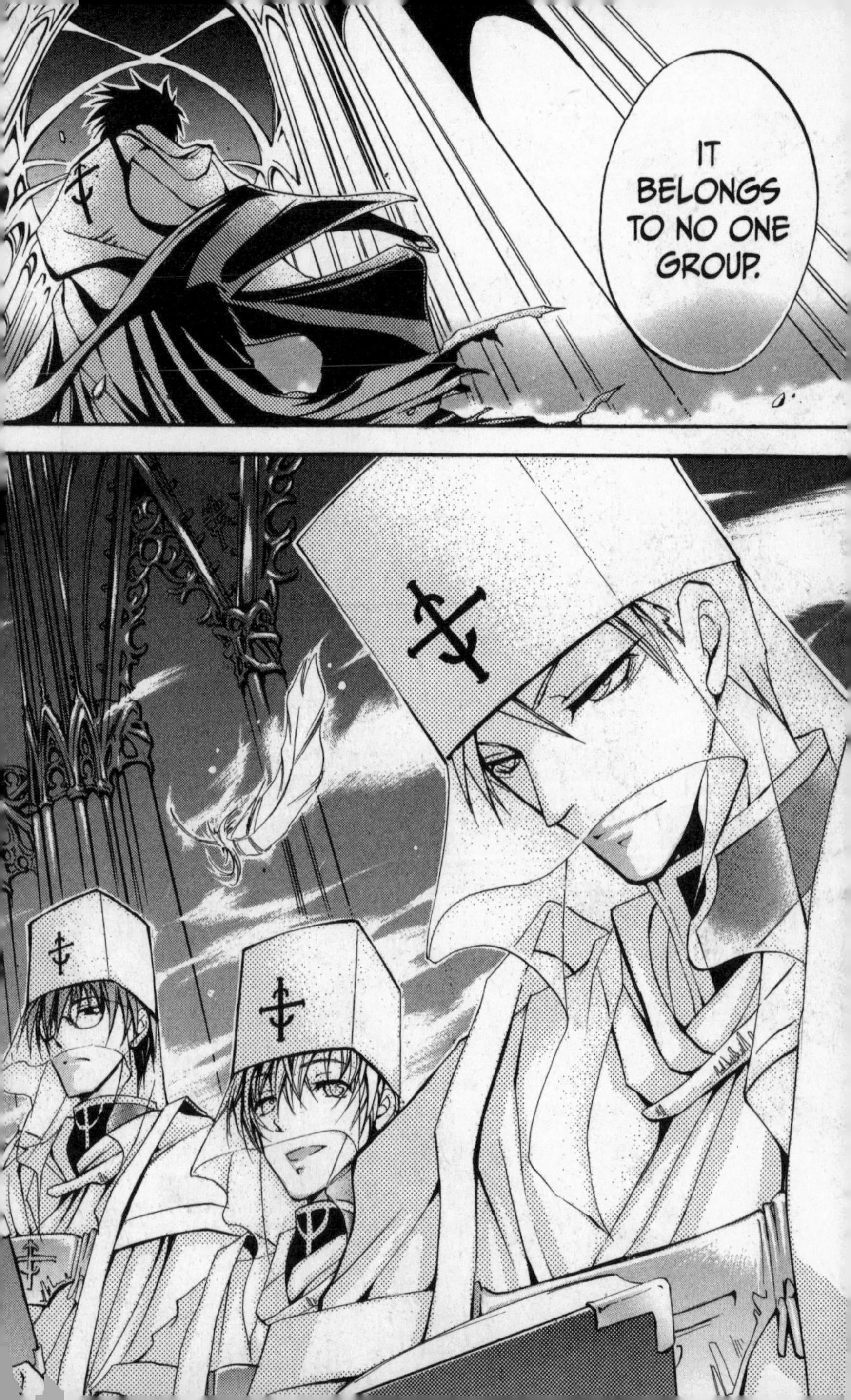
IT BELONGS TO NO ONE GROUP.

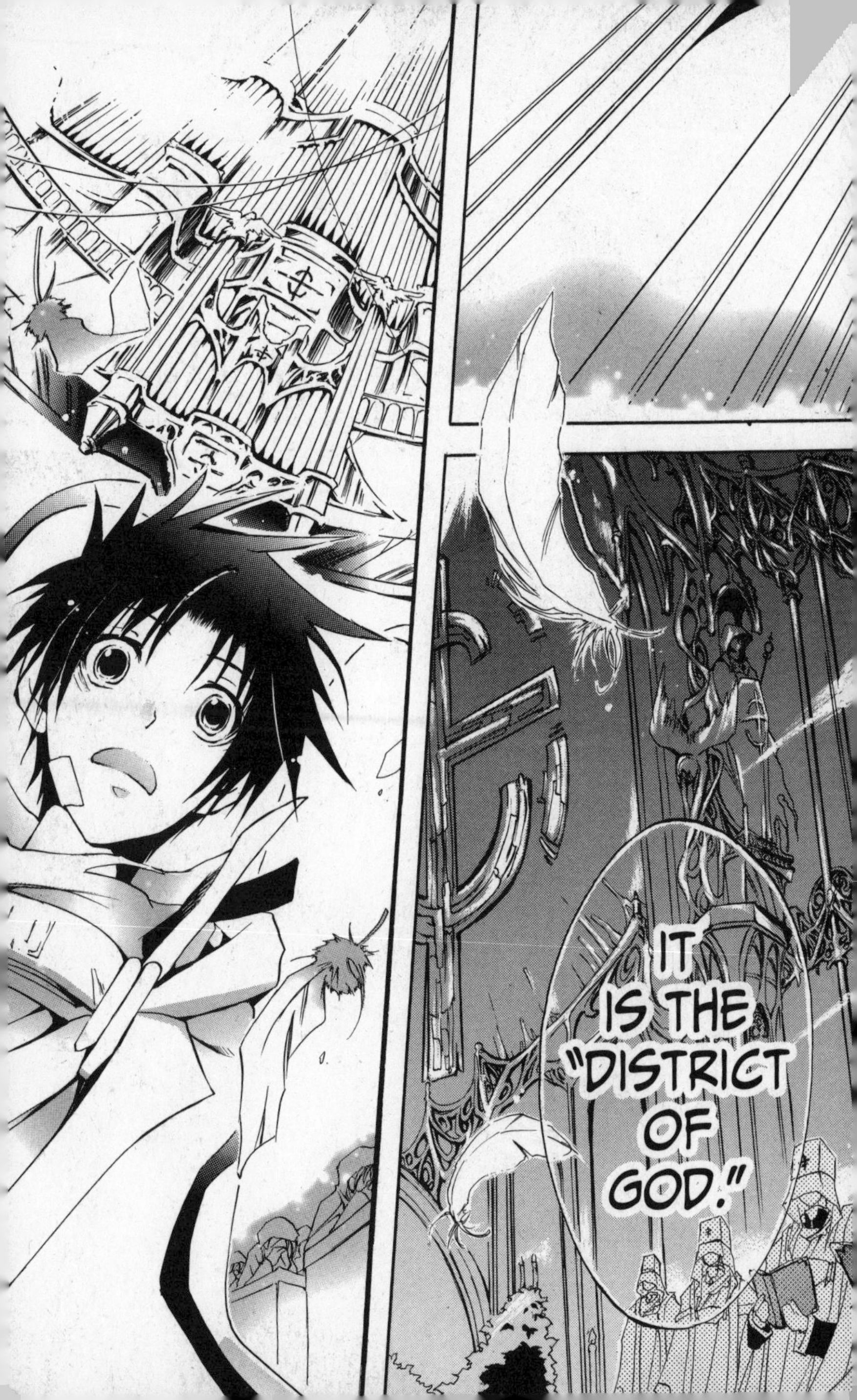
IT IS THE "DISTRICT OF GOD."

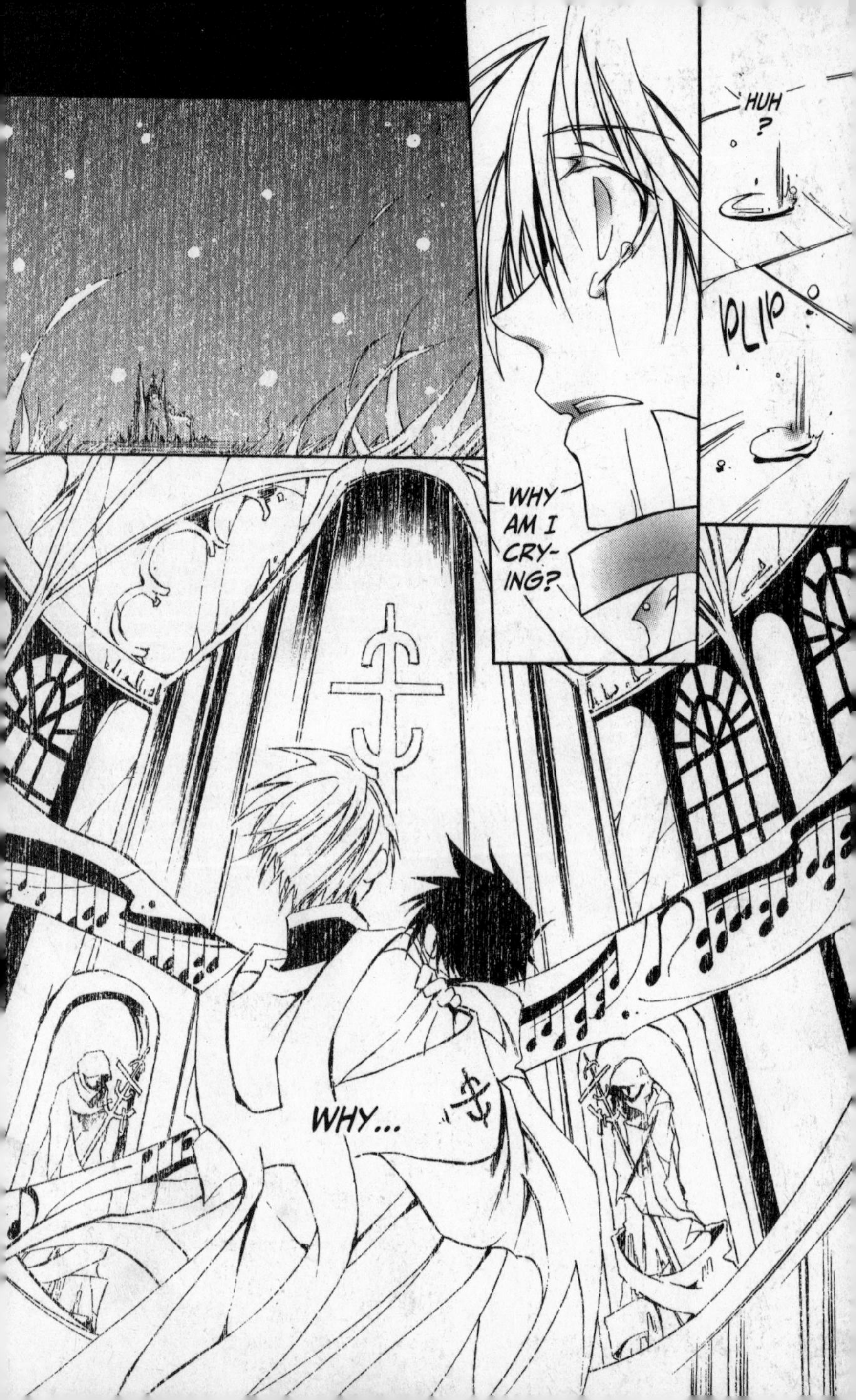
HUH?
PLIP
WHY AM I CRY-ING?
WHY...

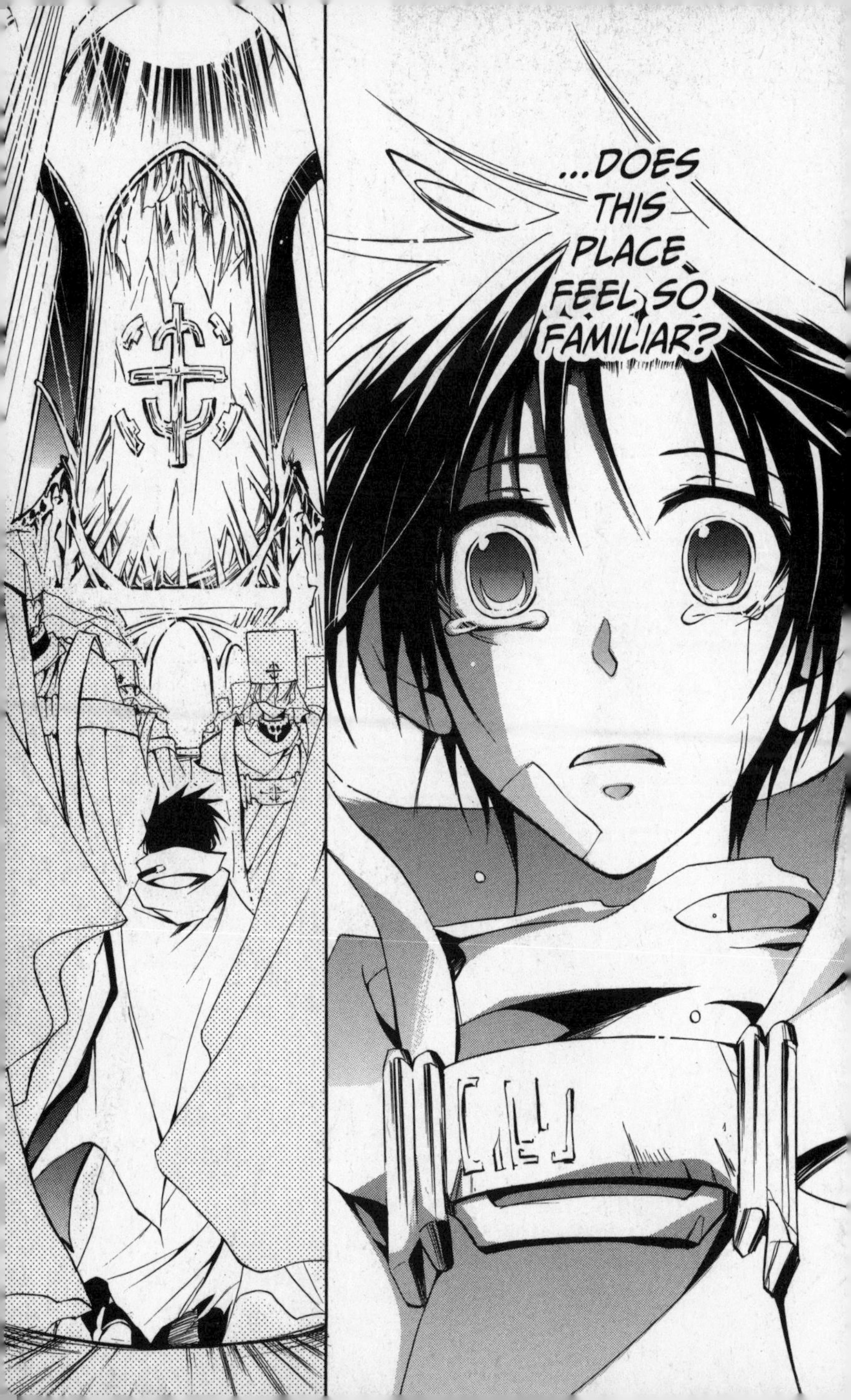
...DOES THIS PLACE FEEL SO FAMILIAR?

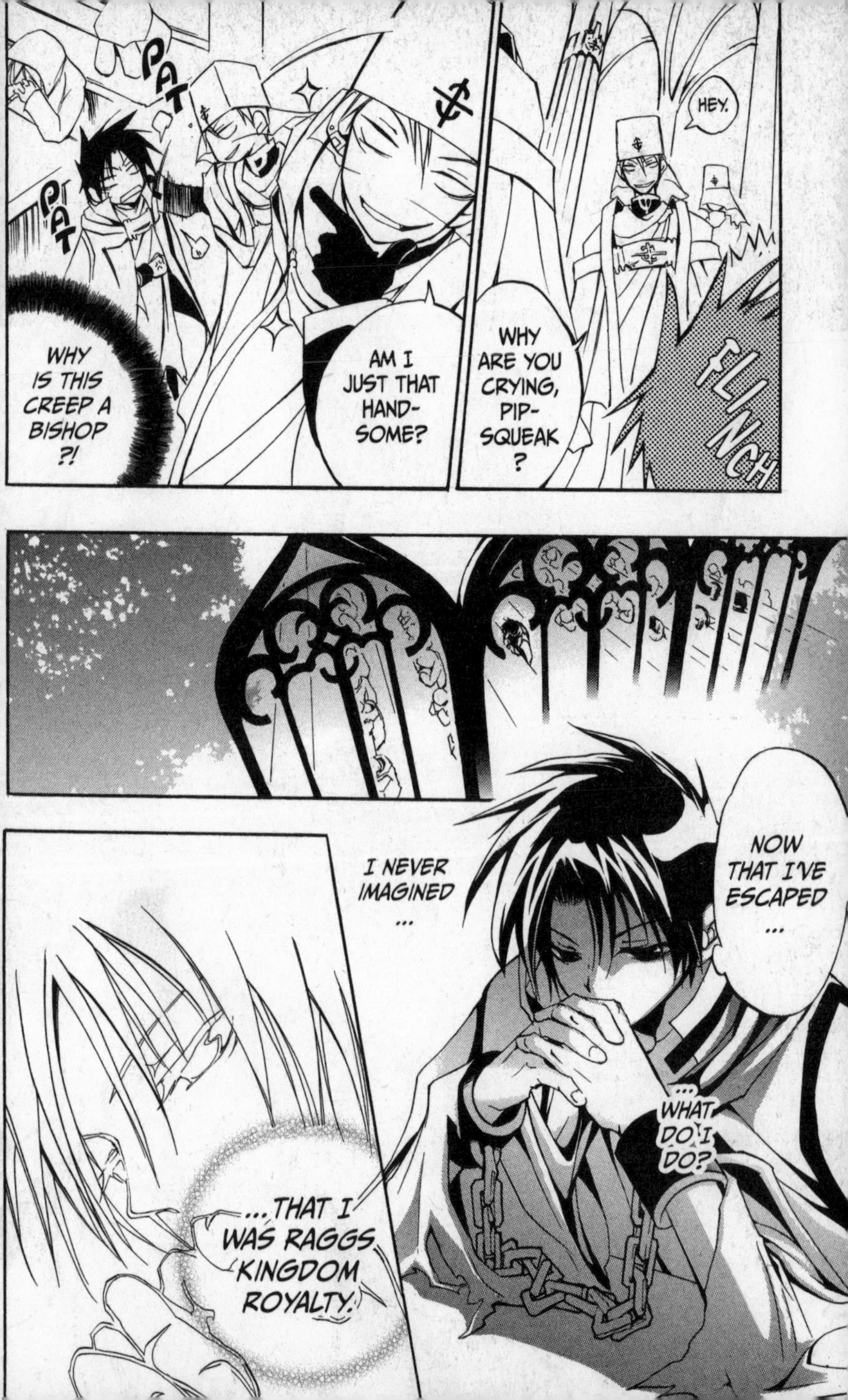
HEY.
FLINCH
WHY ARE YOU CRYING, PIP-SQUEAK?
PAT
PAT PAT
AM I JUST THAT HANDSOME?
WHY IS THIS CREEP A BISHOP?!
NOW THAT I'VE ESCAPED...
I NEVER IMAGINED...
...WHAT DO I DO?
...THAT I WAS RAGGS KINGDOM ROYALTY.

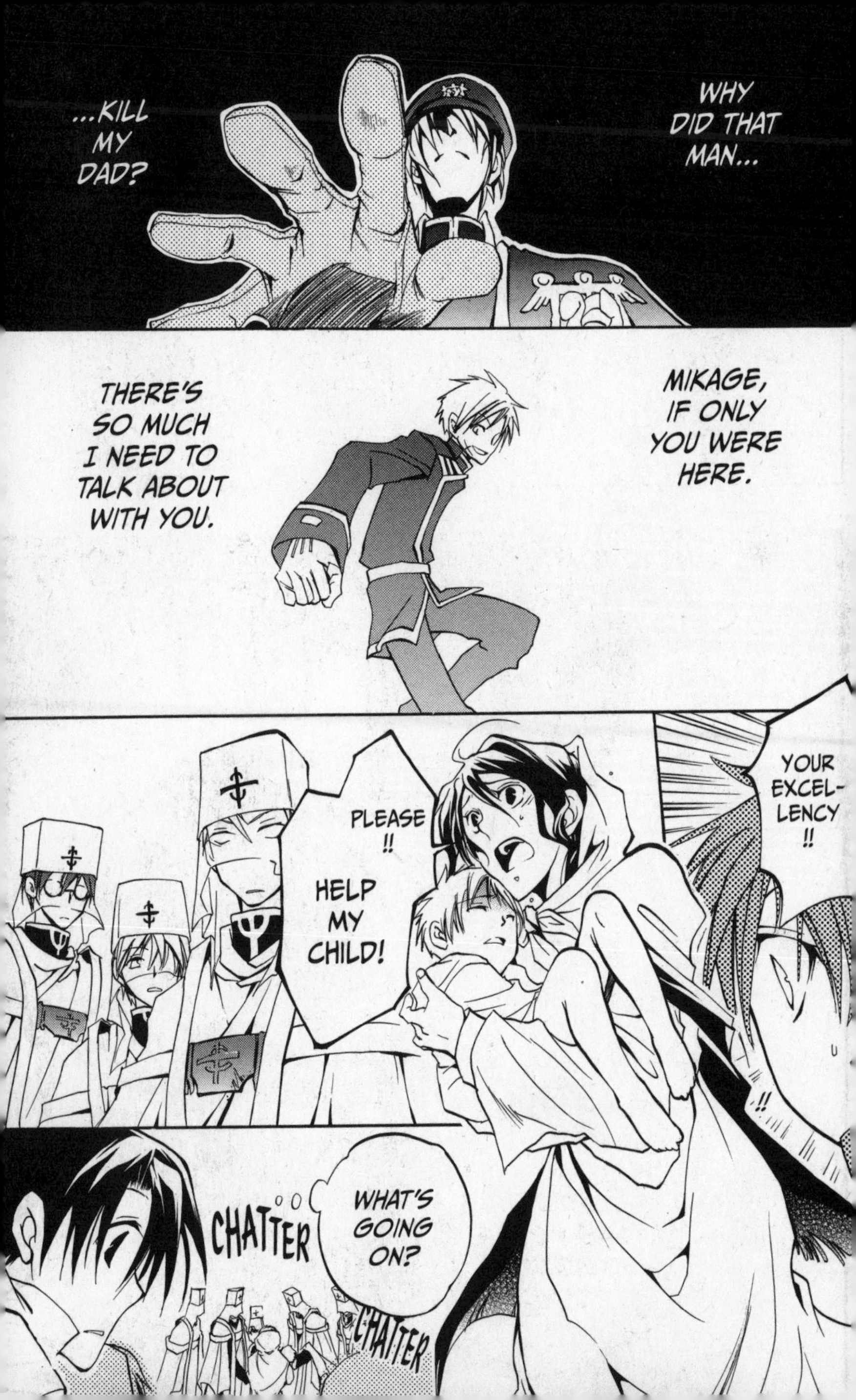
WHY DID THAT MAN...
...KILL MY DAD?
MIKAGE, IF ONLY YOU WERE HERE.
THERE'S SO MUCH I NEED TO TALK ABOUT WITH YOU.
YOUR EXCEL-LENCY !!
PLEASE !!
HELP MY CHILD!
!!
CHATTER
WHAT'S GOING ON?
CHATTER

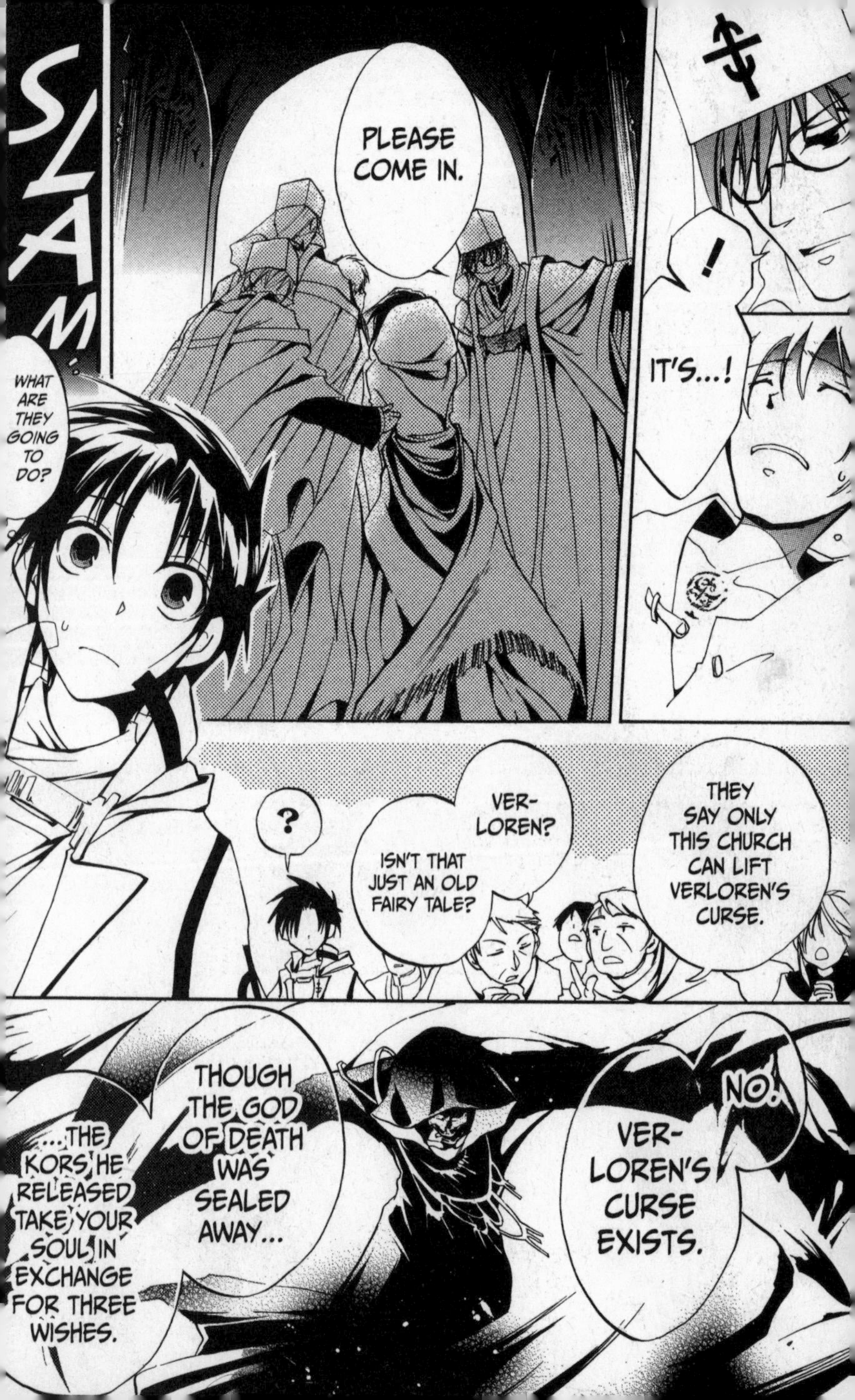
!
IT'S...!
PLEASE COME IN.
SLAM
WHAT ARE THEY GOING TO DO?
THEY SAY ONLY THIS CHURCH CAN LIFT VERLOREN'S CURSE.
VER-LOREN?
ISN'T THAT JUST AN OLD FAIRY TALE?
?
NO.
VER-LOREN'S CURSE EXISTS.
THOUGH THE GOD OF DEATH WAS SEALED AWAY...
...THE KORS HE RELEASED TAKE YOUR SOUL IN EXCHANGE FOR THREE WISHES.

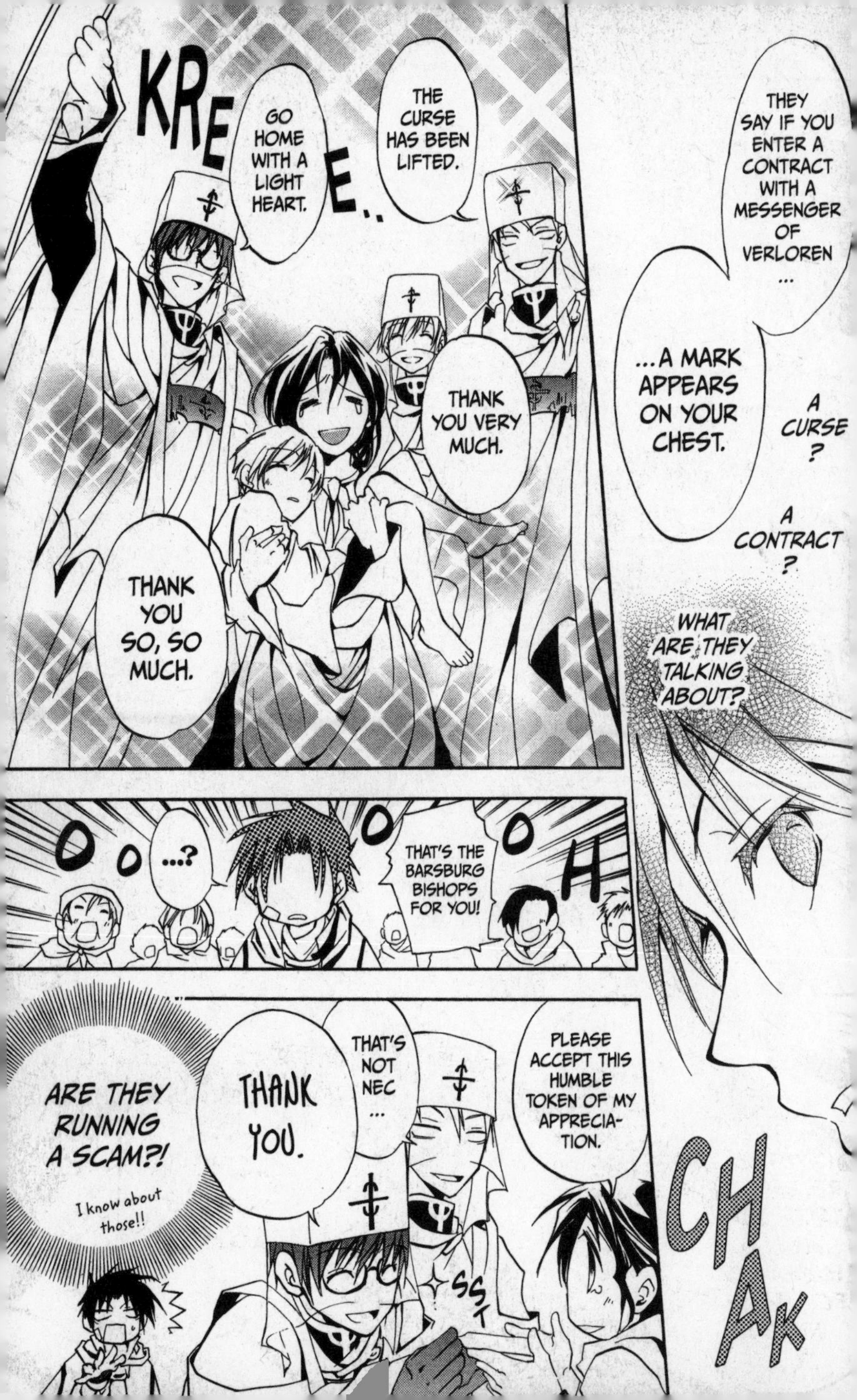
THEY SAY IF YOU ENTER A CONTRACT WITH A MESSENGER OF VERLOREN ...
...A MARK APPEARS ON YOUR CHEST.
A CURSE?
A CONTRACT?
WHAT ARE THEY TALKING ABOUT?
THE CURSE HAS BEEN LIFTED.
GO HOME WITH A LIGHT HEART.
KREEE..
THANK YOU VERY MUCH.
THANK YOU SO, SO MUCH.
OOOOH
THAT'S THE BARSBURG BISHOPS FOR YOU!
...?
CHAK
PLEASE ACCEPT THIS HUMBLE TOKEN OF MY APPRECIATION.
SST
THAT'S NOT NEC ...
THANK YOU.
ARE THEY RUNNING A SCAM?!
I know about those!!

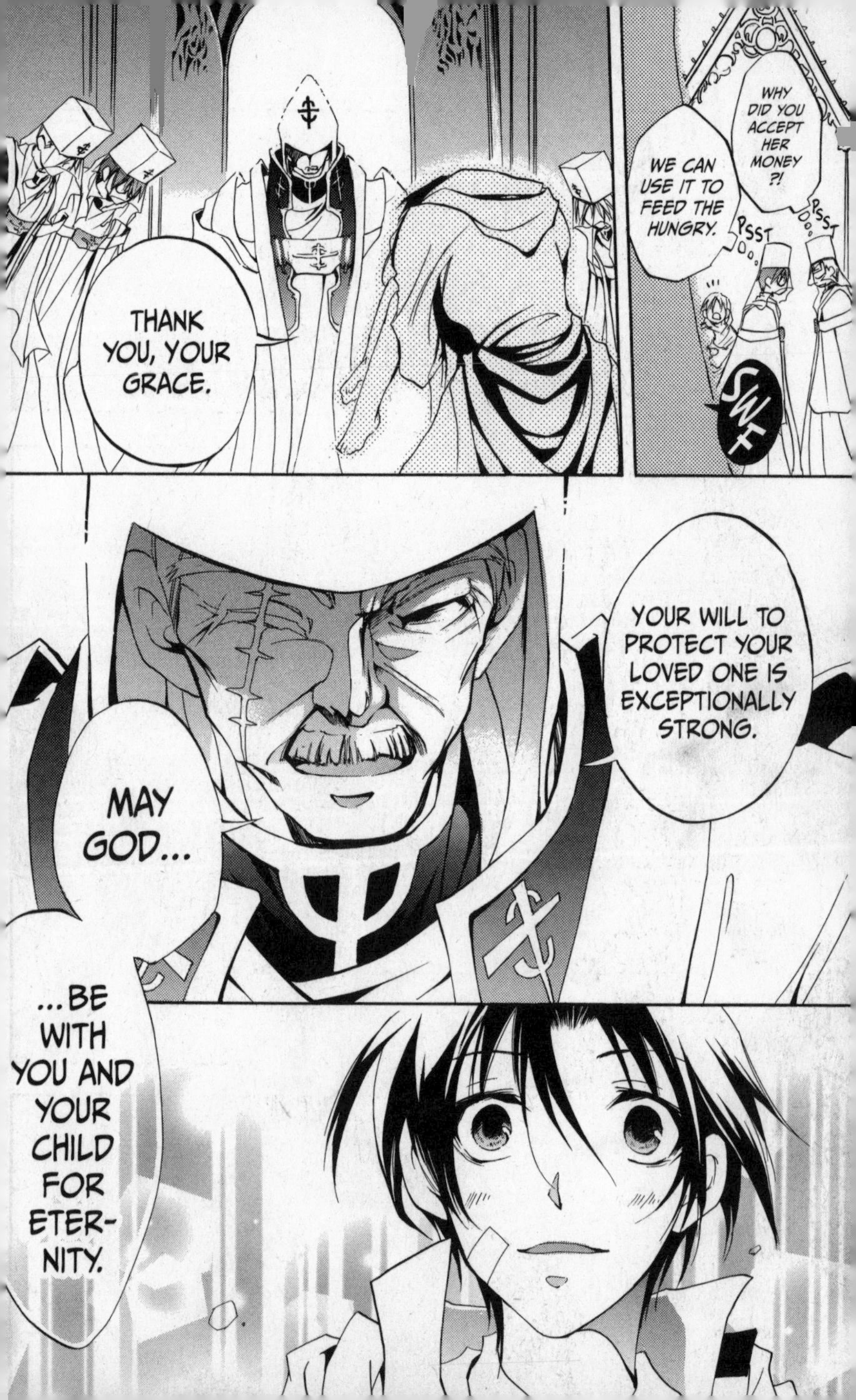
WHY DID YOU ACCEPT HER MONEY ?!
PSST
WE CAN USE IT TO FEED THE HUNGRY.
PSST
SWF
THANK YOU, YOUR GRACE.
YOUR WILL TO PROTECT YOUR LOVED ONE IS EXCEPTIONALLY STRONG.
MAY GOD...
...BE WITH YOU AND YOUR CHILD FOR ETER-NITY.

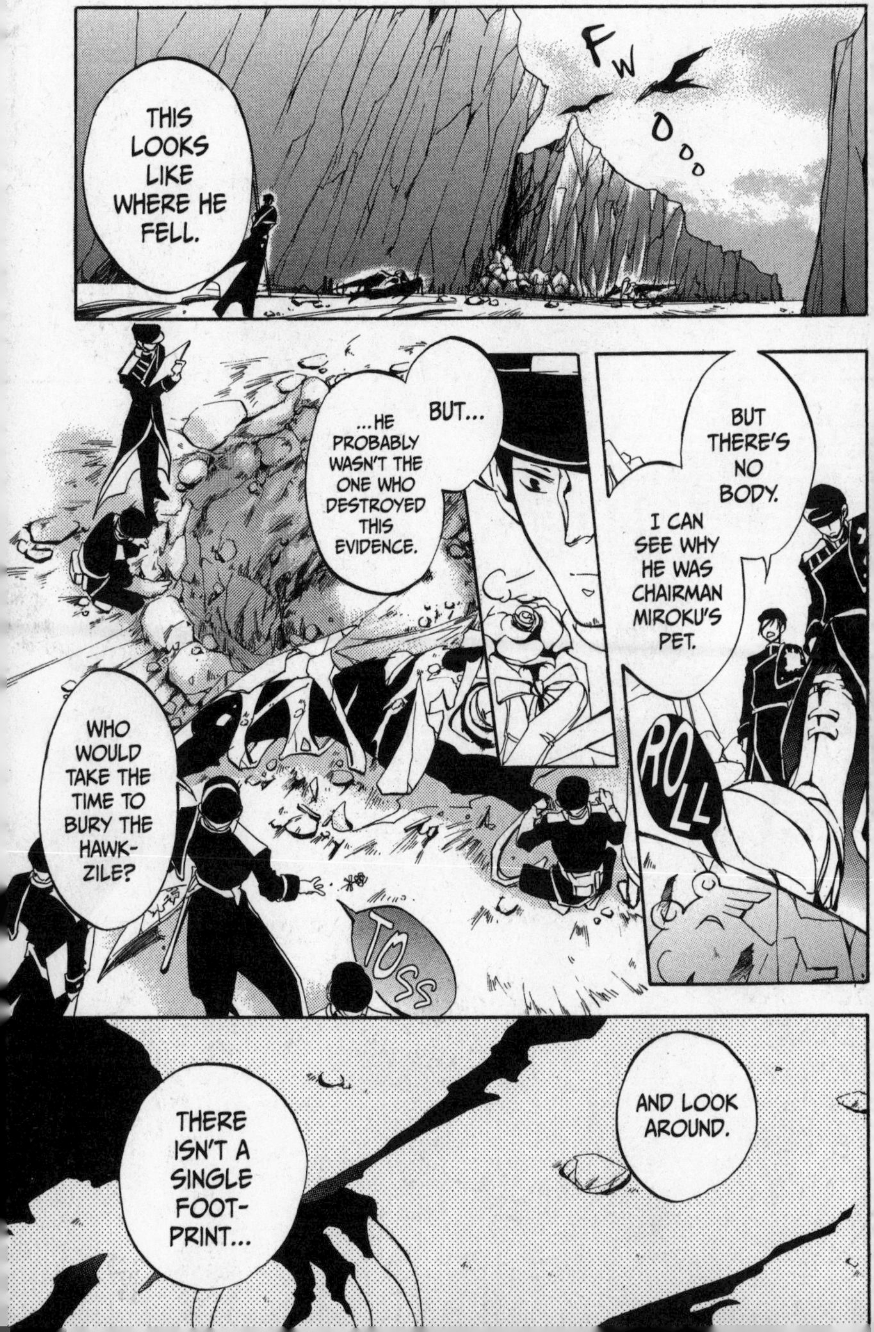
FWOOO
THIS LOOKS LIKE WHERE HE FELL.
BUT THERE'S NO BODY.
I CAN SEE WHY HE WAS CHAIRMAN MIROKU'S PET.
ROLL
BUT...
...HE PROBABLY WASN'T THE ONE WHO DESTROYED THIS EVIDENCE.
WHO WOULD TAKE THE TIME TO BURY THE HAWK-ZILE?
TOSS
AND LOOK AROUND.
THERE ISN'T A SINGLE FOOT-PRINT...

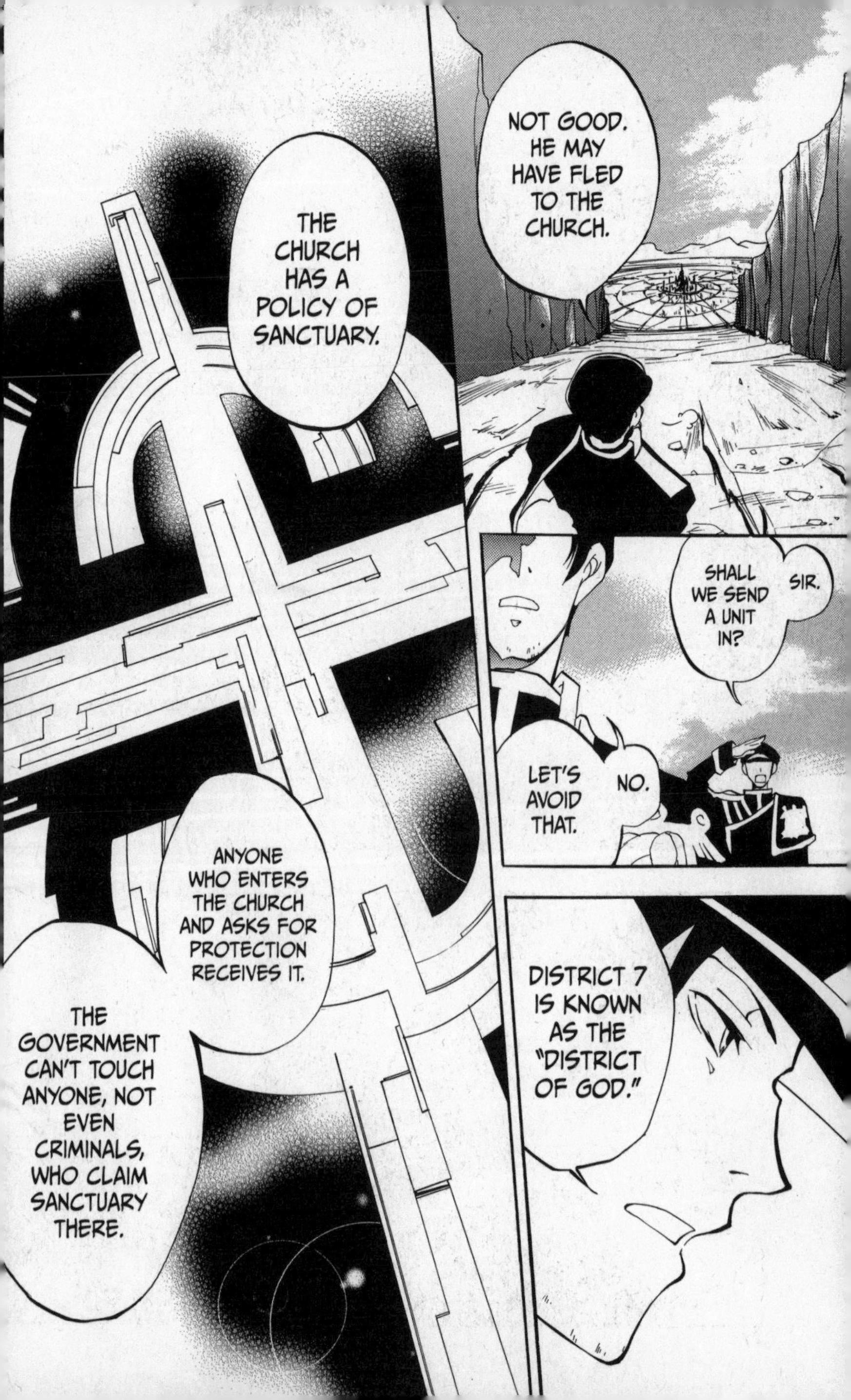
NOT GOOD. HE MAY HAVE FLED TO THE CHURCH.
SIR. SHALL WE SEND A UNIT IN?
NO. LET'S AVOID THAT.
DISTRICT 7 IS KNOWN AS THE "DISTRICT OF GOD."
THE CHURCH HAS A POLICY OF SANCTUARY.
ANYONE WHO ENTERS THE CHURCH AND ASKS FOR PROTECTION RECEIVES IT.
THE GOVERNMENT CAN'T TOUCH ANYONE, NOT EVEN CRIMINALS, WHO CLAIM SANCTUARY THERE.

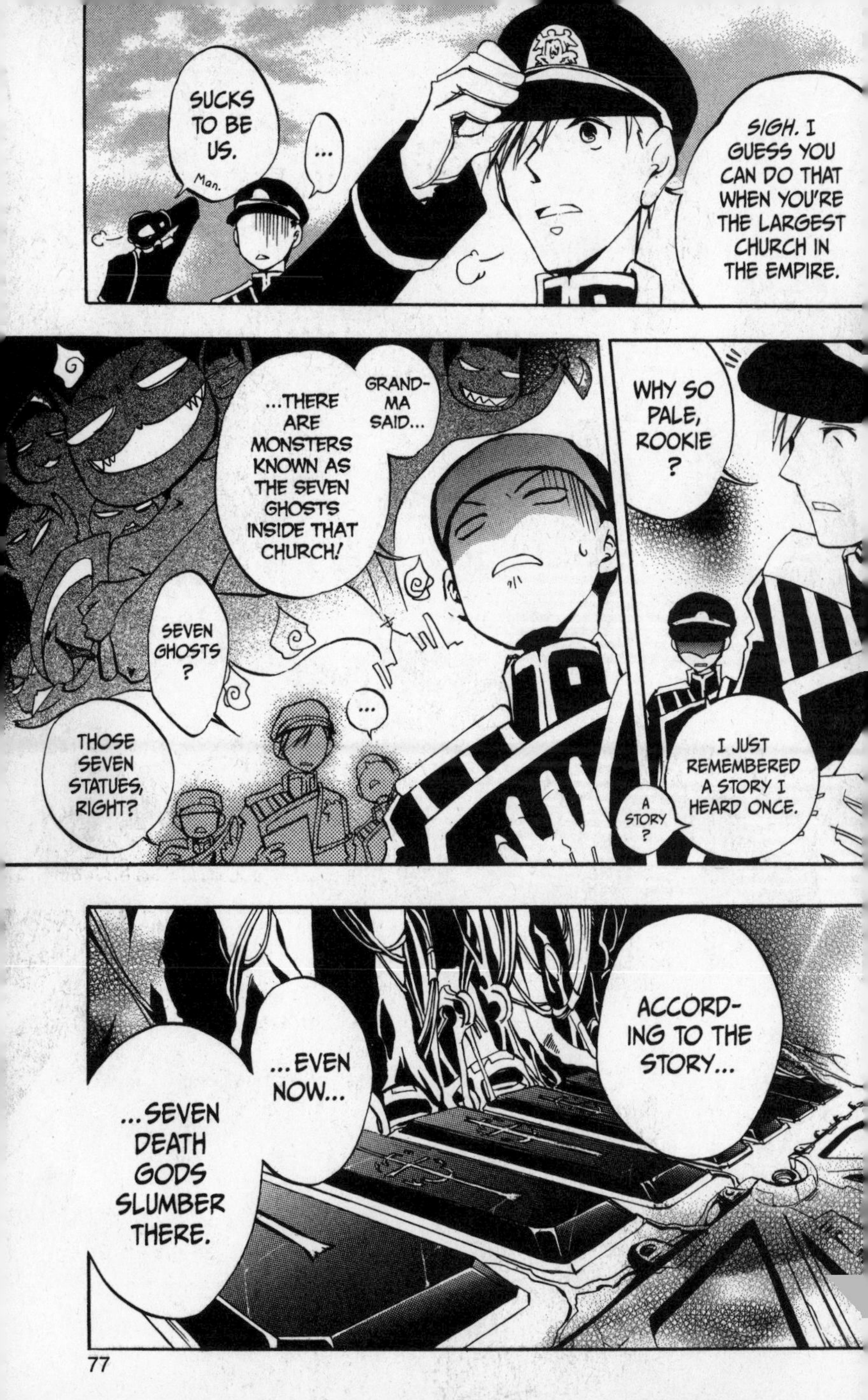
SIGH. I GUESS YOU CAN DO THAT WHEN YOU'RE THE LARGEST CHURCH IN THE EMPIRE.
...
SUCKS TO BE US.
Man.
WHY SO PALE, ROOKIE?
I JUST REMEMBERED A STORY I HEARD ONCE.
A STORY?
GRAND-MA SAID...
...THERE ARE MONSTERS KNOWN AS THE SEVEN GHOSTS INSIDE THAT CHURCH!
...
SEVEN GHOSTS?
THOSE SEVEN STATUES, RIGHT?
ACCORD-ING TO THE STORY...
...EVEN NOW...
...SEVEN DEATH GODS SLUMBER THERE.

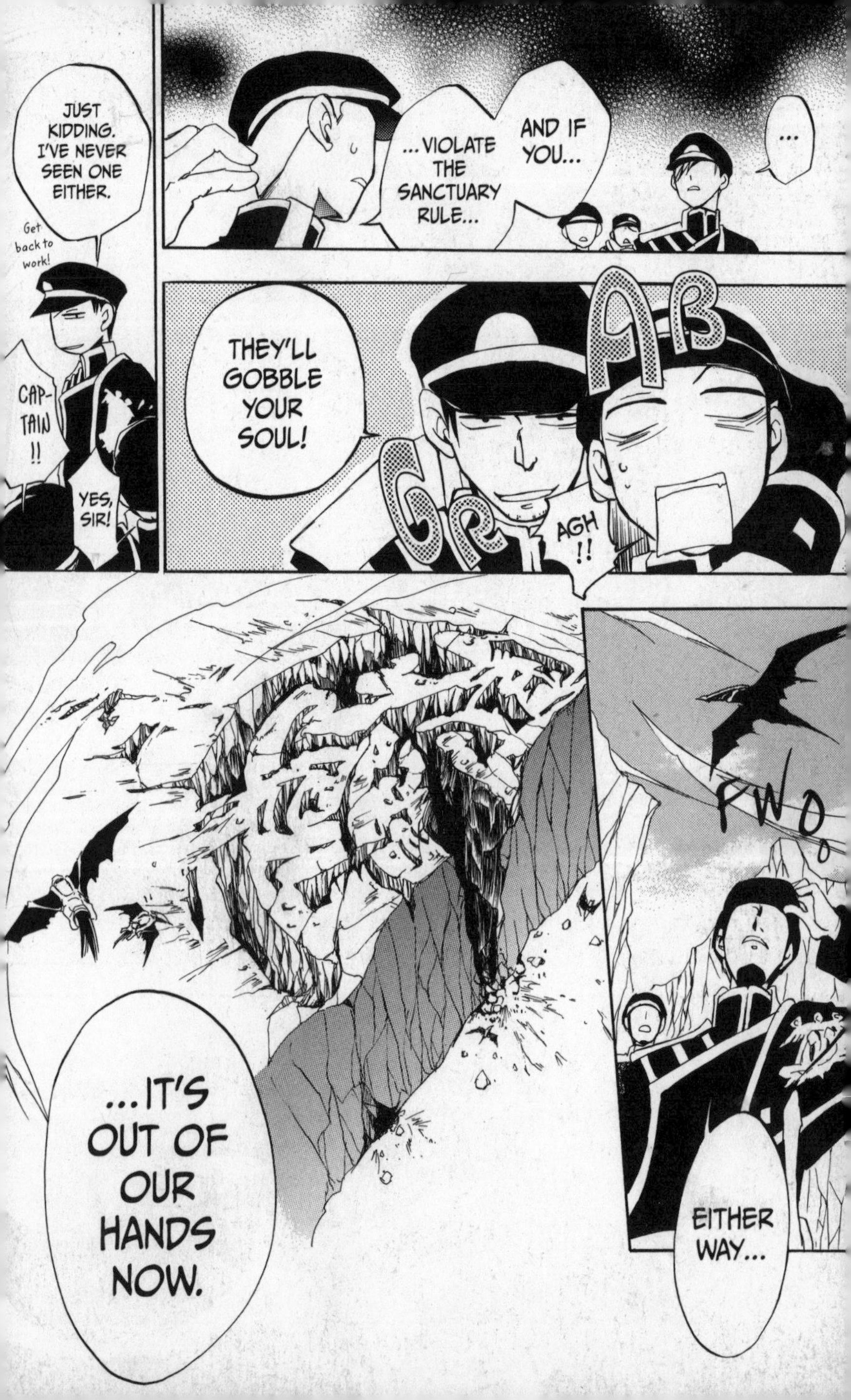
...
AND IF YOU...
...VIOLATE THE SANCTUARY RULE...
THEY'LL GOBBLE YOUR SOUL!
GRAB
AGH !!
JUST KIDDING. I'VE NEVER SEEN ONE EITHER.
Get back to work!
CAP-TAIN !!
YES, SIR!
FWOo
EITHER WAY...
...IT'S OUT OF OUR HANDS NOW.

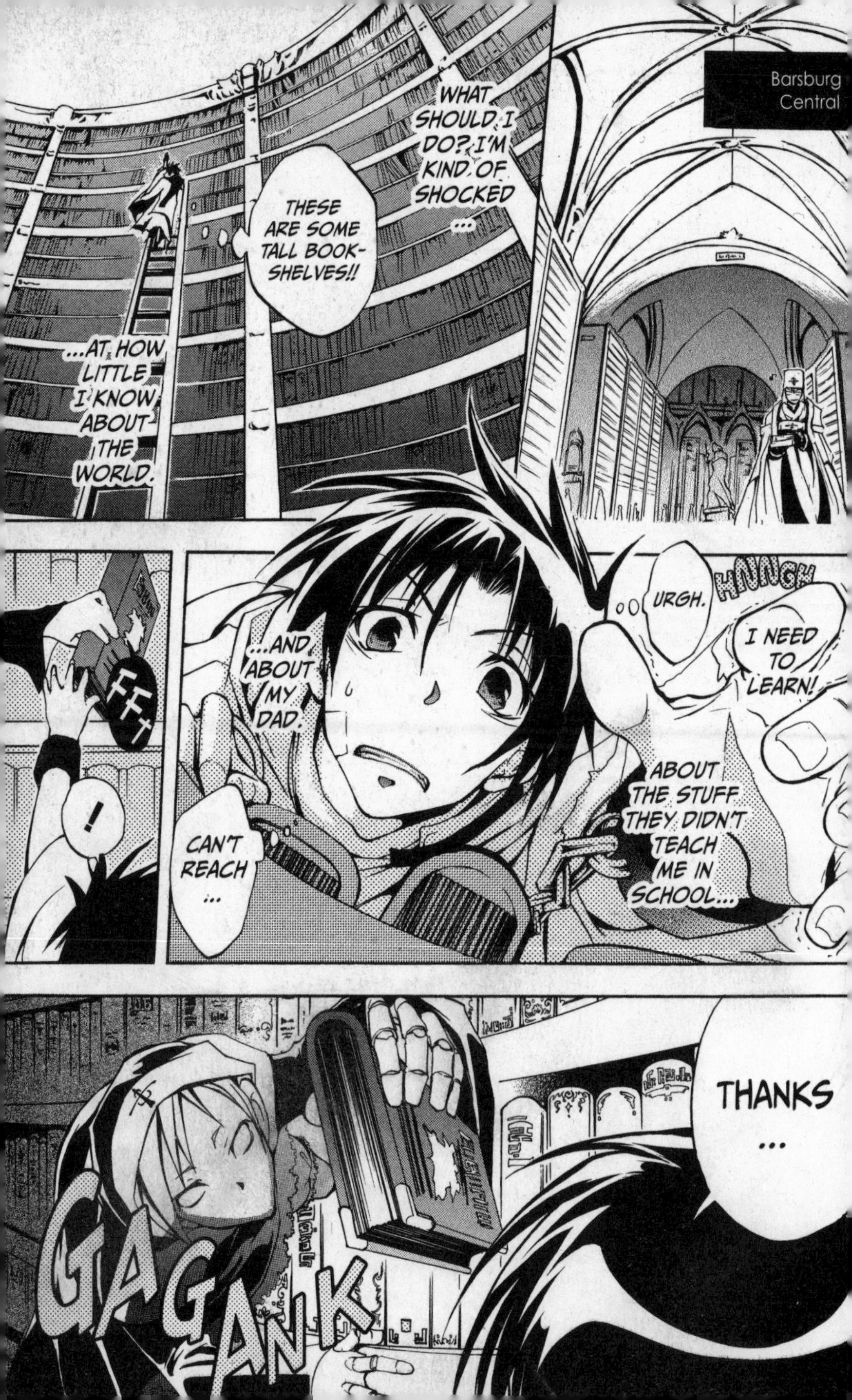
Barsburg Central
WHAT SHOULD I DO? I'M KIND OF SHOCKED...
THESE ARE SOME TALL BOOK-SHELVES!!
...AT HOW LITTLE I KNOW ABOUT THE WORLD.
HNNGH
URGH.
I NEED TO LEARN!
...AND ABOUT MY DAD.
ABOUT THE STUFF THEY DIDN'T TEACH ME IN SCHOOL...
CAN'T REACH...
FFT
!
THANKS...
GAGANK

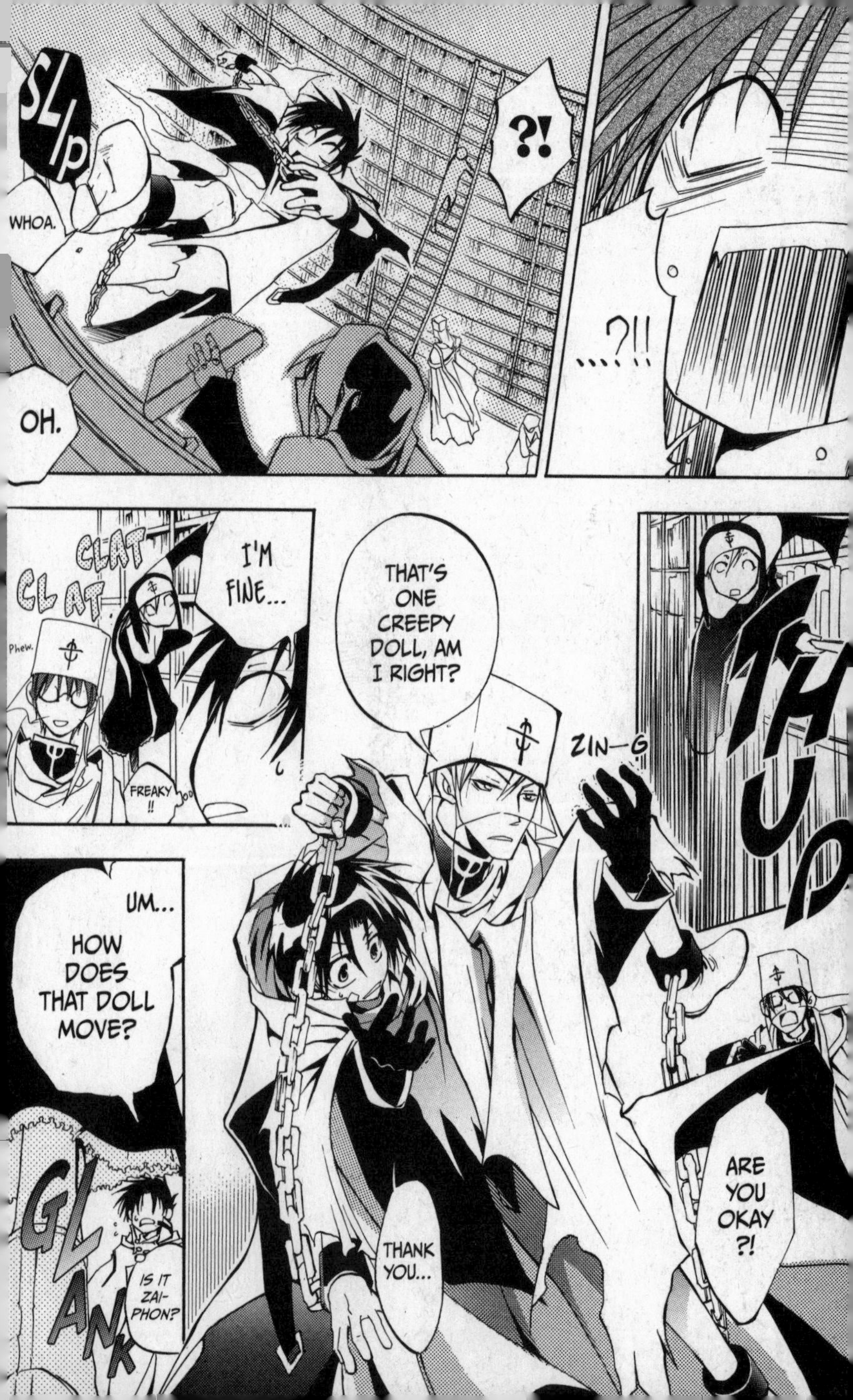
...?!!
?!
SLIP
WHOA.
OH.
THUD
ARE YOU OKAY?!
ZIN-G
THAT'S ONE CREEPY DOLL, AM I RIGHT?
THANK YOU...
I'M FINE...
CLAT CLAT
Phew.
FREAKY!!
UM... HOW DOES THAT DOLL MOVE?
GLANK
IS IT ZAI-PHON?

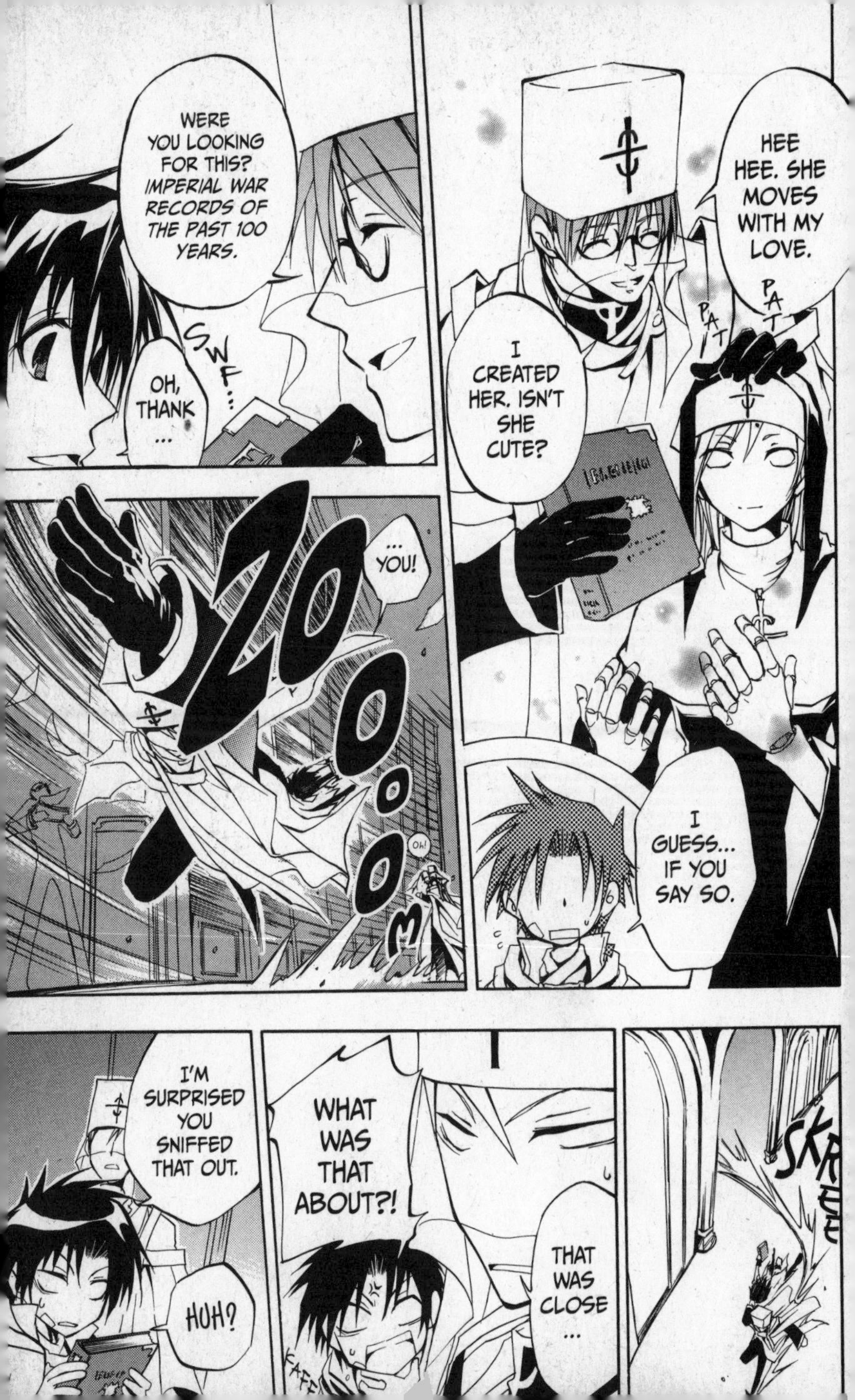
HEE HEE. SHE MOVES WITH MY LOVE.
PAT PAT
I CREATED HER. ISN'T SHE CUTE?
I GUESS... IF YOU SAY SO.
WERE YOU LOOKING FOR THIS? IMPERIAL WAR RECORDS OF THE PAST 100 YEARS.
SWF...
OH, THANK...
ZOOOOOM
... YOU!
OH!
SKREE
WHAT WAS THAT ABOUT?!
THAT WAS CLOSE...
I'M SURPRISED YOU SNIFFED THAT OUT.
HUH?

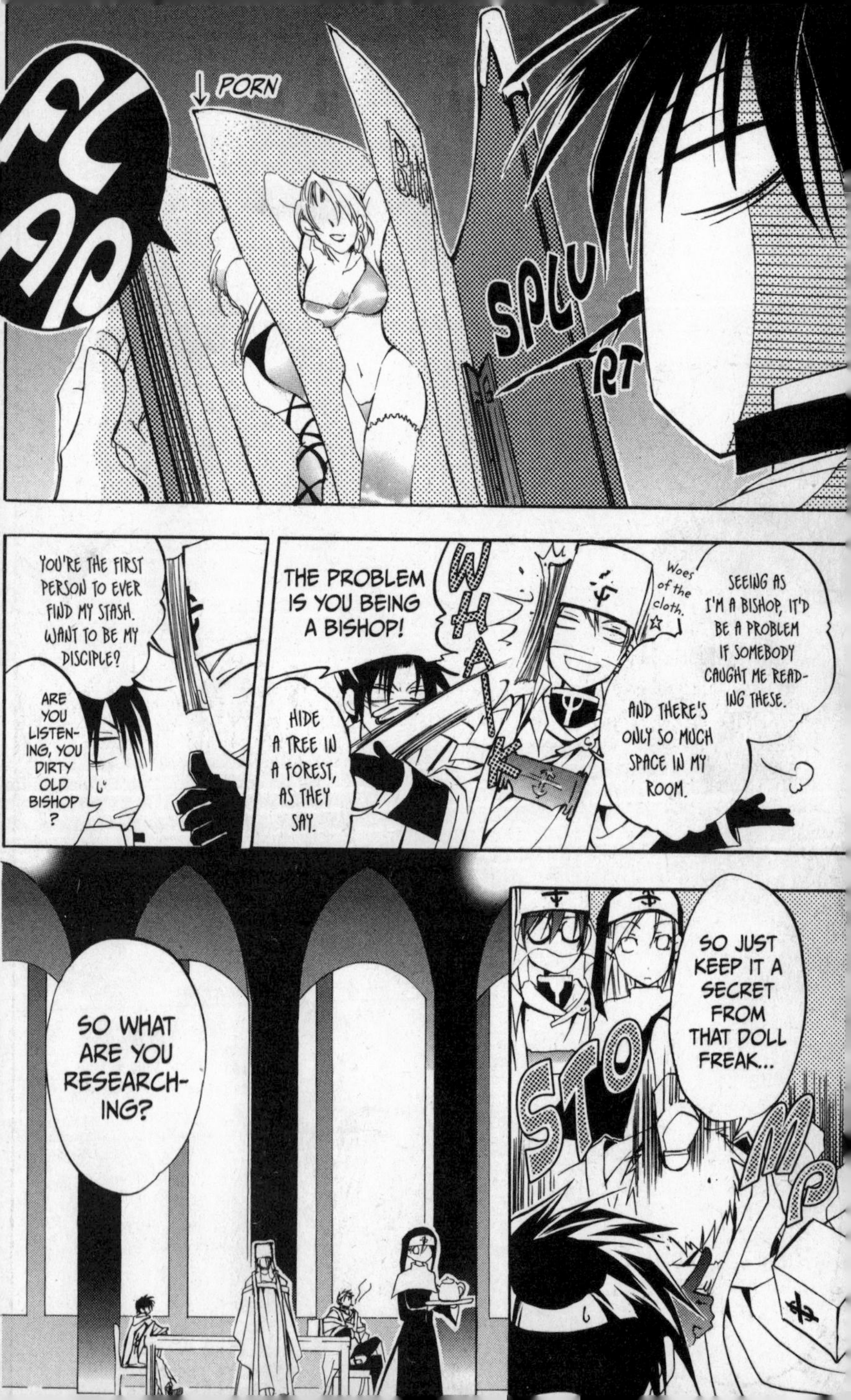
SPLURT
PORN
FLAP
SEEING AS I'M A BISHOP, IT'D BE A PROBLEM IF SOMEBODY CAUGHT ME READING THESE.
Woes of the cloth. ☆
AND THERE'S ONLY SO MUCH SPACE IN MY ROOM.
HIDE A TREE IN A FOREST, AS THEY SAY.
THE PROBLEM IS YOU BEING A BISHOP!
WHACK
YOU'RE THE FIRST PERSON TO EVER FIND MY STASH. WANT TO BE MY DISCIPLE?
ARE YOU LISTENING, YOU DIRTY OLD BISHOP?
SO JUST KEEP IT A SECRET FROM THAT DOLL FREAK...
STOMP
SO WHAT ARE YOU RESEARCHING?

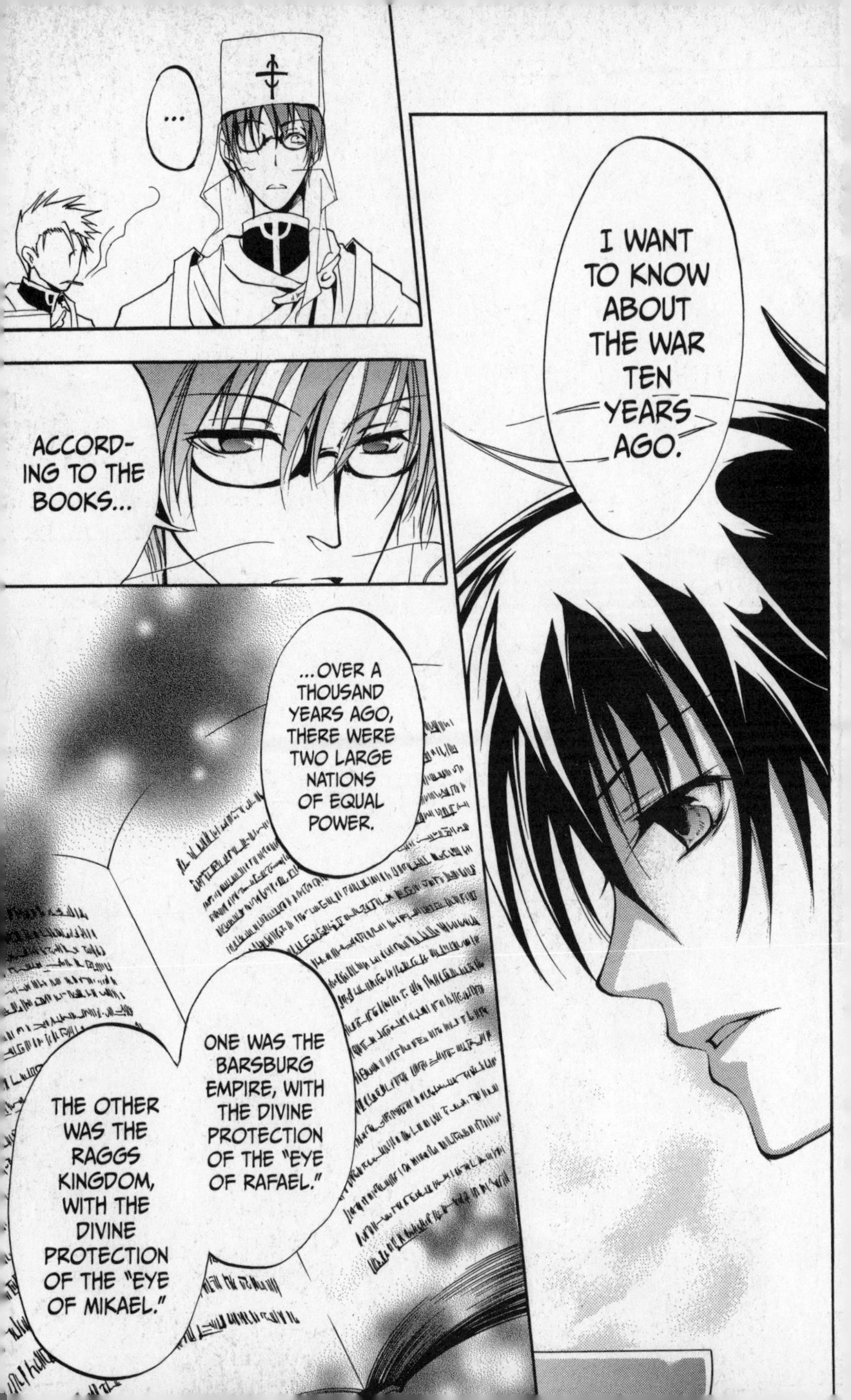
I WANT TO KNOW ABOUT THE WAR TEN YEARS AGO.
...
ACCORDING TO THE BOOKS...
...OVER A THOUSAND YEARS AGO, THERE WERE TWO LARGE NATIONS OF EQUAL POWER.
ONE WAS THE BARSBURG EMPIRE, WITH THE DIVINE PROTECTION OF THE "EYE OF RAFAEL."
THE OTHER WAS THE RAGGS KINGDOM, WITH THE DIVINE PROTECTION OF THE "EYE OF MIKAEL."

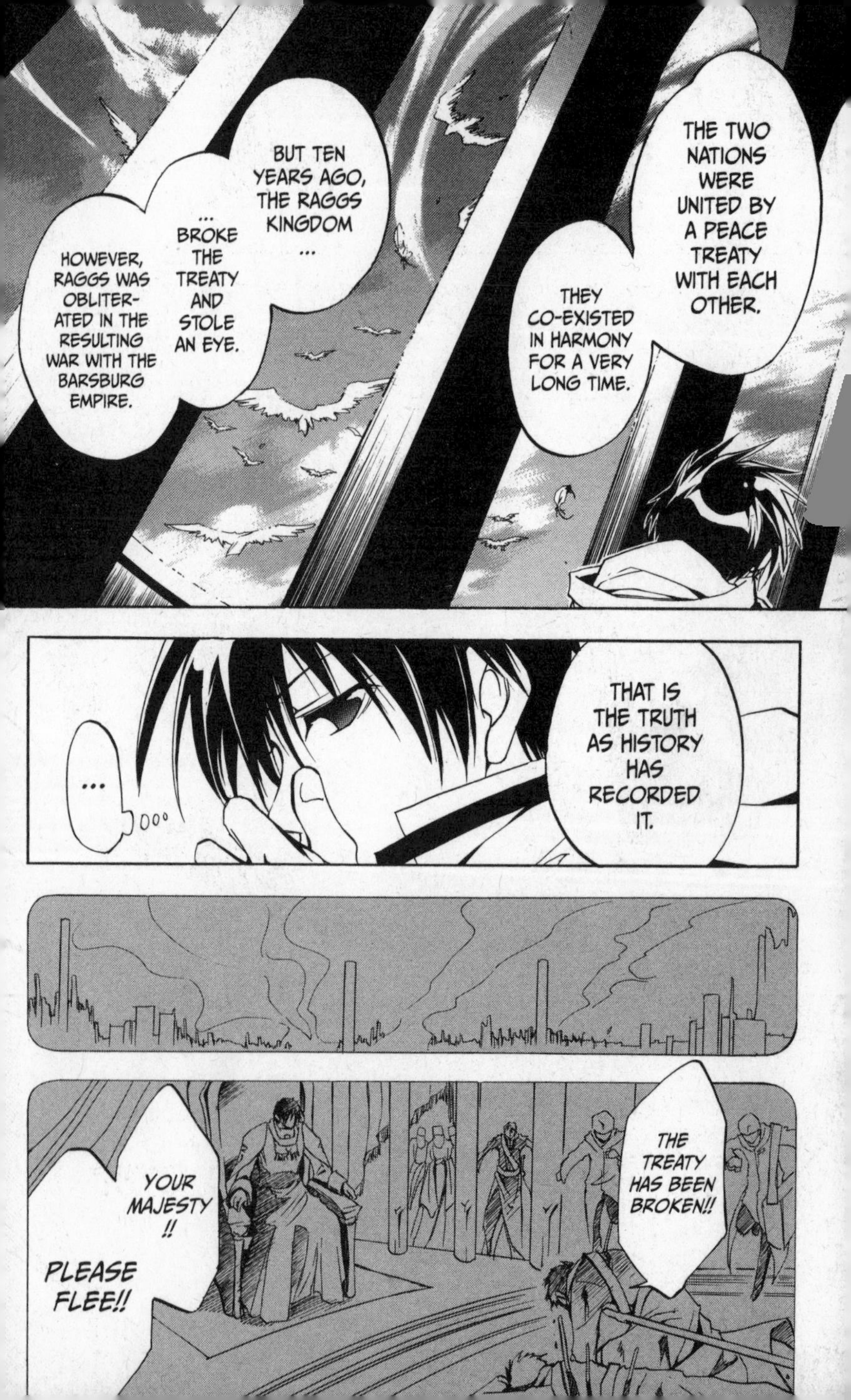
THE TWO NATIONS WERE UNITED BY A PEACE TREATY WITH EACH OTHER.
THEY CO-EXISTED IN HARMONY FOR A VERY LONG TIME.
BUT TEN YEARS AGO, THE RAGGS KINGDOM ...
... BROKE THE TREATY AND STOLE AN EYE.
HOWEVER, RAGGS WAS OBLITERATED IN THE RESULTING WAR WITH THE BARSBURG EMPIRE.
THAT IS THE TRUTH AS HISTORY HAS RECORDED IT.
...
THE TREATY HAS BEEN BROKEN!!
YOUR MAJESTY!!
PLEASE FLEE!!

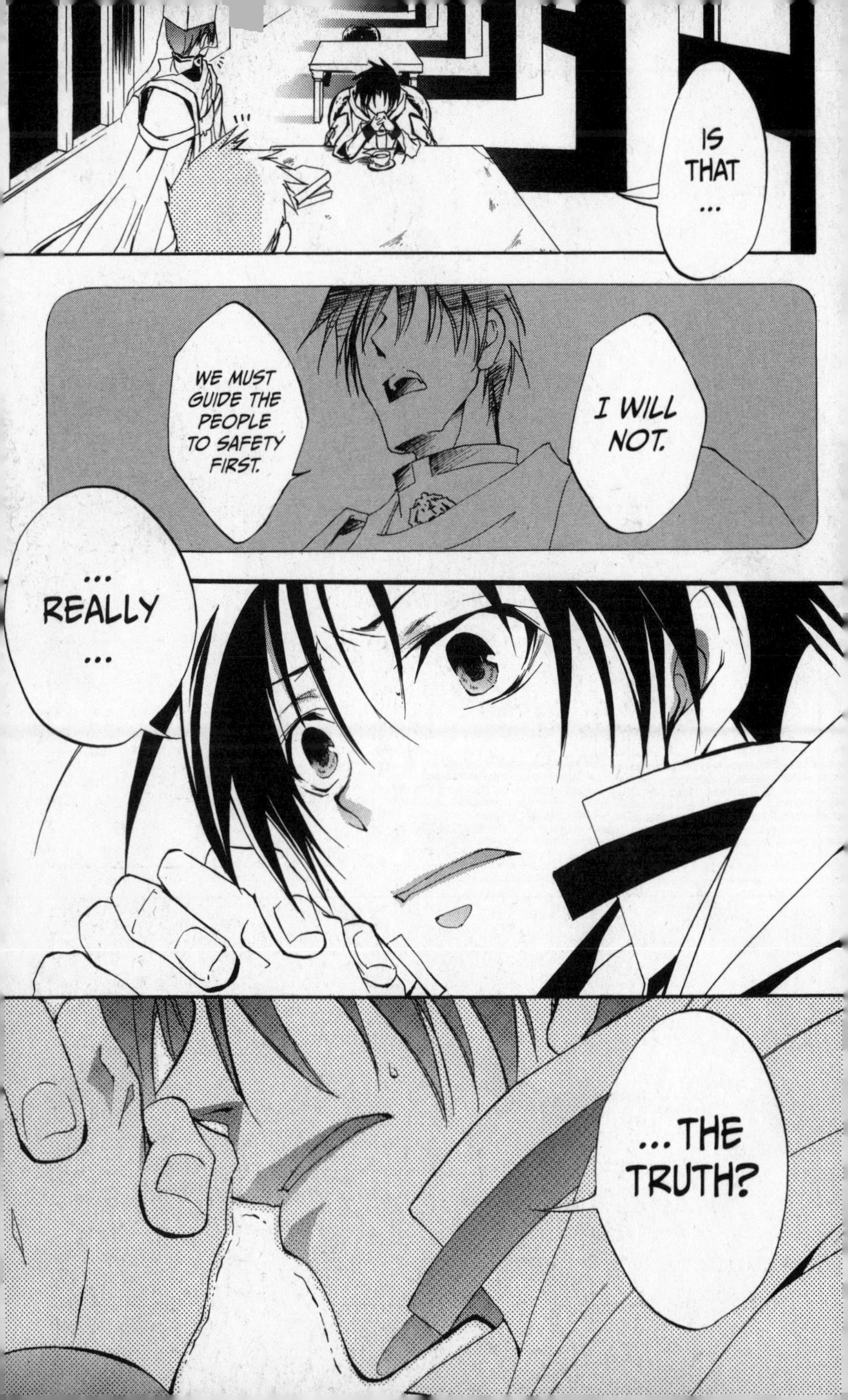
IS THAT ...
I WILL NOT.
WE MUST GUIDE THE PEOPLE TO SAFETY FIRST.
... REALLY ...
... THE TRUTH?

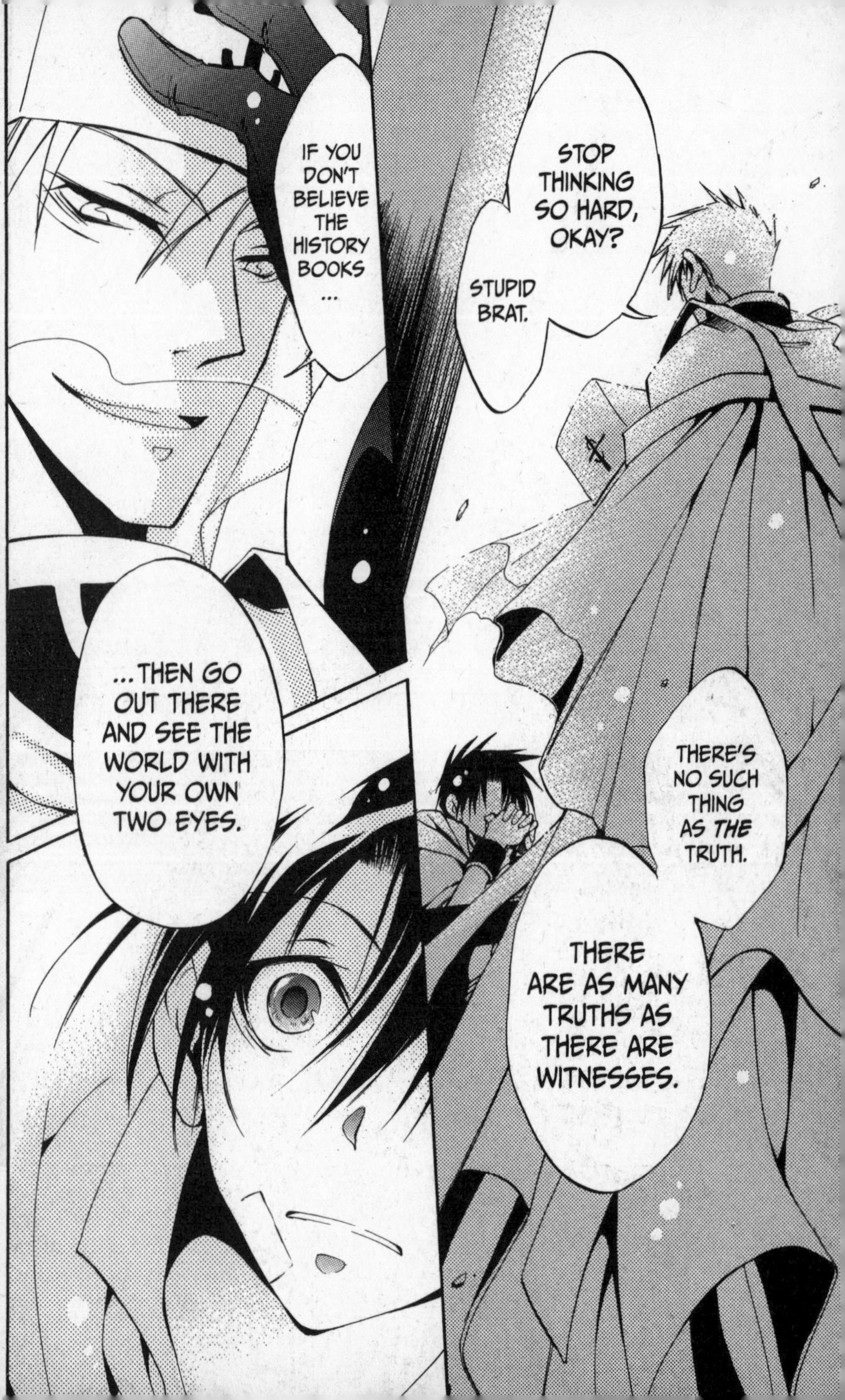
STOP THINKING SO HARD, OKAY?
STUPID BRAT.
IF YOU DON'T BELIEVE THE HISTORY BOOKS...
...THEN GO OUT THERE AND SEE THE WORLD WITH YOUR OWN TWO EYES.
THERE'S NO SUCH THING AS *THE* TRUTH.
THERE ARE AS MANY TRUTHS AS THERE ARE WITNESSES.

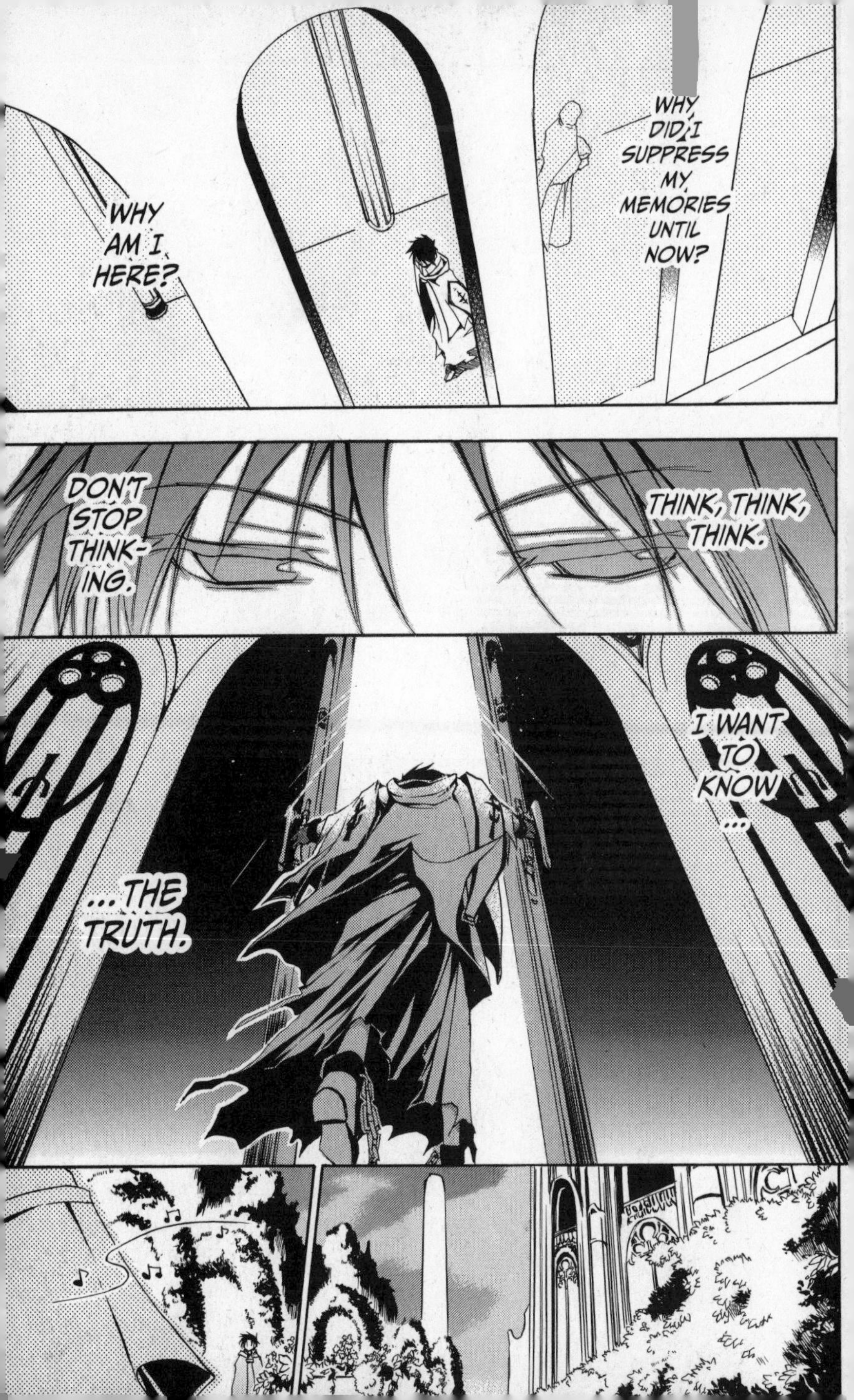
WHY DID I SUPPRESS MY MEMORIES UNTIL NOW?
WHY AM I HERE?
THINK, THINK, THINK.
DON'T STOP THINK-ING.
I WANT TO KNOW...
...THE TRUTH.

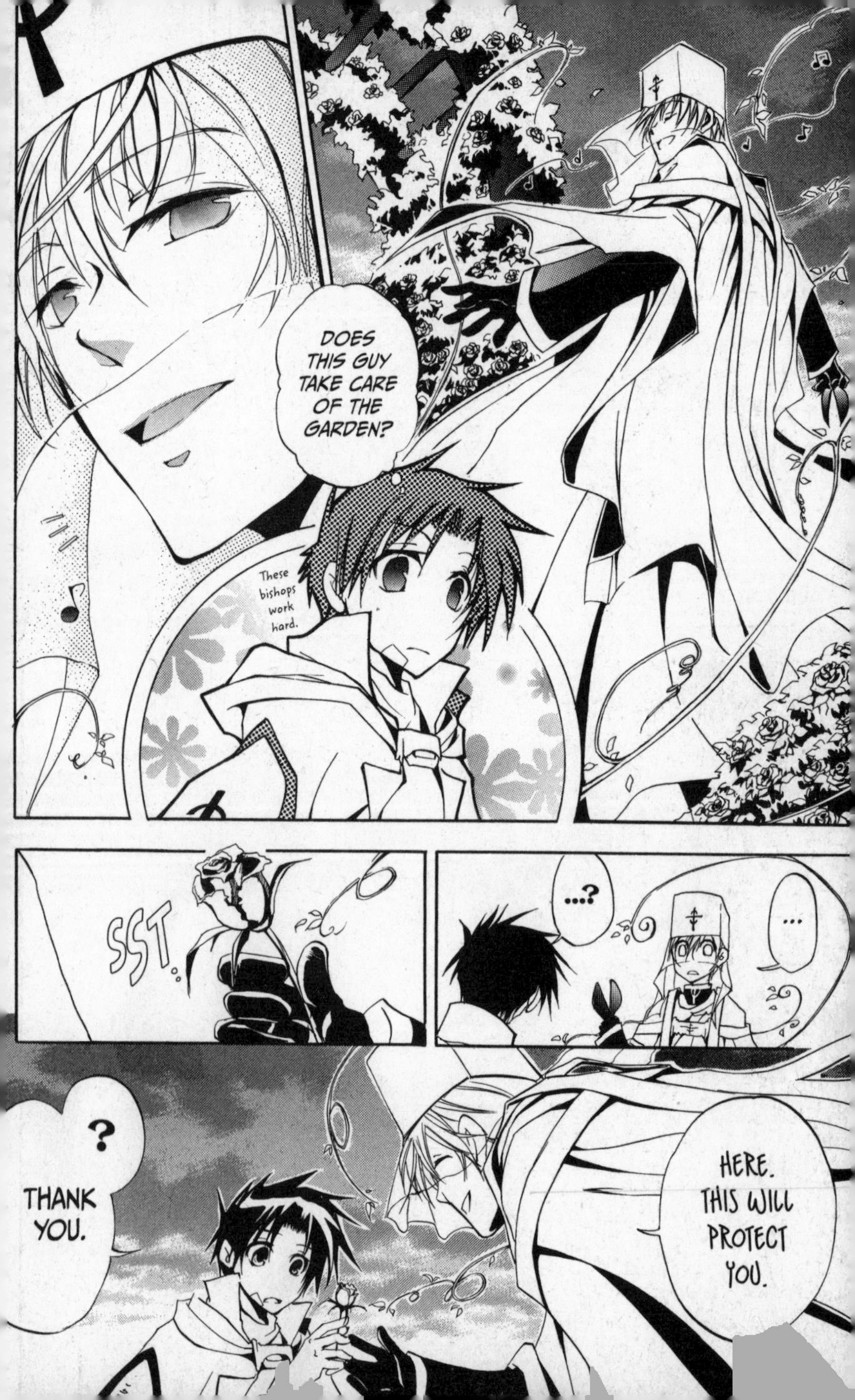

DOES THIS GUY TAKE CARE OF THE GARDEN?
These bishops work hard.
...
...?
SST
HERE. THIS WILL PROTECT YOU.
?
THANK YOU.

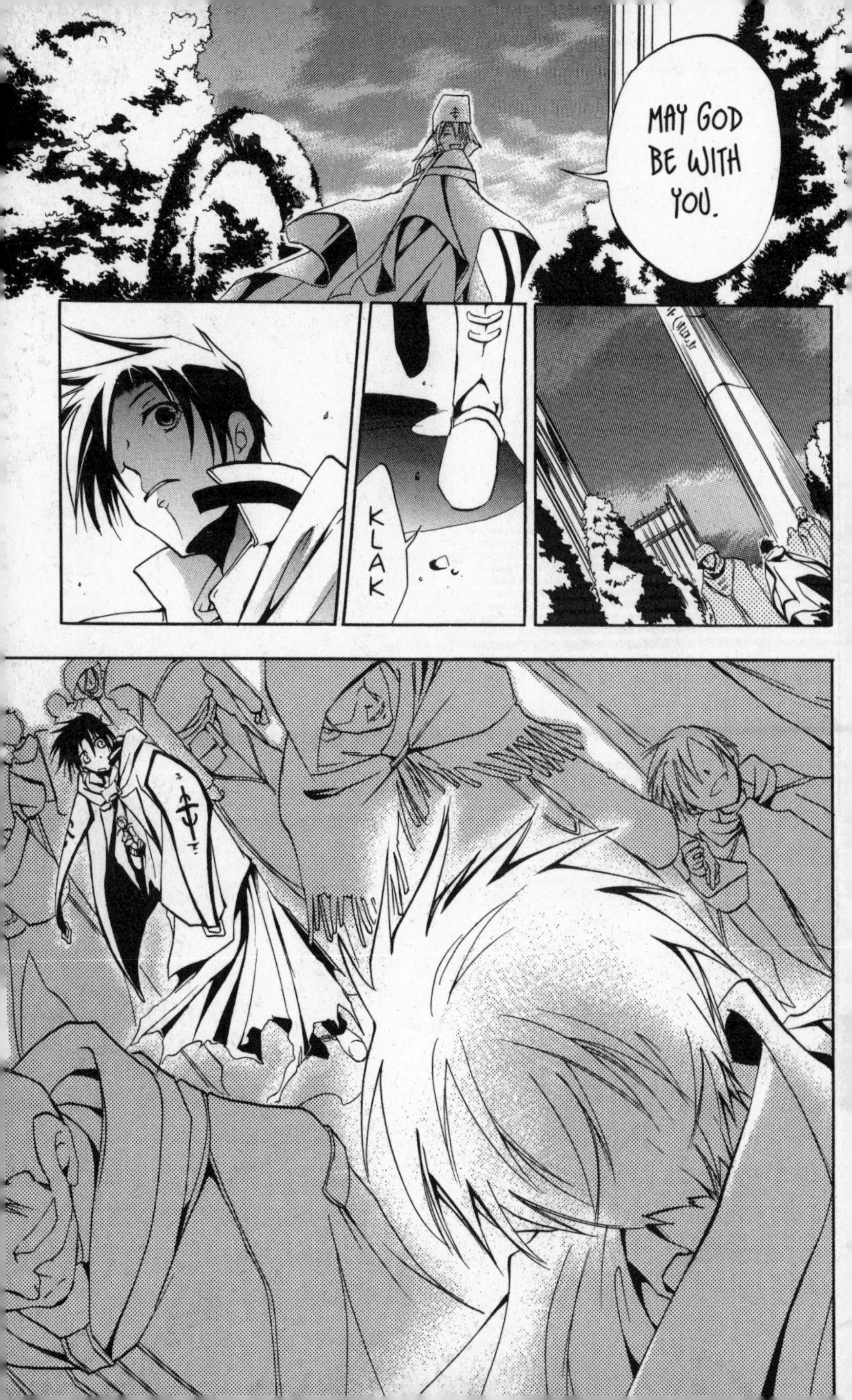
MAY GOD BE WITH YOU.
KLAK

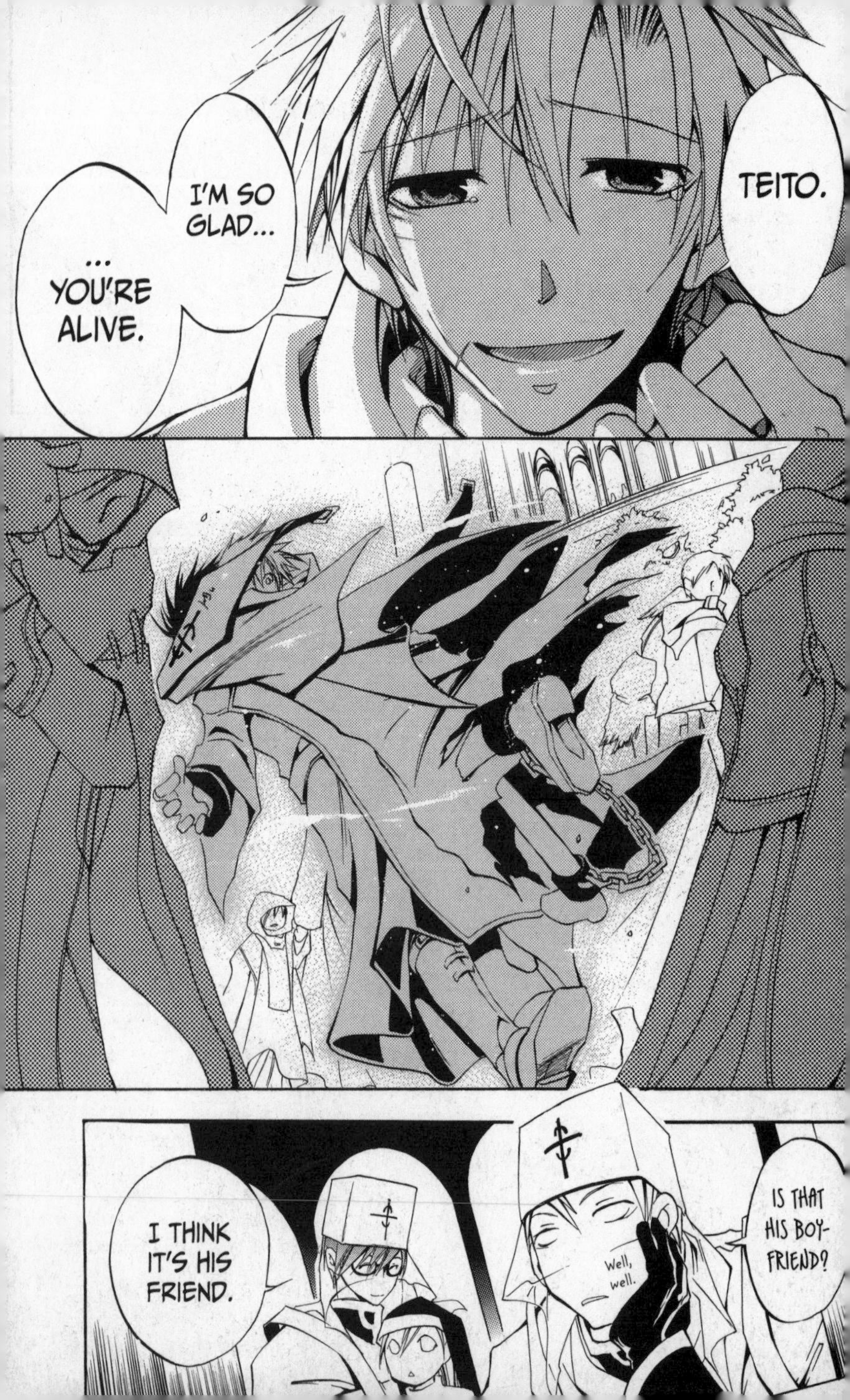
TEITO.
I'M SO GLAD...
... YOU'RE ALIVE.
IS THAT HIS BOY-FRIEND?
Well, well.
I THINK IT'S HIS FRIEND.

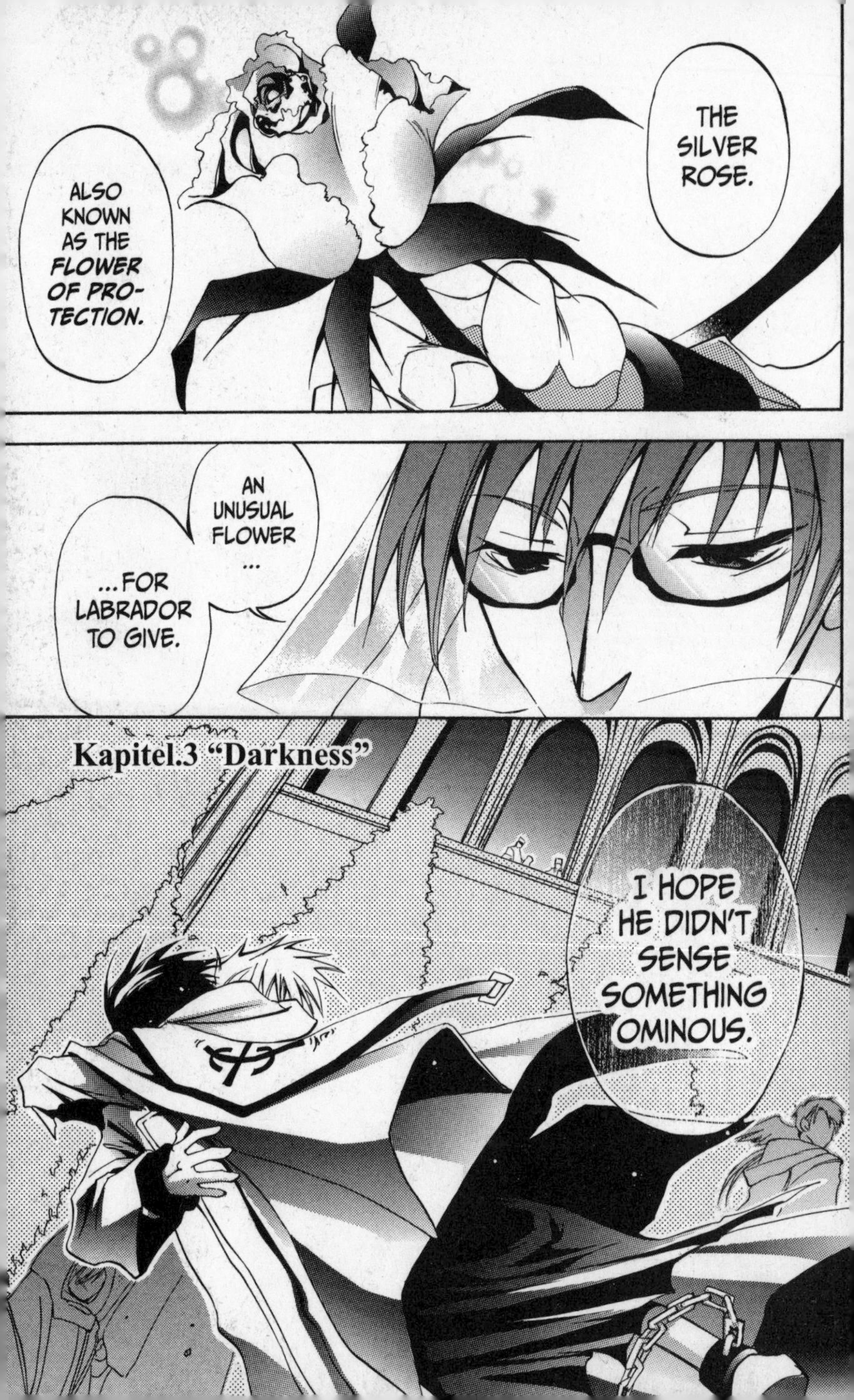
THE SILVER ROSE.
ALSO KNOWN AS THE FLOWER OF PROTECTION.
AN UNUSUAL FLOWER ...
...FOR LABRADOR TO GIVE.
I HOPE HE DIDN'T SENSE SOMETHING OMINOUS.
Kapitel.3 “Darkness”

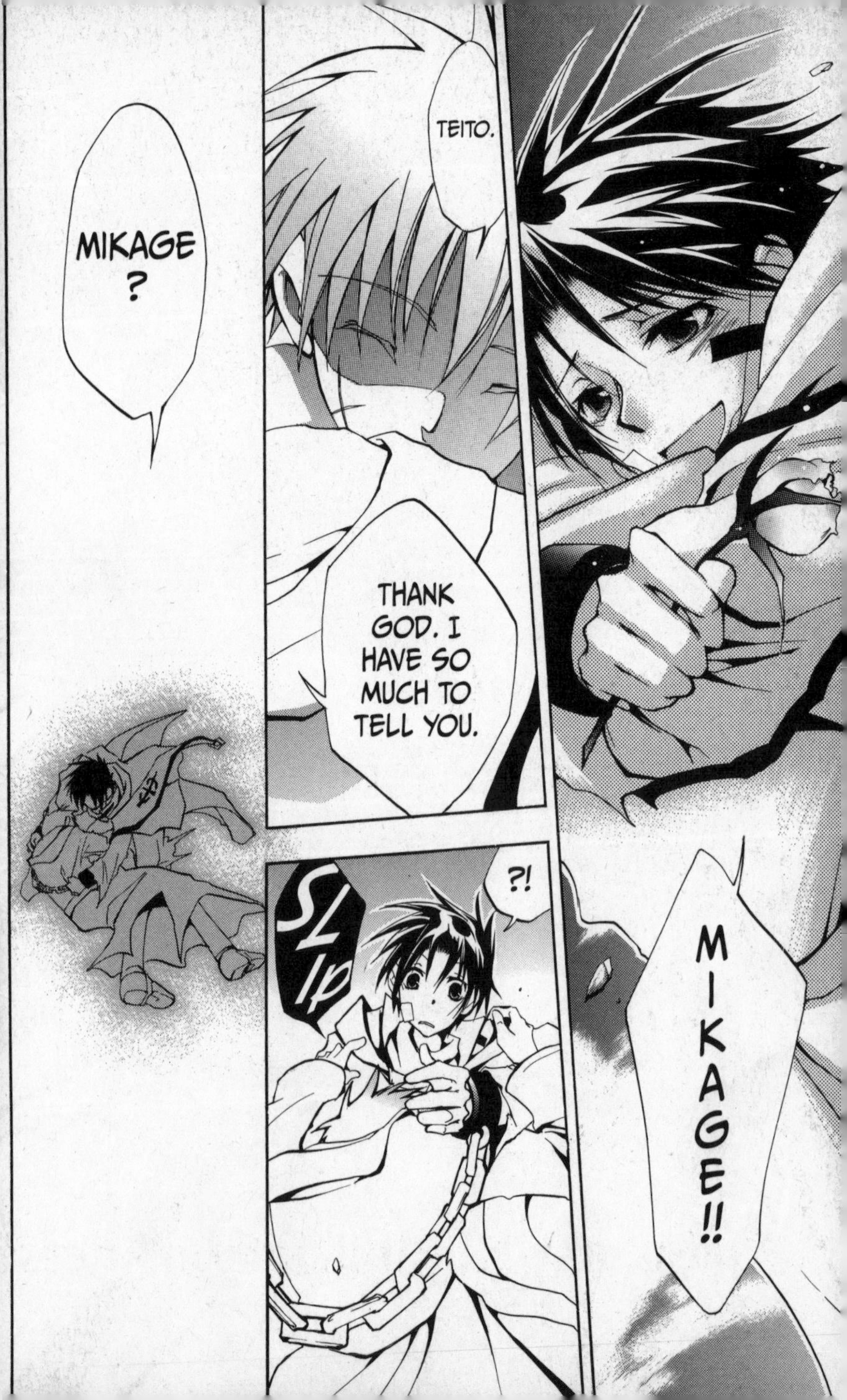
TEITO.
THANK GOD. I HAVE SO MUCH TO TELL YOU.
?!
SLIP
MIKAGE!!
MIKAGE?

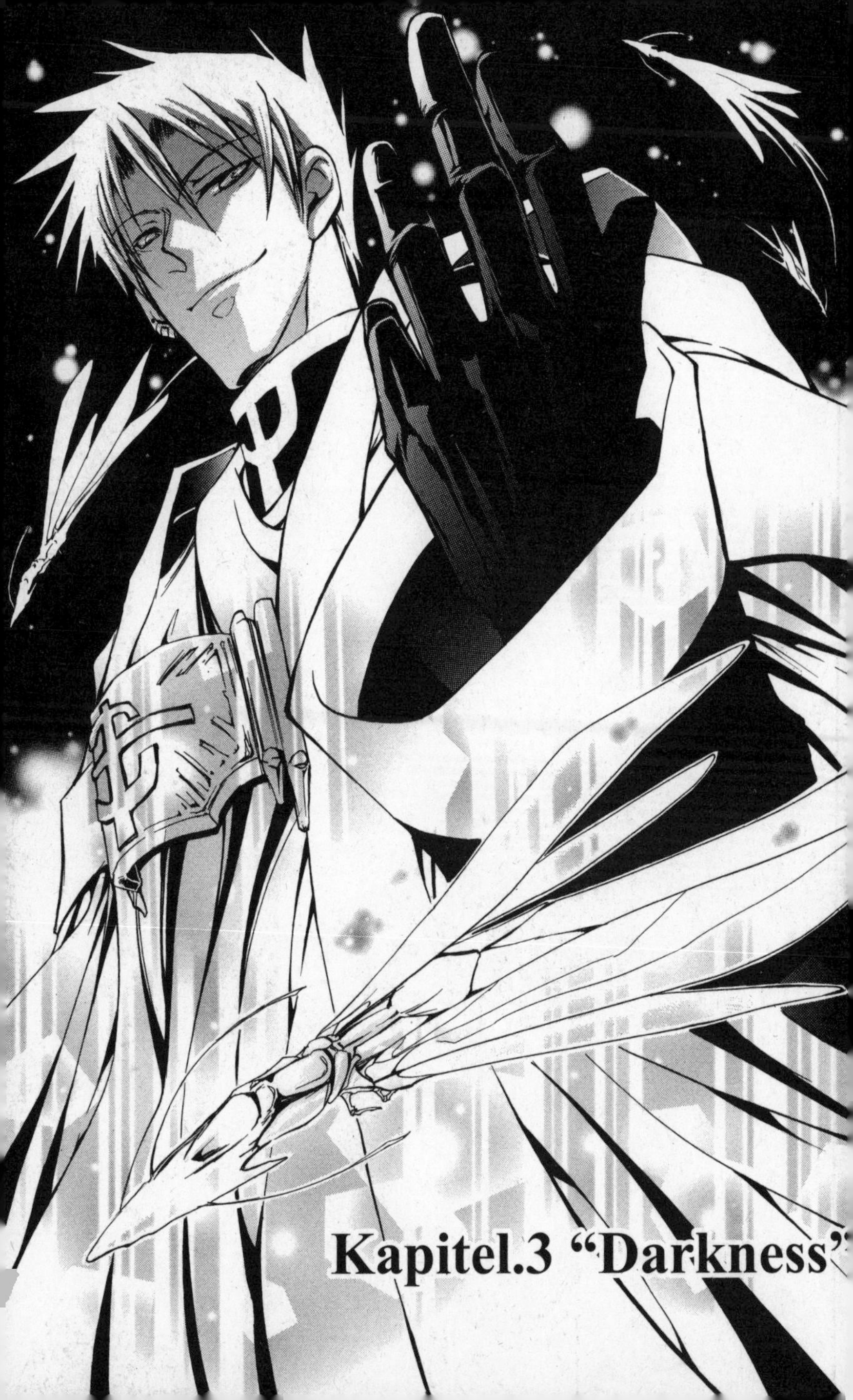
Kapitel.3 “Darkness”

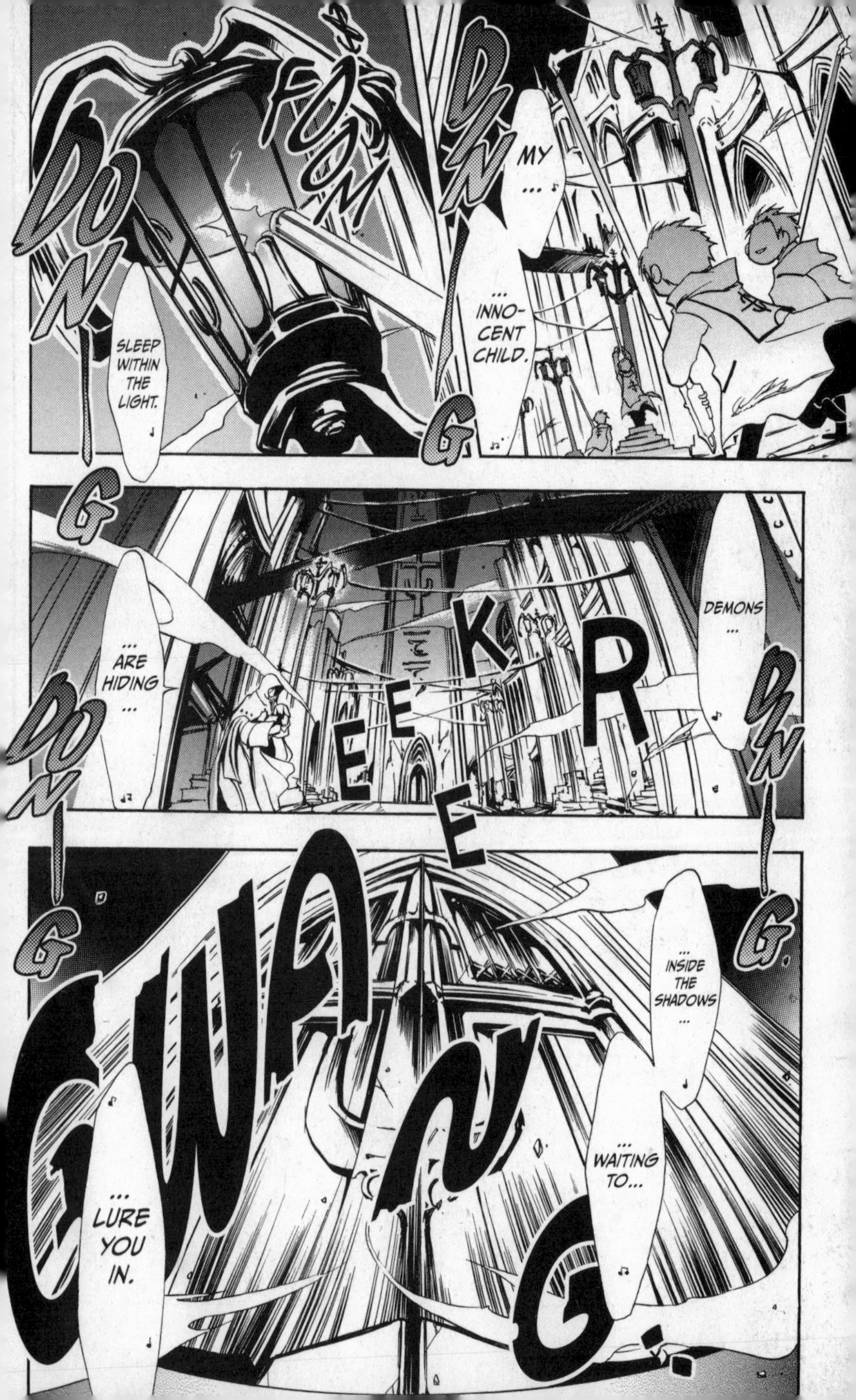
FOOM
MY...
...INNOCENT CHILD.
SLEEP WITHIN THE LIGHT.
DEMONS...
...ARE HIDING...
...INSIDE THE SHADOWS...
...WAITING TO...
...LURE YOU IN.

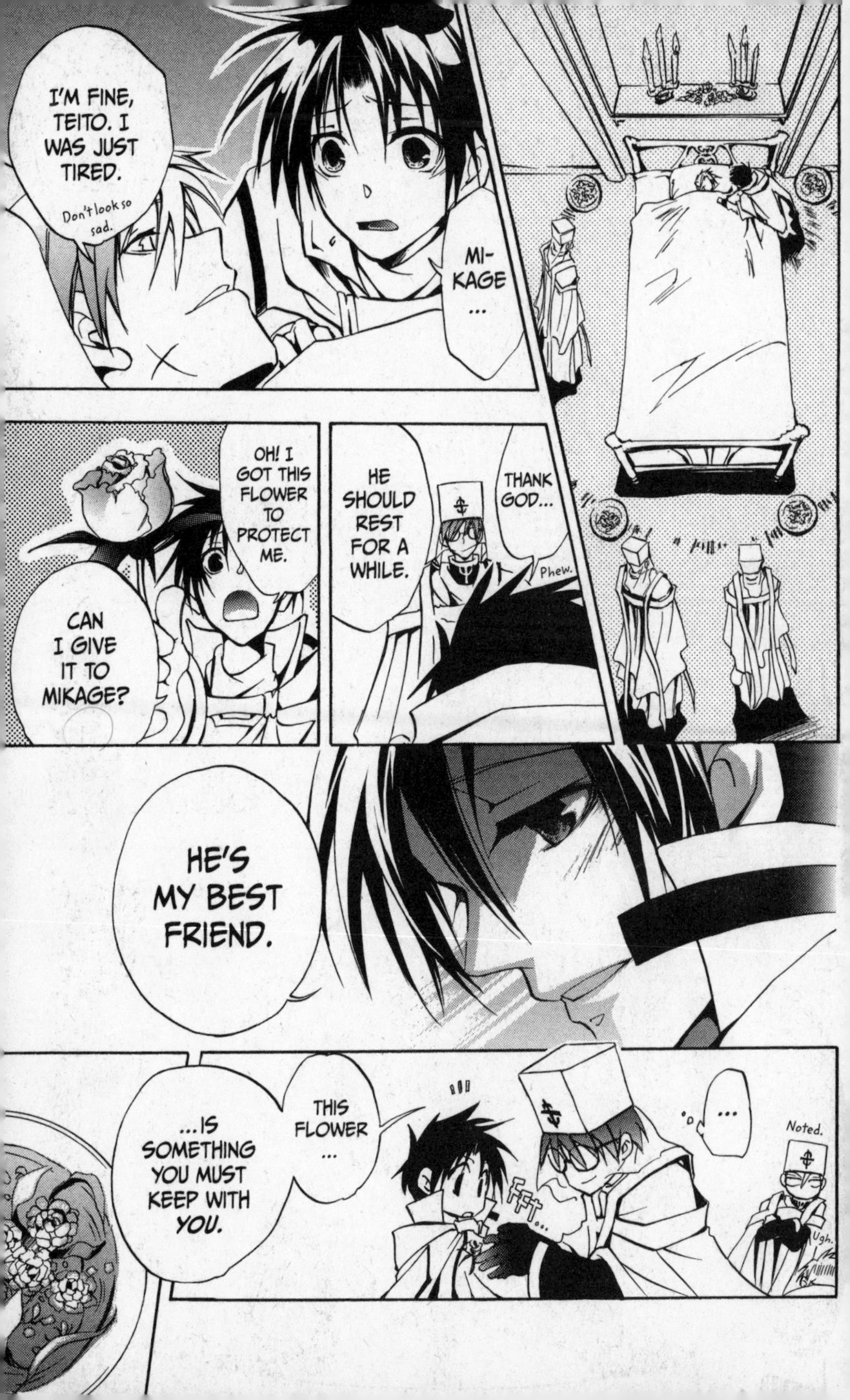
MI-KAGE...
I'M FINE, TEITO. I WAS JUST TIRED.
Don't look so sad.
THANK GOD...
Phew.
HE SHOULD REST FOR A WHILE.
OH! I GOT THIS FLOWER TO PROTECT ME.
CAN I GIVE IT TO MIKAGE?
HE'S MY BEST FRIEND.
Noted.
Ugh.
...
THIS FLOWER...
...IS SOMETHING YOU MUST KEEP WITH YOU.
FFT...

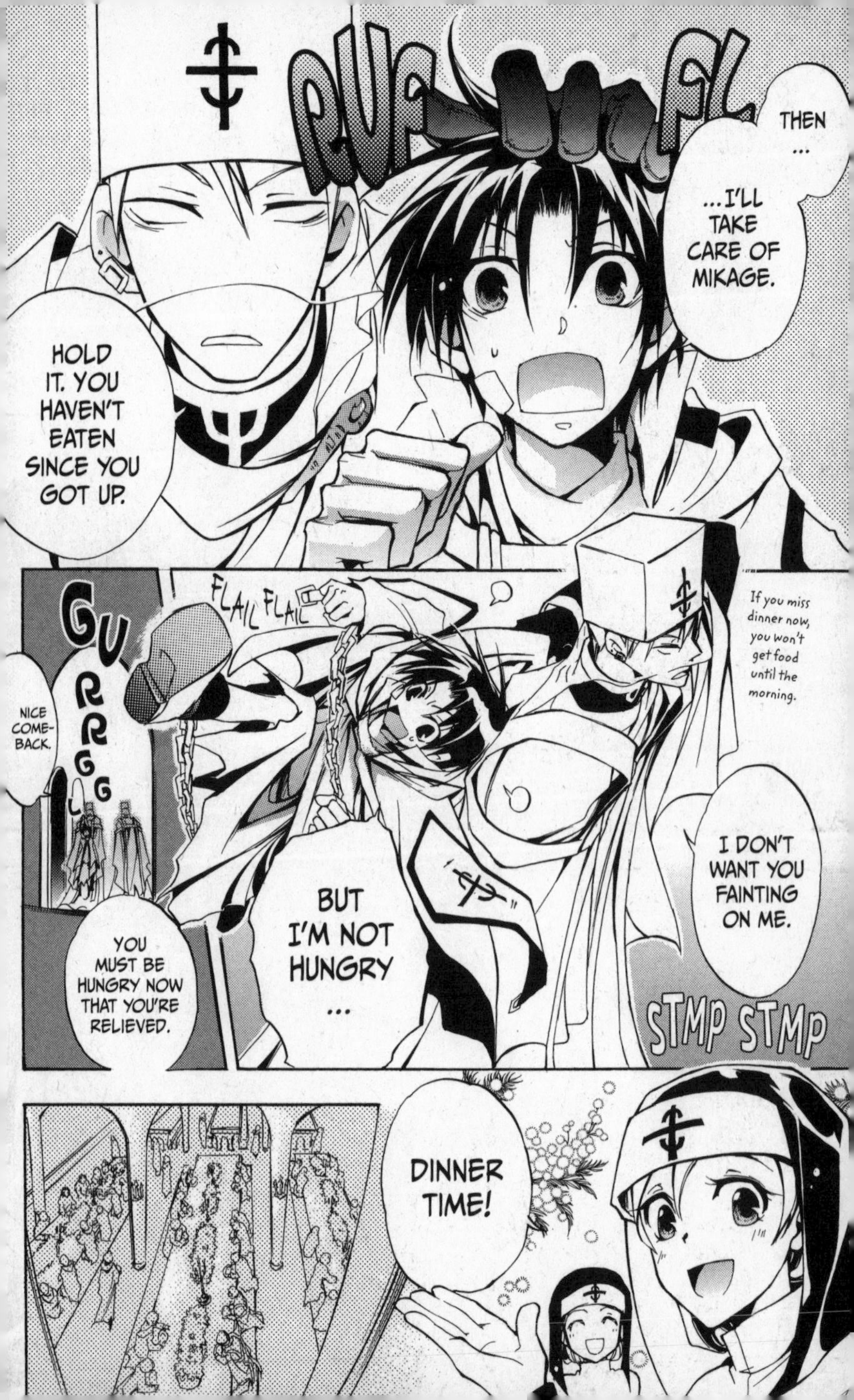
RUFFL
THEN ...
...I'LL TAKE CARE OF MIKAGE.
HOLD IT. YOU HAVEN'T EATEN SINCE YOU GOT UP.
If you miss dinner now, you won't get food until the morning.
I DON'T WANT YOU FAINTING ON ME.
STMP STMP
FLAIL FLAIL
BUT I'M NOT HUNGRY ...
GURRGGL
NICE COME-BACK.
YOU MUST BE HUNGRY NOW THAT YOU'RE RELIEVED.
DINNER TIME!

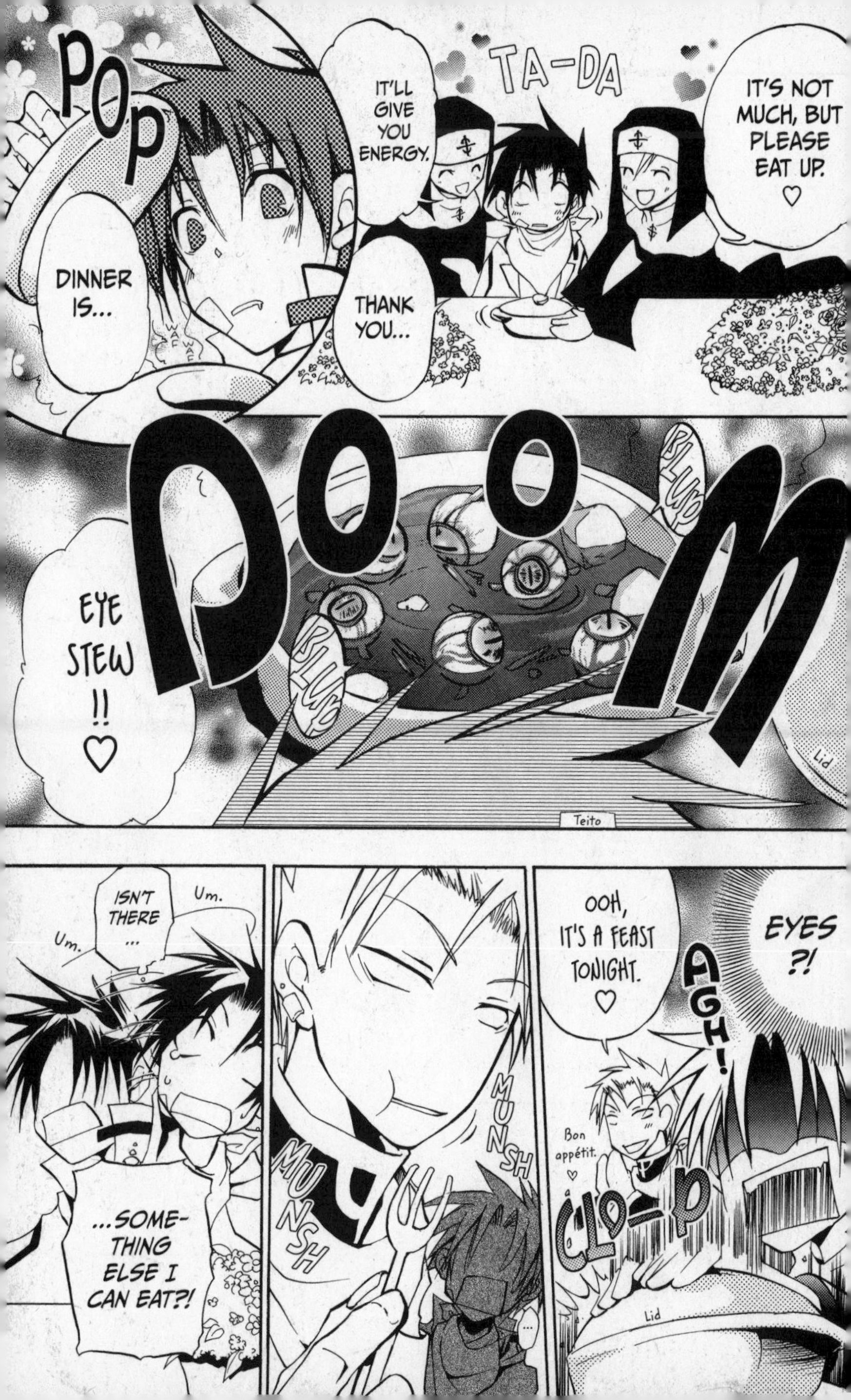
IT'S NOT MUCH, BUT PLEASE EAT UP. ♡
TA-DA
IT'LL GIVE YOU ENERGY.
THANK YOU...
POP
DINNER IS...
BLUP
DOOM
Lid
Teito
BLUP
EYE STEW !! ♡
EYES ?!
AGH!
OOH, IT'S A FEAST TONIGHT. ♡
Bon appétit. ♡
CLO-P
Lid
...
MUNSH
MUNSH
Um.
ISN'T THERE ...
Um.
...SOME-THING ELSE I CAN EAT?!

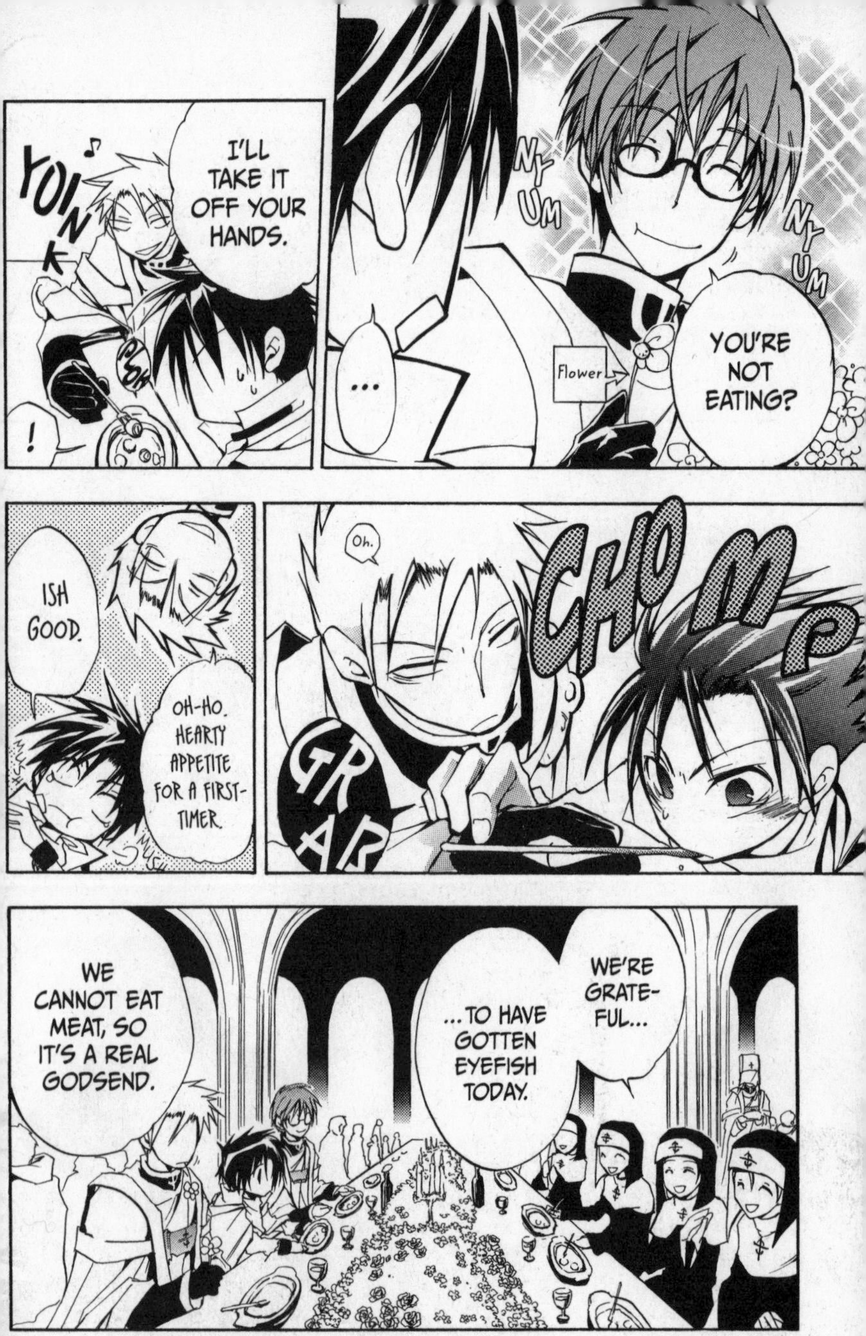
NYUM NYUM
YOU'RE NOT EATING?
Flower
...
YOINK
♪
I'LL TAKE IT OFF YOUR HANDS.
PLOK
!
CHOMP
Oh.
GRAR
ISH GOOD.
OH-HO. HEARTY APPETITE FOR A FIRST-TIMER.
MUSH MUSH
WE'RE GRATEFUL...
...TO HAVE GOTTEN EYEFISH TODAY.
WE CANNOT EAT MEAT, SO IT'S A REAL GODSEND.

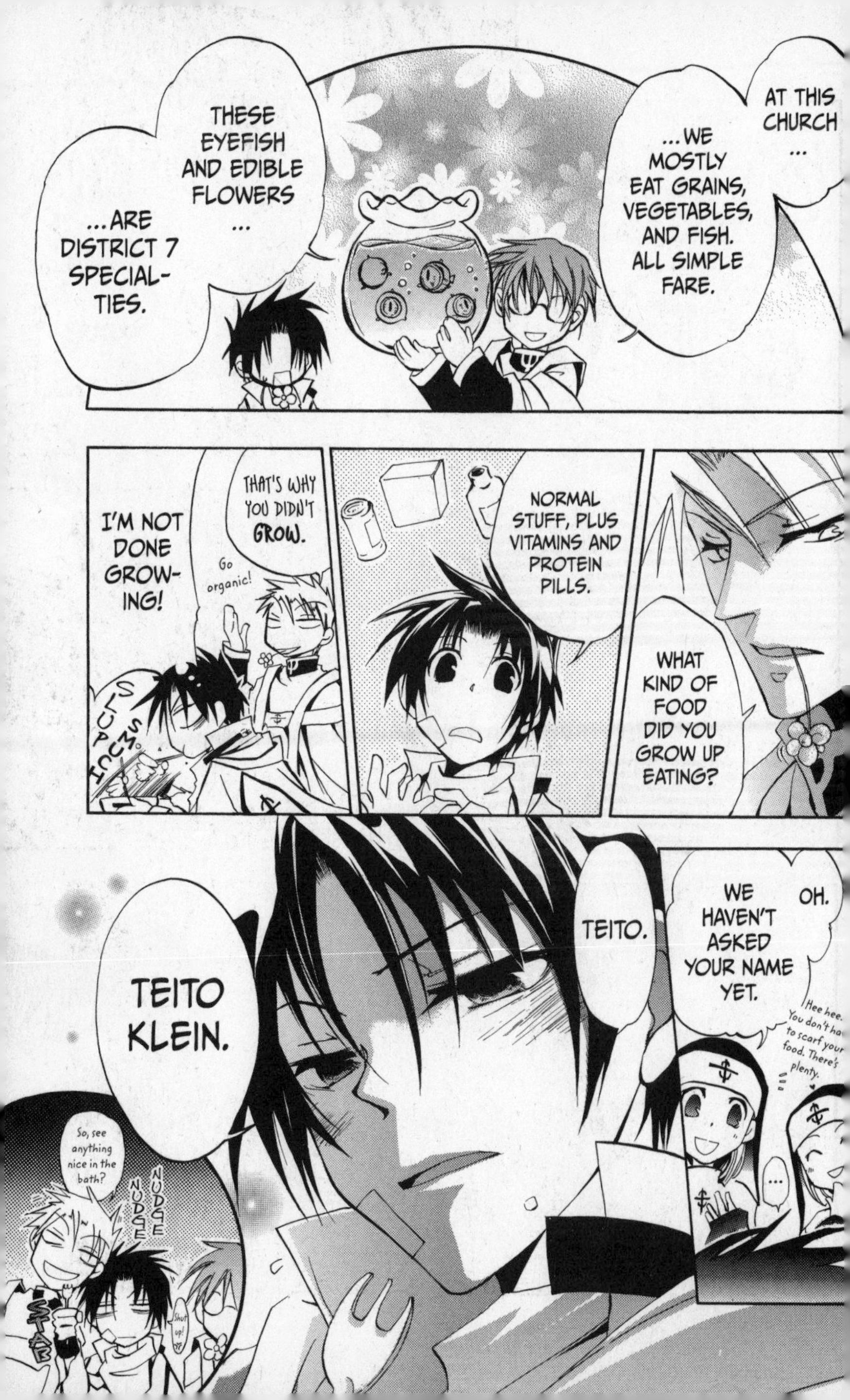
AT THIS CHURCH ...
...WE MOSTLY EAT GRAINS, VEGETABLES, AND FISH. ALL SIMPLE FARE.
THESE EYEFISH AND EDIBLE FLOWERS ...
...ARE DISTRICT 7 SPECIAL-TIES.
WHAT KIND OF FOOD DID YOU GROW UP EATING?
NORMAL STUFF, PLUS VITAMINS AND PROTEIN PILLS.
THAT'S WHY YOU DIDN'T GROW.
Go organic!
I'M NOT DONE GROW-ING!
SLUPCH
OH.
WE HAVEN'T ASKED YOUR NAME YET.
Hee hee. You don't have to scarf your food. There's plenty.
...
TEITO.
TEITO KLEIN.
So, see anything nice in the bath?
NUDGE NUDGE
Shut up!
STAB

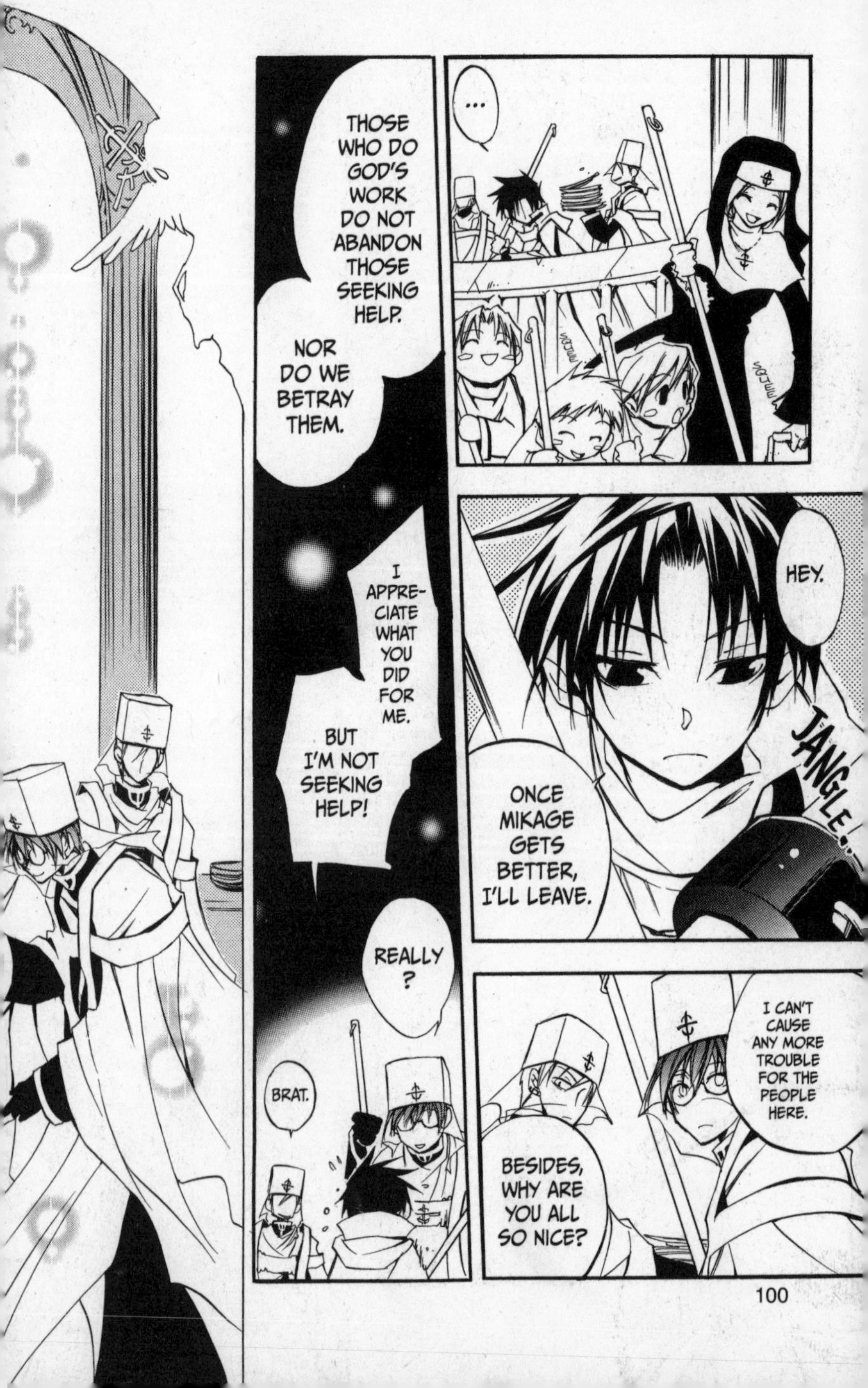
...
HEY.
ONCE MIKAGE GETS BETTER, I'LL LEAVE.
JANGLE...
I CAN'T CAUSE ANY MORE TROUBLE FOR THE PEOPLE HERE.
BESIDES, WHY ARE YOU ALL SO NICE?
THOSE WHO DO GOD'S WORK DO NOT ABANDON THOSE SEEKING HELP.
NOR DO WE BETRAY THEM.
I APPRECIATE WHAT YOU DID FOR ME.
BUT I'M NOT SEEKING HELP!
REALLY?
BRAT.

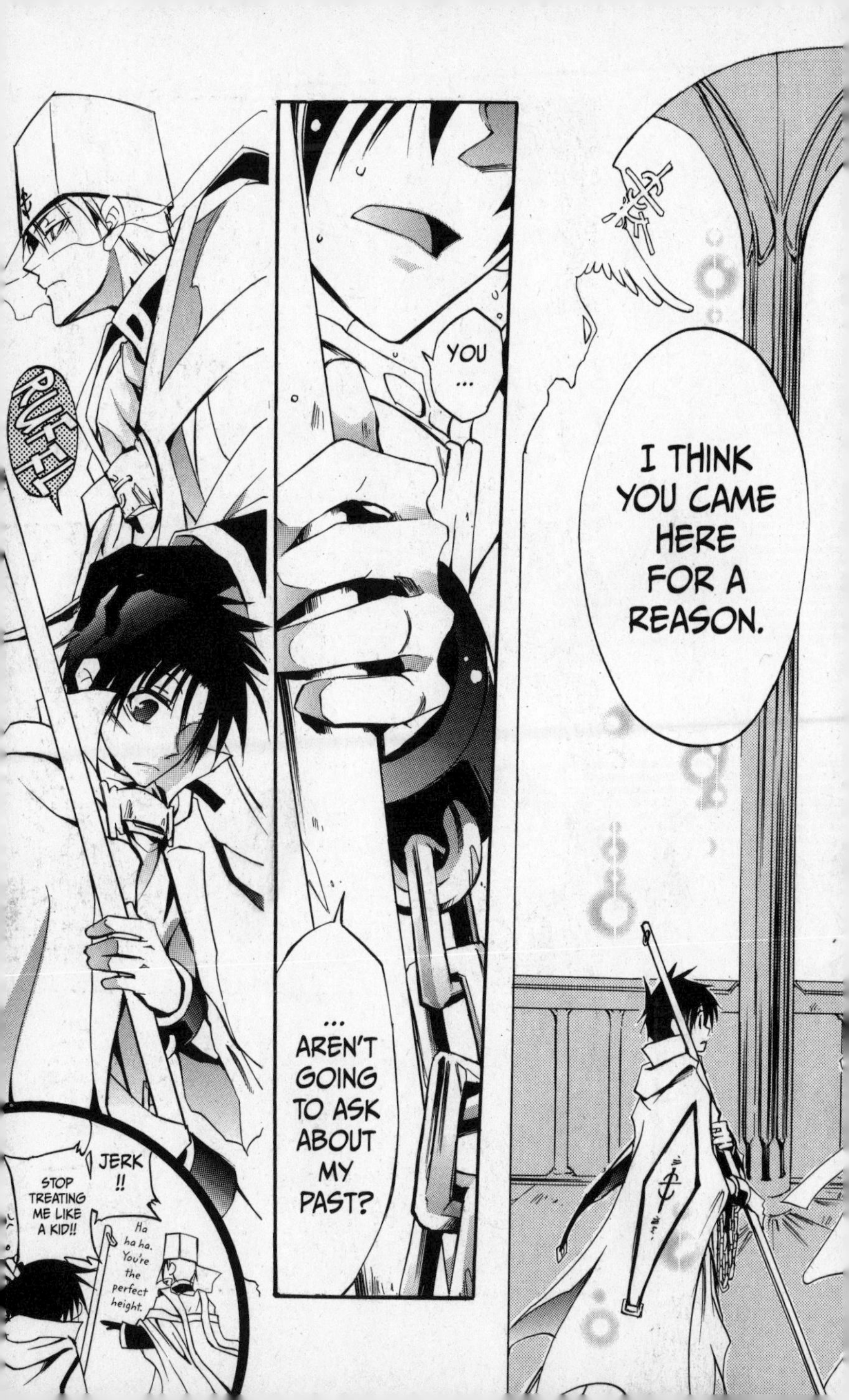
I THINK YOU CAME HERE FOR A REASON.
YOU ...
... AREN'T GOING TO ASK ABOUT MY PAST?
RUFFL
JERK!!
STOP TREATING ME LIKE A KID!!
Ha ha ha. You're the perfect height.

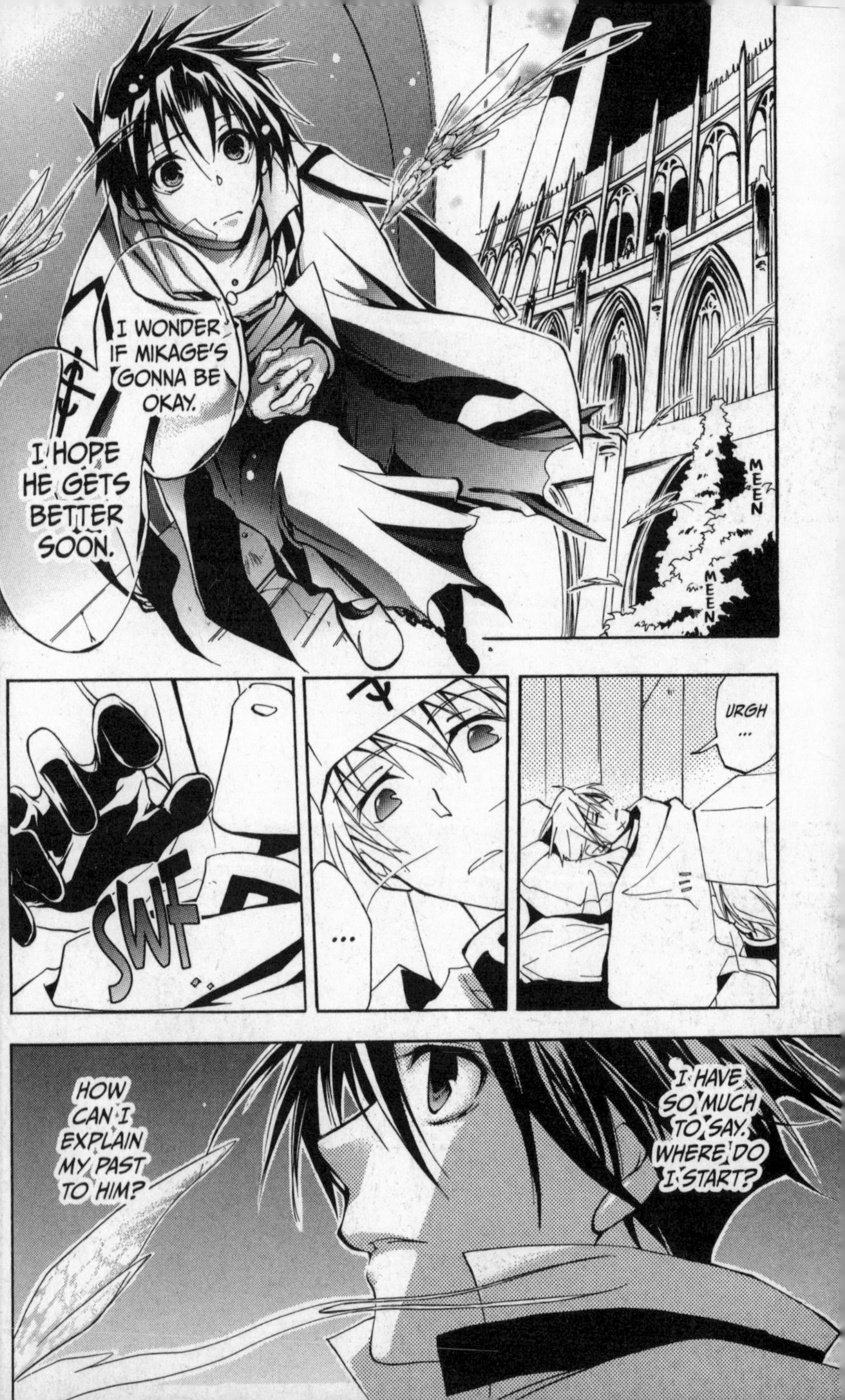
I WONDER IF MIKAGE'S GONNA BE OKAY.
I HOPE HE GETS BETTER SOON.
MEEN
MEEN
URGH ...
...
SWF
I HAVE SO MUCH TO SAY. WHERE DO I START?
HOW CAN I EXPLAIN MY PAST TO HIM?

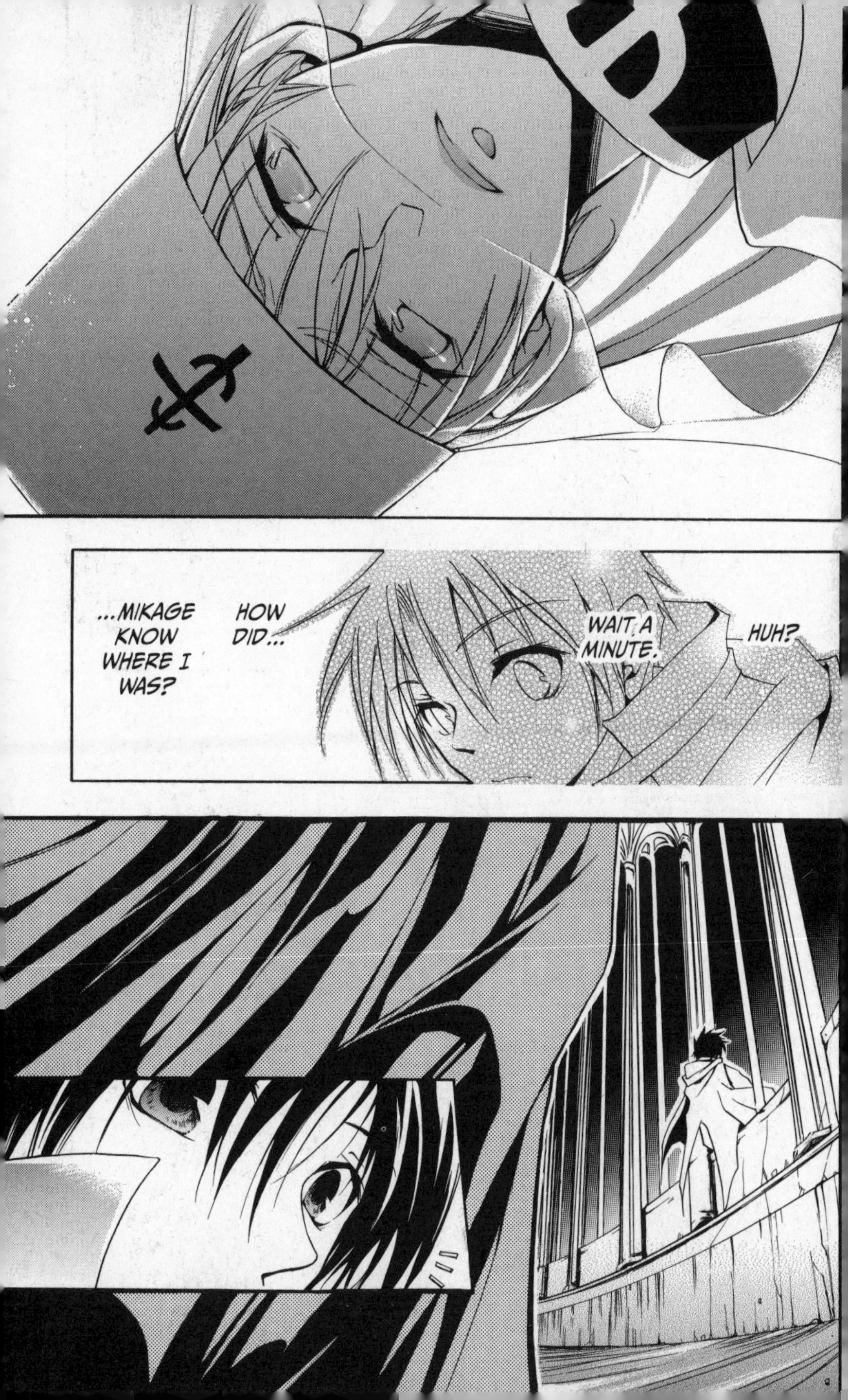
HUH?
WAIT A MINUTE.
HOW DID...
...MIKAGE KNOW WHERE I WAS?

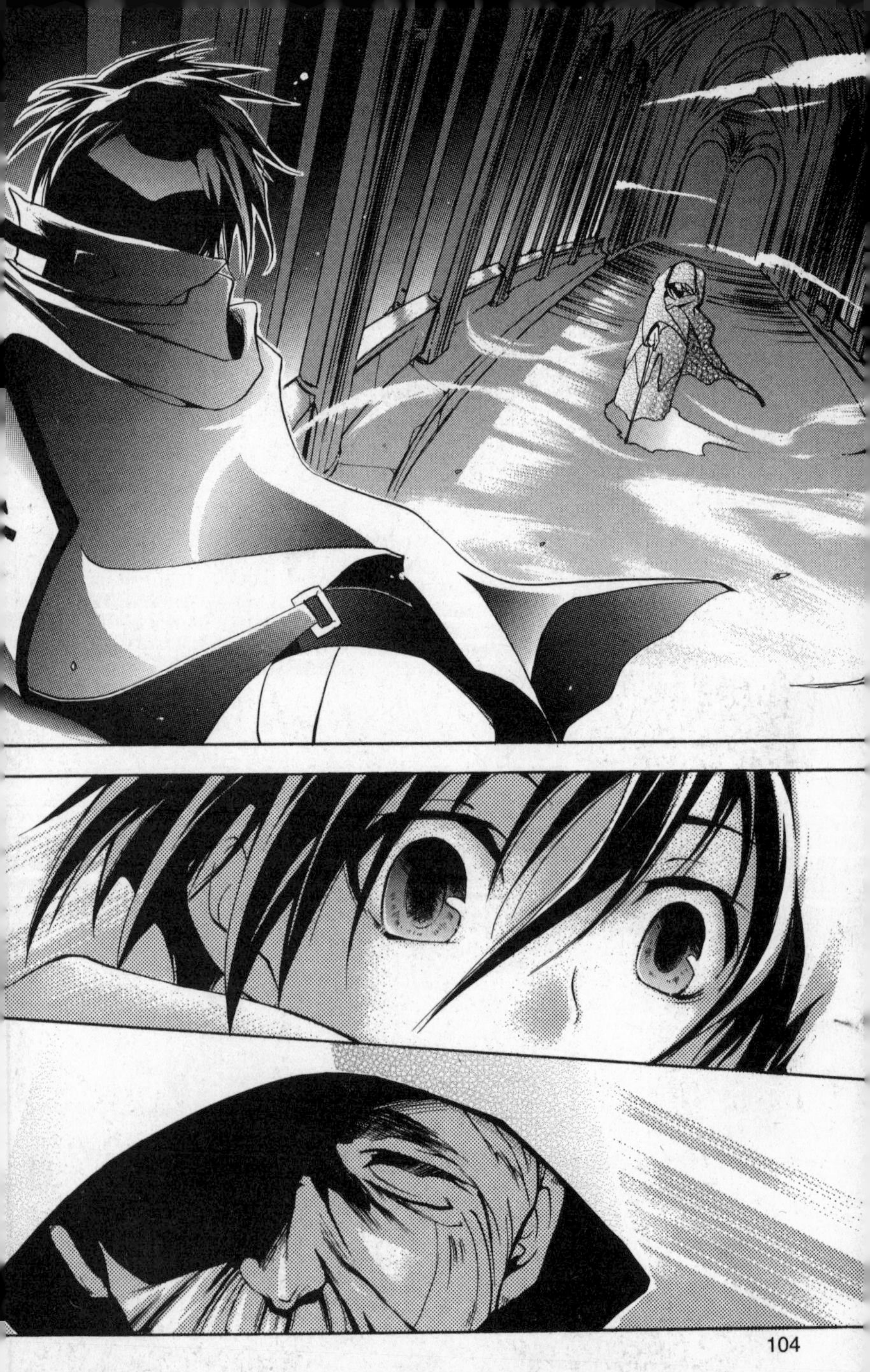

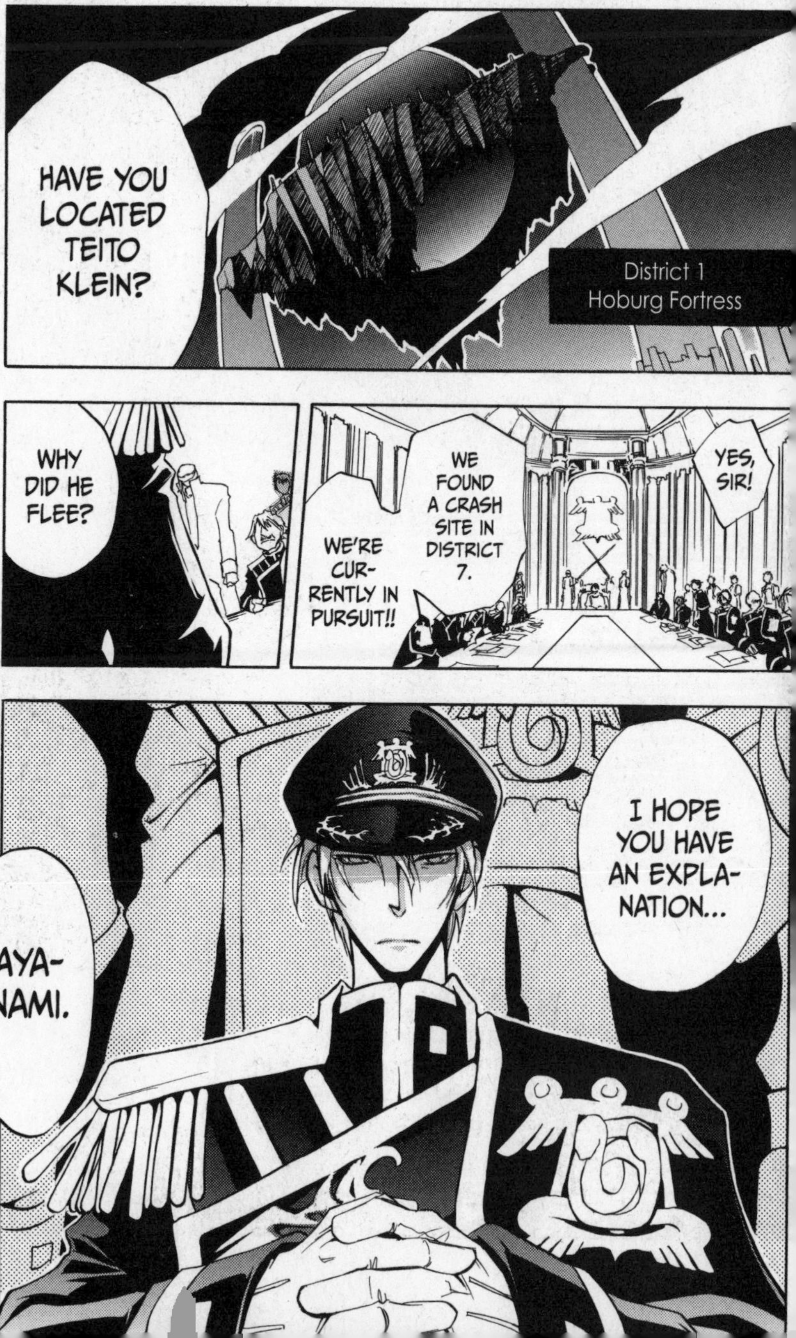
District 1 Hoburg Fortress
HAVE YOU LOCATED TEITO KLEIN?
YES, SIR!
WE FOUND A CRASH SITE IN DISTRICT 7.
WE'RE CURRENTLY IN PURSUIT!!
WHY DID HE FLEE?
I HOPE YOU HAVE AN EXPLANATION...
AYANAMI.

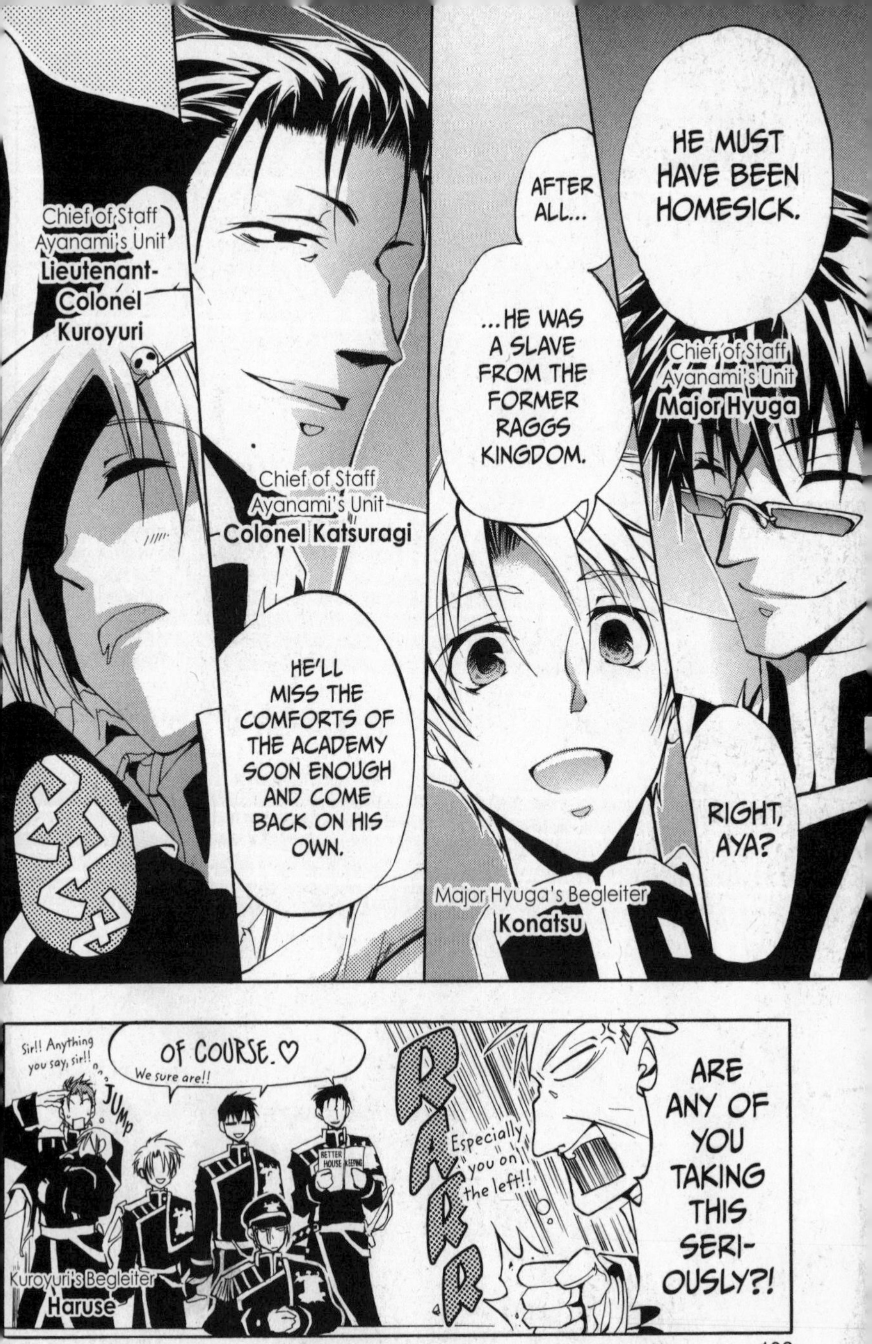
HE MUST HAVE BEEN HOMESICK.
Chief of Staff Ayanami's Unit Major Hyuga
RIGHT, AYA?
AFTER ALL...
...HE WAS A SLAVE FROM THE FORMER RAGGS KINGDOM.
Major Hyuga's Begleiter Konatsu
Chief of Staff Ayanami's Unit Colonel Katsuragi
HE'LL MISS THE COMFORTS OF THE ACADEMY SOON ENOUGH AND COME BACK ON HIS OWN.
Chief of Staff Ayanami's Unit Lieutenant-Colonel Kuroyuri
ARE ANY OF YOU TAKING THIS SERI-OUSLY?!
RARR
Especially you on the left!!
BETTER HOUSE KEEPING
OF COURSE. ♡
We sure are!!
Sir!! Anything you say, sir!!
JUMP
Kuroyuri's Begleiter Haruse

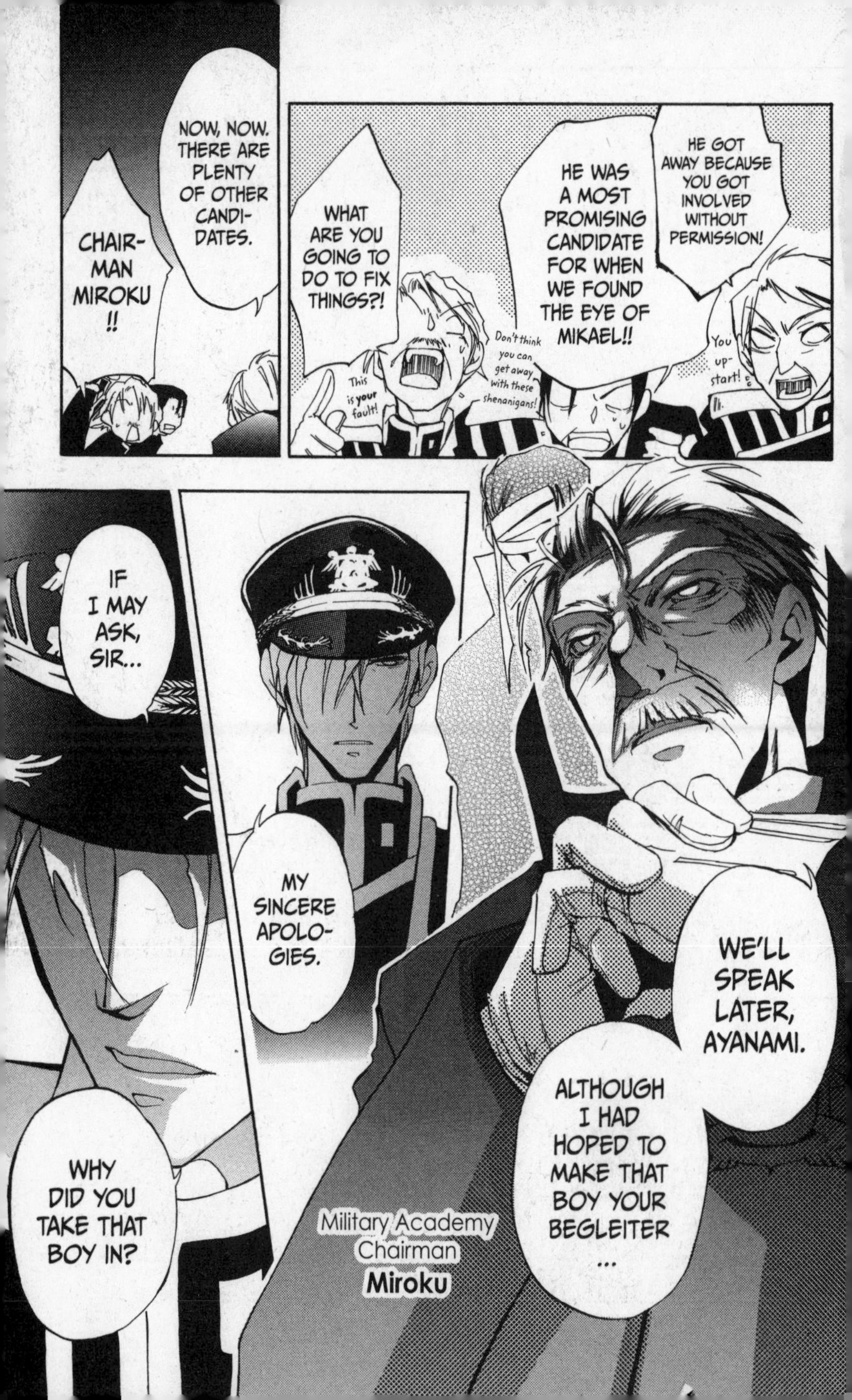
HE GOT AWAY BECAUSE YOU GOT INVOLVED WITHOUT PERMISSION!
You upstart!
HE WAS A MOST PROMISING CANDIDATE FOR WHEN WE FOUND THE EYE OF MIKAEL!!
Don't think you can get away with these shenanigans!
WHAT ARE YOU GOING TO DO TO FIX THINGS?!
This is your fault!
NOW, NOW. THERE ARE PLENTY OF OTHER CANDI-DATES.
CHAIR-MAN MIROKU!!
WE'LL SPEAK LATER, AYANAMI.
ALTHOUGH I HAD HOPED TO MAKE THAT BOY YOUR BEGLEITER...
Military Academy Chairman
Miroku
MY SINCERE APOLO-GIES.
IF I MAY ASK, SIR...
WHY DID YOU TAKE THAT BOY IN?

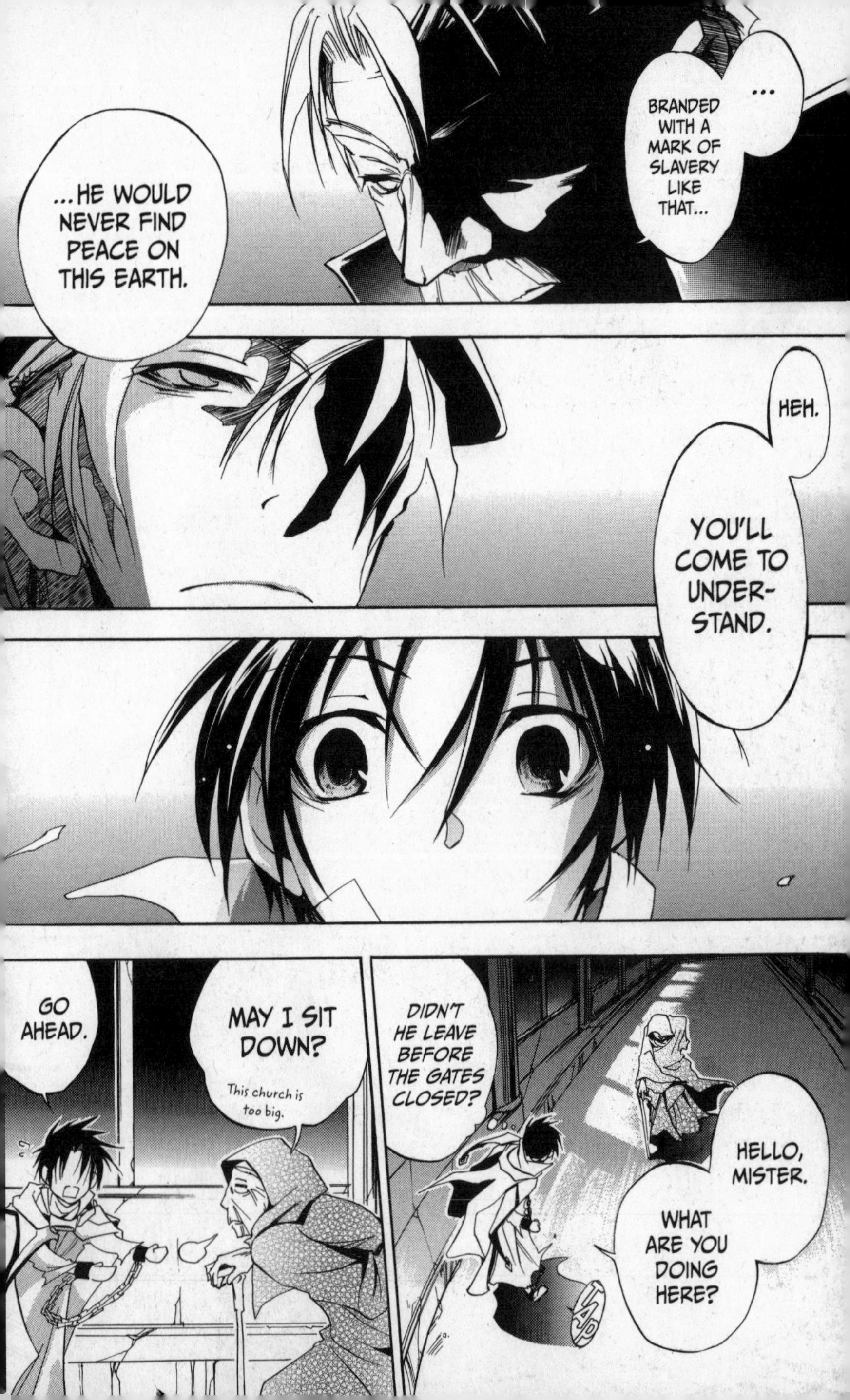
...
BRANDED WITH A MARK OF SLAVERY LIKE THAT...
...HE WOULD NEVER FIND PEACE ON THIS EARTH.
HEH.
YOU'LL COME TO UNDERSTAND.
HELLO, MISTER.
WHAT ARE YOU DOING HERE?
DIDN'T HE LEAVE BEFORE THE GATES CLOSED?
MAY I SIT DOWN?
This church is too big.
GO AHEAD.

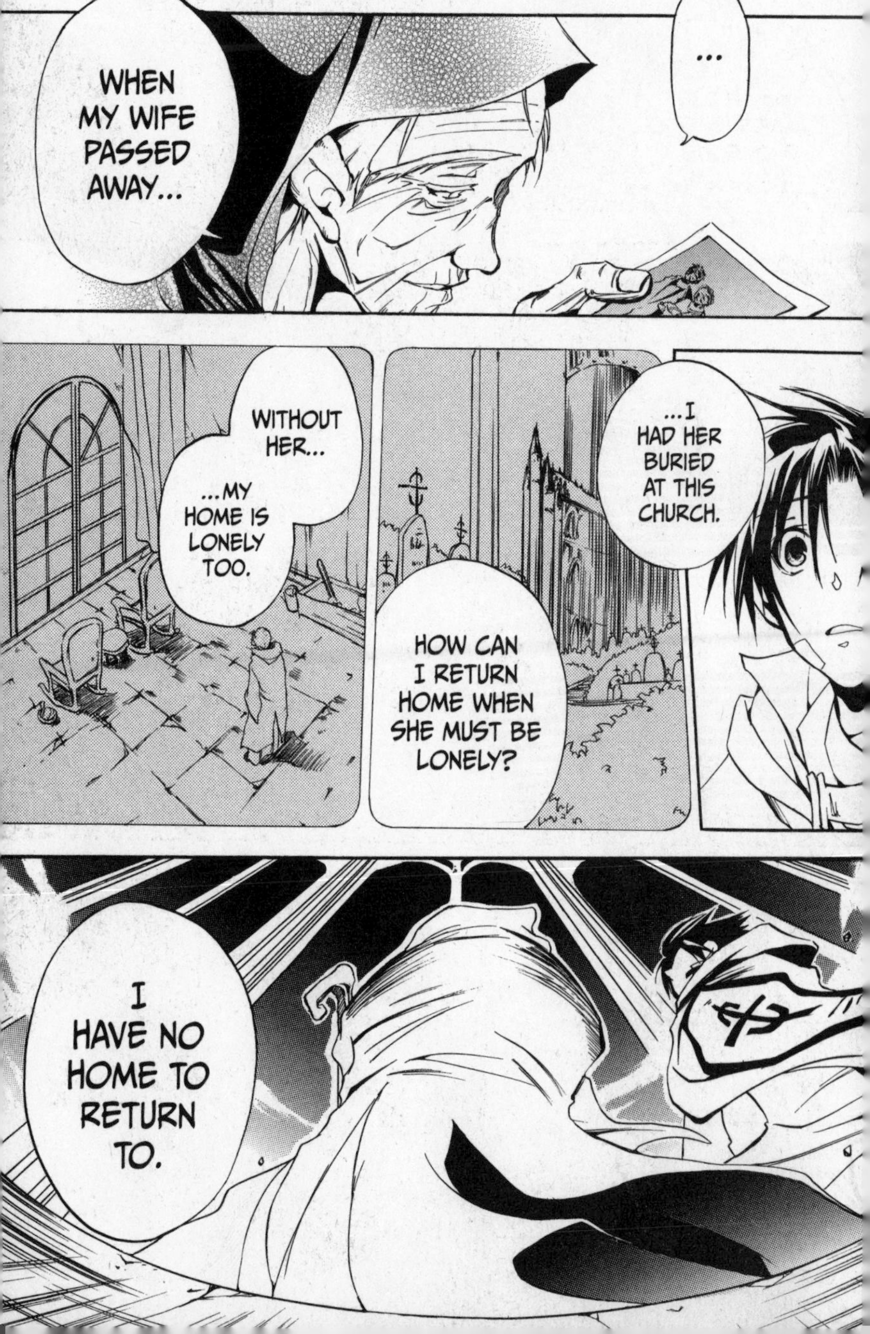
...
WHEN MY WIFE PASSED AWAY...
...I HAD HER BURIED AT THIS CHURCH.
HOW CAN I RETURN HOME WHEN SHE MUST BE LONELY?
WITHOUT HER...
...MY HOME IS LONELY TOO.
I HAVE NO HOME TO RETURN TO.

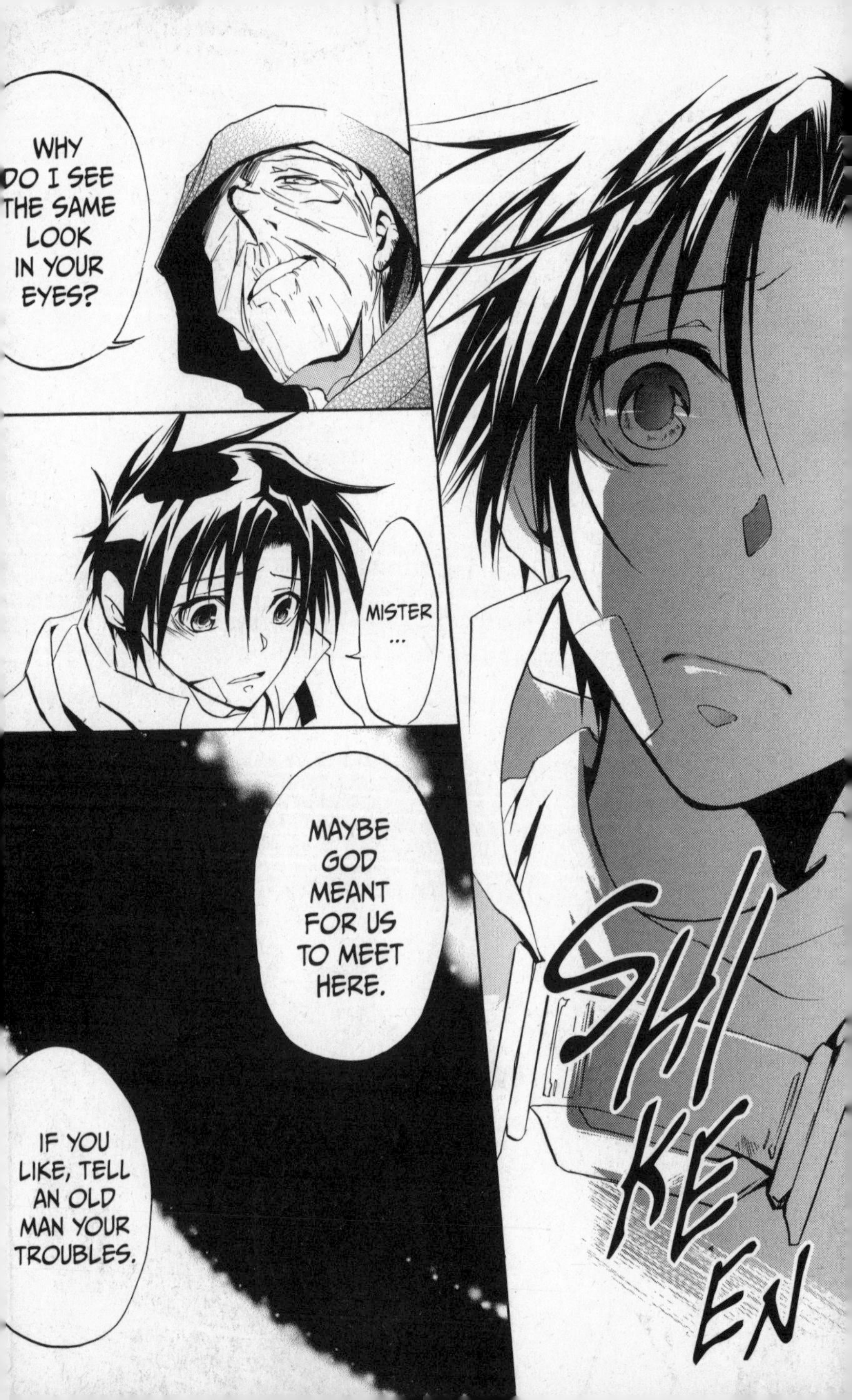

SHIKEEN
WHY DO I SEE THE SAME LOOK IN YOUR EYES?
MISTER ...
MAYBE GOD MEANT FOR US TO MEET HERE.
IF YOU LIKE, TELL AN OLD MAN YOUR TROUBLES.

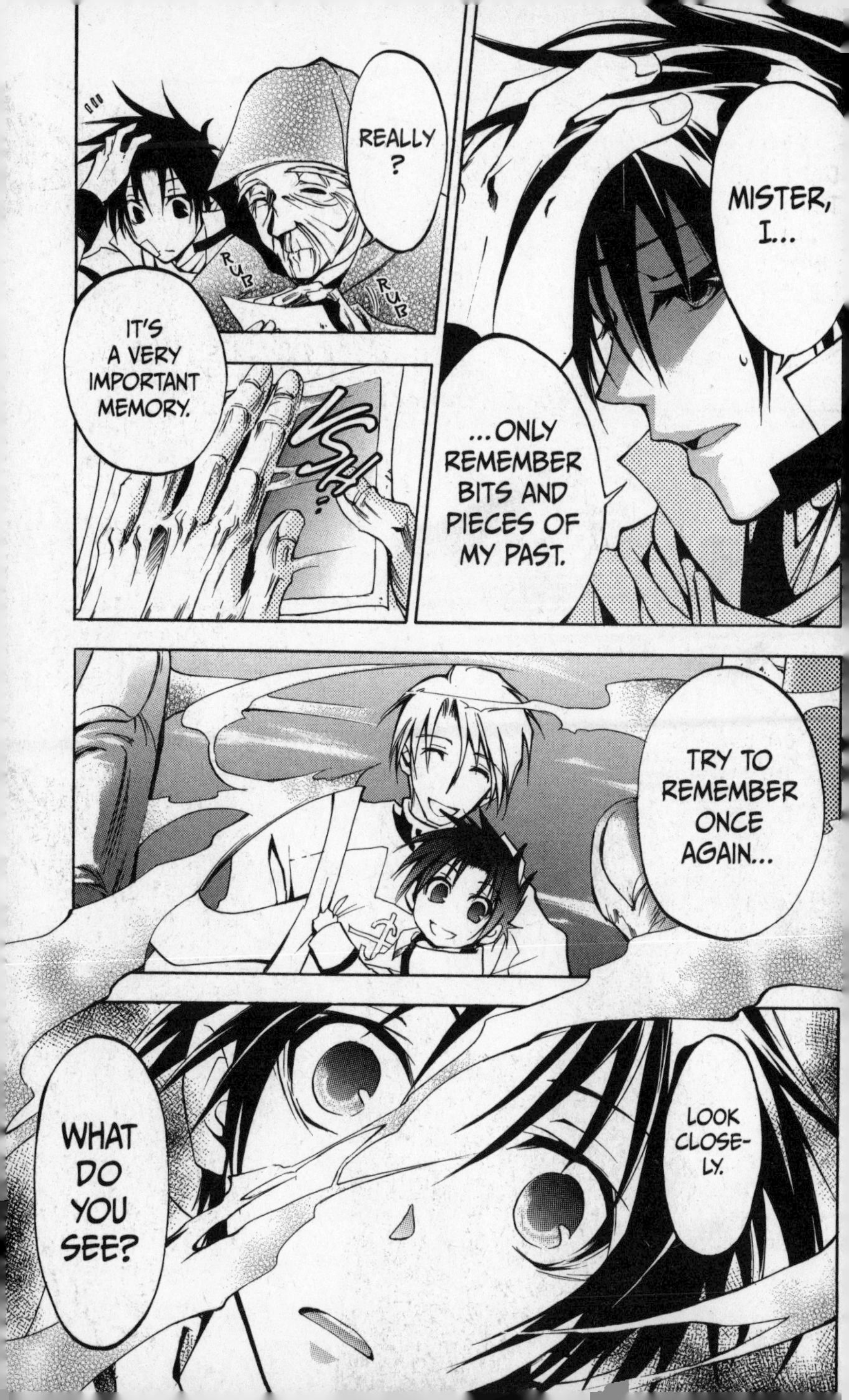
MISTER, I...
...ONLY REMEMBER BITS AND PIECES OF MY PAST.
REALLY?
RUB
RUB
IT'S A VERY IMPORTANT MEMORY.
VSH!
TRY TO REMEMBER ONCE AGAIN...
LOOK CLOSE-LY.
WHAT DO YOU SEE?

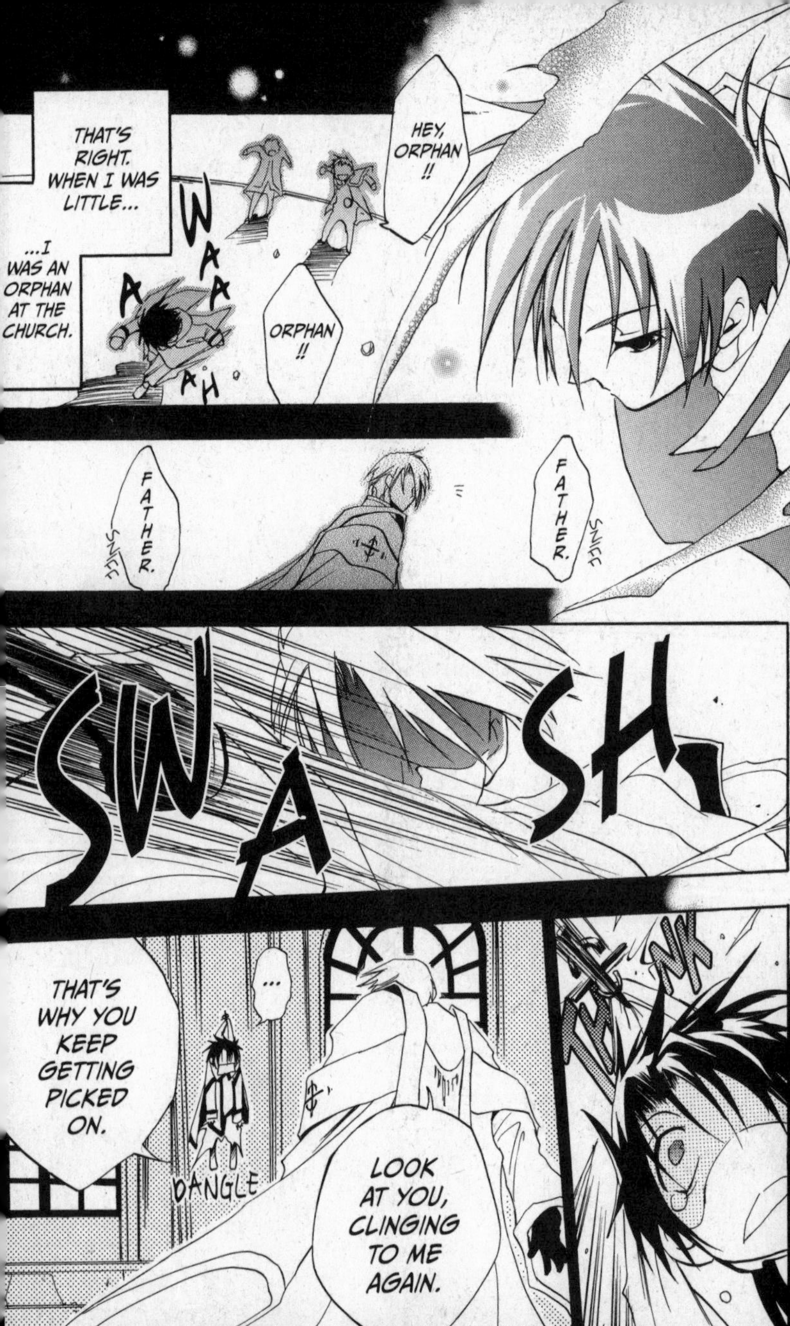
HEY, ORPHAN!!
THAT'S RIGHT. WHEN I WAS LITTLE...
WAAAAH
ORPHAN!!
...I WAS AN ORPHAN AT THE CHURCH.
FATHER.
SNIFF
FATHER.
SNIFF
SWASH
...
THAT'S WHY YOU KEEP GETTING PICKED ON.
LOOK AT YOU, CLINGING TO ME AGAIN.
DANGLE

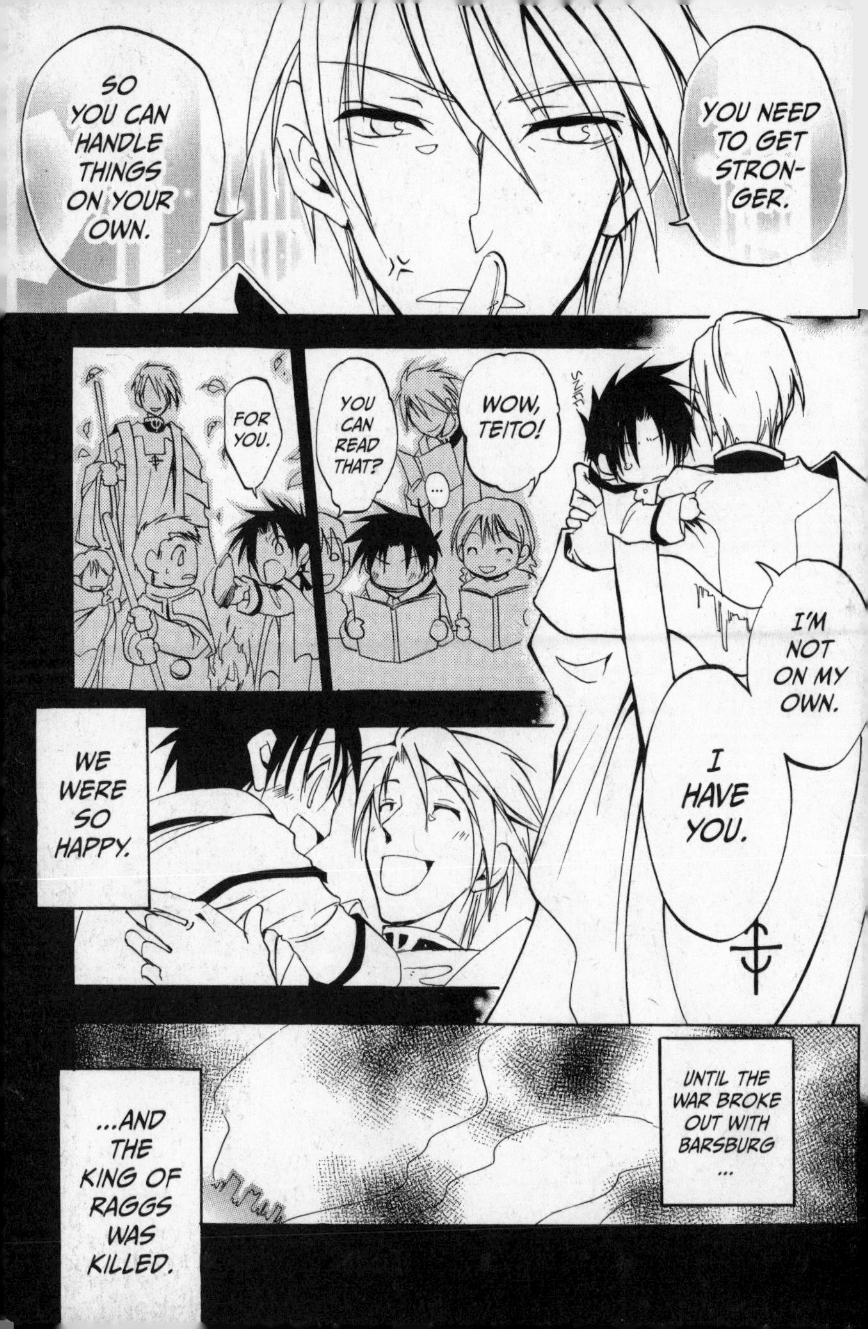
YOU NEED TO GET STRONGER.
SO YOU CAN HANDLE THINGS ON YOUR OWN.
SNIFF
I'M NOT ON MY OWN.
I HAVE YOU.
WOW, TEITO!
YOU CAN READ THAT?
...
FOR YOU.
WE WERE SO HAPPY.
UNTIL THE WAR BROKE OUT WITH BARSBURG ...
...AND THE KING OF RAGGS WAS KILLED.

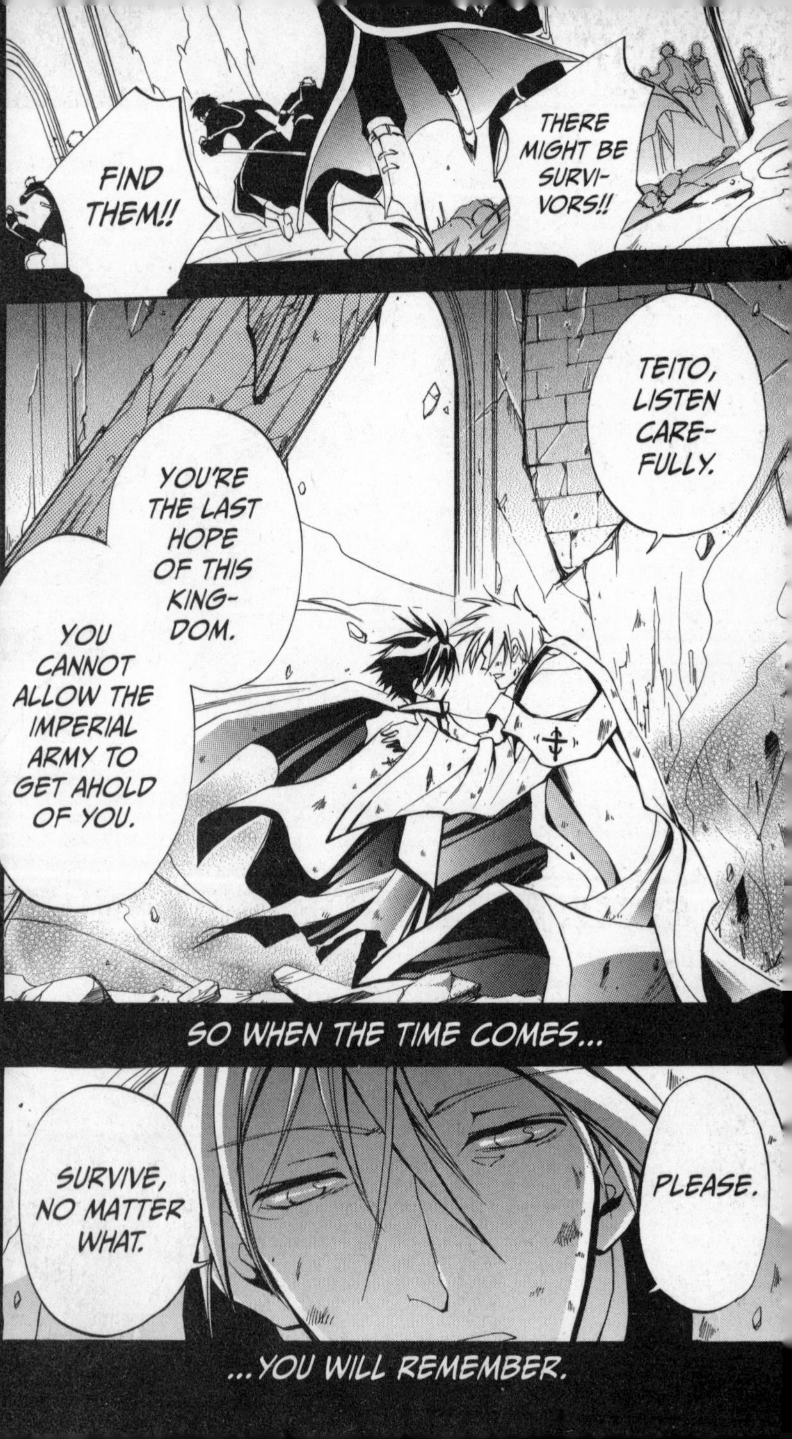
THERE MIGHT BE SURVIVORS!!
FIND THEM!!
TEITO, LISTEN CAREFULLY.
YOU'RE THE LAST HOPE OF THIS KINGDOM.
YOU CANNOT ALLOW THE IMPERIAL ARMY TO GET AHOLD OF YOU.
SO WHEN THE TIME COMES...
PLEASE.
SURVIVE, NO MATTER WHAT.
...YOU WILL REMEMBER.

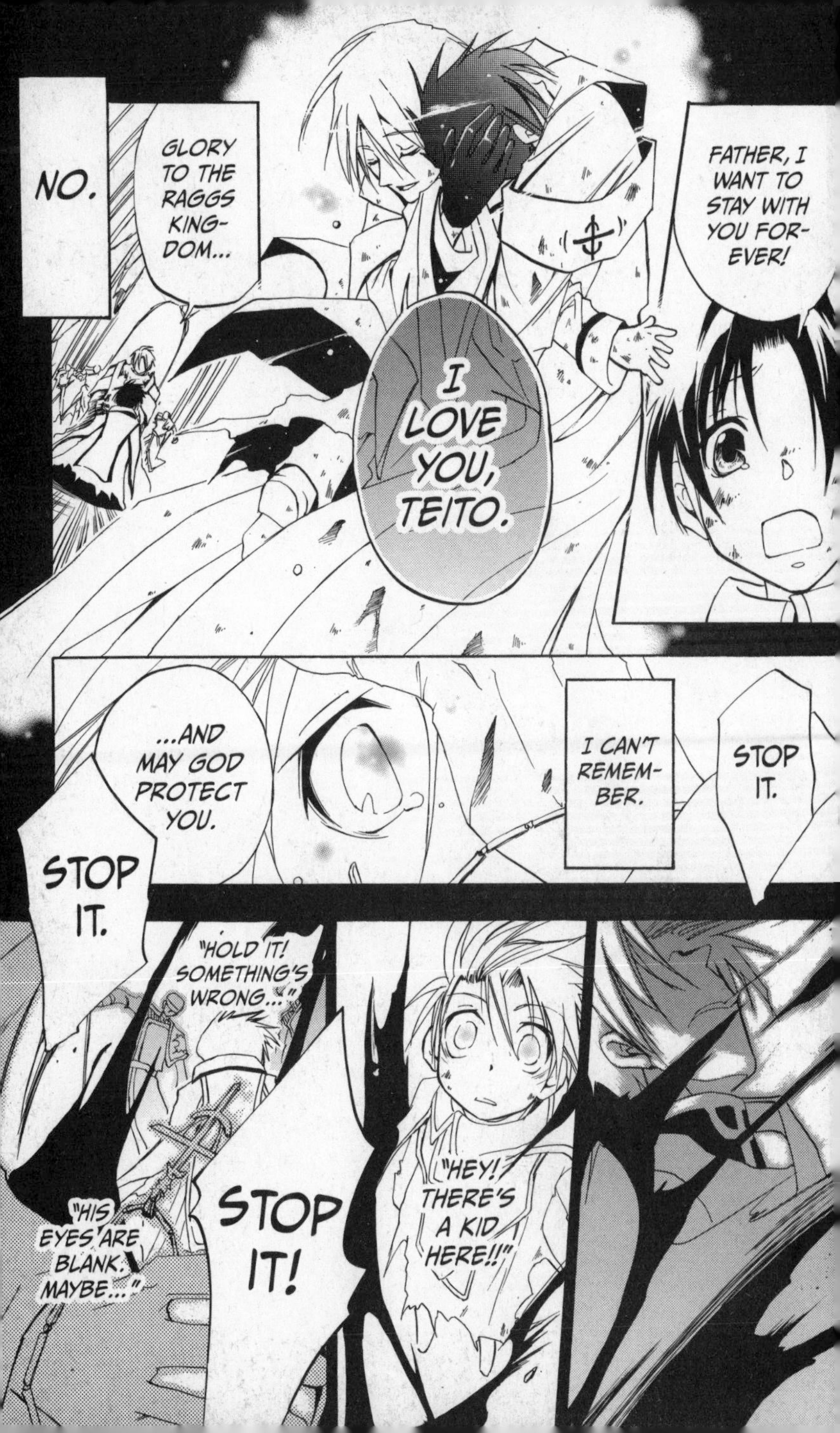
FATHER, I WANT TO STAY WITH YOU FOREVER!
I LOVE YOU, TEITO.
GLORY TO THE RAGGS KINGDOM...
NO.
STOP IT.
I CAN'T REMEMBER.
...AND MAY GOD PROTECT YOU.
STOP IT.
"HEY! THERE'S A KID HERE!!"
STOP IT!
"HOLD IT! SOMETHING'S WRONG..."
"HIS EYES ARE BLANK. MAYBE..."

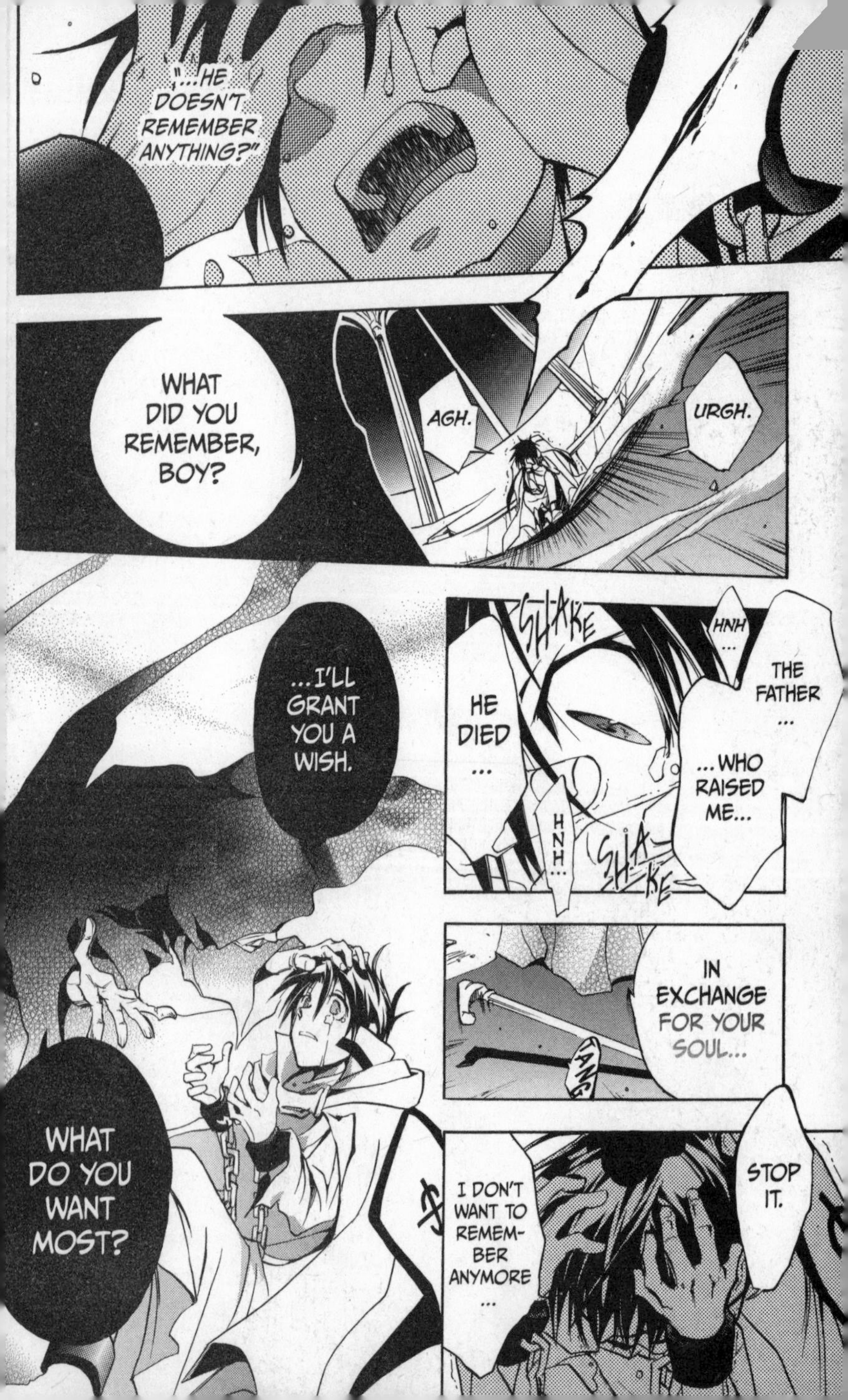
"...HE DOESN'T REMEMBER ANYTHING?"
URGH.
AGH.
WHAT DID YOU REMEMBER, BOY?
HNH...
THE FATHER...
...WHO RAISED ME...
HE DIED...
SHAKE
HNH...
SHAKE
IN EXCHANGE FOR YOUR SOUL...
TANG
STOP IT.
I DON'T WANT TO REMEMBER ANYMORE...
...I'LL GRANT YOU A WISH.
WHAT DO YOU WANT MOST?

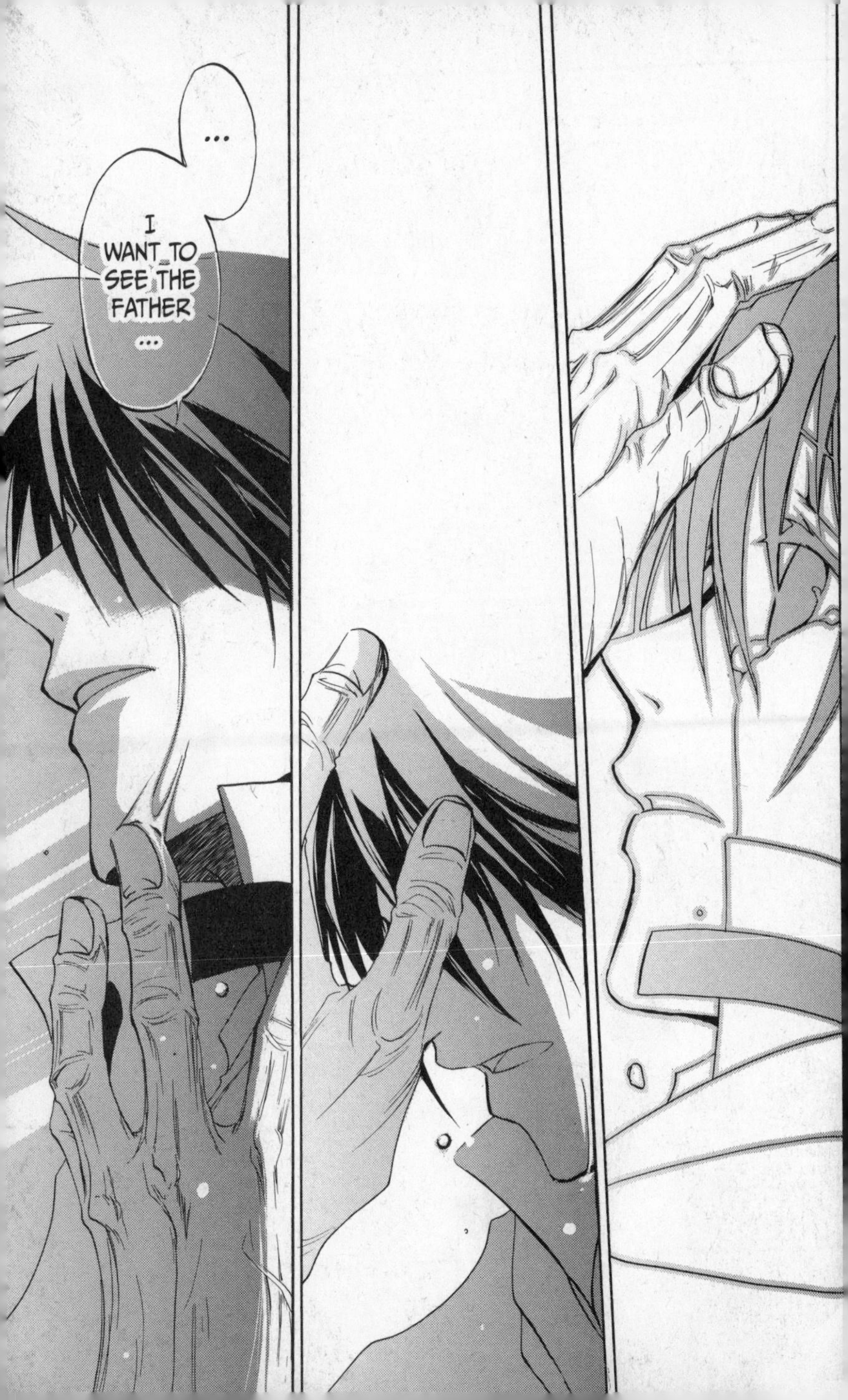
...
I WANT TO SEE THE FATHER ...

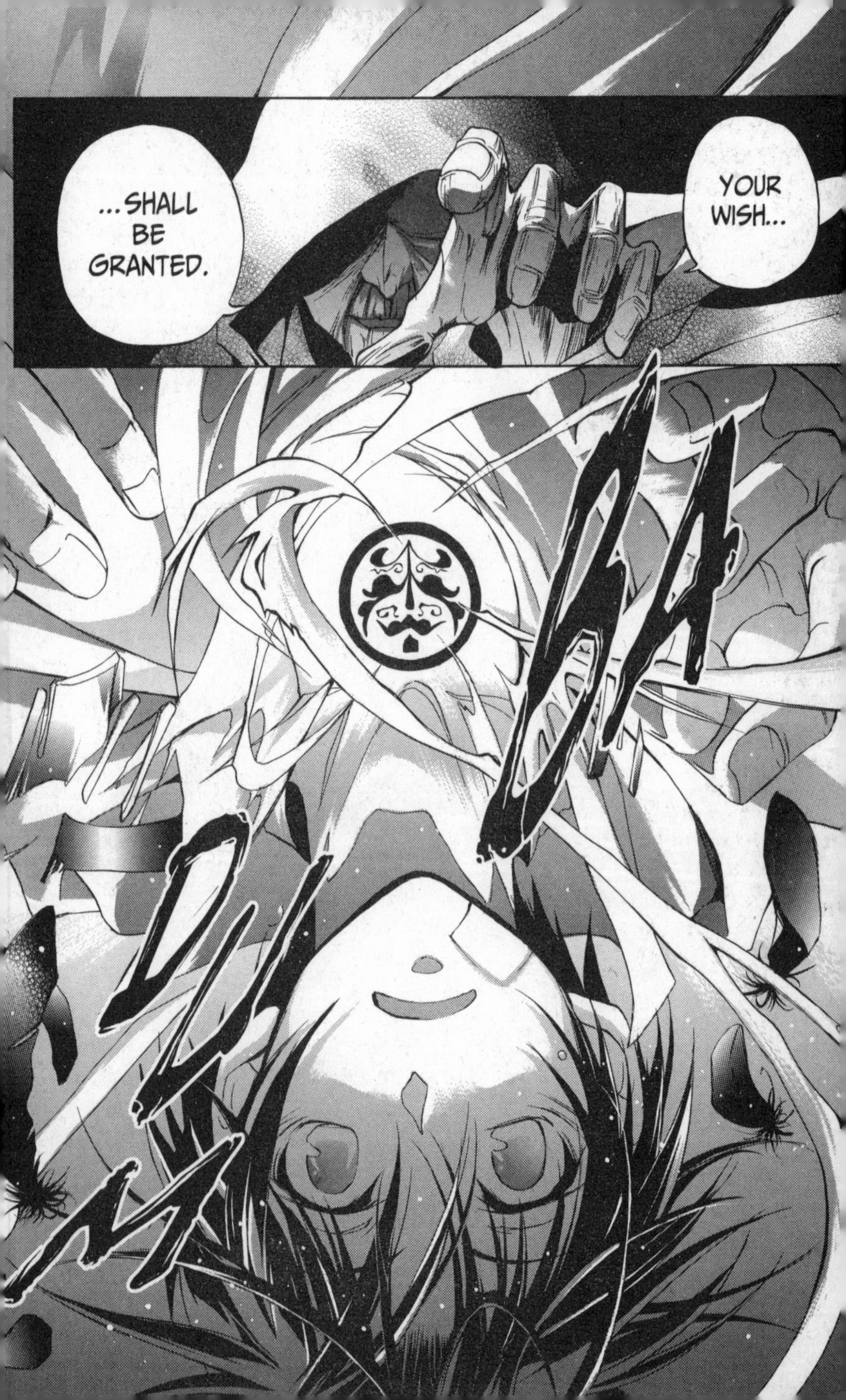
YOUR WISH...
...SHALL BE GRANTED.

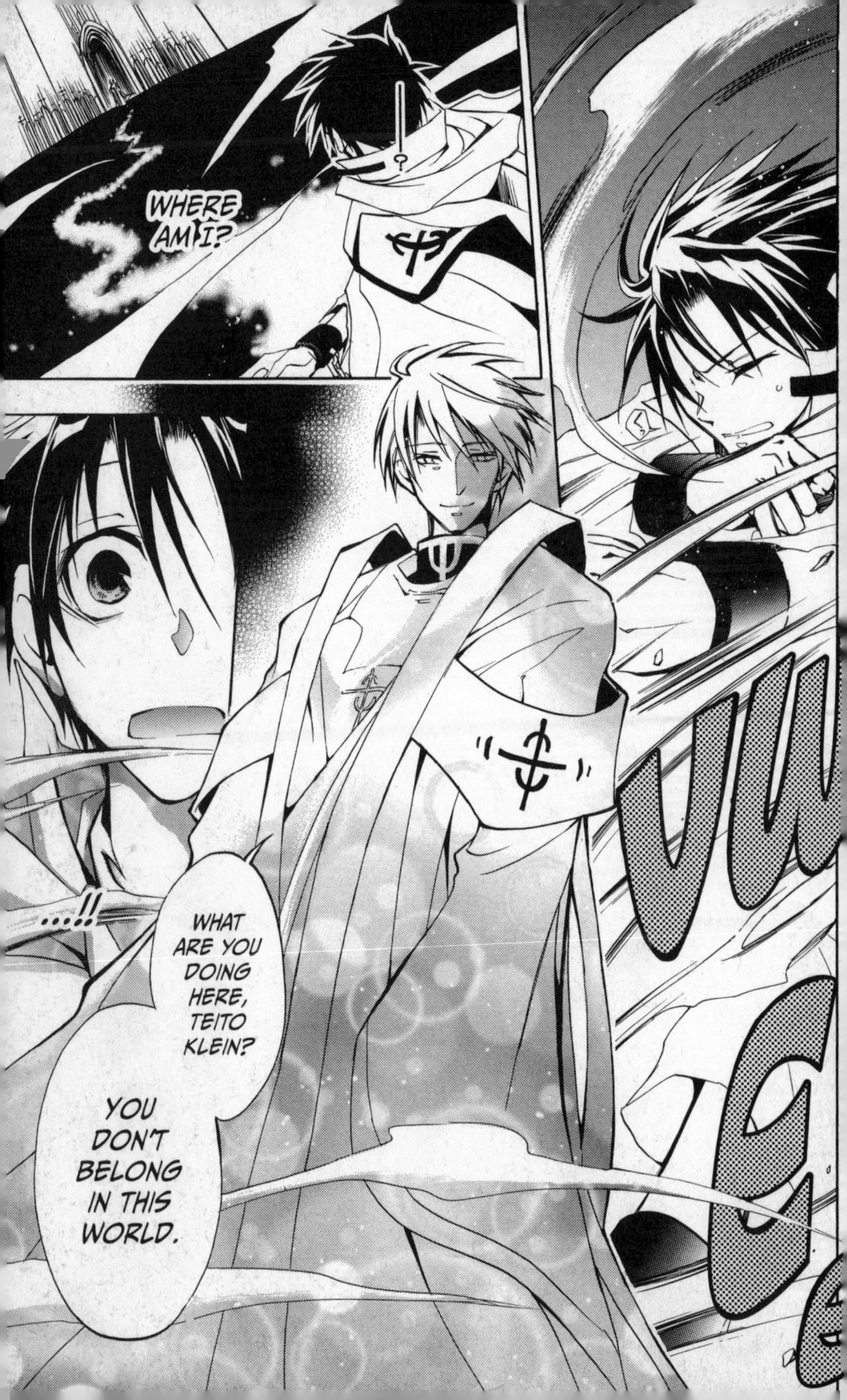
WHERE AM I?
...!!
WHAT ARE YOU DOING HERE, TEITO KLEIN?
YOU DON'T BELONG IN THIS WORLD.

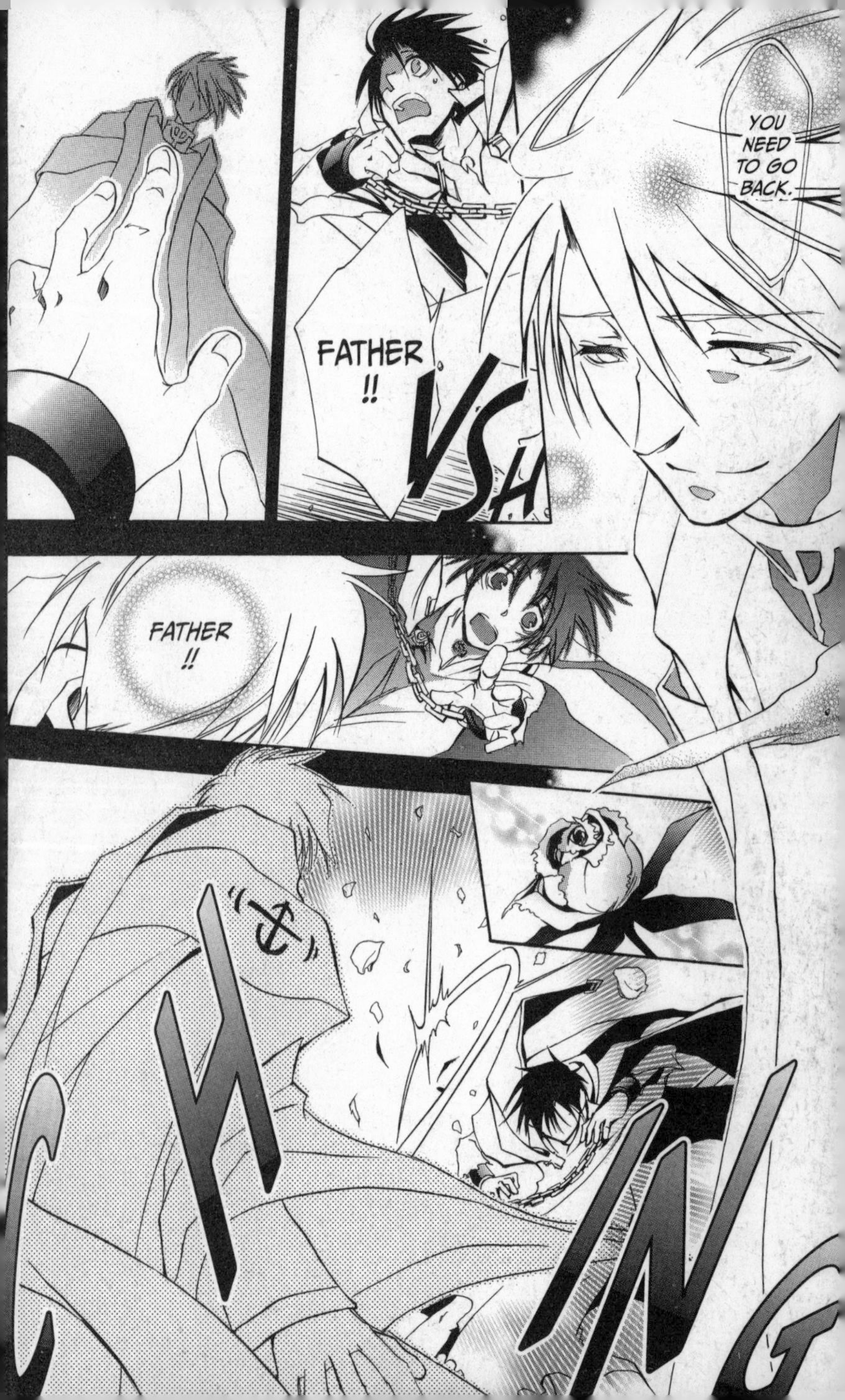
YOU NEED TO GO BACK.
FATHER !!
VSH
FATHER !!
CHING

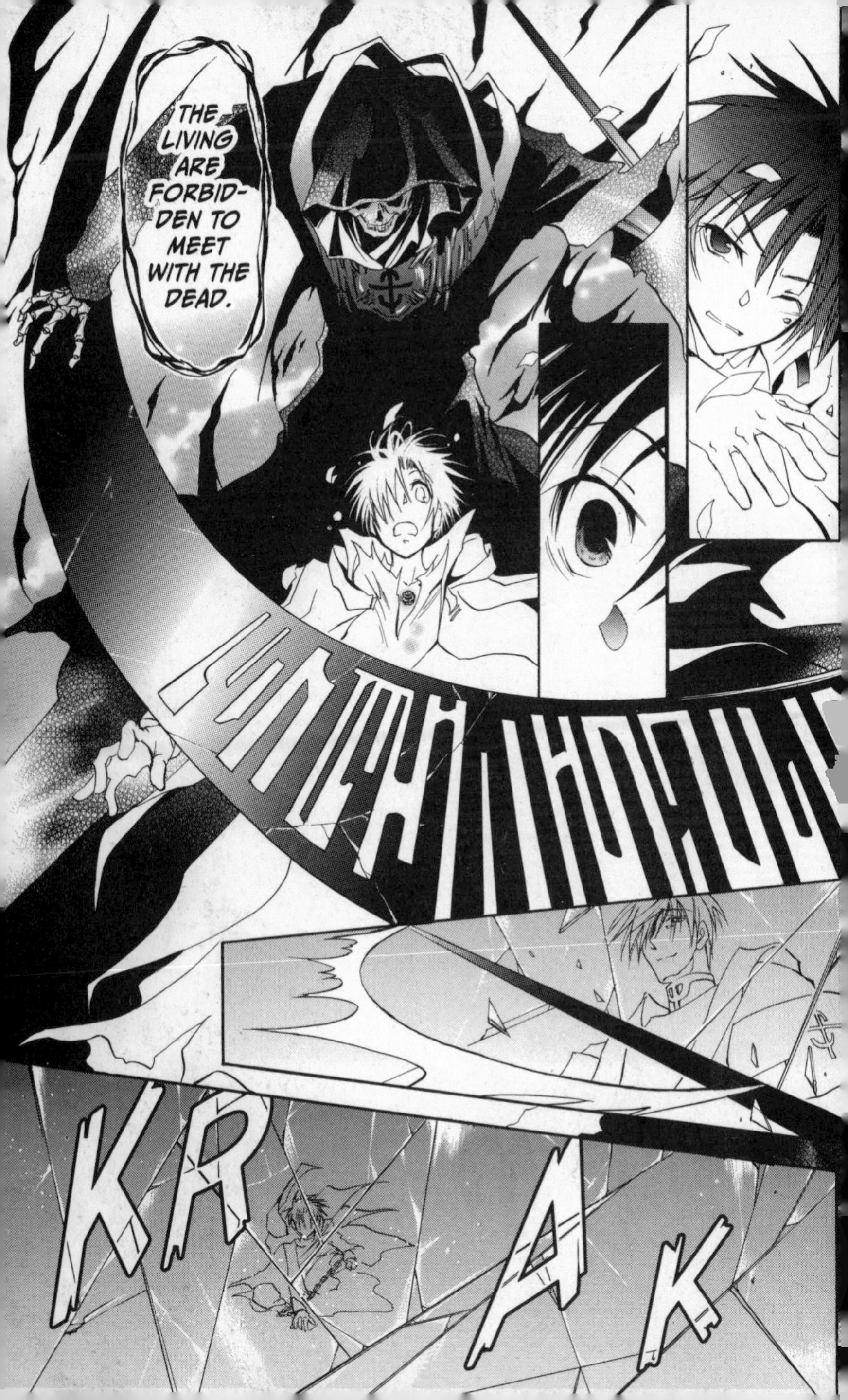
THE LIVING ARE FORBIDDEN TO MEET WITH THE DEAD.
KRAK

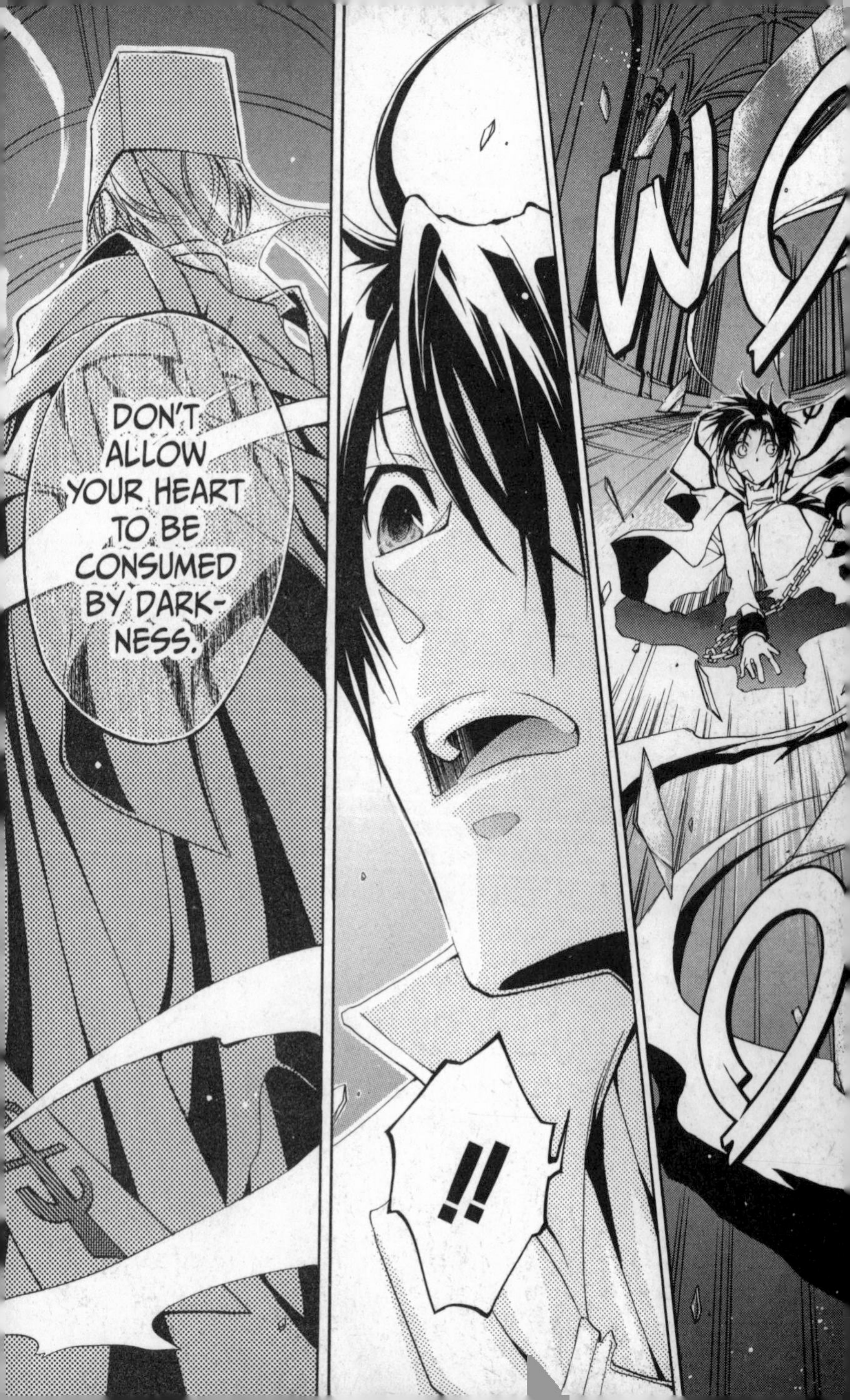
!!
DON'T ALLOW YOUR HEART TO BE CONSUMED BY DARK-NESS.

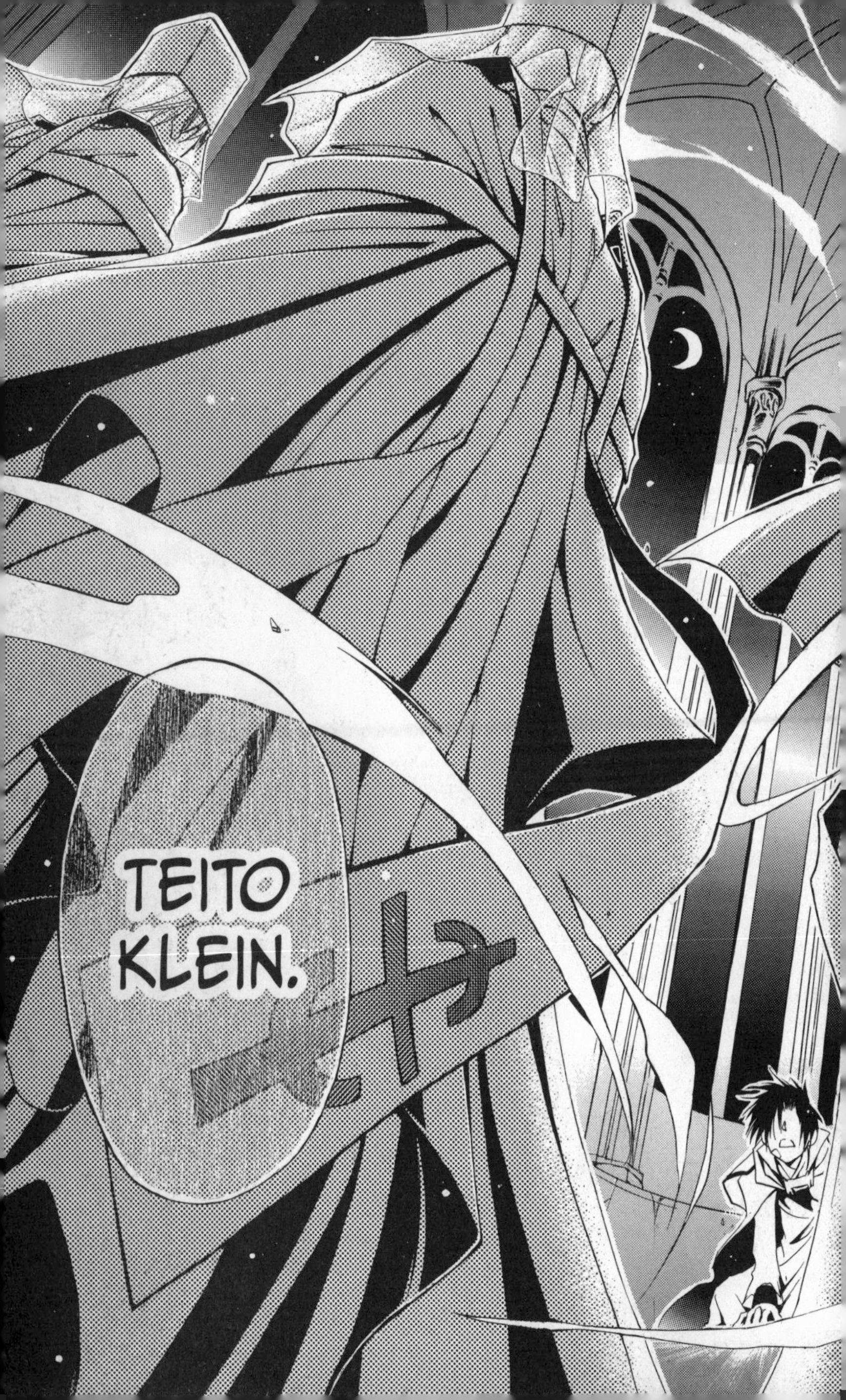
TEITO KLEIN.

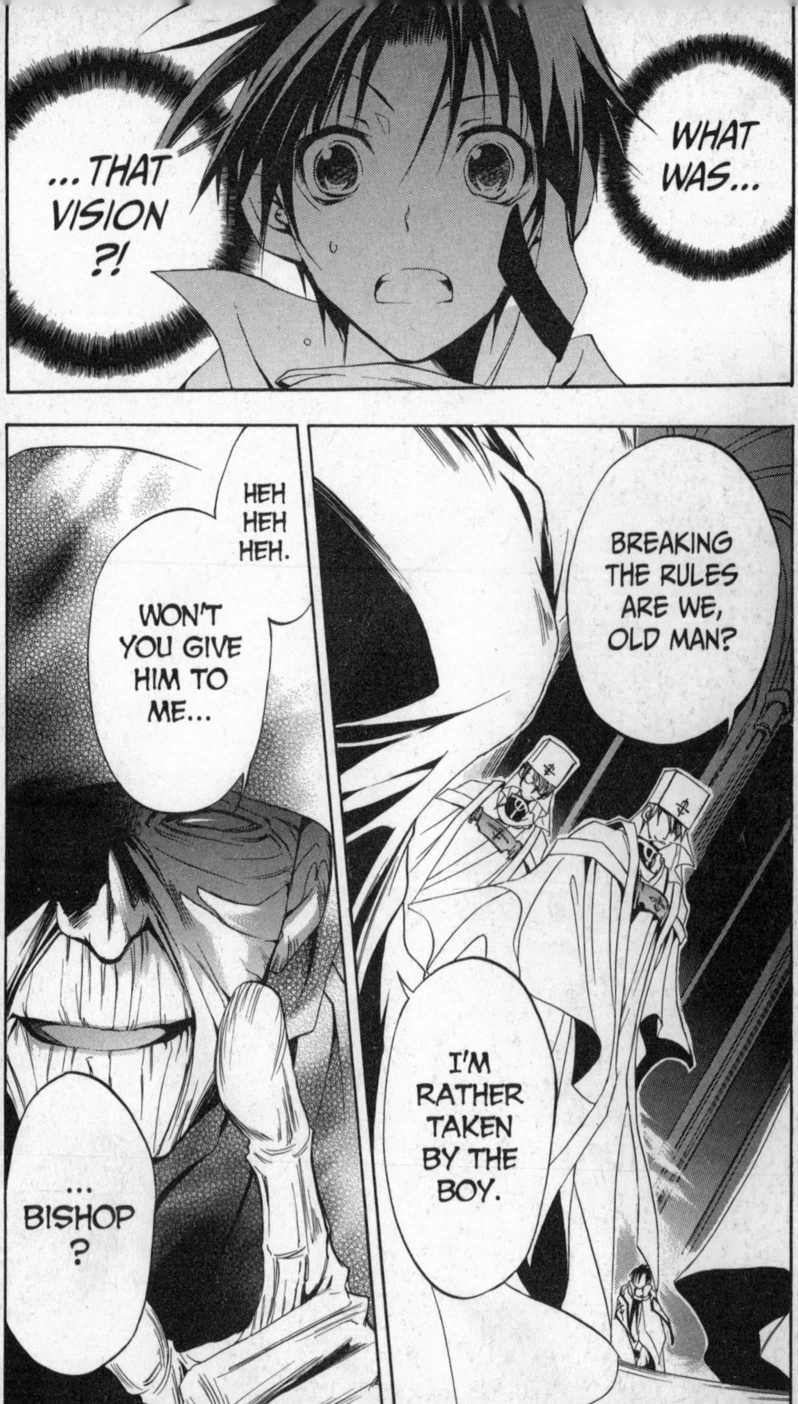
WHAT WAS...
...THAT VISION ?!
BREAKING THE RULES ARE WE, OLD MAN?
I'M RATHER TAKEN BY THE BOY.
HEH HEH HEH.
WON'T YOU GIVE HIM TO ME...
...BISHOP ?

Kapitel.4 "Kor"

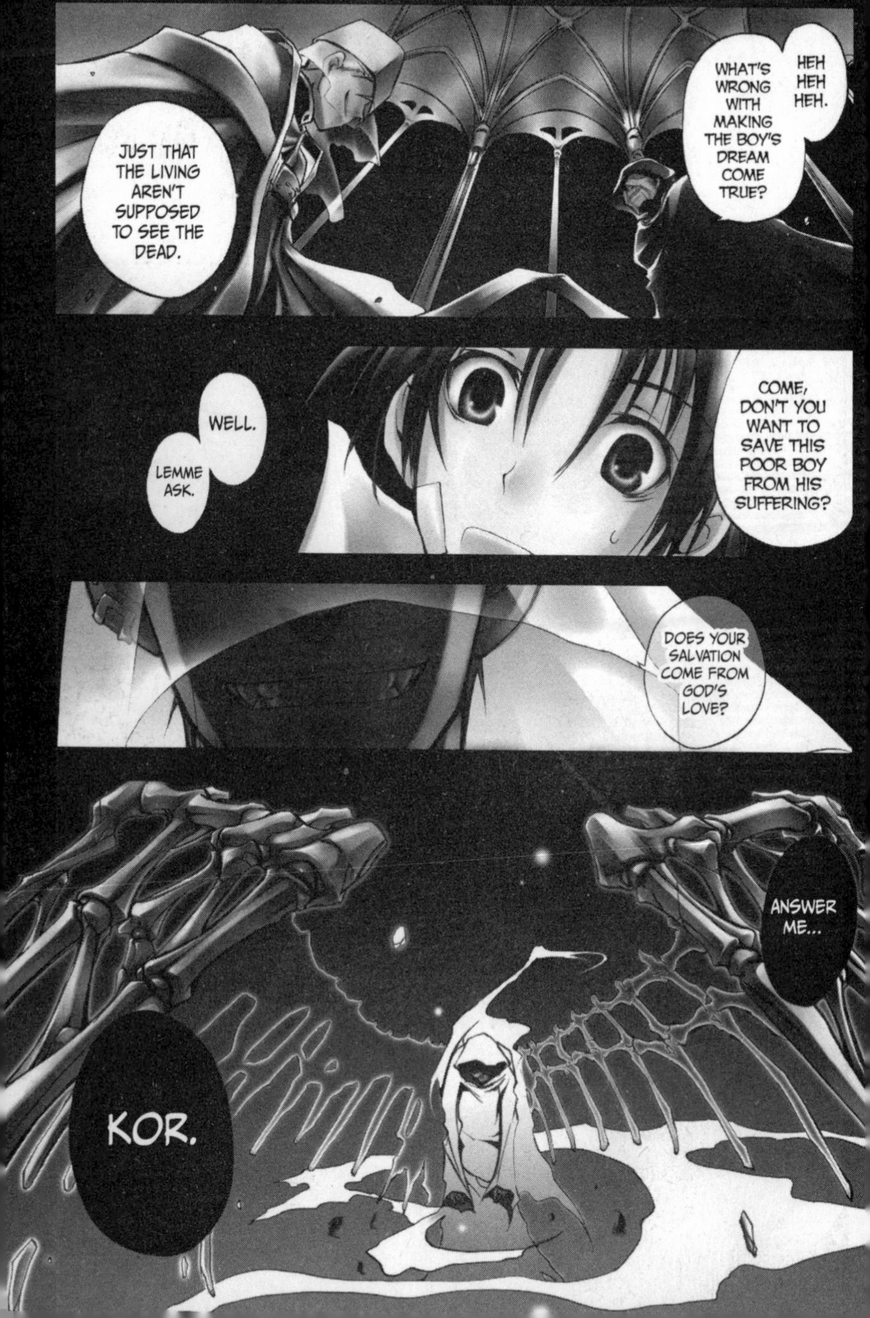

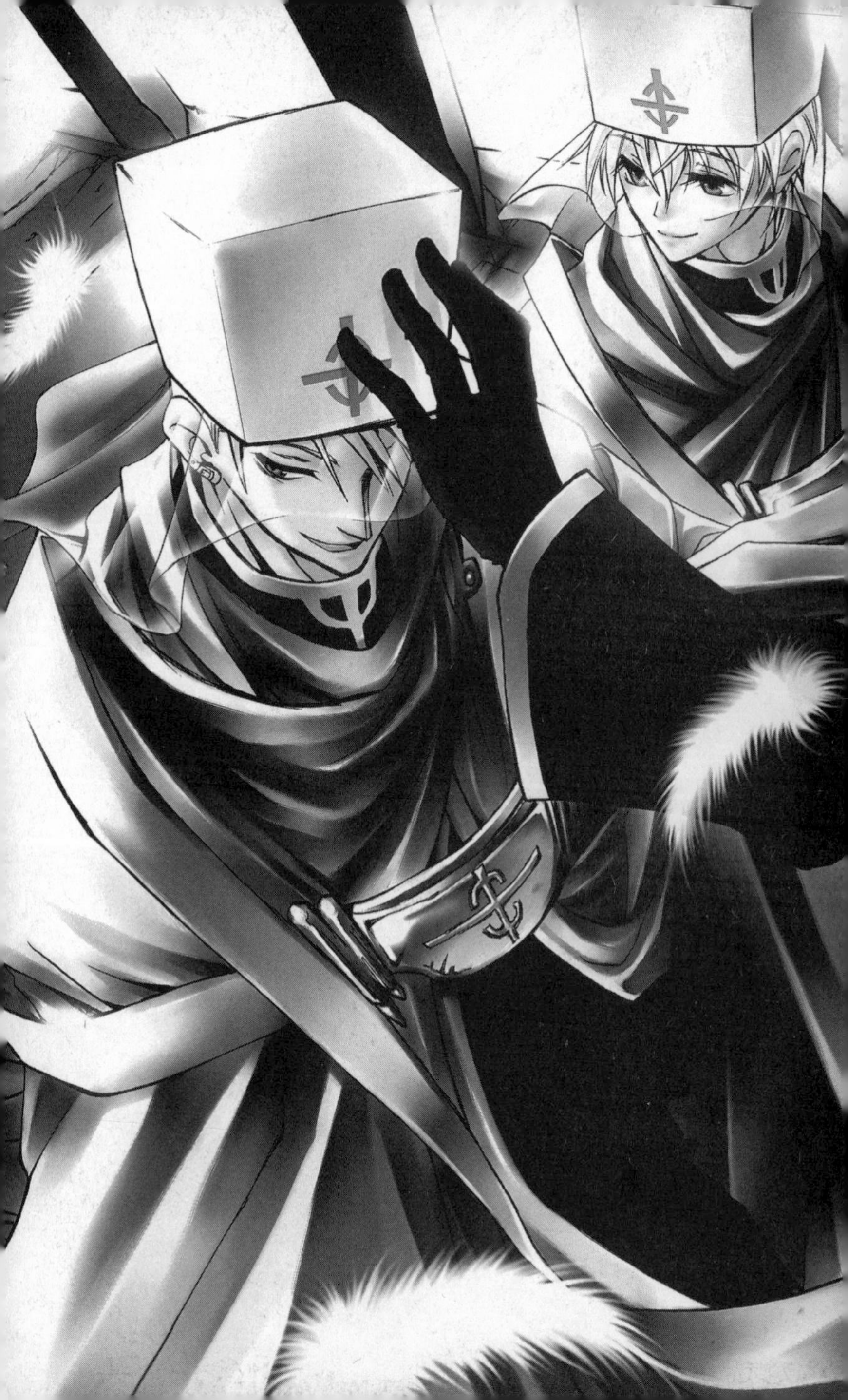

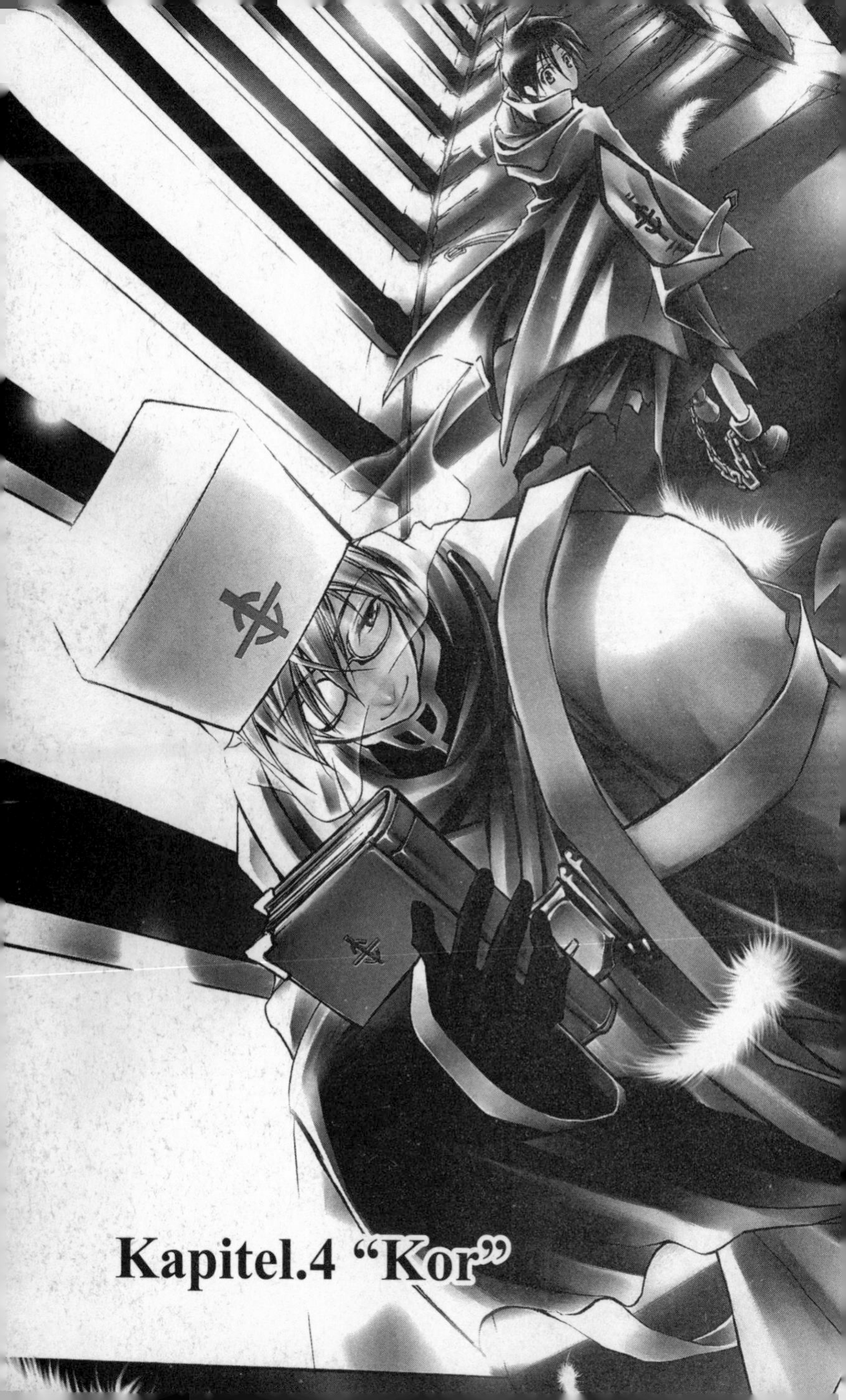
Kapitel.4 “Kor”

ONLY
THROUGH
DEVOUT
PRAYER
CAN YOU
ACHIEVE
YOUR
GREATEST
DREAMS.

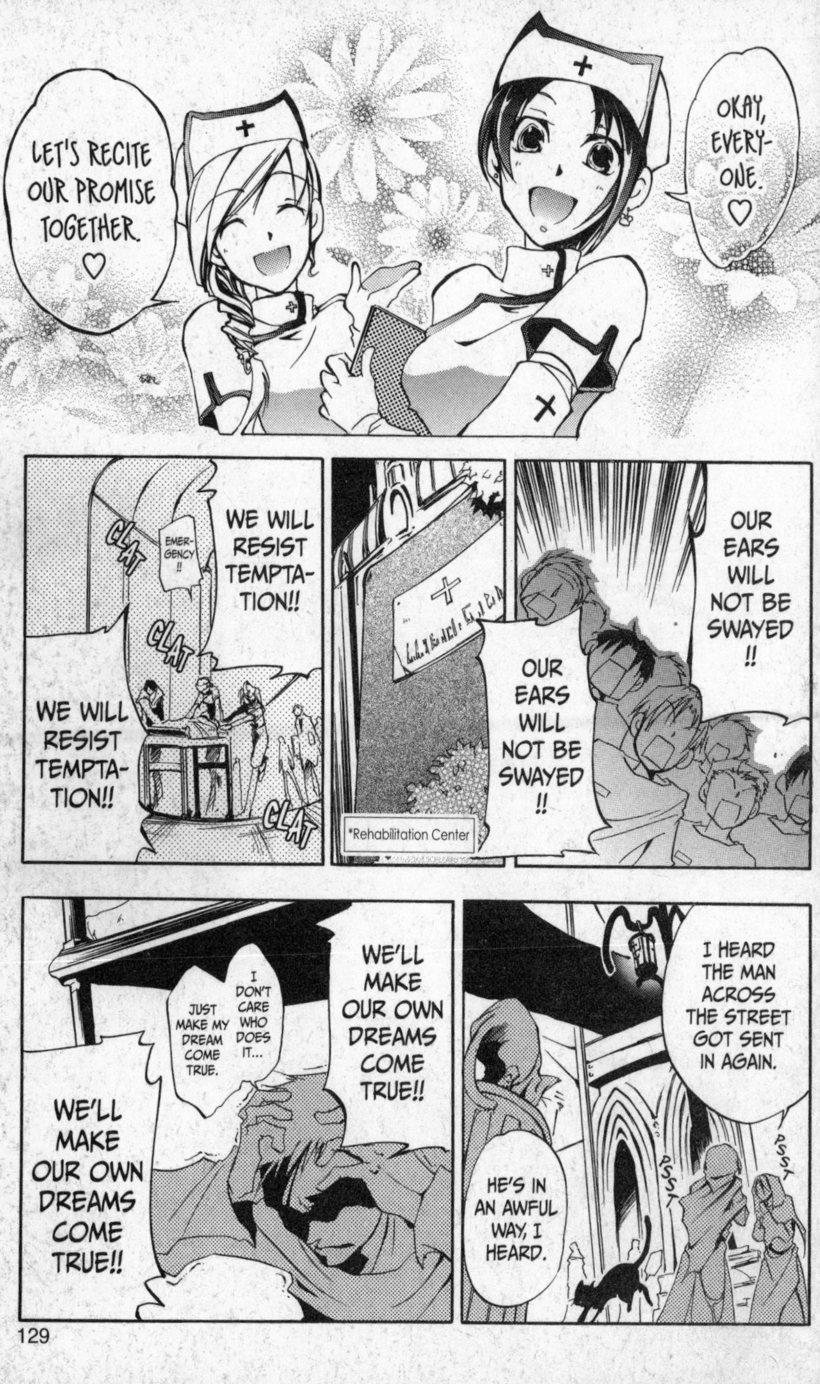
OKAY, EVERY-ONE. ♡
LET'S RECITE OUR PROMISE TOGETHER. ♡
OUR EARS WILL NOT BE SWAYED!!
OUR EARS WILL NOT BE SWAYED!!
*Rehabilitation Center
WE WILL RESIST TEMPTA-TION!!
EMER-GENCY!!
CLAT
CLAT
WE WILL RESIST TEMPTA-TION!!
CLAT
I HEARD THE MAN ACROSS THE STREET GOT SENT IN AGAIN.
PSST
HE'S IN AN AWFUL WAY, I HEARD.
PSST
WE'LL MAKE OUR OWN DREAMS COME TRUE!!
I DON'T CARE WHO DOES IT...
JUST MAKE MY DREAM COME TRUE.
WE'LL MAKE OUR OWN DREAMS COME TRUE!!

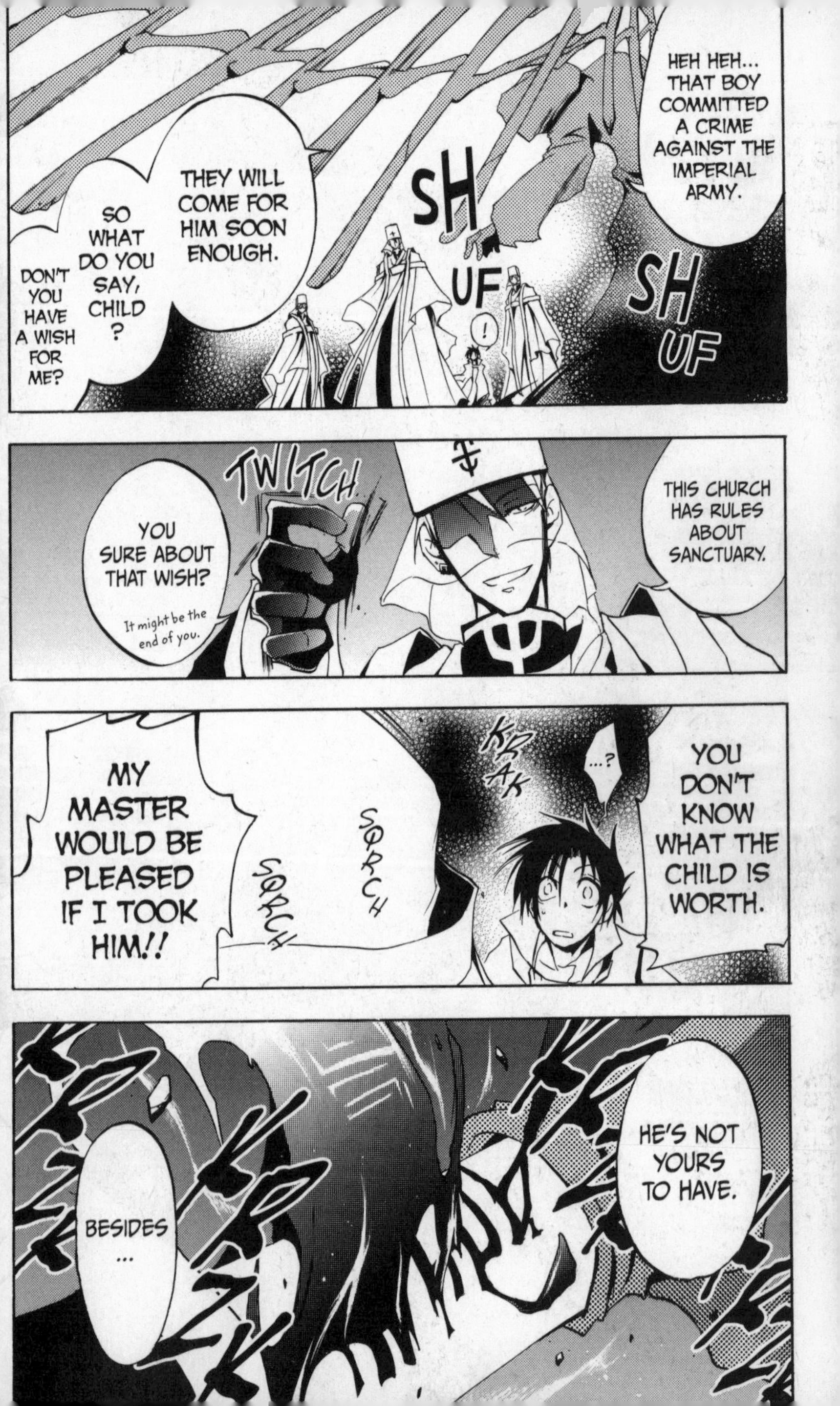
HEH HEH... THAT BOY COMMITTED A CRIME AGAINST THE IMPERIAL ARMY.
SH UF
SH UF
!
THEY WILL COME FOR HIM SOON ENOUGH.
SO WHAT DO YOU SAY, CHILD?
DON'T YOU HAVE A WISH FOR ME?
THIS CHURCH HAS RULES ABOUT SANCTUARY.
TWITCH
YOU SURE ABOUT THAT WISH? It might be the end of you.
YOU DON'T KNOW WHAT THE CHILD IS WORTH.
...?
KRAK
SQRCH
SQRCH
MY MASTER WOULD BE PLEASED IF I TOOK HIM!!
HE'S NOT YOURS TO HAVE.
BESIDES...

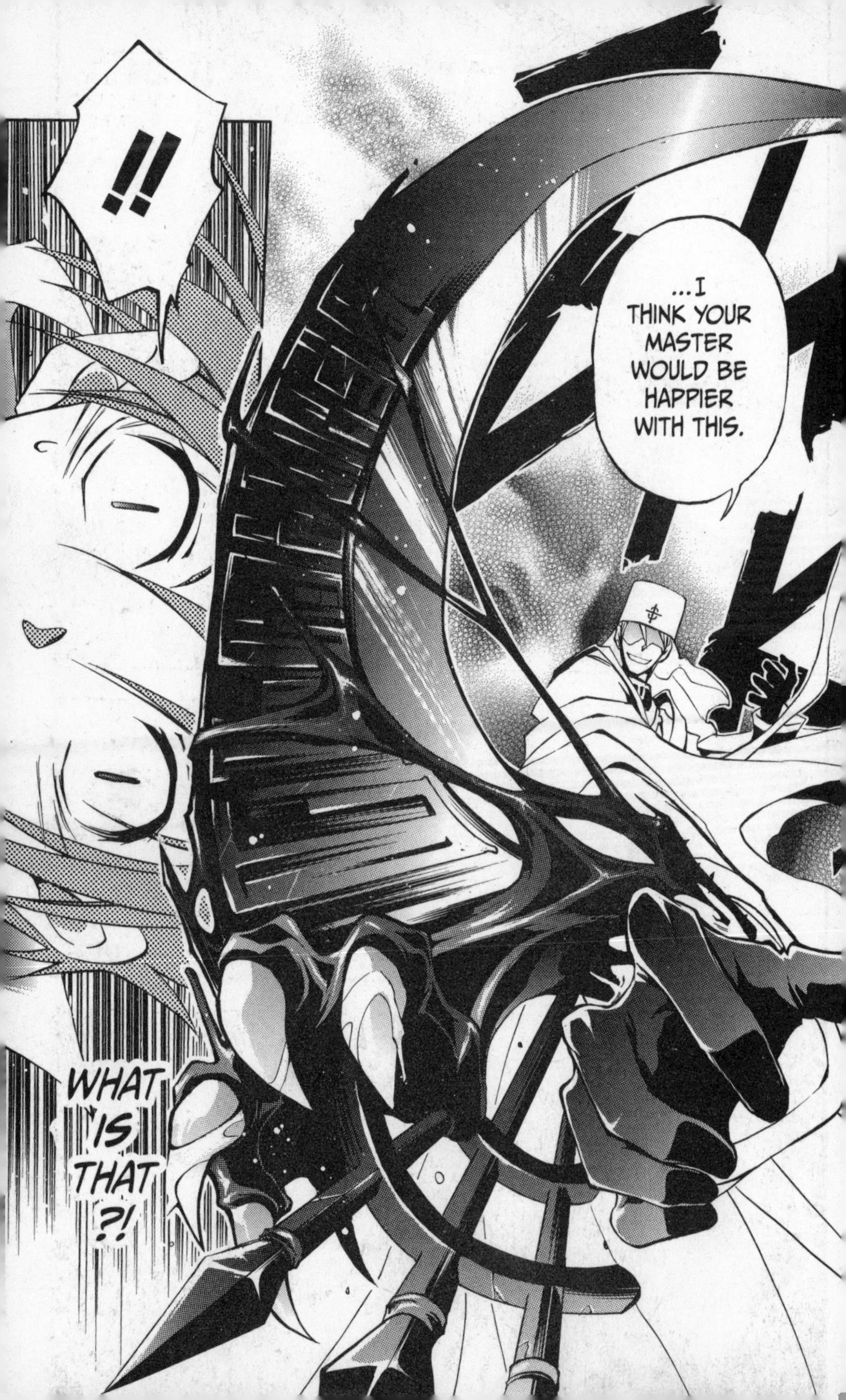
...I THINK YOUR MASTER WOULD BE HAPPIER WITH THIS.
!!
WHAT IS THAT ?!

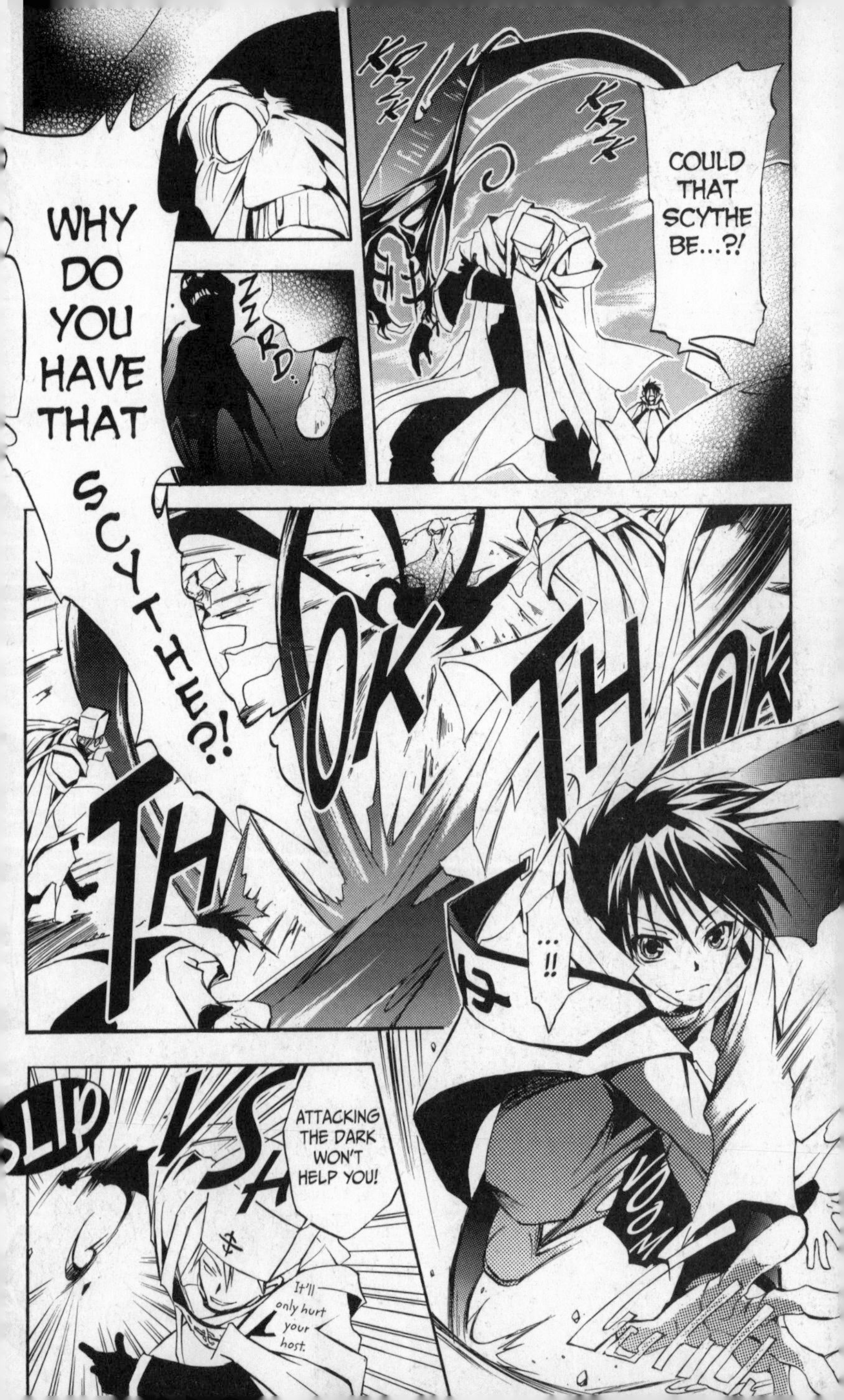
COULD THAT SCYTHE BE...?!
ZZRD.
WHY DO YOU HAVE THAT SCYTHE?!
THOK
THOK
...!!
ATTACKING THE DARK WON'T HELP YOU!
It'll only hurt your host.
SLIP

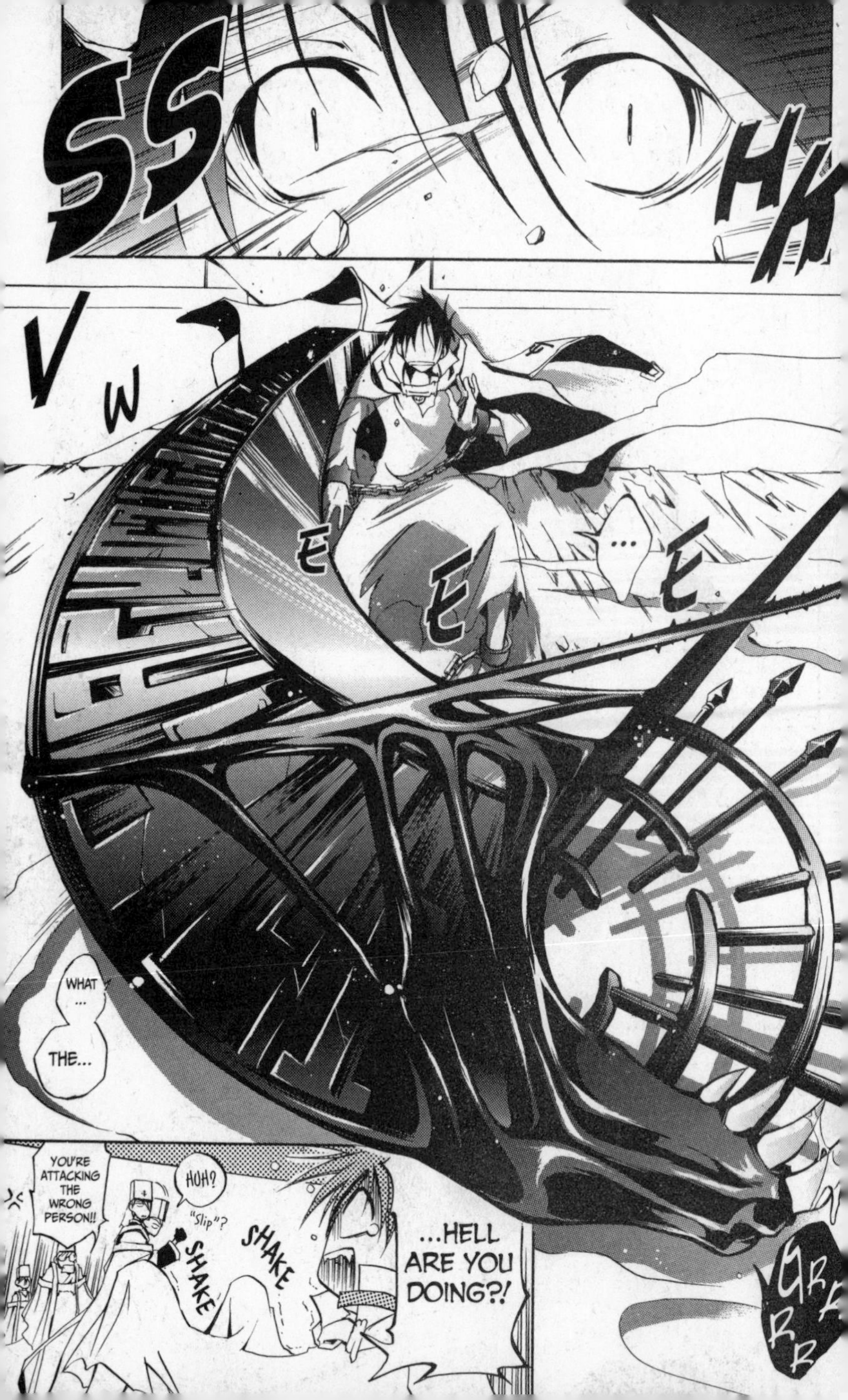
SS
HK
VW
...
E
E
E
WHAT ... THE...
GRR RRR
...HELL ARE YOU DOING?!
SHAKE
SHAKE
SHAKE
HUH?
"Slip"?
YOU'RE ATTACKING THE WRONG PERSON!!

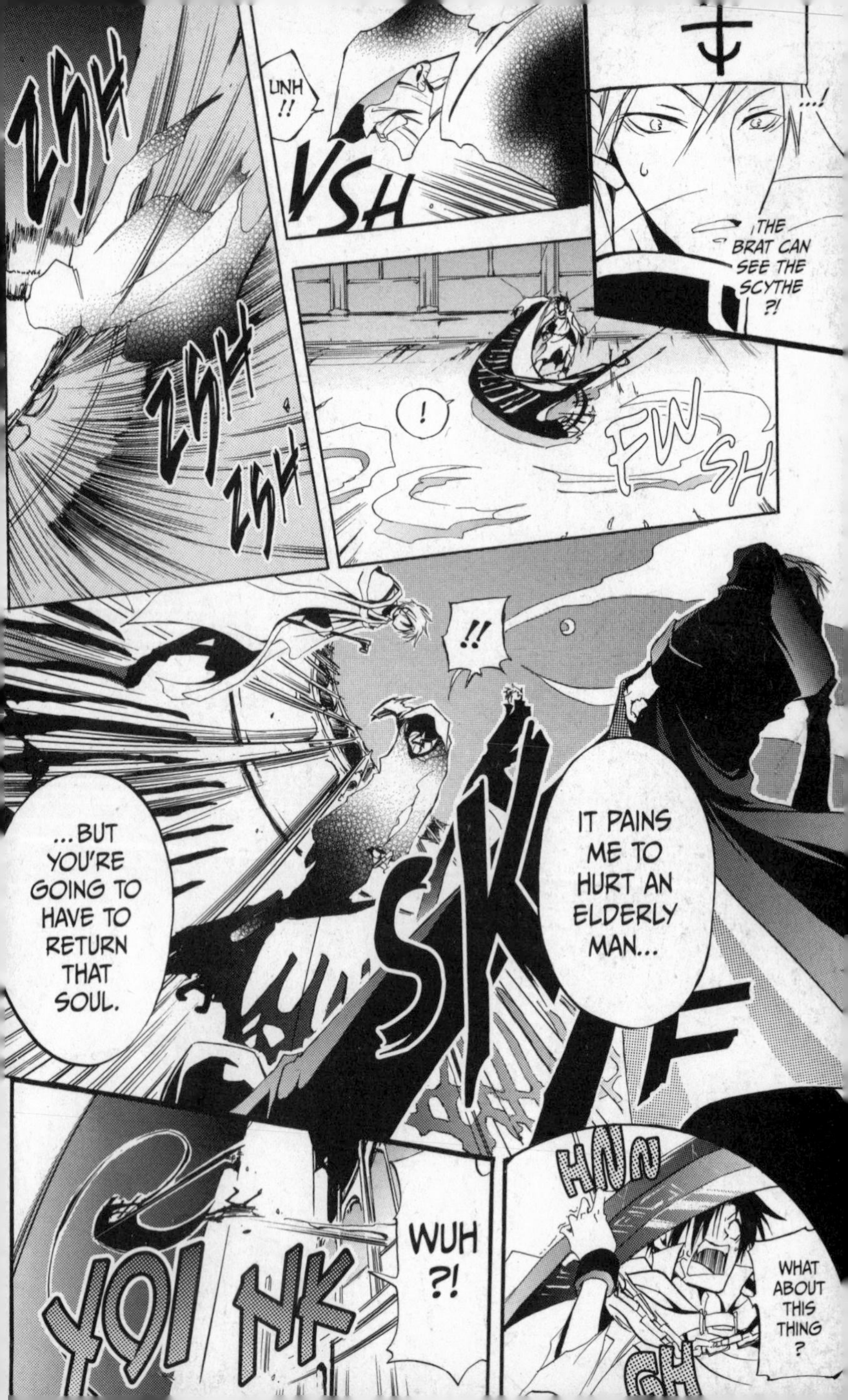
....!
THE BRAT CAN SEE THE SCYTHE ?!
UNH !!
VSH
!
FWSH
ZSH
ZSH
ZSH
ZSH
!!
IT PAINS ME TO HURT AN ELDERLY MAN...
...BUT YOU'RE GOING TO HAVE TO RETURN THAT SOUL.
SKF
HNN
WHAT ABOUT THIS THING ?
CH
WUH ?!
YOINK

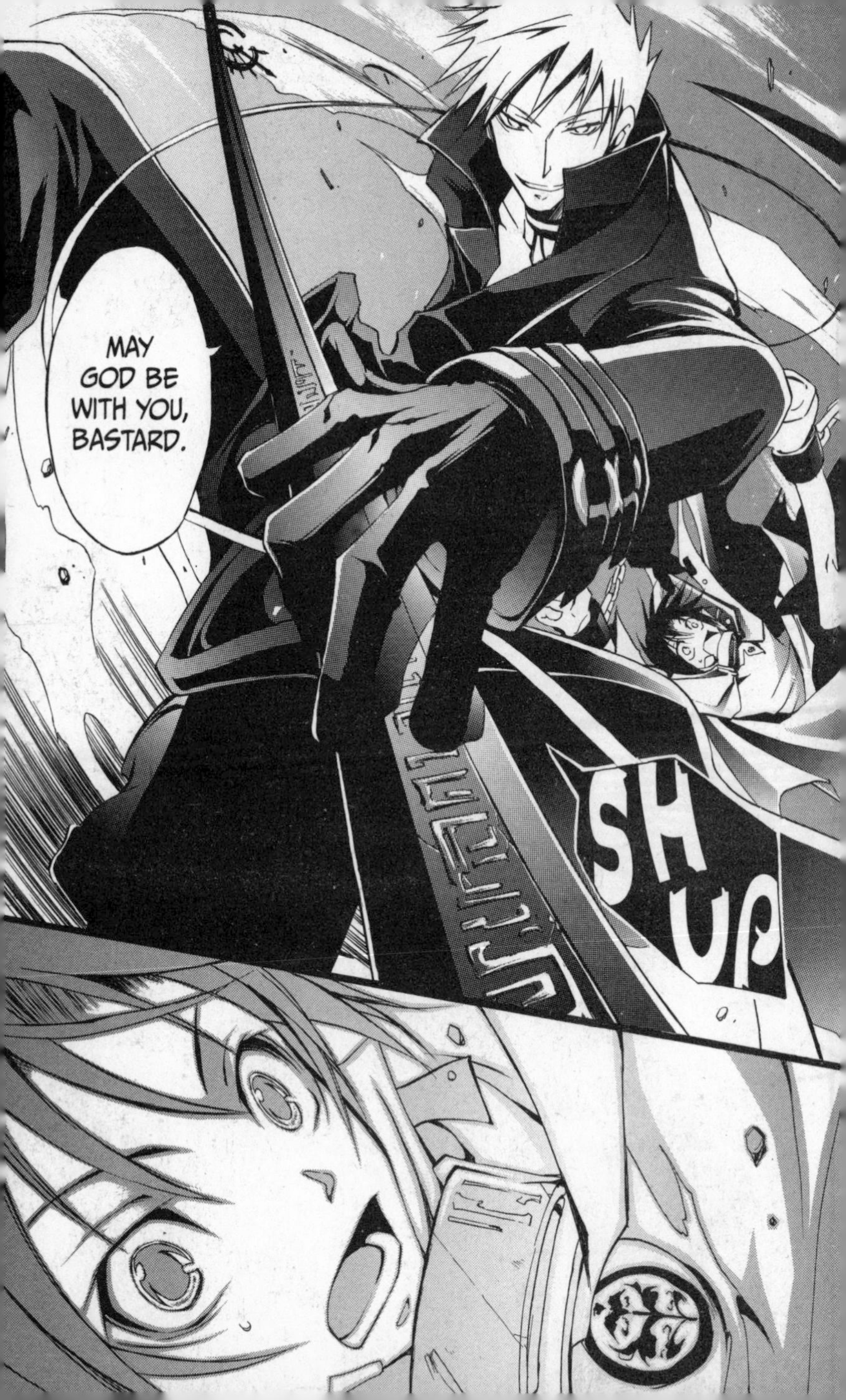
MAY GOD BE WITH YOU, BASTARD.
SHUP

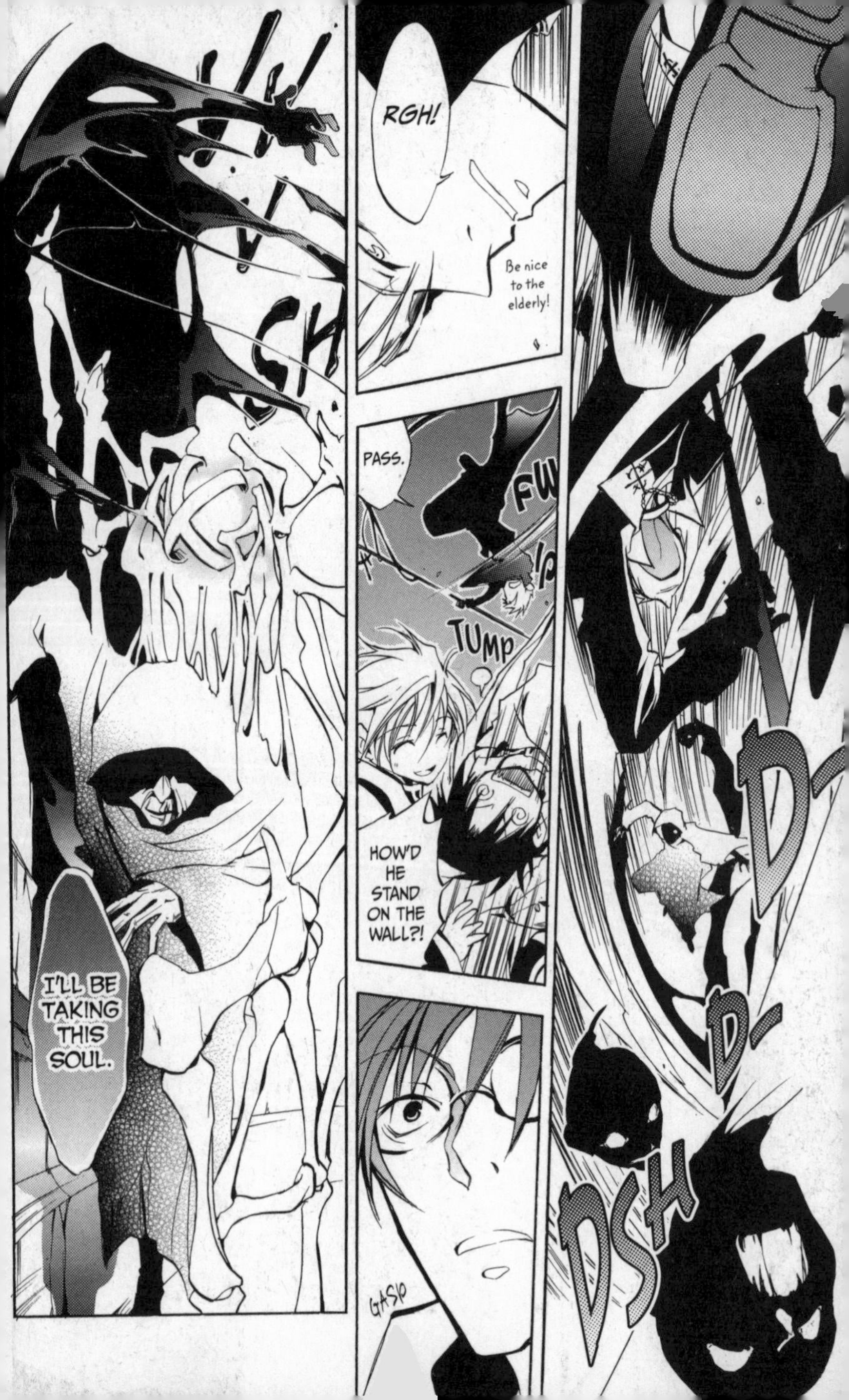
D-
D-
DSH
RGH!
Be nice to the elderly!
PASS.
TUMP
HOW'D HE STAND ON THE WALL?!
GASP
I'LL BE TAKING THIS SOUL.

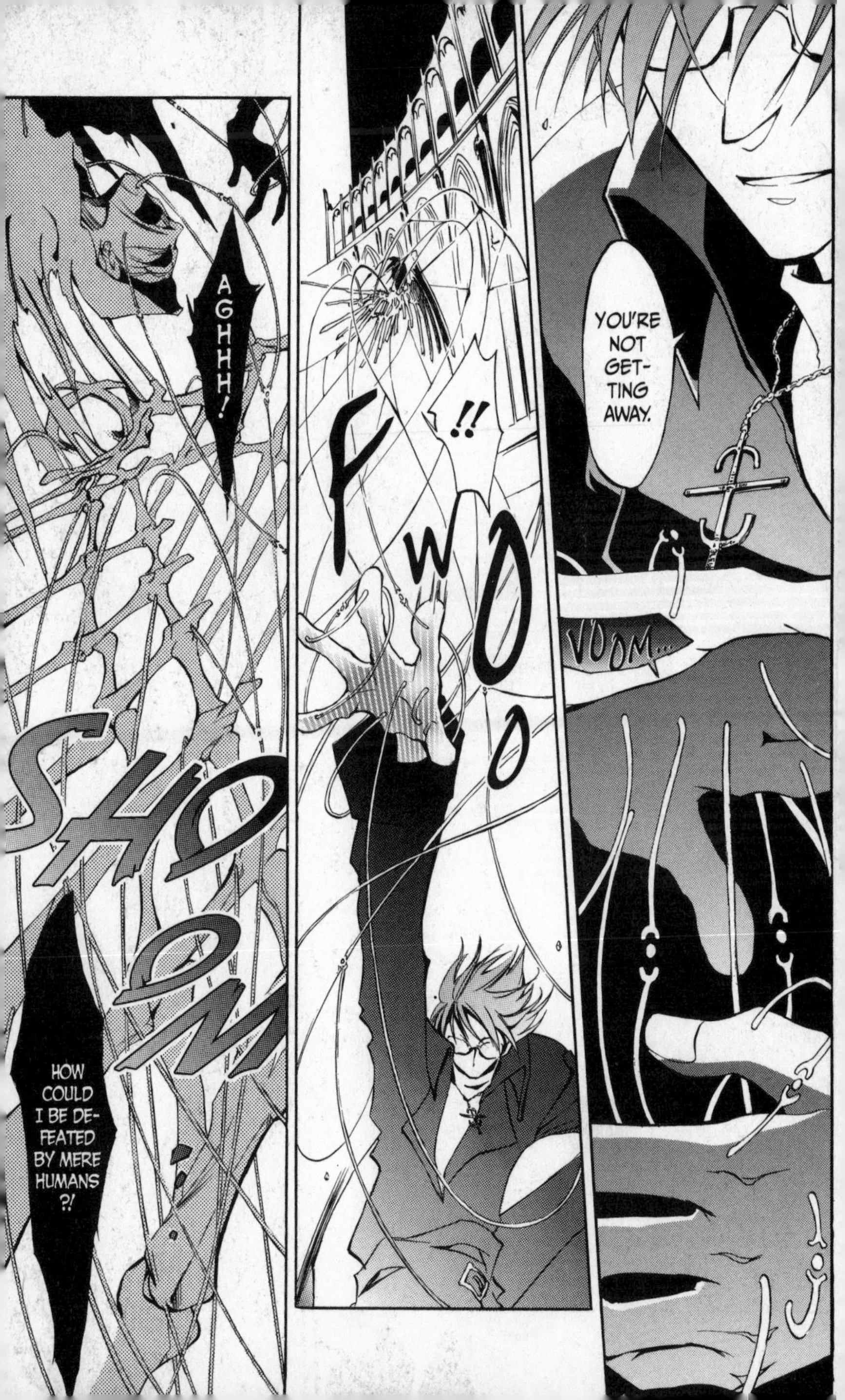
YOU'RE NOT GET-TING AWAY.
VOOM...
!!
FWOOO
AGHHH!
SHOOM
HOW COULD I BE DE-FEATED BY MERE HUMANS?!

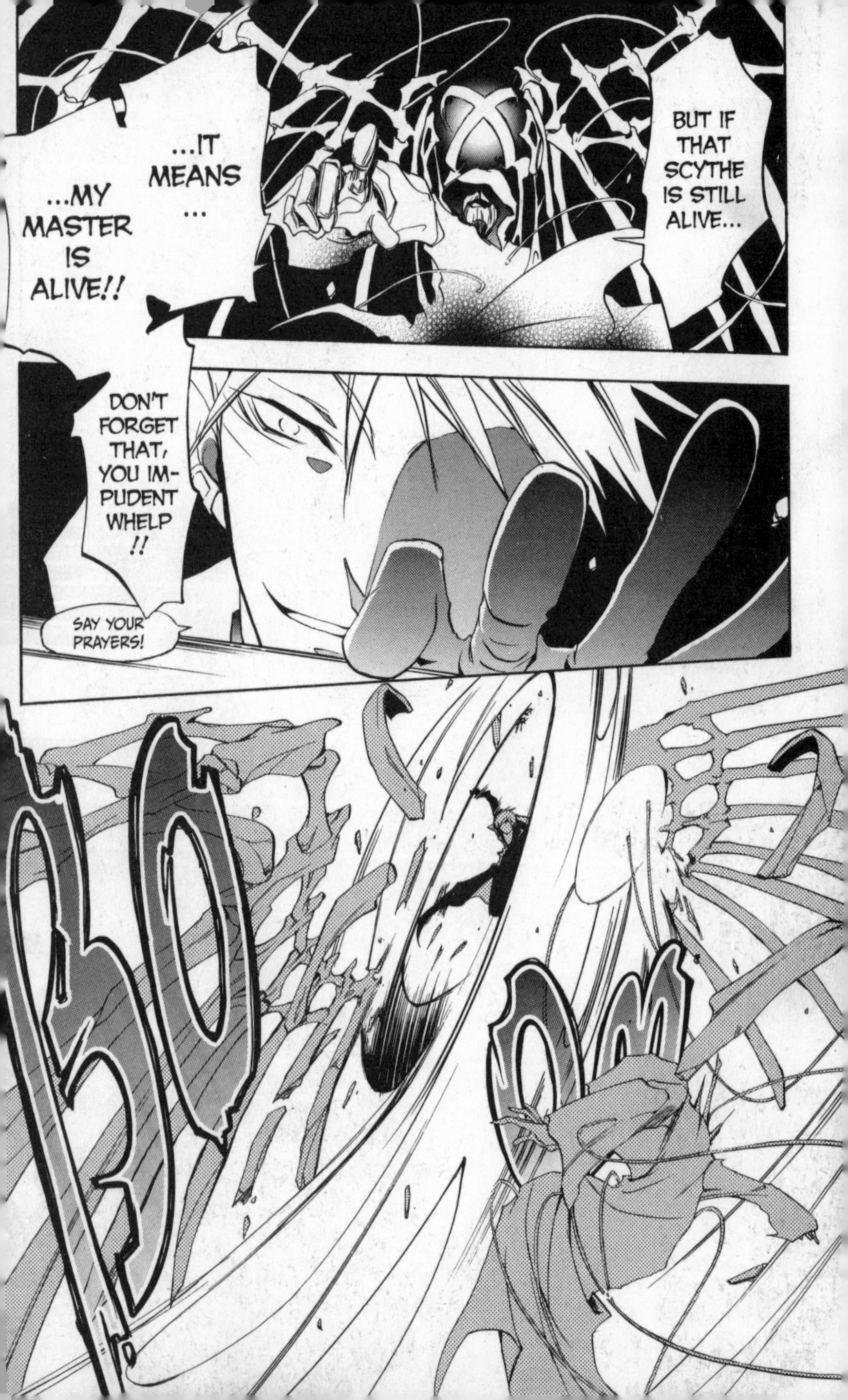
BUT IF THAT SCYTHE IS STILL ALIVE...
...IT MEANS...
...MY MASTER IS ALIVE!!
DON'T FORGET THAT, YOU IMPUDENT WHELP!!
SAY YOUR PRAYERS!
BOOOM

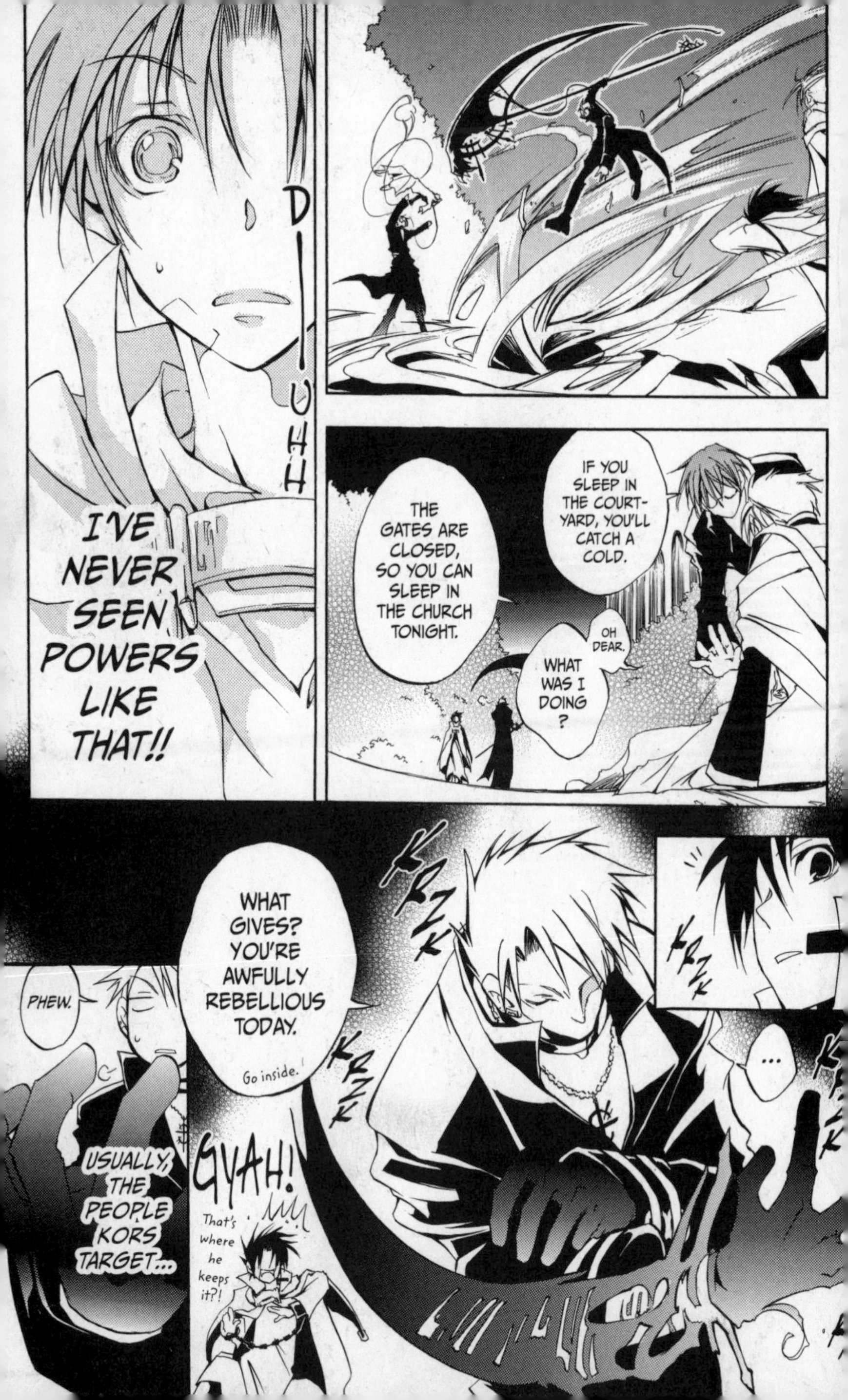
IF YOU SLEEP IN THE COURTYARD, YOU'LL CATCH A COLD.
THE GATES ARE CLOSED, SO YOU CAN SLEEP IN THE CHURCH TONIGHT.
OH DEAR.
WHAT WAS I DOING?
D-UHH
I'VE NEVER SEEN POWERS LIKE THAT!!
KRNK
KRNK
...
KRNK
KRNK
WHAT GIVES? YOU'RE AWFULLY REBELLIOUS TODAY.
Go inside.
KRNK
GYAH!
That's where he keeps it?!
PHEW.
USUALLY, THE PEOPLE KORS TARGET...

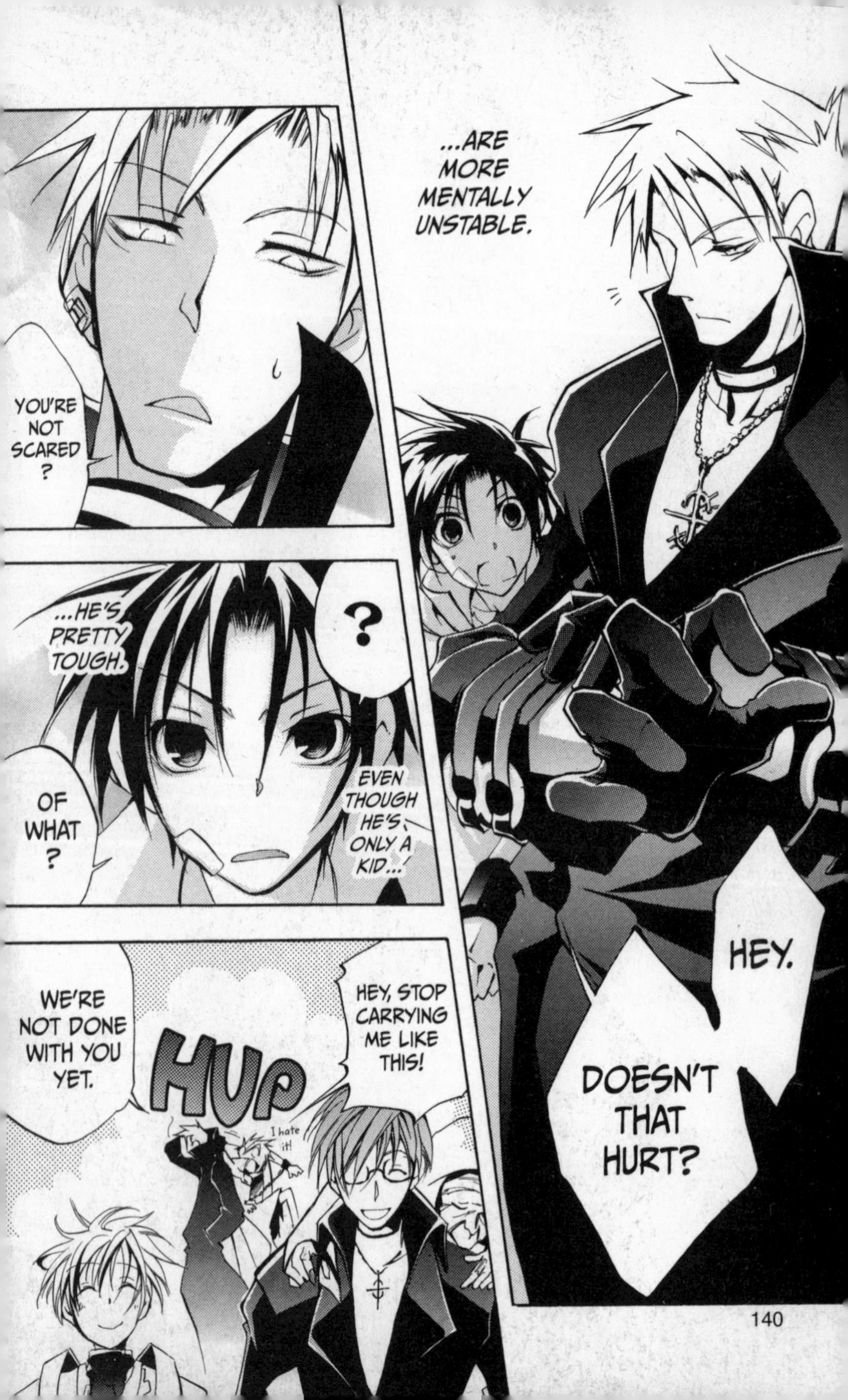
...ARE MORE MENTALLY UNSTABLE.
HEY. DOESN'T THAT HURT?
YOU'RE NOT SCARED?
?
...HE'S PRETTY TOUGH.
EVEN THOUGH HE'S ONLY A KID...!
OF WHAT?
HEY, STOP CARRYING ME LIKE THIS!
WE'RE NOT DONE WITH YOU YET.
HUP
I hate it!

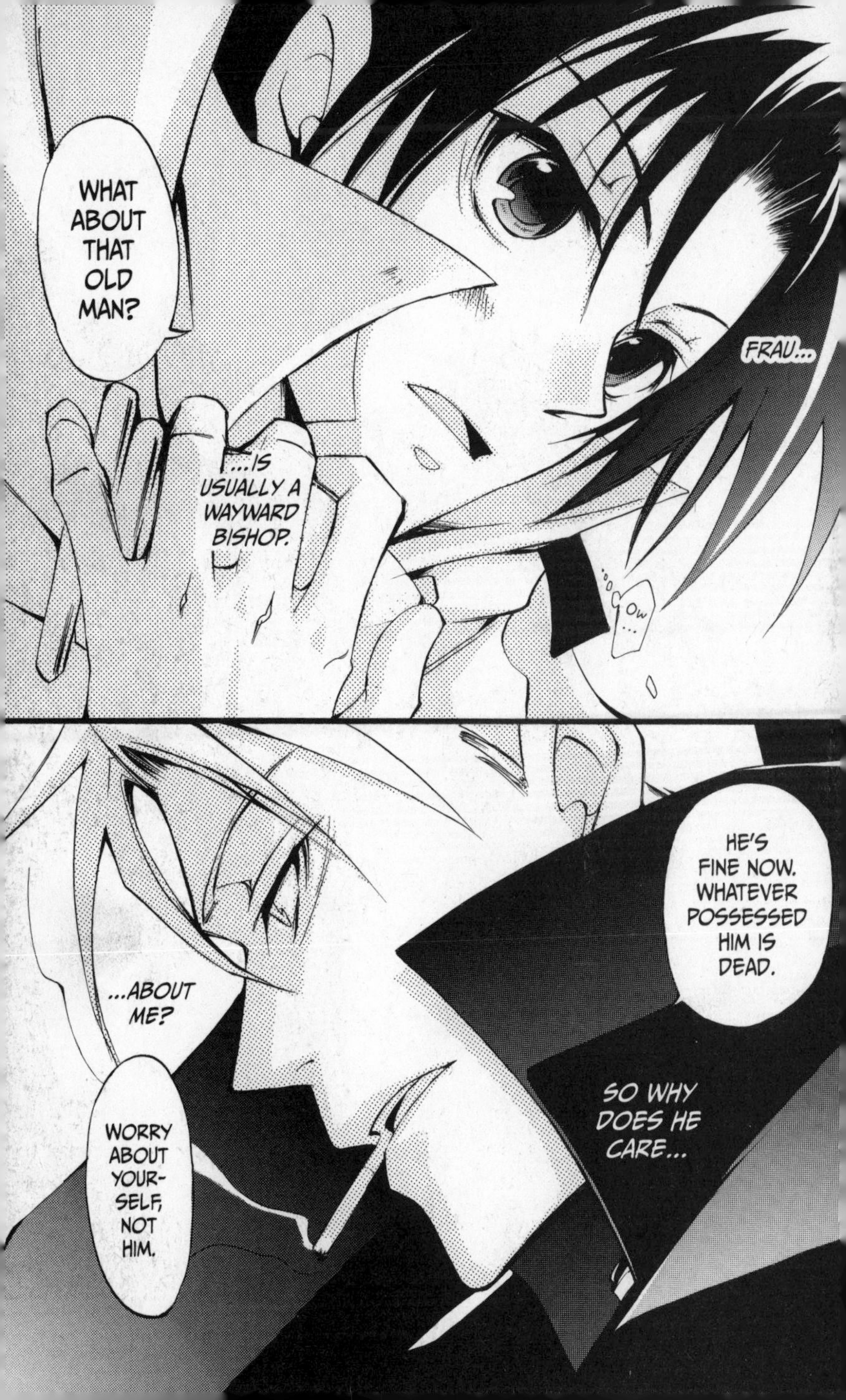
FRAU...
WHAT ABOUT THAT OLD MAN?
...IS USUALLY A WAYWARD BISHOP.
OW...
HE'S FINE NOW. WHATEVER POSSESSED HIM IS DEAD.
SO WHY DOES HE CARE...
...ABOUT ME?
WORRY ABOUT YOURSELF, NOT HIM.

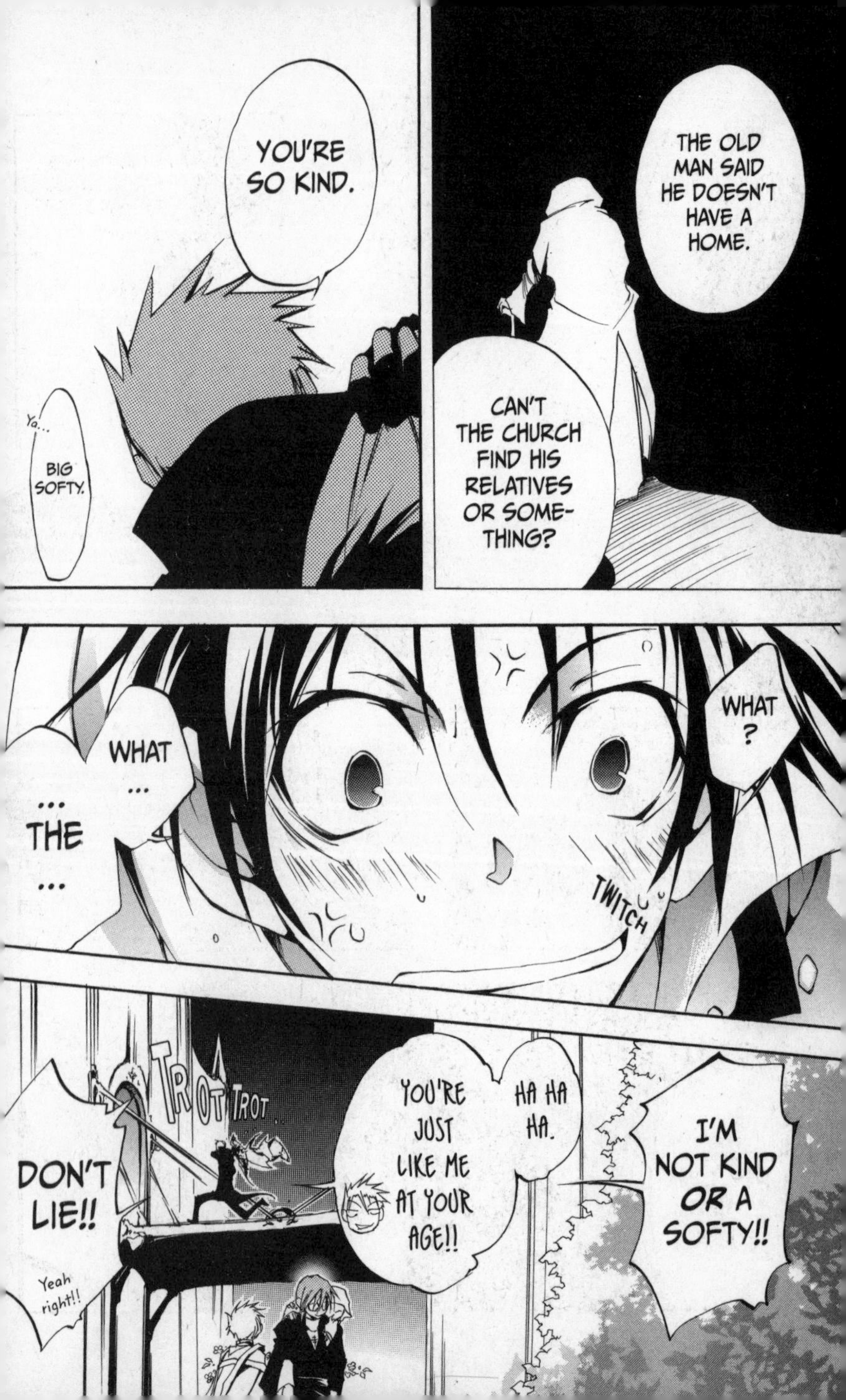

THE OLD MAN SAID HE DOESN'T HAVE A HOME.
CAN'T THE CHURCH FIND HIS RELATIVES OR SOME-THING?
YOU'RE SO KIND.
Ya...
BIG SOFTY.
WHAT?
TWITCH
WHAT...
...THE...
I'M NOT KIND OR A SOFTY!!
HA HA HA.
YOU'RE JUST LIKE ME AT YOUR AGE!!
TROT TROT
DON'T LIE!!
Yeah right!!

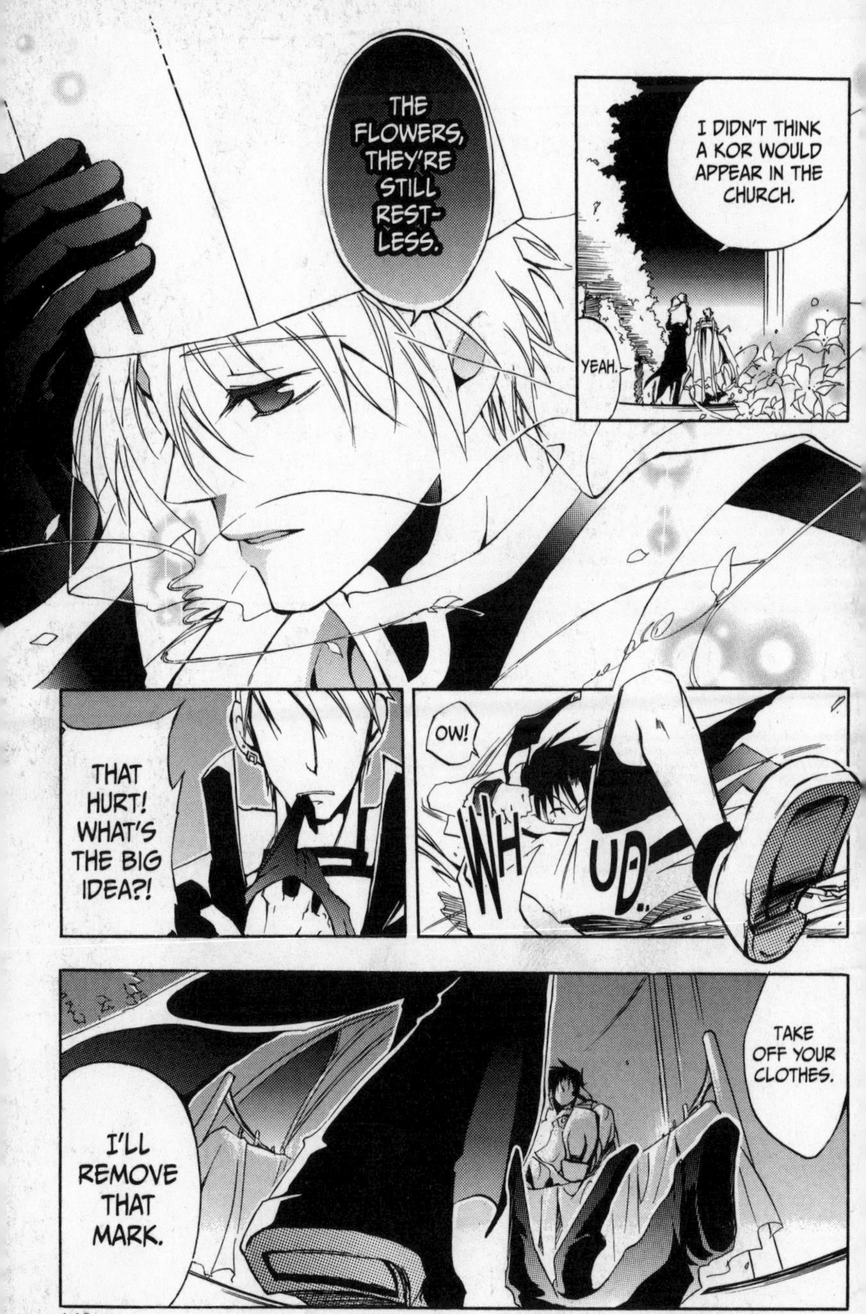
I DIDN'T THINK A KOR WOULD APPEAR IN THE CHURCH.
YEAH.
THE FLOWERS, THEY'RE STILL RESTLESS.
OW!
WHUD..
THAT HURT! WHAT'S THE BIG IDEA?!
TAKE OFF YOUR CLOTHES.
I'LL REMOVE THAT MARK.

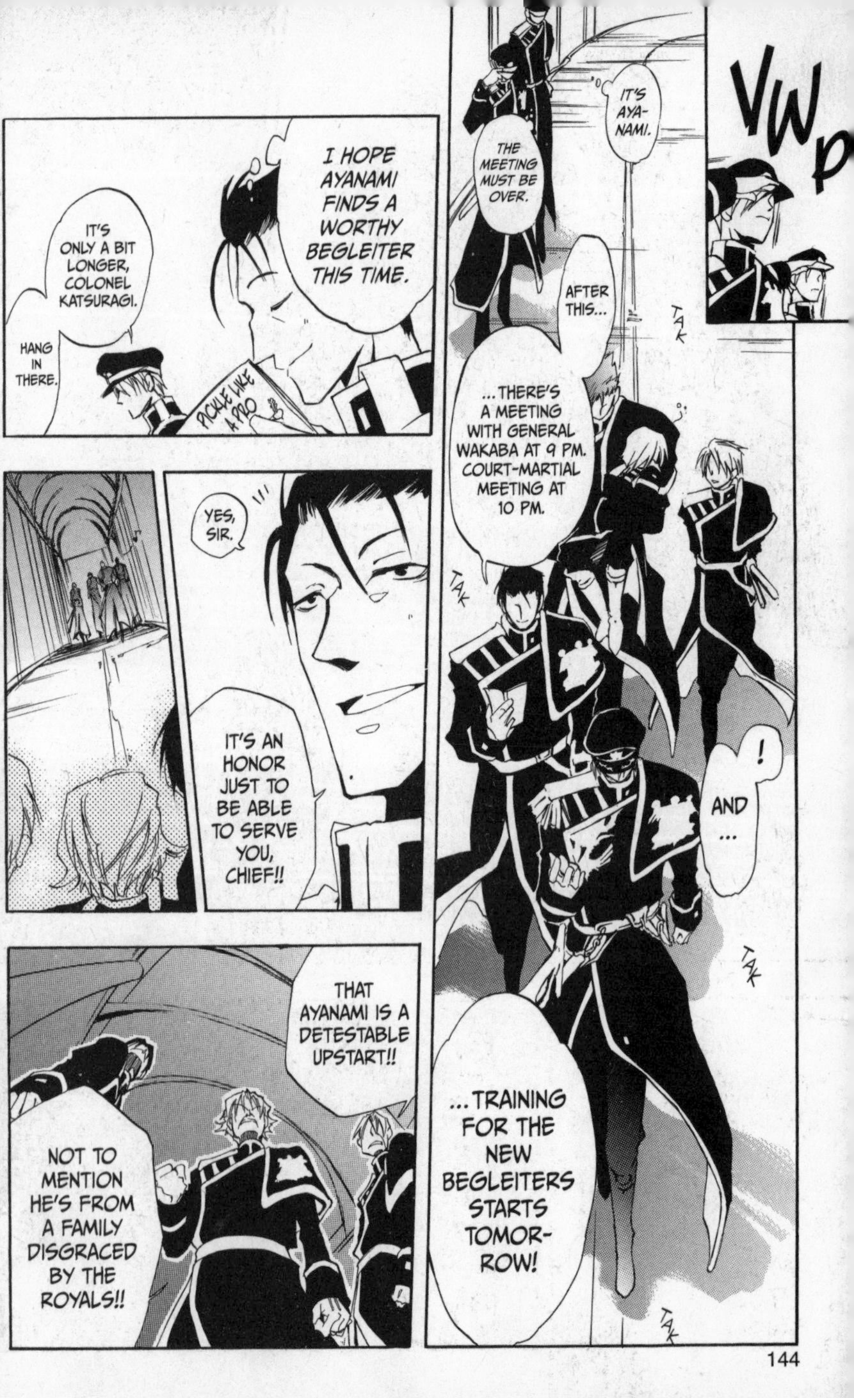
VWP
IT'S AYANAMI.
THE MEETING MUST BE OVER.
TAK
AFTER THIS...
...THERE'S A MEETING WITH GENERAL WAKABA AT 9 PM. COURT-MARTIAL MEETING AT 10 PM.
TAK
!
AND...
TAK
...TRAINING FOR THE NEW BEGLEITERS STARTS TOMOR-ROW!
TAK
I HOPE AYANAMI FINDS A WORTHY BEGLEITER THIS TIME.
IT'S ONLY A BIT LONGER, COLONEL KATSURAGI.
HANG IN THERE.
PICKLE LIKE A PRO
YES, SIR.
IT'S AN HONOR JUST TO BE ABLE TO SERVE YOU, CHIEF!!
THAT AYANAMI IS A DETESTABLE UPSTART!!
NOT TO MENTION HE'S FROM A FAMILY DISGRACED BY THE ROYALS!!

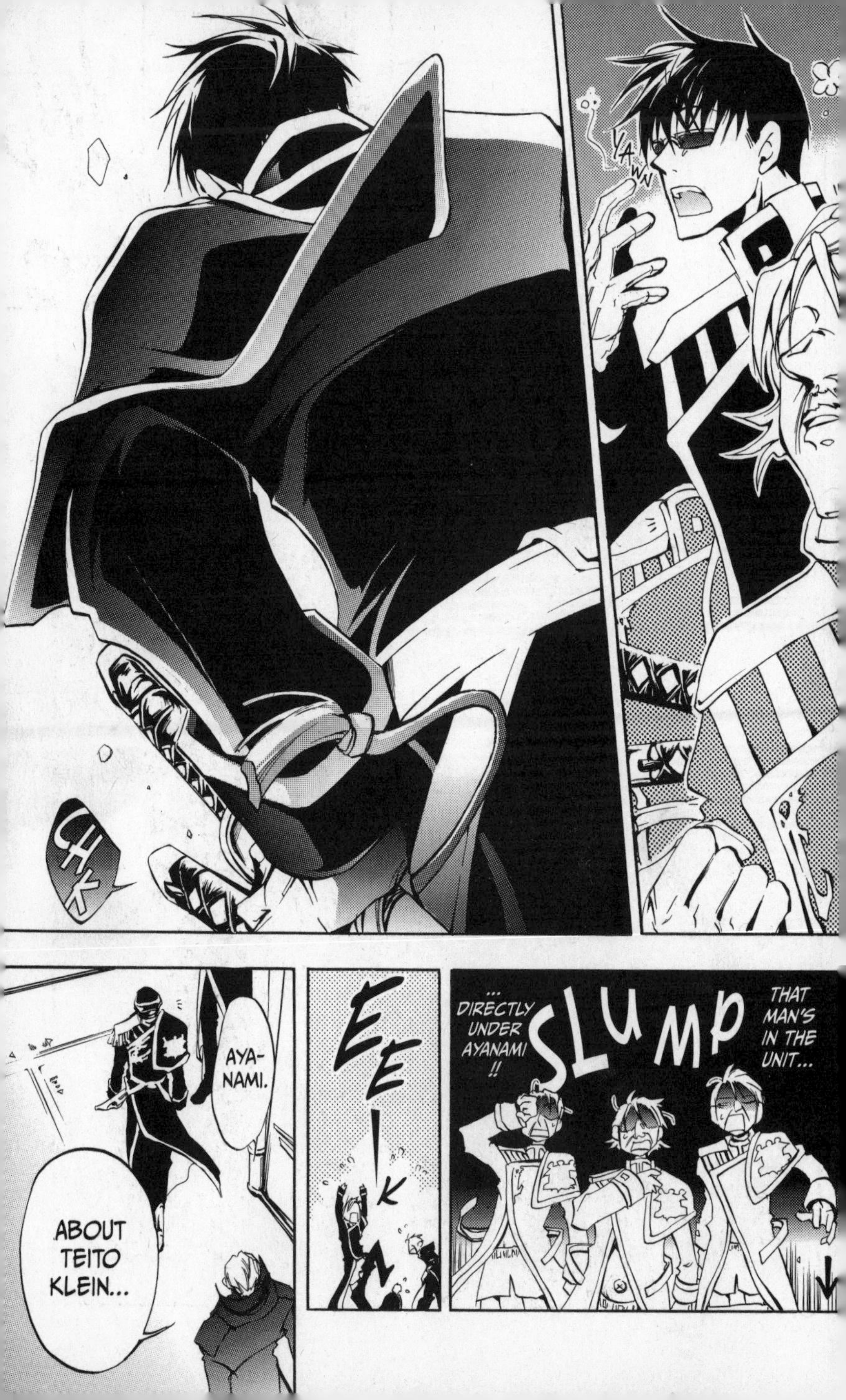
YAWN
CHK
THAT MAN'S IN THE UNIT...
SLUMP
...DIRECTLY UNDER AYANAMI!!
EEIK
AYA-NAMI.
ABOUT TEITO KLEIN...

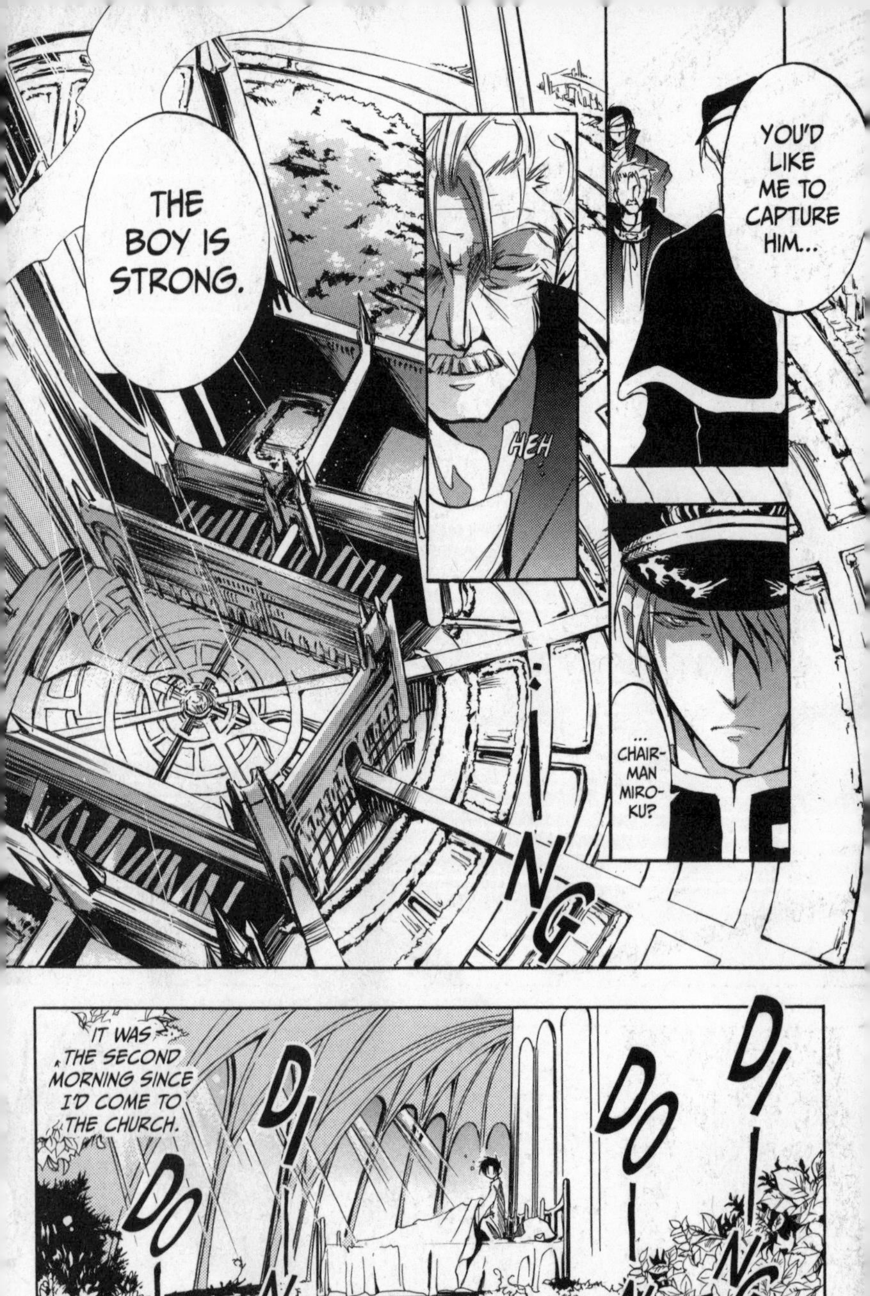
YOU'D LIKE ME TO CAPTURE HIM...
...CHAIRMAN MIROKU?
HEH
THE BOY IS STRONG.
ING!
DIING
DOING
IT WAS THE SECOND MORNING SINCE I'D COME TO THE CHURCH.
DIING
DOING.

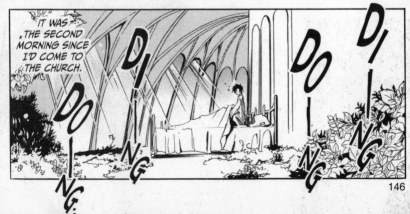

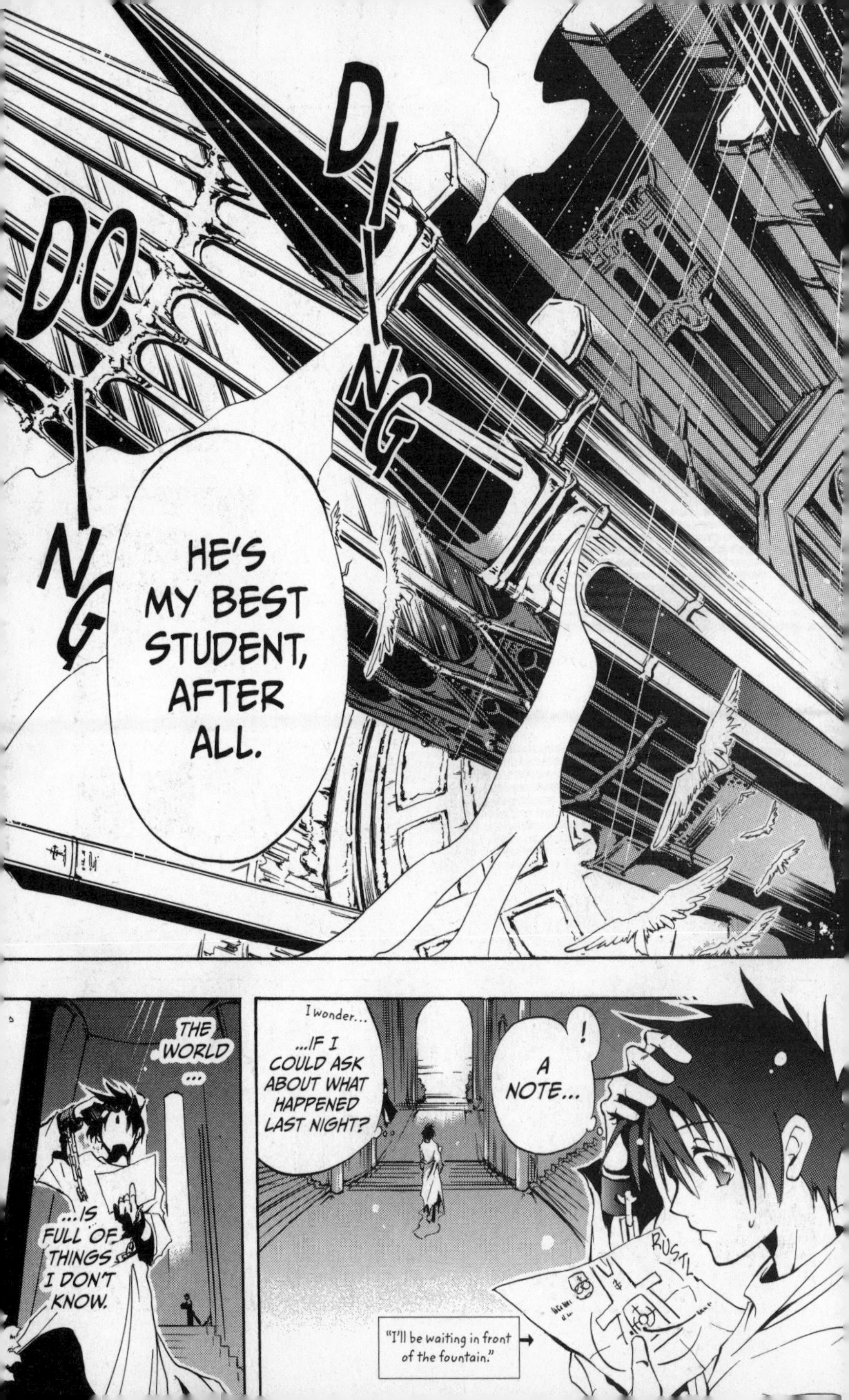
DING
HE'S MY BEST STUDENT, AFTER ALL.
DOING
!
A NOTE...
"I'll be waiting in front of the fountain."
I wonder...
...IF I COULD ASK ABOUT WHAT HAPPENED LAST NIGHT?
THE WORLD...
...IS FULL OF THINGS I DON'T KNOW.

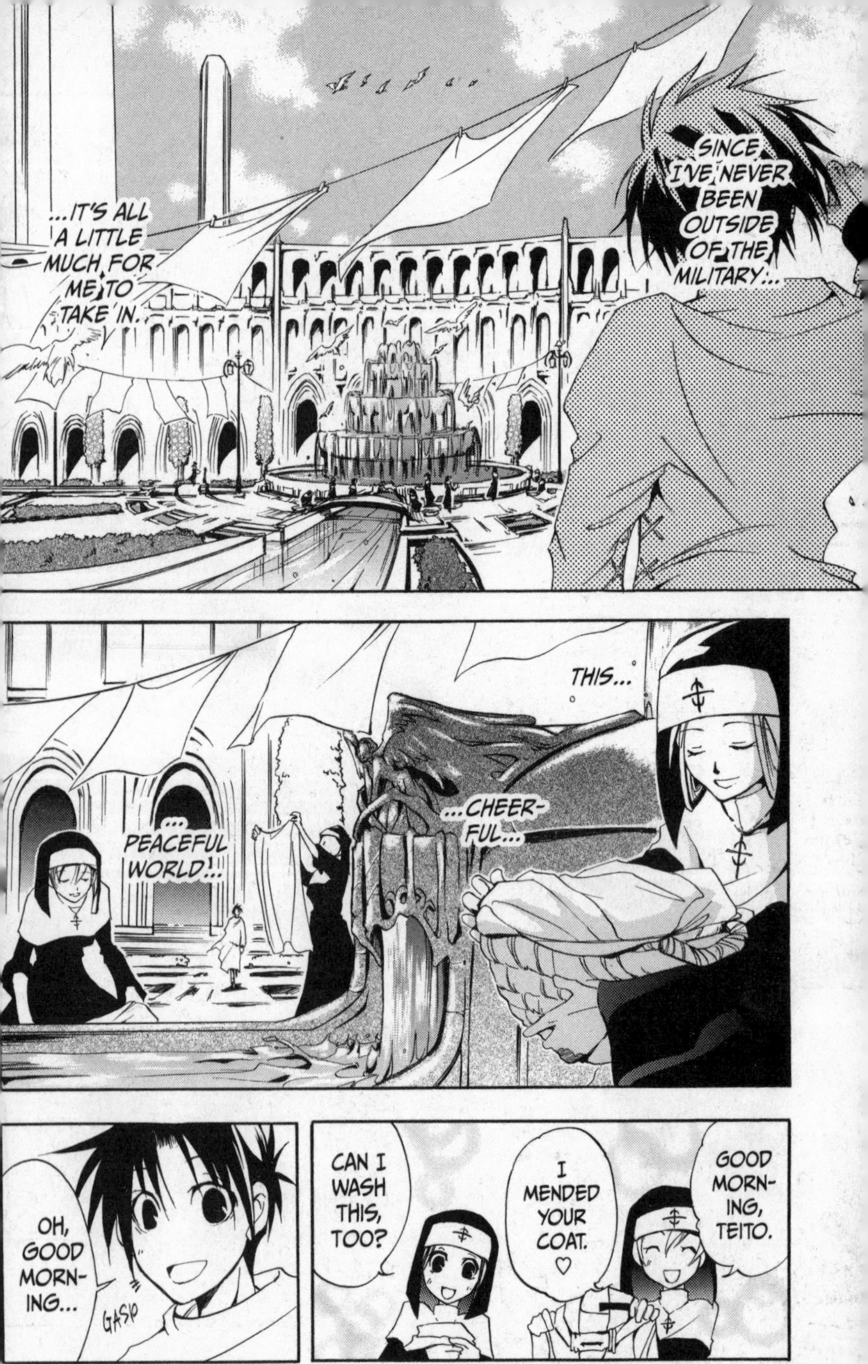
SINCE I'VE NEVER BEEN OUTSIDE OF THE MILITARY...
...IT'S ALL A LITTLE MUCH FOR ME TO TAKE IN.
THIS...
...CHEERFUL...
...PEACEFUL WORLD!...
GOOD MORNING, TEITO.
I MENDED YOUR COAT. ♡
CAN I WASH THIS, TOO?
OH, GOOD MORNING...
GASP

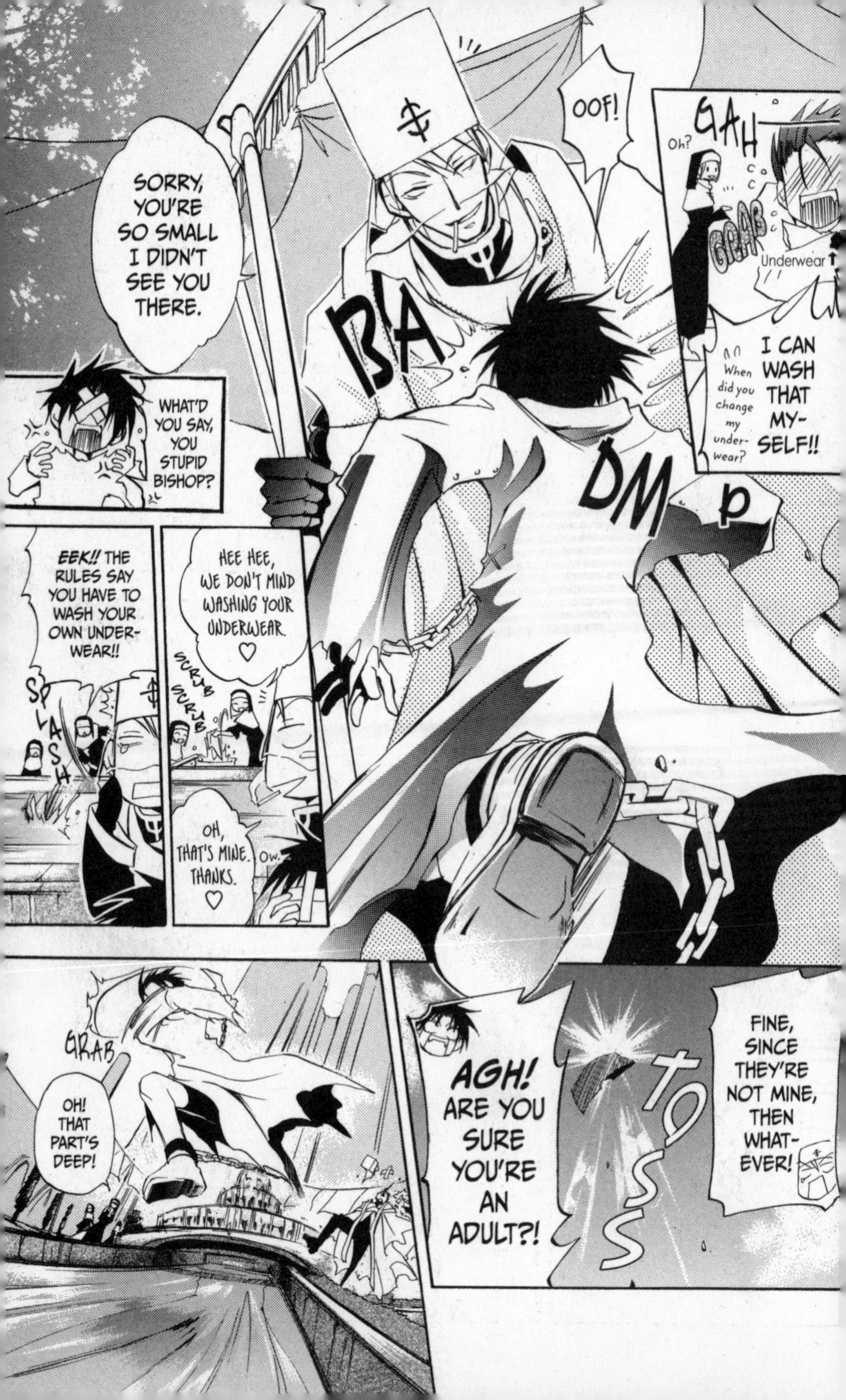
GAH
Oh?
GRAB
Underwear↑
I CAN WASH THAT MYSELF!!
When did you change my under-wear?
OOF!
SORRY, YOU'RE SO SMALL I DIDN'T SEE YOU THERE.
BA
DMP
WHAT'D YOU SAY, YOU STUPID BISHOP?
HEE HEE, WE DON'T MIND WASHING YOUR UNDERWEAR. ♡
SCRUB SCRUB
OH, THAT'S MINE. THANKS. ♡
Ow.
EEK!! THE RULES SAY YOU HAVE TO WASH YOUR OWN UNDER-WEAR!!
SPLASH
FINE, SINCE THEY'RE NOT MINE, THEN WHAT-EVER!
TOSS
AGH! ARE YOU SURE YOU'RE AN ADULT?!
GRAB
OH! THAT PART'S DEEP!

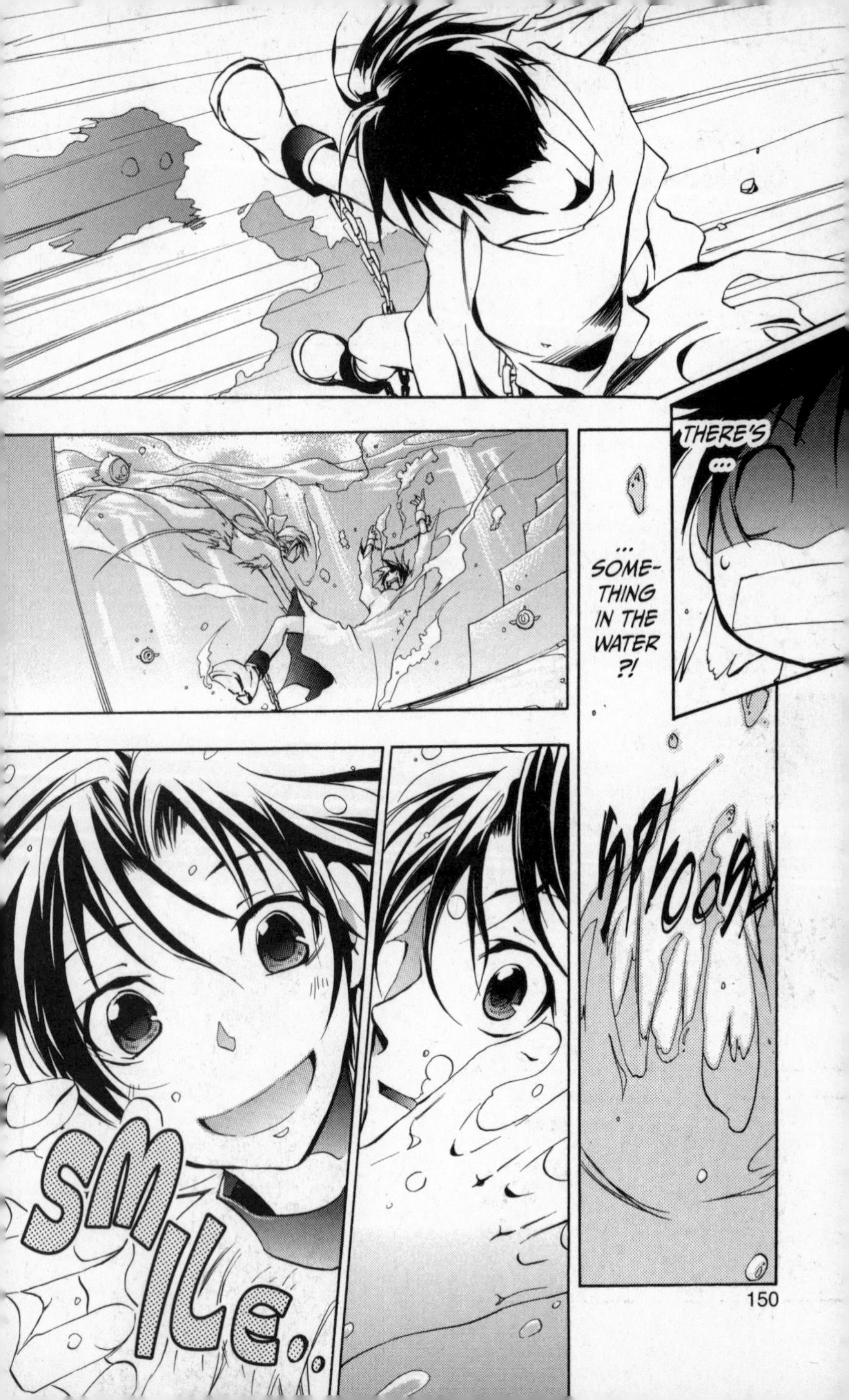
THERE'S ...
... SOMETHING IN THE WATER ?!
SPLOOSH
SMILE..

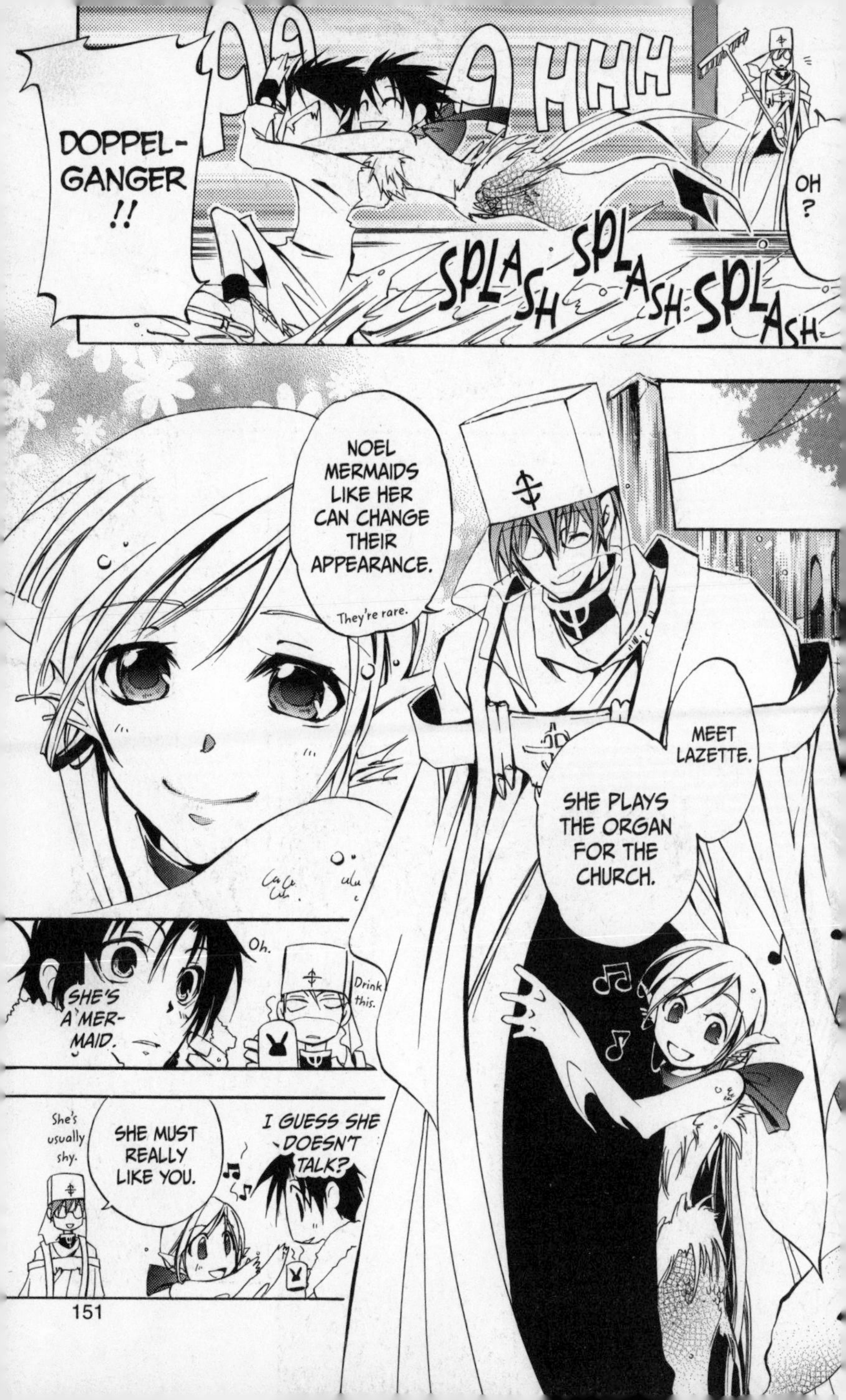
OH?
AAAHHH
DOPPEL-GANGER!!
SPLASH SPLASH SPLASH
MEET LAZETTE.
SHE PLAYS THE ORGAN FOR THE CHURCH.
NOEL MERMAIDS LIKE HER CAN CHANGE THEIR APPEARANCE.
They're rare.
Drink this.
Oh.
SHE'S A MER-MAID.
I GUESS SHE DOESN'T TALK?
SHE MUST REALLY LIKE YOU.
She's usually shy.

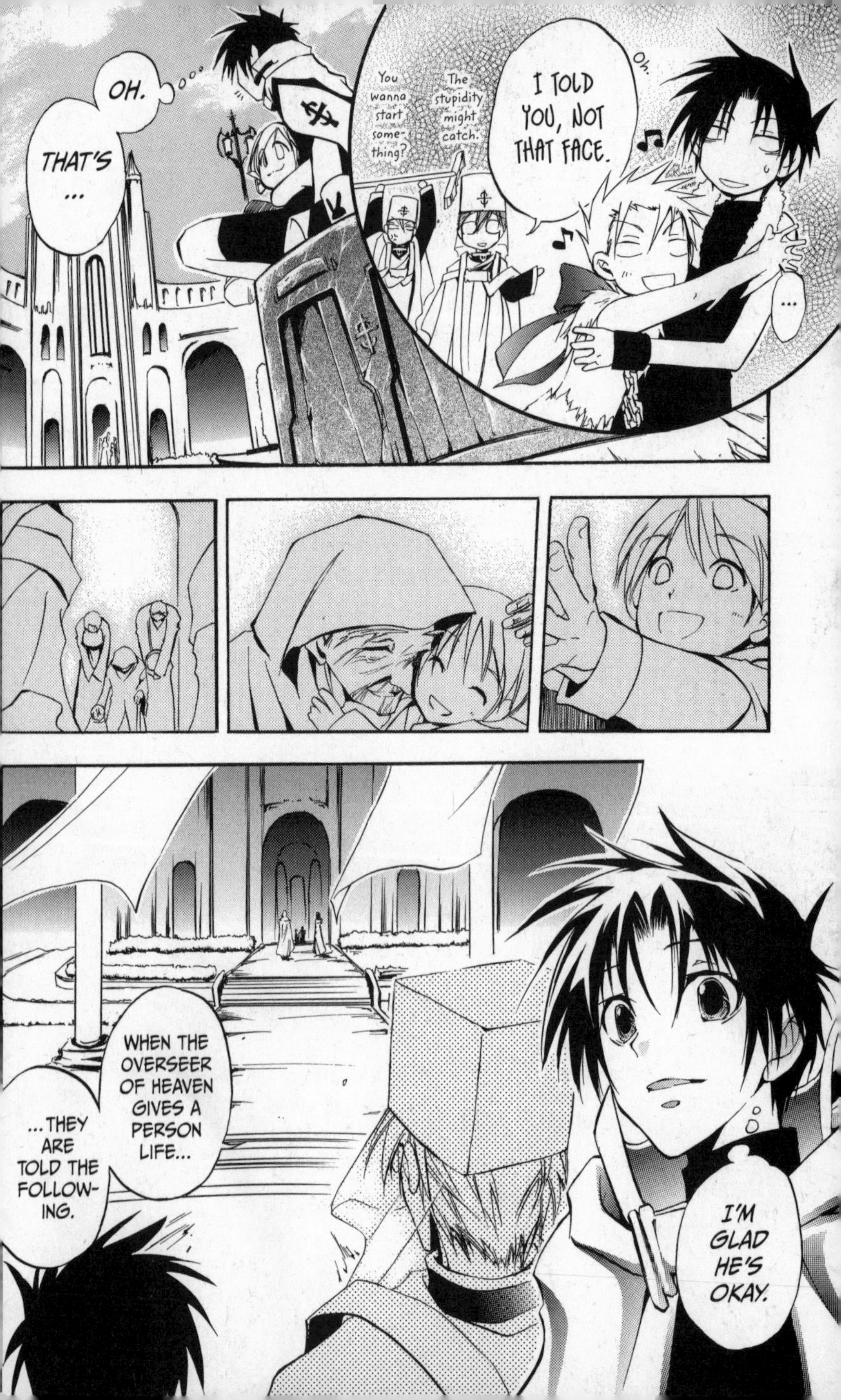
Oh.
I TOLD YOU, NOT THAT FACE.
...
The stupidity might catch.
You wanna start some-thing?
OH.
THAT'S ...
I'M GLAD HE'S OKAY.
WHEN THE OVERSEER OF HEAVEN GIVES A PERSON LIFE...
...THEY ARE TOLD THE FOLLOW-ING.

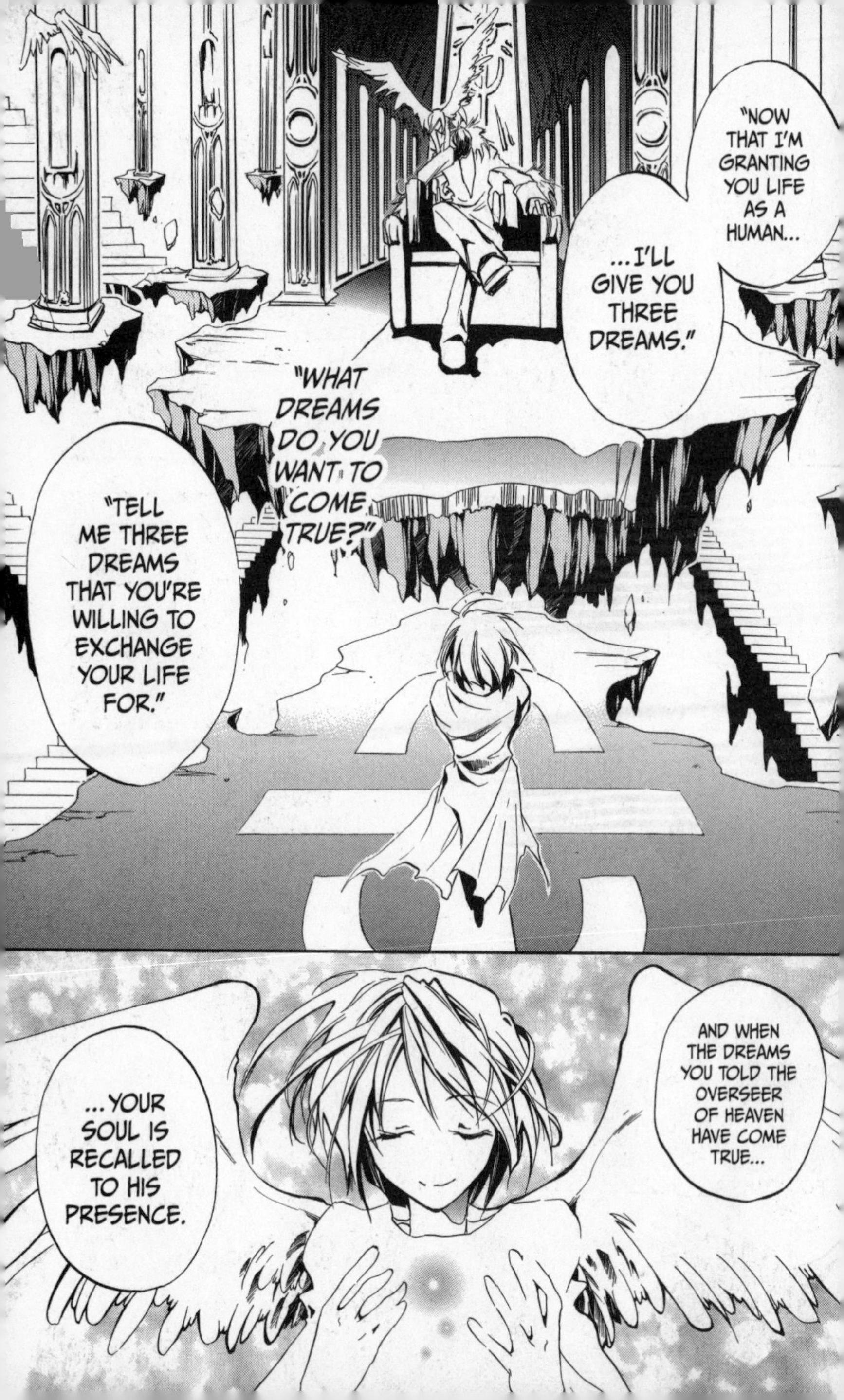
"NOW THAT I'M GRANTING YOU LIFE AS A HUMAN...
...I'LL GIVE YOU THREE DREAMS."
"WHAT DREAMS DO YOU WANT TO COME TRUE?"
"TELL ME THREE DREAMS THAT YOU'RE WILLING TO EXCHANGE YOUR LIFE FOR."
AND WHEN THE DREAMS YOU TOLD THE OVERSEER OF HEAVEN HAVE COME TRUE...
...YOUR SOUL IS RECALLED TO HIS PRESENCE.

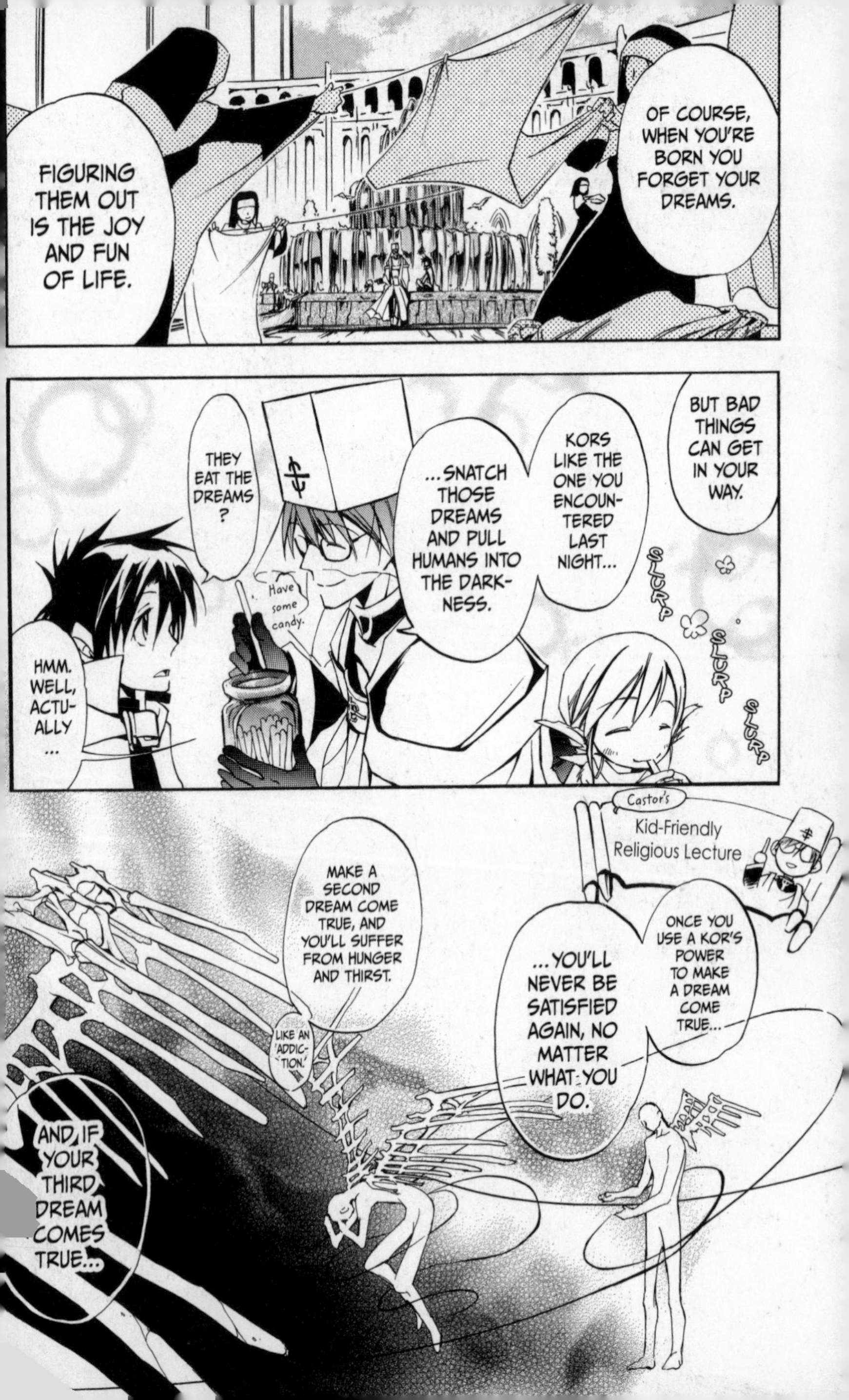
OF COURSE, WHEN YOU'RE BORN YOU FORGET YOUR DREAMS.
FIGURING THEM OUT IS THE JOY AND FUN OF LIFE.
BUT BAD THINGS CAN GET IN YOUR WAY.
KORS LIKE THE ONE YOU ENCOUN-TERED LAST NIGHT...
...SNATCH THOSE DREAMS AND PULL HUMANS INTO THE DARK-NESS.
SLURP
SLURP
SLURP
THEY EAT THE DREAMS?
Have some candy.
HMM. WELL, ACTU-ALLY...
Castor's Kid-Friendly Religious Lecture
ONCE YOU USE A KOR'S POWER TO MAKE A DREAM COME TRUE...
...YOU'LL NEVER BE SATISFIED AGAIN, NO MATTER WHAT YOU DO.
MAKE A SECOND DREAM COME TRUE, AND YOU'LL SUFFER FROM HUNGER AND THIRST.
LIKE AN 'ADDIC-TION.'
AND IF YOUR THIRD DREAM COMES TRUE...

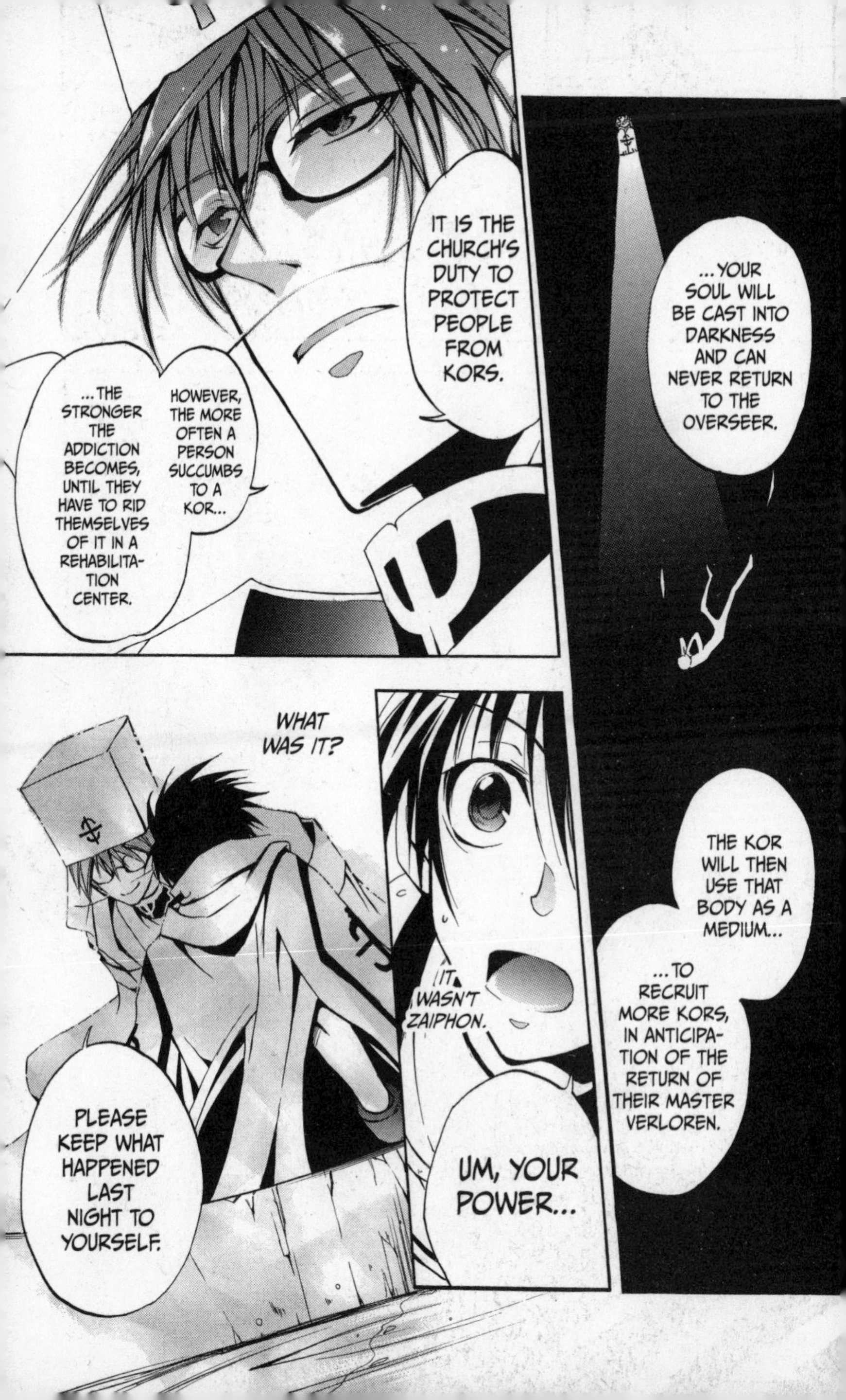
...YOUR SOUL WILL BE CAST INTO DARKNESS AND CAN NEVER RETURN TO THE OVERSEER.
THE KOR WILL THEN USE THAT BODY AS A MEDIUM...
...TO RECRUIT MORE KORS, IN ANTICIPATION OF THE RETURN OF THEIR MASTER VERLOREN.
IT IS THE CHURCH'S DUTY TO PROTECT PEOPLE FROM KORS.
HOWEVER, THE MORE OFTEN A PERSON SUCCUMBS TO A KOR...
...THE STRONGER THE ADDICTION BECOMES, UNTIL THEY HAVE TO RID THEMSELVES OF IT IN A REHABILITATION CENTER.
UM, YOUR POWER...
IT WASN'T ZAIPHON.
WHAT WAS IT?
PLEASE KEEP WHAT HAPPENED LAST NIGHT TO YOURSELF.

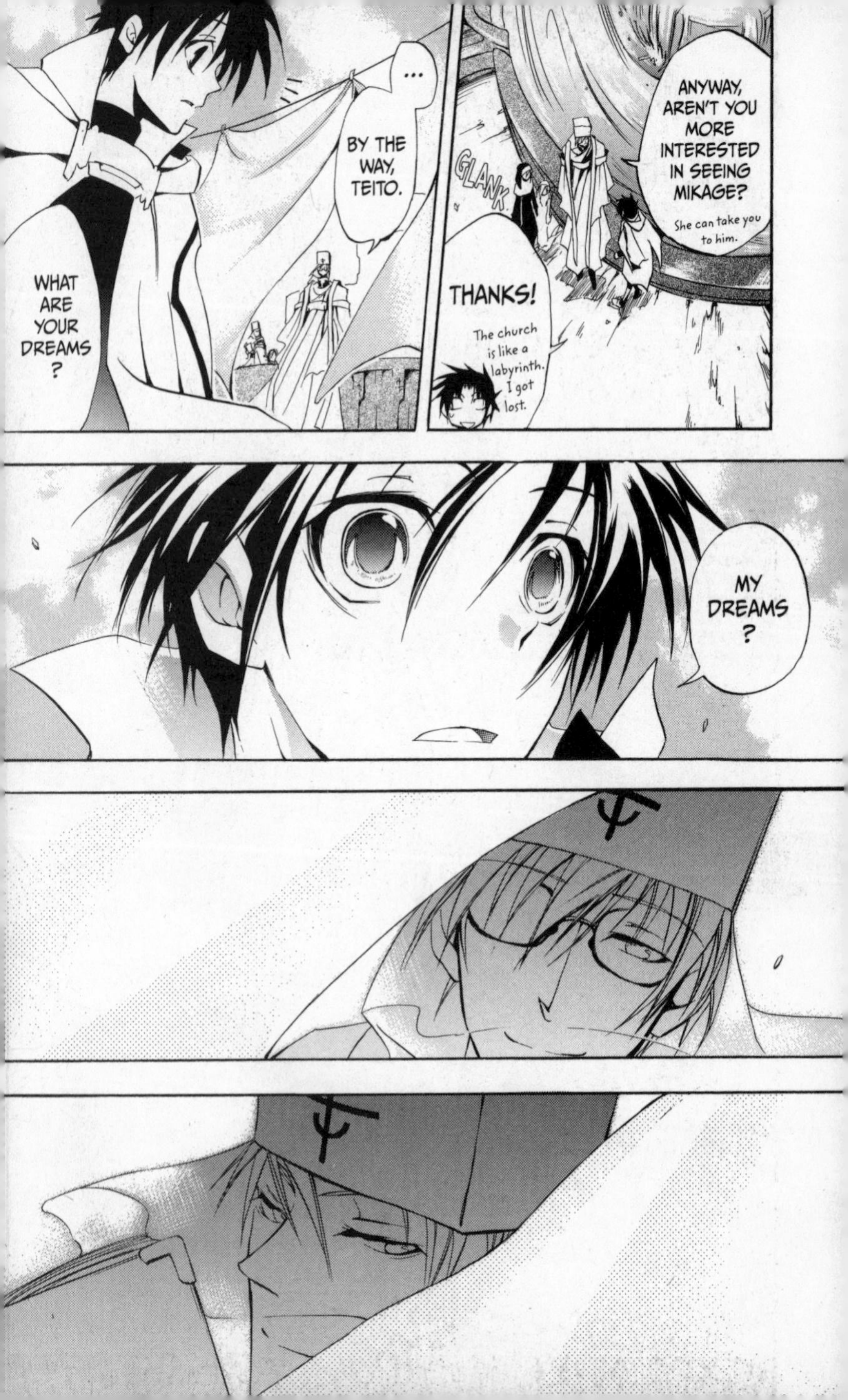
ANYWAY, AREN'T YOU MORE INTERESTED IN SEEING MIKAGE?
She can take you to him.
GLANK
THANKS!
The church is like a labyrinth. I got lost.
...
BY THE WAY, TEITO.
WHAT ARE YOUR DREAMS?
MY DREAMS?

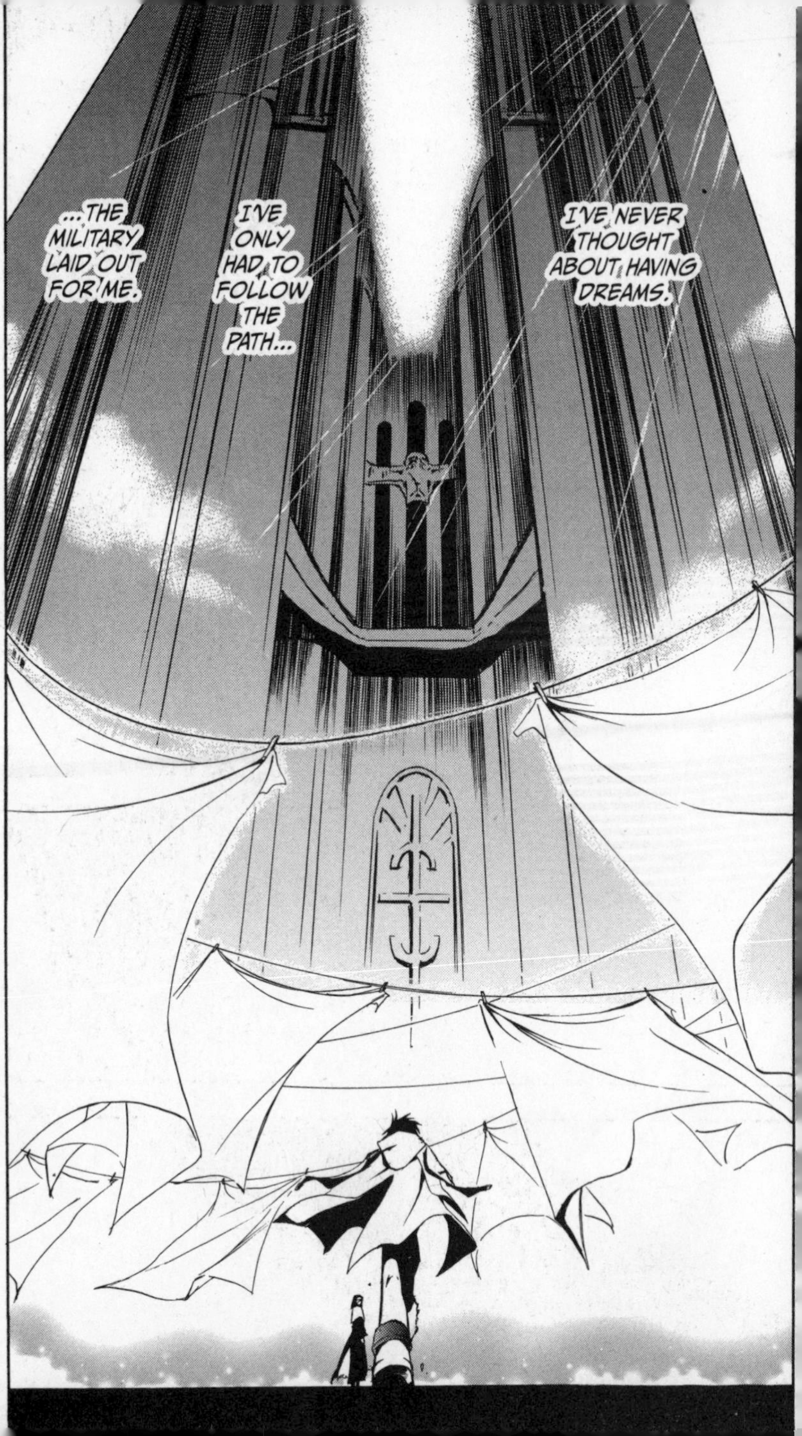
I'VE NEVER THOUGHT ABOUT HAVING DREAMS.
I'VE ONLY HAD TO FOLLOW THE PATH...
...THE MILITARY LAID OUT FOR ME.

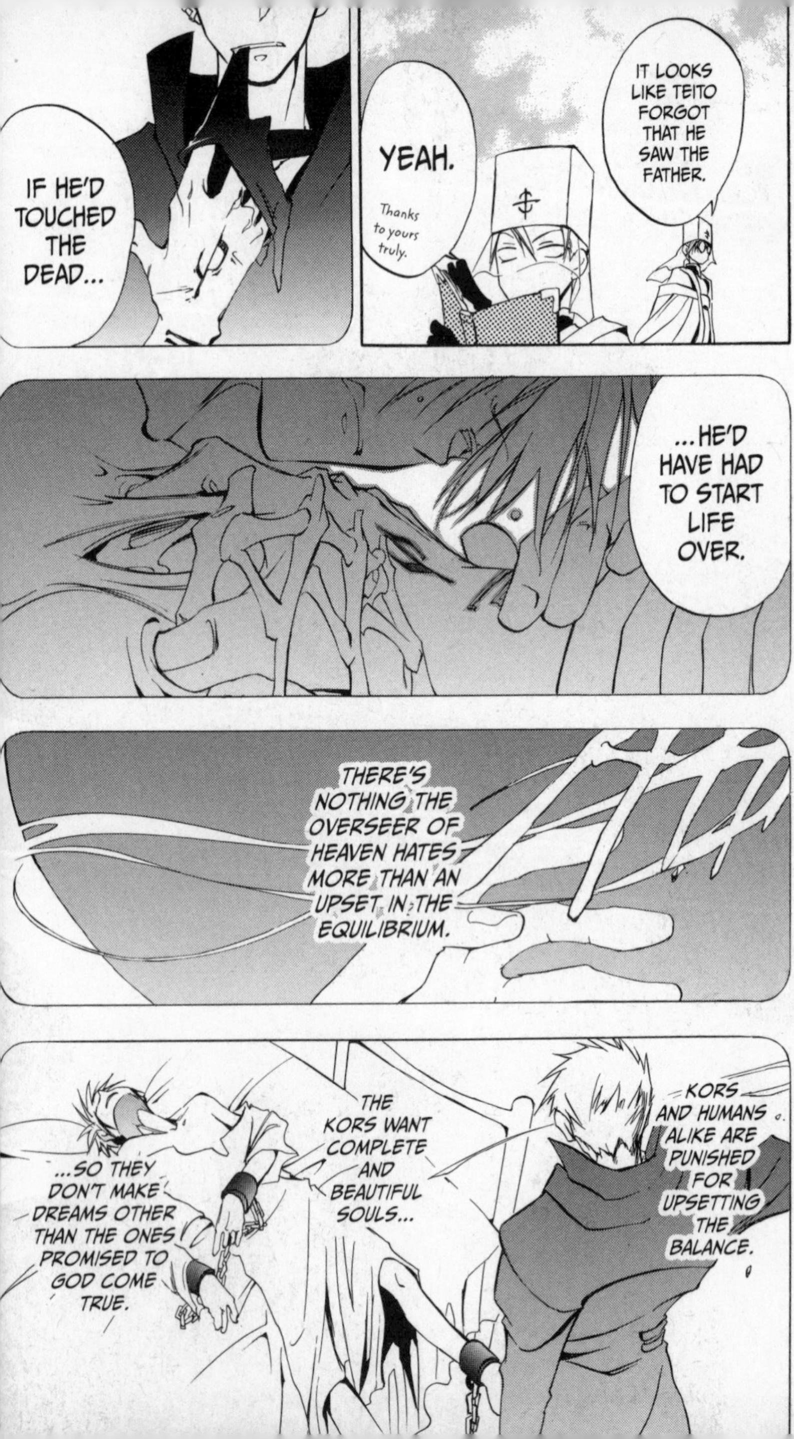
IT LOOKS LIKE TEITO FORGOT THAT HE SAW THE FATHER.
YEAH.
Thanks to yours truly.
IF HE'D TOUCHED THE DEAD...
...HE'D HAVE HAD TO START LIFE OVER.
THERE'S NOTHING THE OVERSEER OF HEAVEN HATES MORE THAN AN UPSET IN THE EQUILIBRIUM.
KORS AND HUMANS ALIKE ARE PUNISHED FOR UPSETTING THE BALANCE.
THE KORS WANT COMPLETE AND BEAUTIFUL SOULS...
...SO THEY DON'T MAKE DREAMS OTHER THAN THE ONES PROMISED TO GOD COME TRUE.

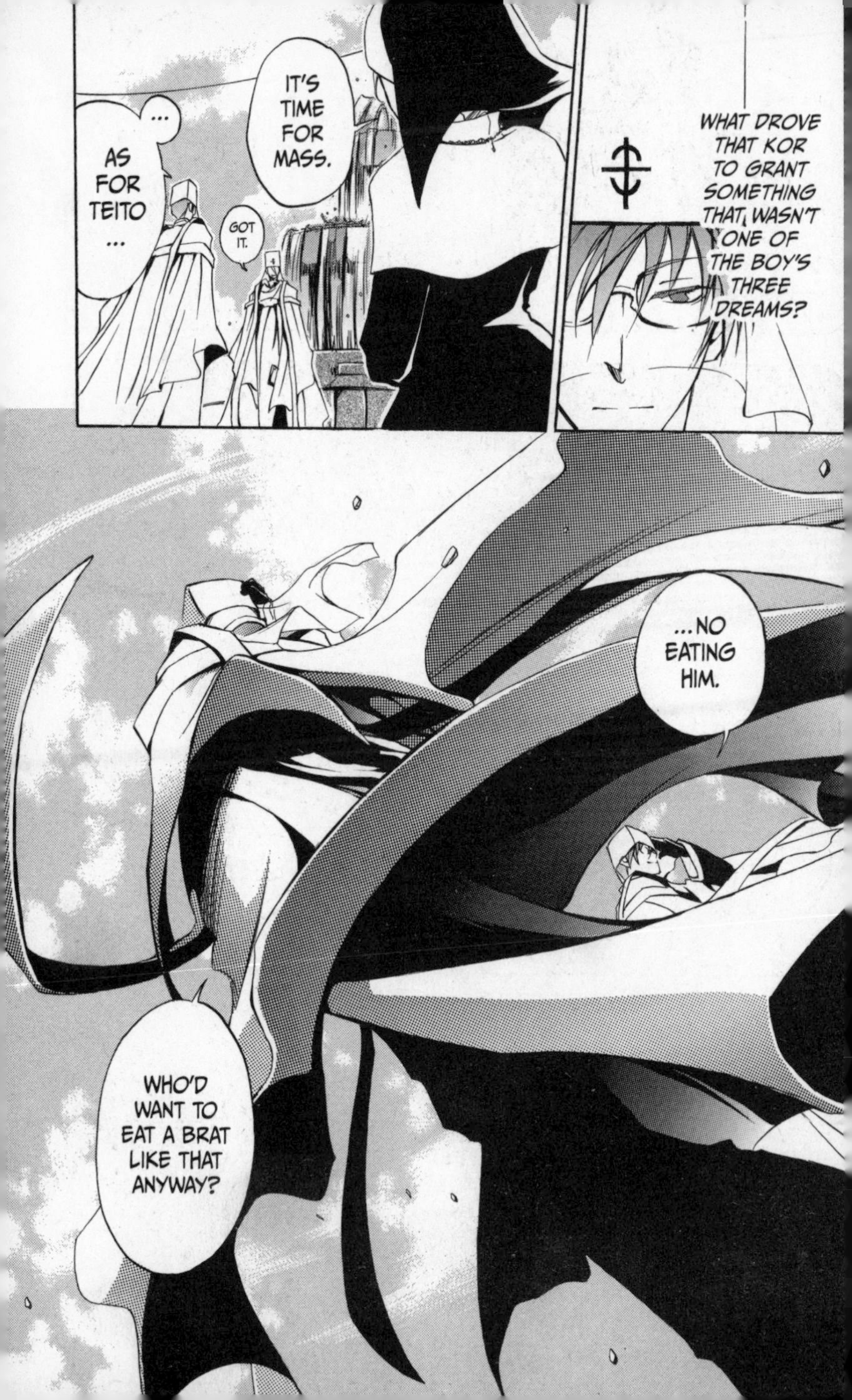
WHAT DROVE THAT KOR TO GRANT SOMETHING THAT WASN'T ONE OF THE BOY'S THREE DREAMS?
IT'S TIME FOR MASS.
GOT IT.
...
AS FOR TEITO ...
...NO EATING HIM.
WHO'D WANT TO EAT A BRAT LIKE THAT ANYWAY?

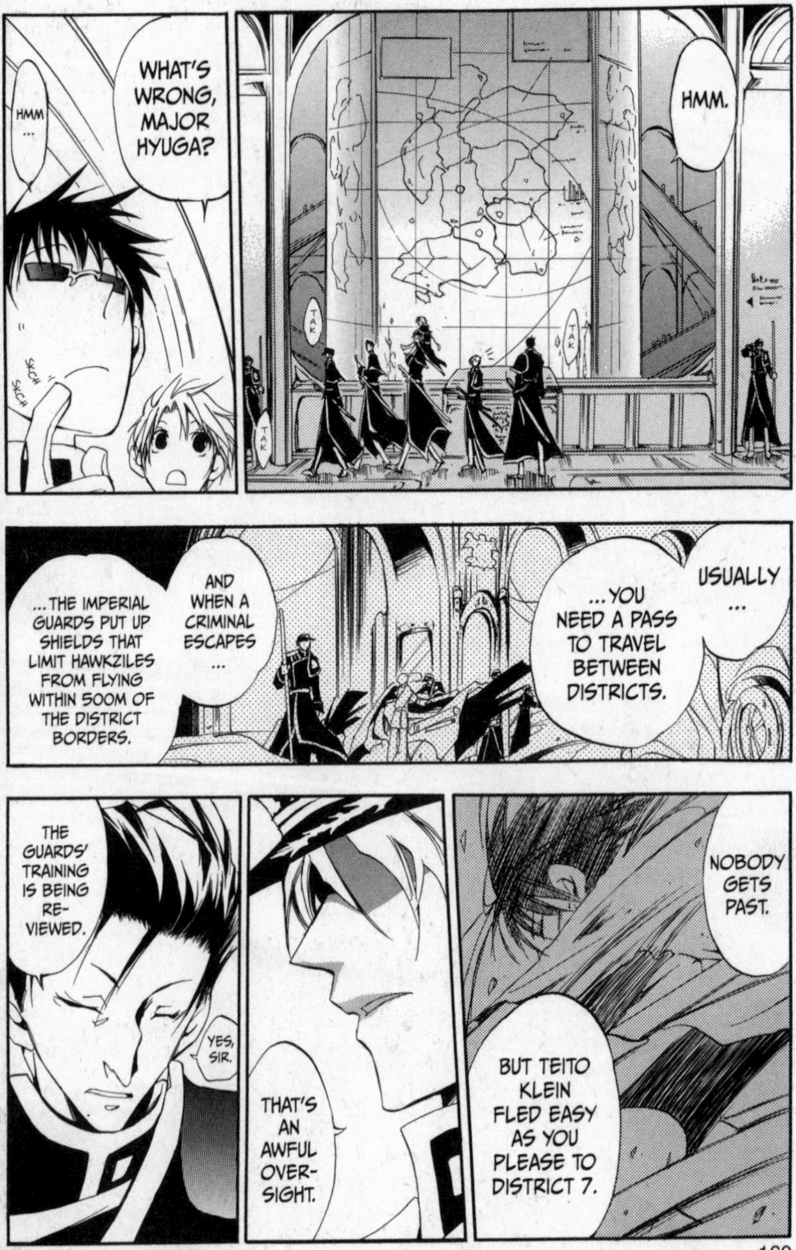
HMM.
TAK
TAK
TAK
WHAT'S WRONG, MAJOR HYUGA?
HMM ...
SKCH SKCH
USUALLY ...
... YOU NEED A PASS TO TRAVEL BETWEEN DISTRICTS.
AND WHEN A CRIMINAL ESCAPES ...
... THE IMPERIAL GUARDS PUT UP SHIELDS THAT LIMIT HAWKZILES FROM FLYING WITHIN 500M OF THE DISTRICT BORDERS.
NOBODY GETS PAST.
BUT TEITO KLEIN FLED EASY AS YOU PLEASE TO DISTRICT 7.
THAT'S AN AWFUL OVER-SIGHT.
THE GUARDS' TRAINING IS BEING RE-VIEWED.
YES, SIR.

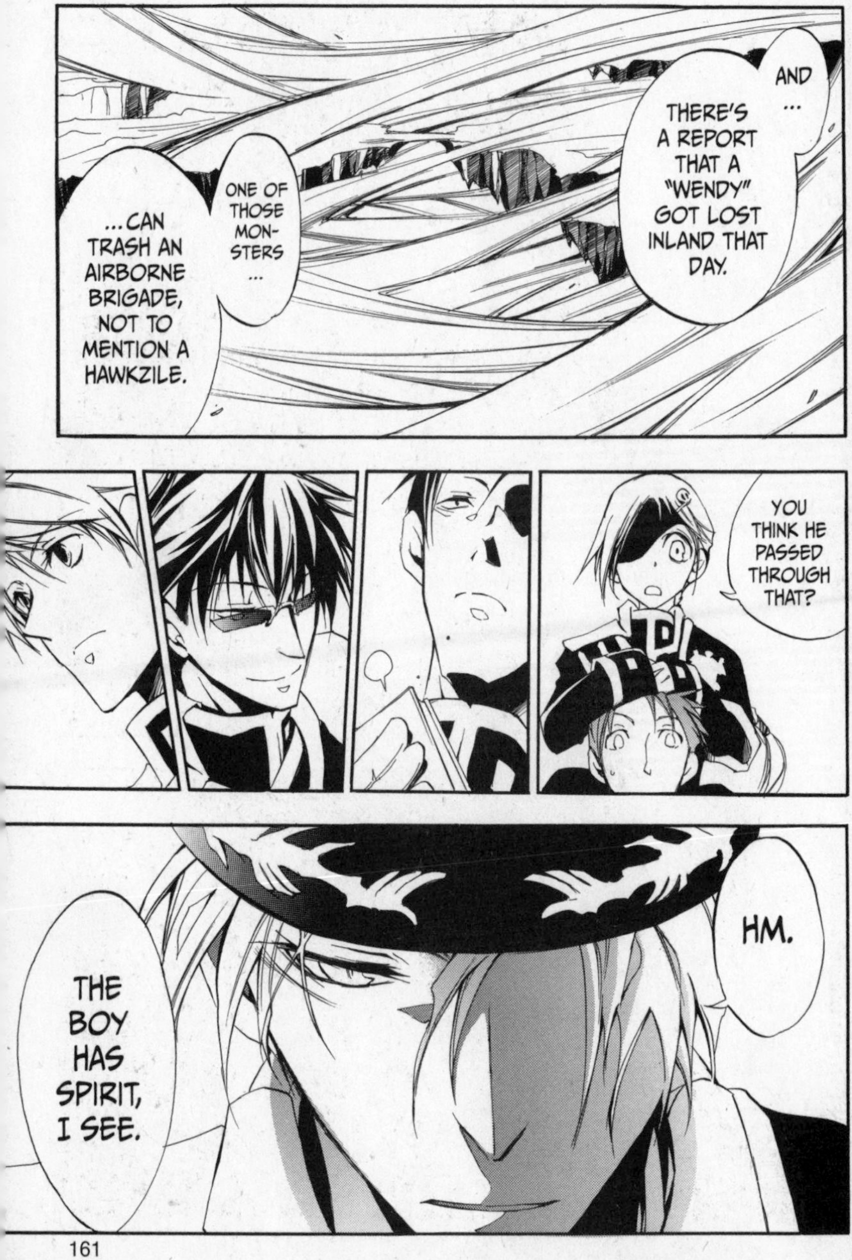
AND ...
THERE'S A REPORT THAT A "WENDY" GOT LOST INLAND THAT DAY.
ONE OF THOSE MONSTERS ...
...CAN TRASH AN AIRBORNE BRIGADE, NOT TO MENTION A HAWKZILE.
YOU THINK HE PASSED THROUGH THAT?
HM.
THE BOY HAS SPIRIT, I SEE.

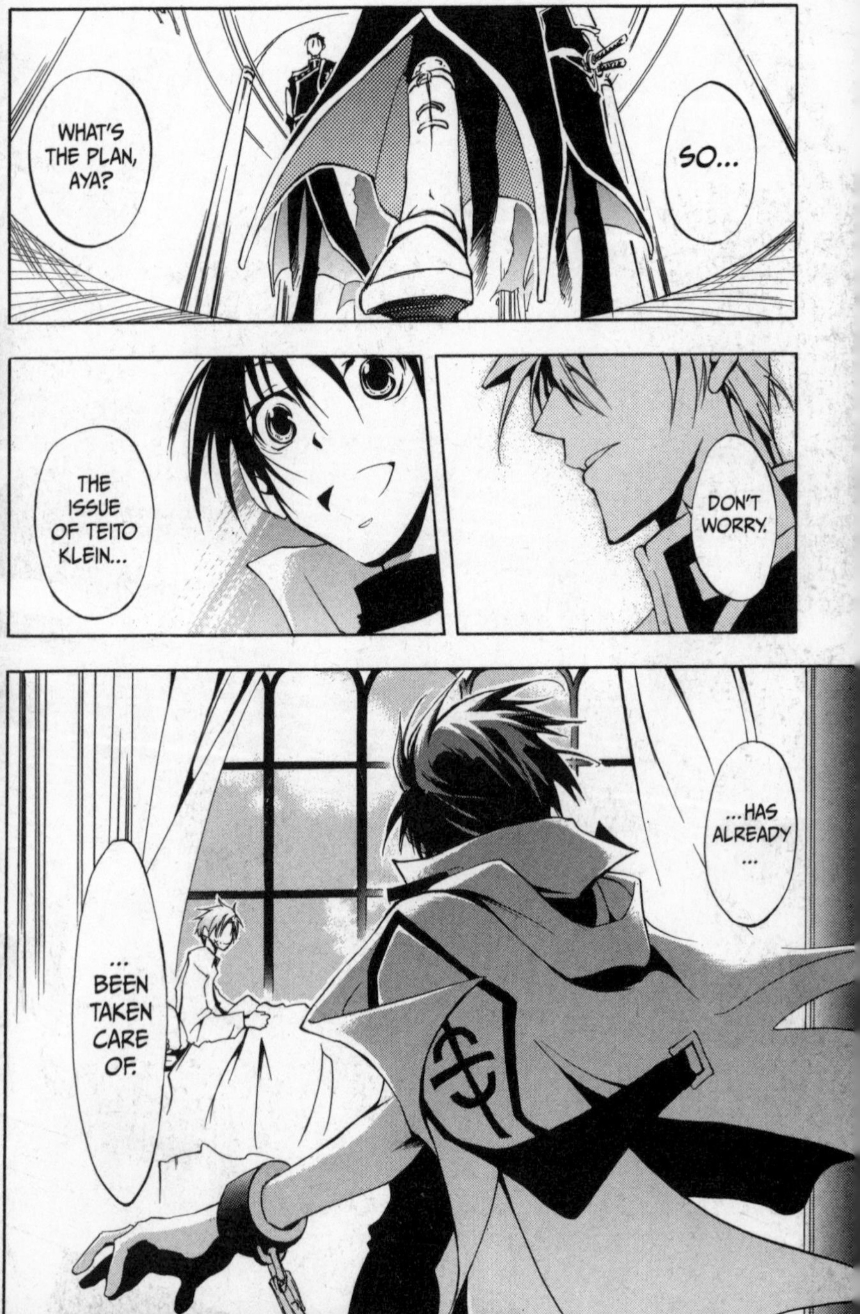
SO...
WHAT'S THE PLAN, AYA?
DON'T WORRY.
THE ISSUE OF TEITO KLEIN...
...HAS ALREADY...
...BEEN TAKEN CARE OF.

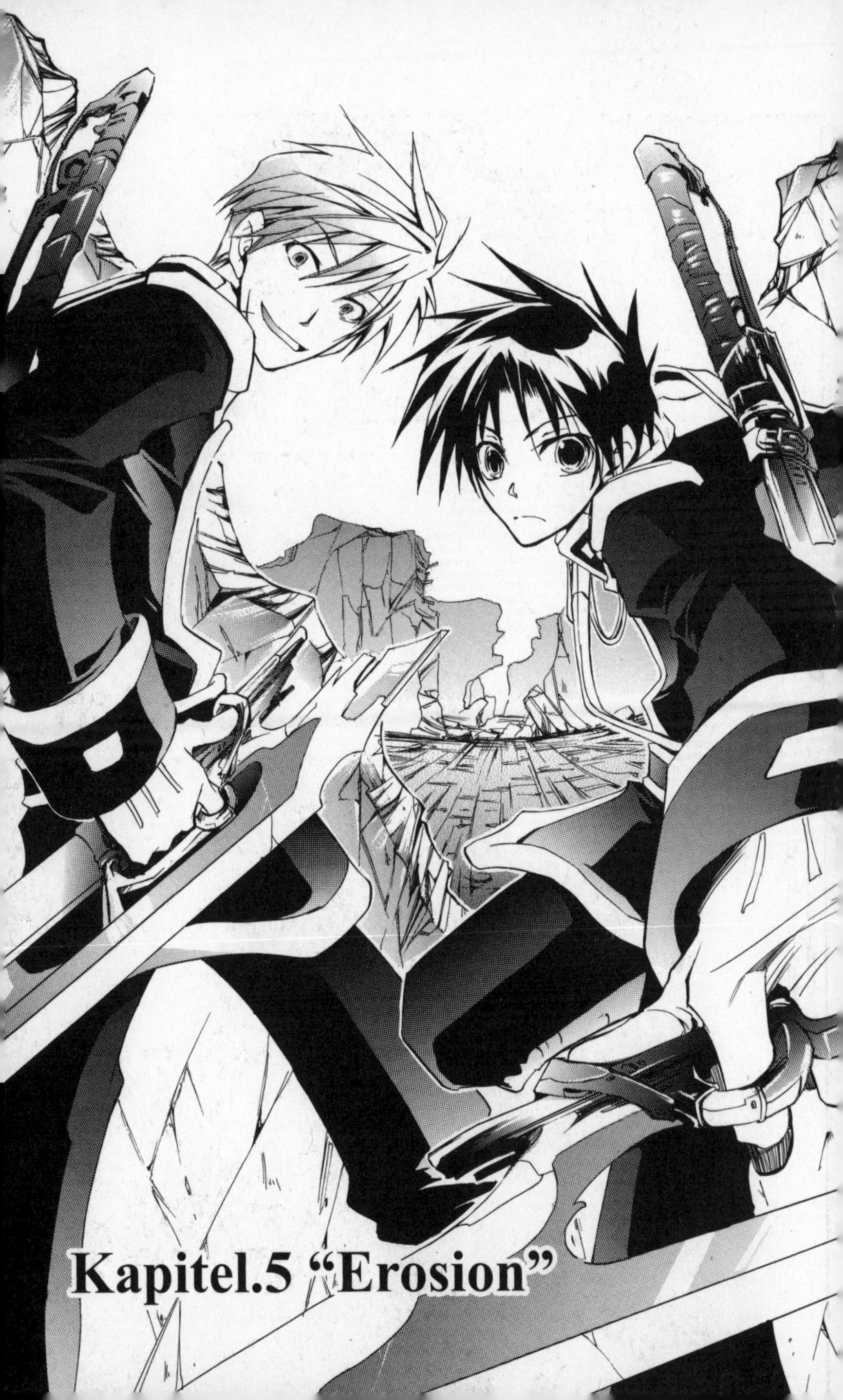

Kapitel.5 “Erosion”

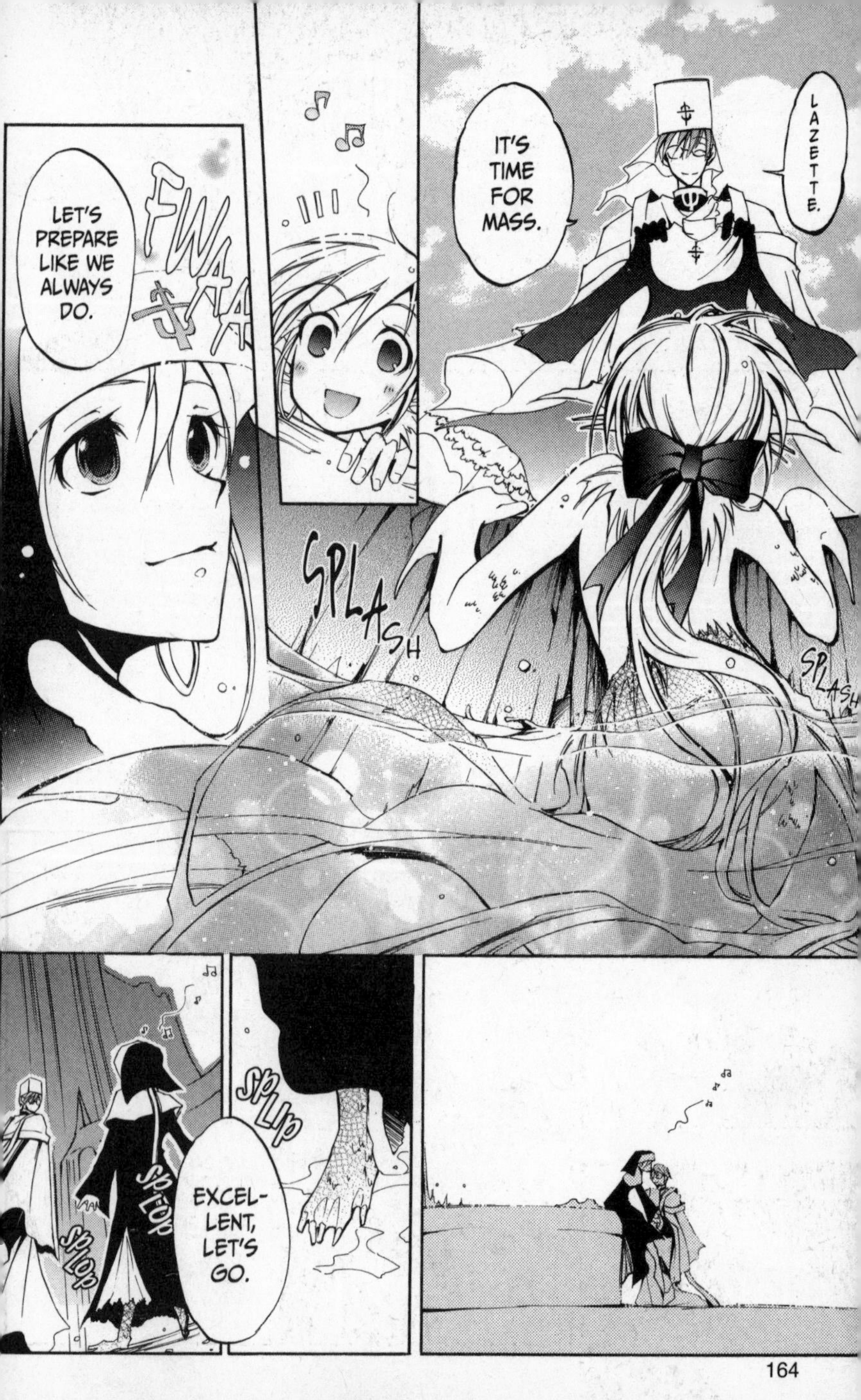
LAZETTE.
IT'S TIME FOR MASS.
SPLASH
SPLASH
FWAA
LET'S PREPARE LIKE WE ALWAYS DO.
SPLIP
EXCEL-LENT, LET'S GO.
SPLOP
SPLOP

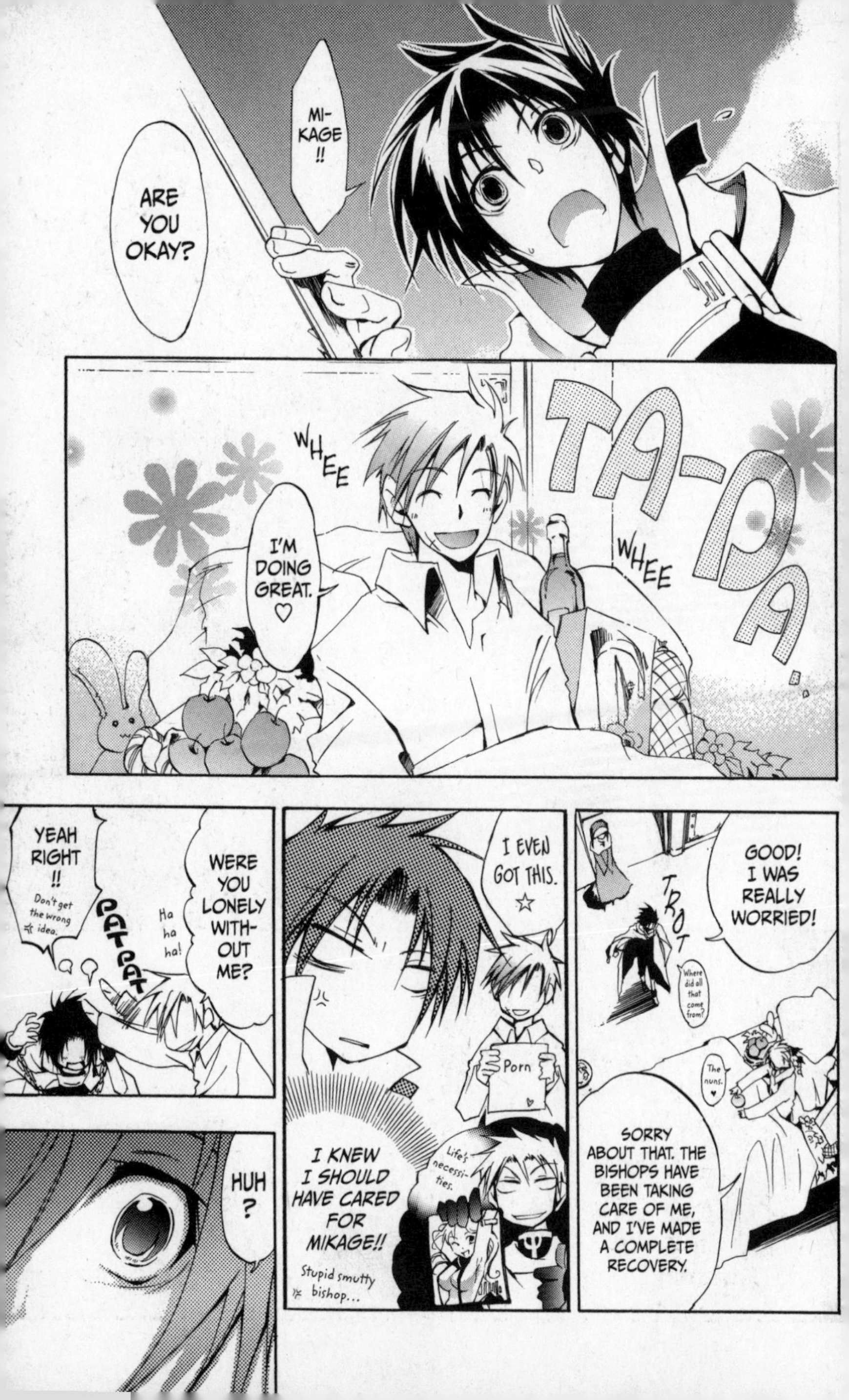
MI-KAGE!!
ARE YOU OKAY?
TA-DA.
WHEE
WHEE
I'M DOING GREAT. ♡
GOOD! I WAS REALLY WORRIED!
TROT
Where did all that come from?
The nuns. ♥
SORRY ABOUT THAT. THE BISHOPS HAVE BEEN TAKING CARE OF ME, AND I'VE MADE A COMPLETE RECOVERY.
I EVEN GOT THIS. ☆
Porn
Life's necessities.
I KNEW I SHOULD HAVE CARED FOR MIKAGE!!
Stupid smutty bishop...
WERE YOU LONELY WITHOUT ME?
Ha ha ha!
PAT PAT
YEAH RIGHT!!
Don't get the wrong idea.
HUH?

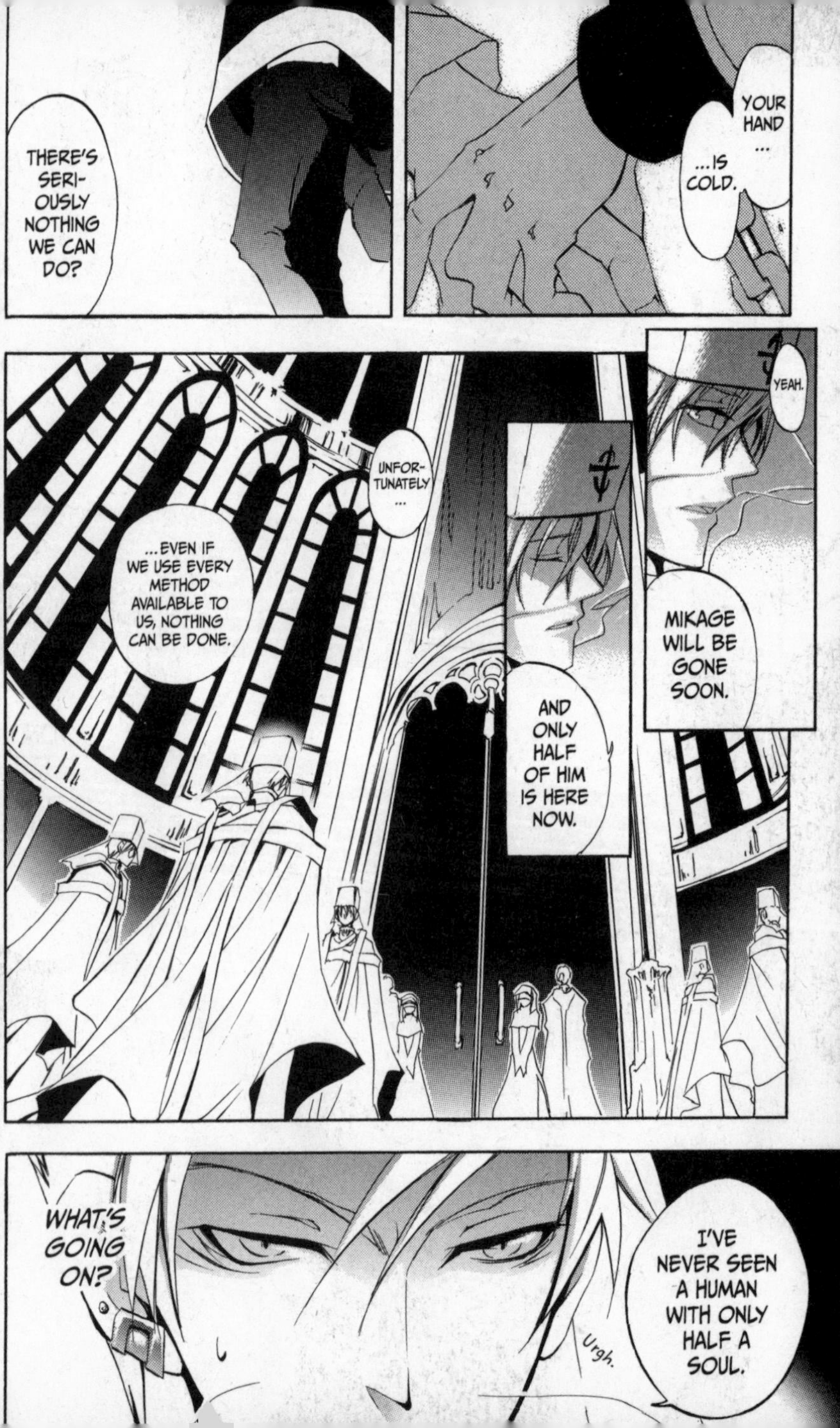
YOUR HAND ... ...IS COLD.
THERE'S SERIOUSLY NOTHING WE CAN DO?
YEAH.
MIKAGE WILL BE GONE SOON.
AND ONLY HALF OF HIM IS HERE NOW.
UNFORTUNATELY ...
...EVEN IF WE USE EVERY METHOD AVAILABLE TO US, NOTHING CAN BE DONE.
I'VE NEVER SEEN A HUMAN WITH ONLY HALF A SOUL.
Urgh.
WHAT'S GOING ON?

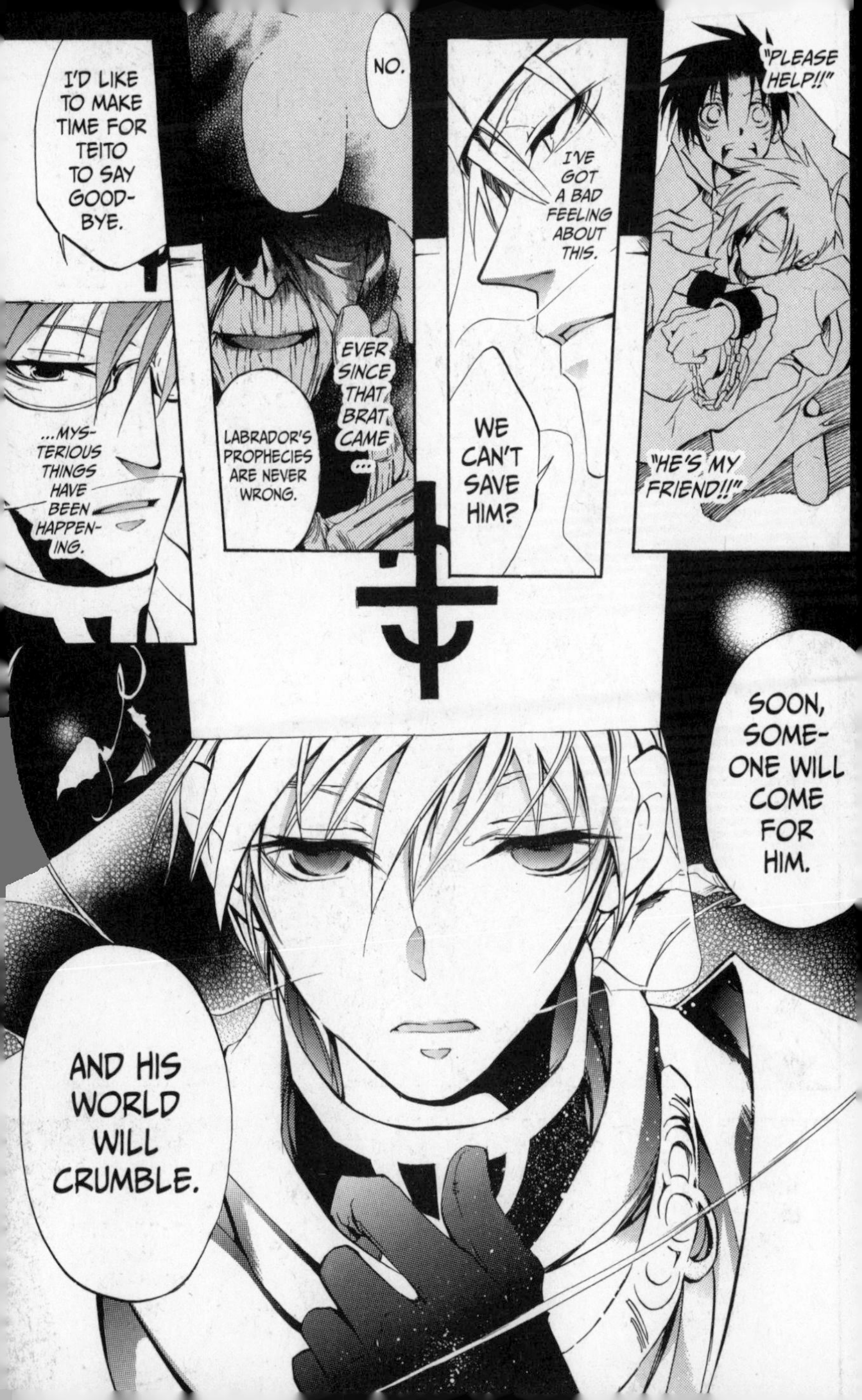
"PLEASE HELP!!"
"HE'S MY FRIEND!!"
I'VE GOT A BAD FEELING ABOUT THIS.
WE CAN'T SAVE HIM?
NO.
EVER SINCE THAT BRAT CAME...
LABRADOR'S PROPHECIES ARE NEVER WRONG.
I'D LIKE TO MAKE TIME FOR TEITO TO SAY GOOD-BYE.
...MYS-TERIOUS THINGS HAVE BEEN HAPPEN-ING.
SOON, SOME-ONE WILL COME FOR HIM.
AND HIS WORLD WILL CRUMBLE.

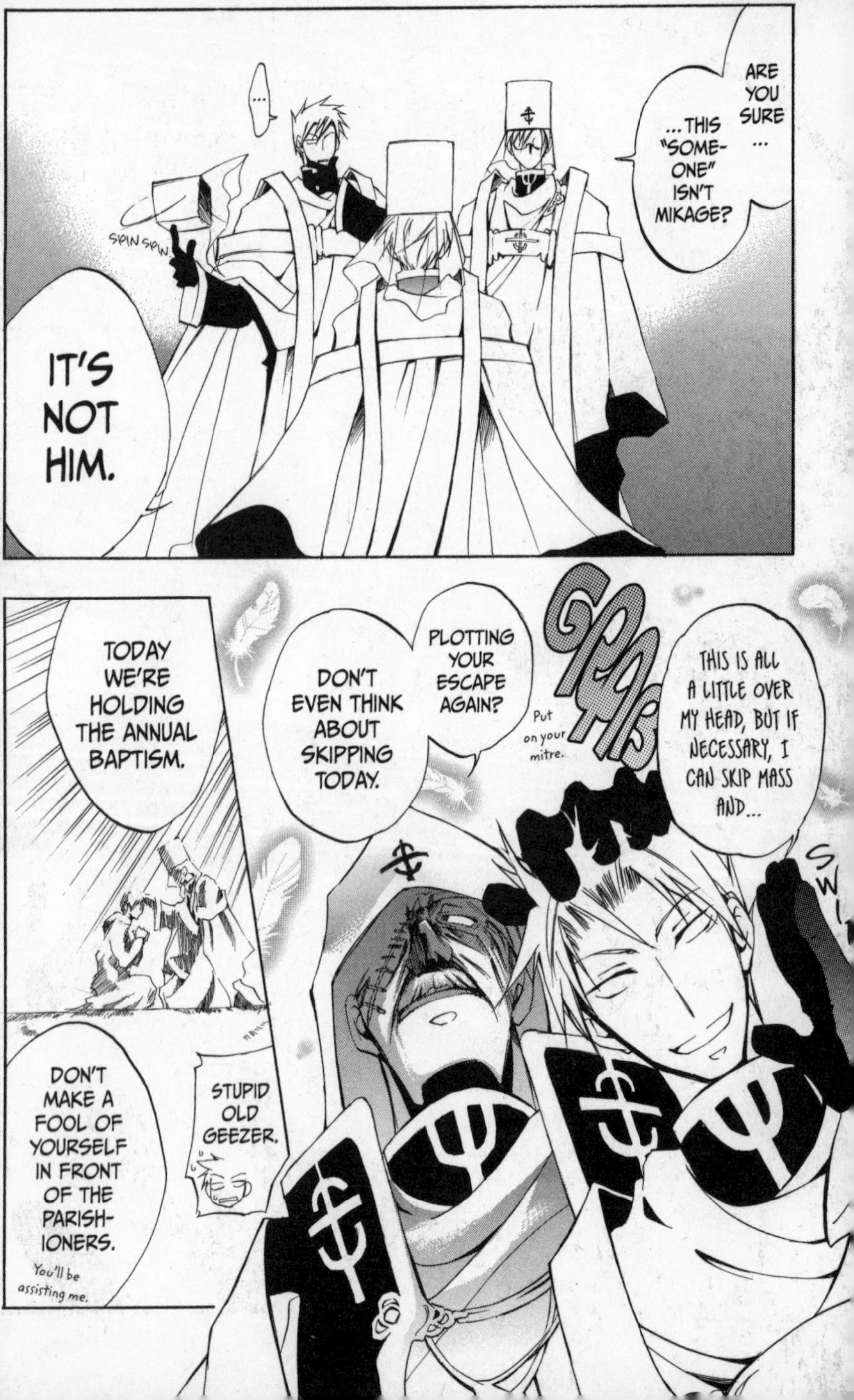
ARE YOU SURE ...
...THIS "SOME-ONE" ISN'T MIKAGE?
...
SPIN SPIN
IT'S NOT HIM.
THIS IS ALL A LITTLE OVER MY HEAD, BUT IF NECESSARY, I CAN SKIP MASS AND...
GRAB
SWI
PLOTTING YOUR ESCAPE AGAIN?
Put on your mitre.
DON'T EVEN THINK ABOUT SKIPPING TODAY.
TODAY WE'RE HOLDING THE ANNUAL BAPTISM.
STUPID OLD GEEZER.
DON'T MAKE A FOOL OF YOURSELF IN FRONT OF THE PARISH-IONERS.
You'll be assisting me.

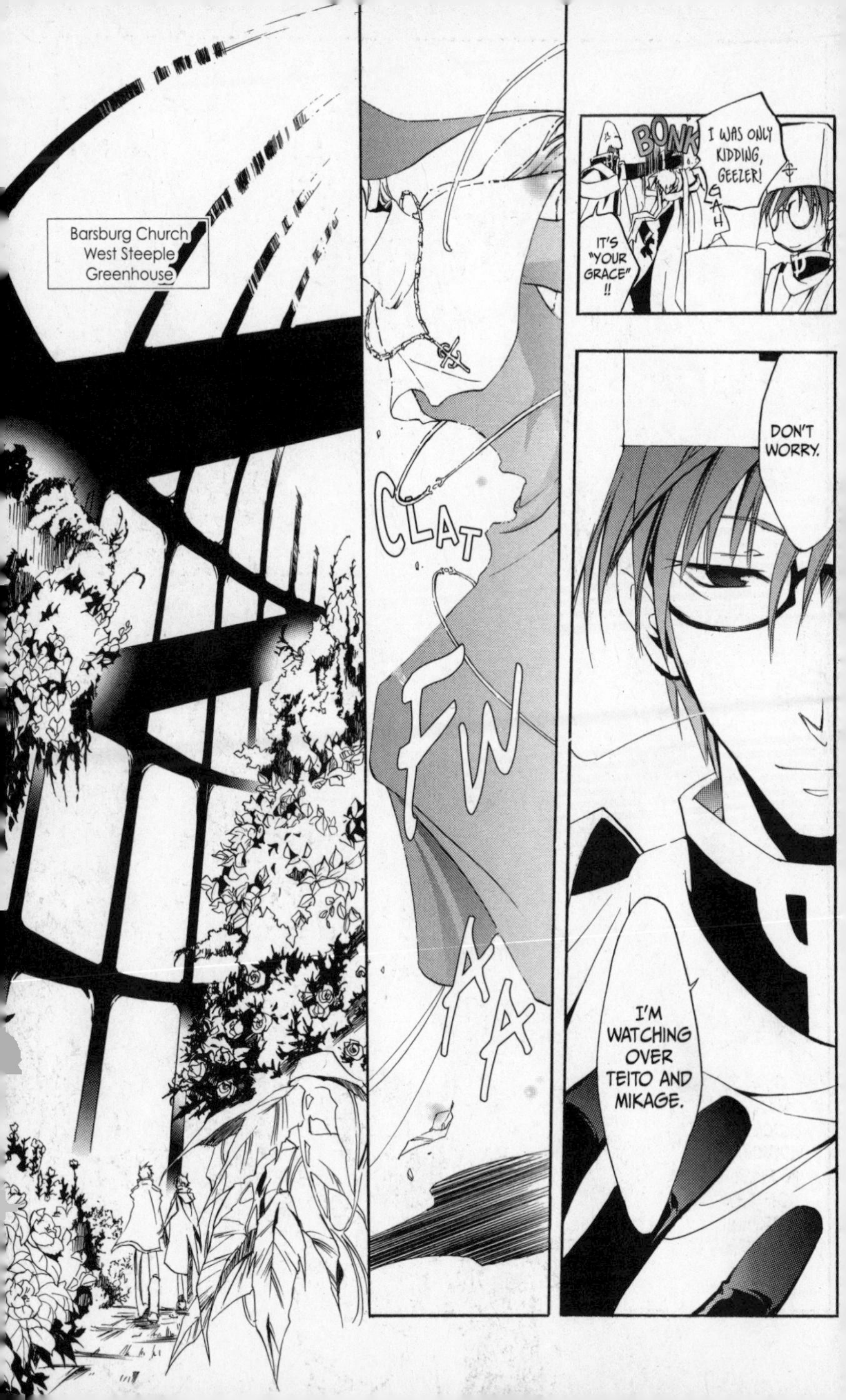
I WAS ONLY KIDDING, GEEZER!
BONK
GAH
IT'S "YOUR GRACE" !!
DON'T WORRY.
I'M WATCHING OVER TEITO AND MIKAGE.
CLAT
FWAA
Barsburg Church West Steeple Greenhouse

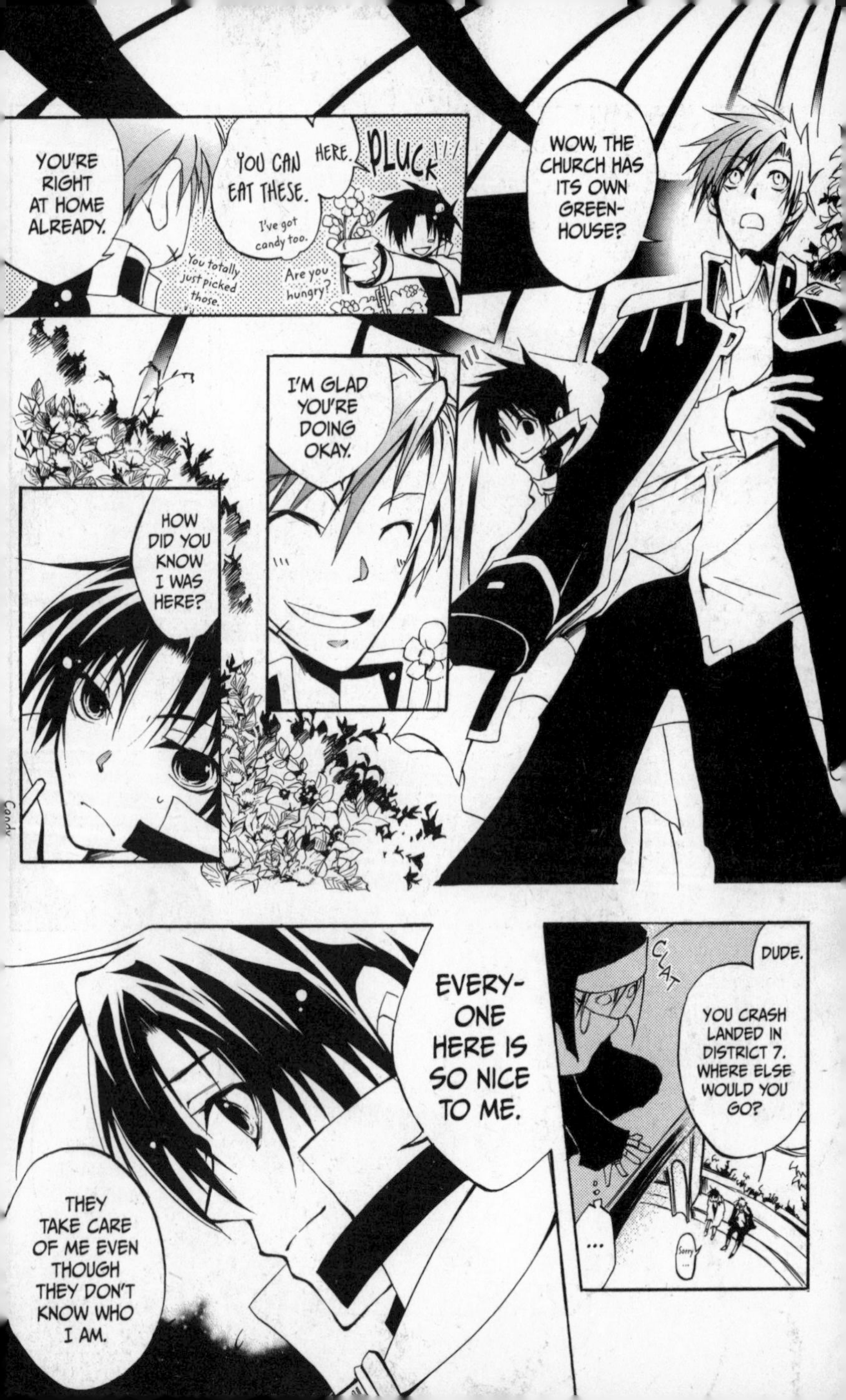
WOW, THE CHURCH HAS ITS OWN GREEN-HOUSE?
PLUCK
HERE.
YOU CAN EAT THESE.
I've got candy too.
Are you hungry?
YOU'RE RIGHT AT HOME ALREADY.
You totally just picked those.
I'M GLAD YOU'RE DOING OKAY.
HOW DID YOU KNOW I WAS HERE?
CLAT
DUDE.
YOU CRASH LANDED IN DISTRICT 7. WHERE ELSE WOULD YOU GO?
...
Sorry...
EVERY-ONE HERE IS SO NICE TO ME.
THEY TAKE CARE OF ME EVEN THOUGH THEY DON'T KNOW WHO I AM.

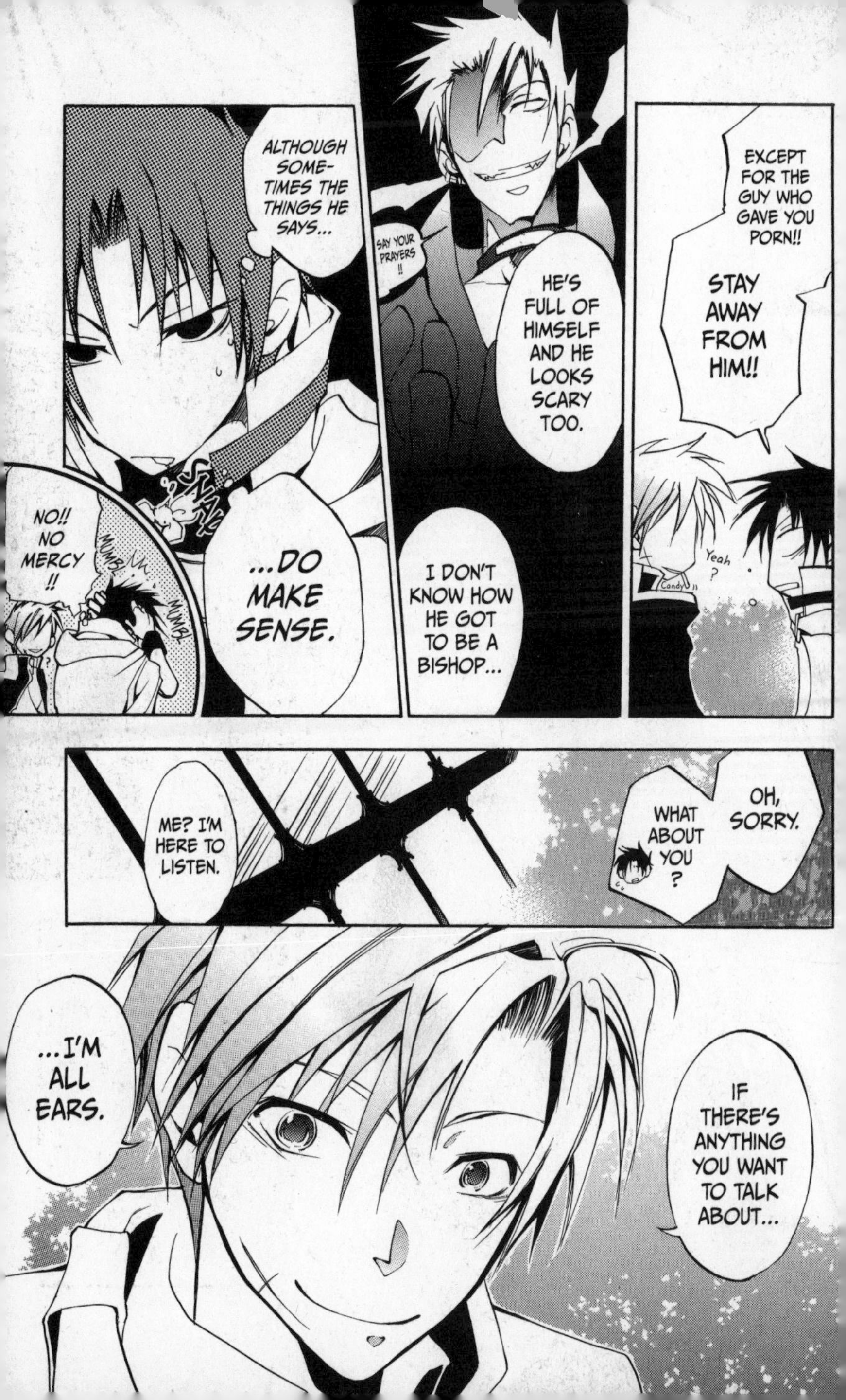
EXCEPT FOR THE GUY WHO GAVE YOU PORN!!
STAY AWAY FROM HIM!!
Yeah?
Candy
SAY YOUR PRAYERS!!
HE'S FULL OF HIMSELF AND HE LOOKS SCARY TOO.
I DON'T KNOW HOW HE GOT TO BE A BISHOP...
ALTHOUGH SOME-TIMES THE THINGS HE SAYS...
...DO MAKE SENSE.
MUMBL MUMBL
NO!! NO MERCY!!
OH, SORRY.
WHAT ABOUT YOU?
ME? I'M HERE TO LISTEN.
IF THERE'S ANYTHING YOU WANT TO TALK ABOUT...
...I'M ALL EARS.

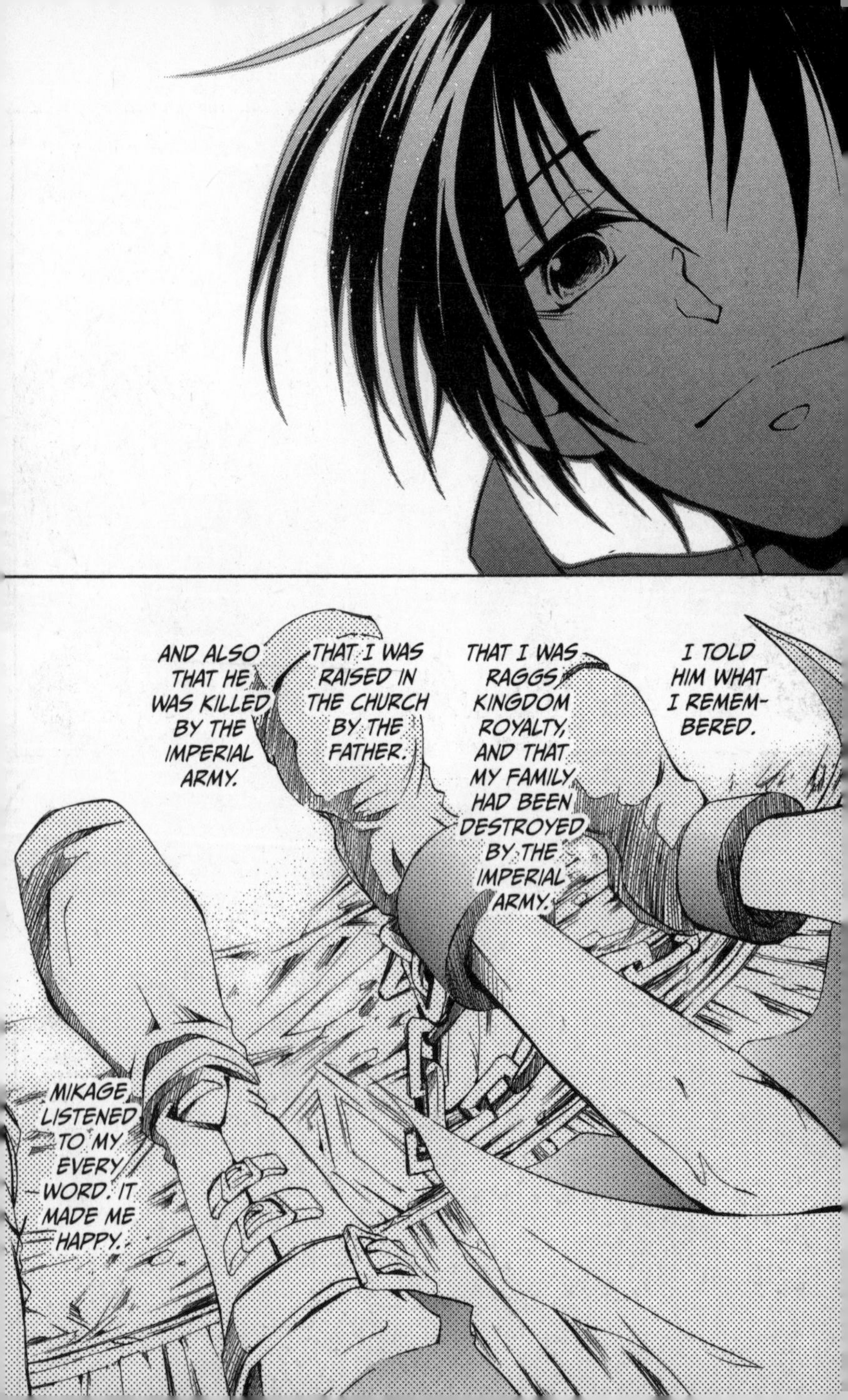
I TOLD HIM WHAT I REMEMBERED.
THAT I WAS RAGGS KINGDOM ROYALTY, AND THAT MY FAMILY HAD BEEN DESTROYED BY THE IMPERIAL ARMY.
THAT I WAS RAISED IN THE CHURCH BY THE FATHER.
AND ALSO THAT HE WAS KILLED BY THE IMPERIAL ARMY.
MIKAGE LISTENED TO MY EVERY WORD. IT MADE ME HAPPY.

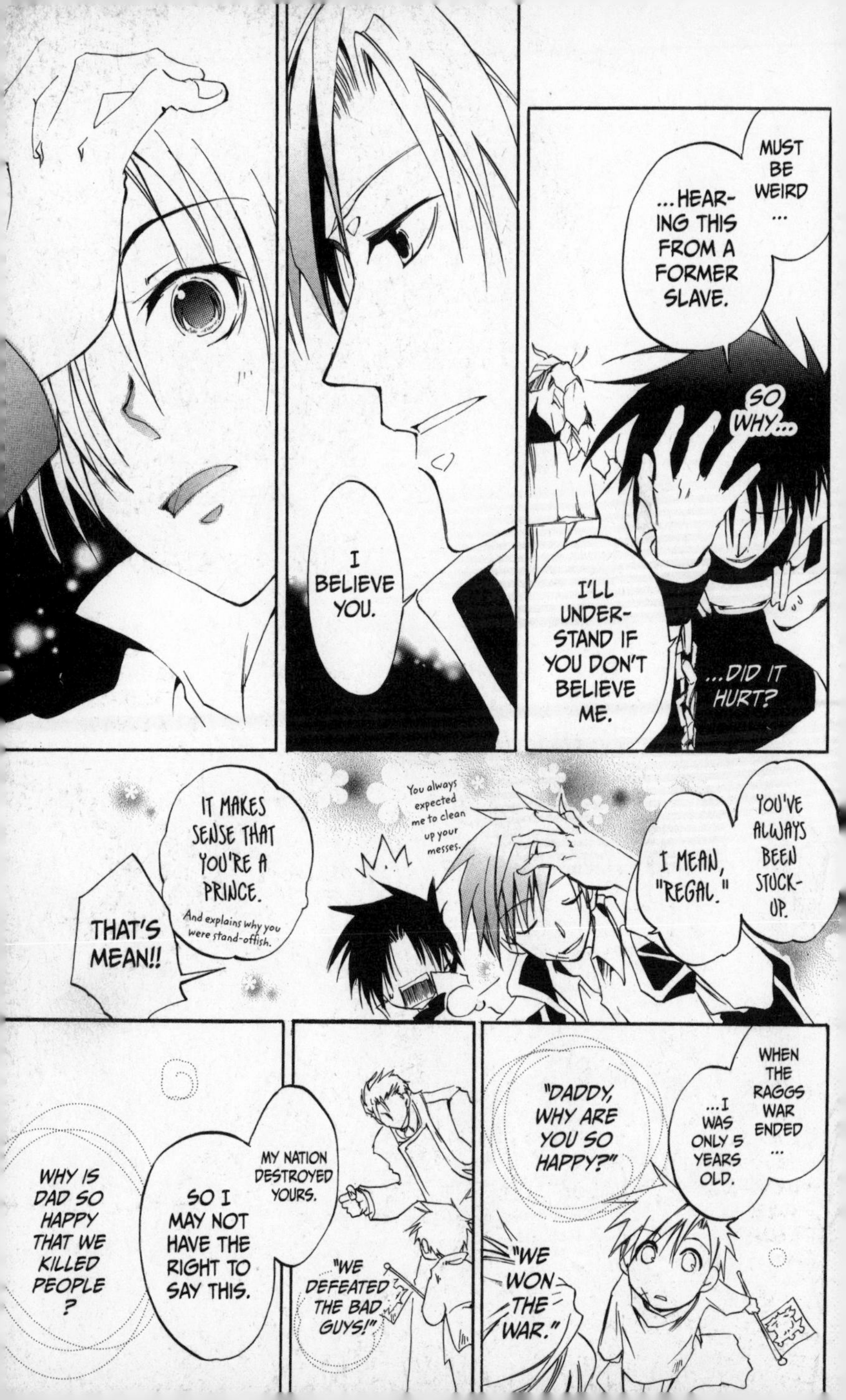
MUST BE WEIRD...
...HEARING THIS FROM A FORMER SLAVE.
SO WHY...
I'LL UNDERSTAND IF YOU DON'T BELIEVE ME.
...DID IT HURT?
I BELIEVE YOU.
YOU'VE ALWAYS BEEN STUCK-UP.
I MEAN, "REGAL."
You always expected me to clean up your messes.
IT MAKES SENSE THAT YOU'RE A PRINCE.
And explains why you were stand-offish.
THAT'S MEAN!!
WHEN THE RAGGS WAR ENDED...
...I WAS ONLY 5 YEARS OLD.
"DADDY, WHY ARE YOU SO HAPPY?"
"WE WON THE WAR."
MY NATION DESTROYED YOURS.
"WE DEFEATED THE BAD GUYS!"
SO I MAY NOT HAVE THE RIGHT TO SAY THIS.
WHY IS DAD SO HAPPY THAT WE KILLED PEOPLE?

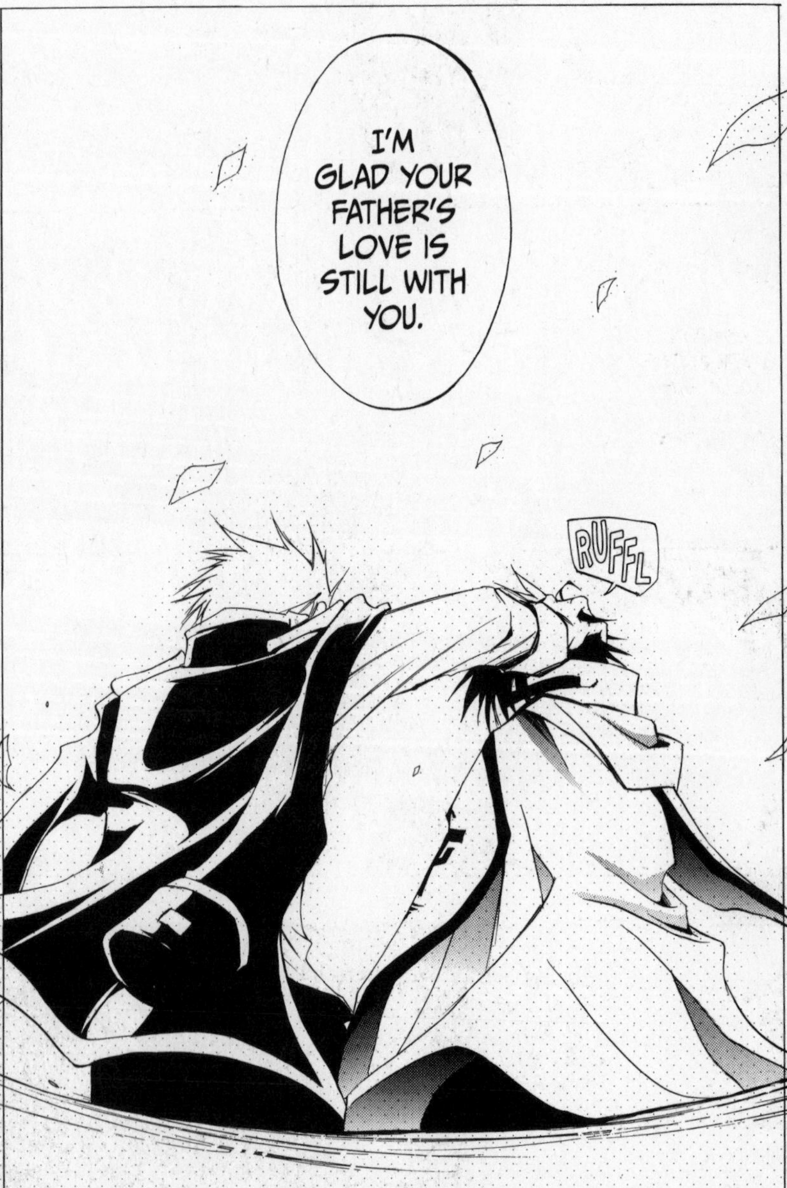
I'M GLAD YOUR FATHER'S LOVE IS STILL WITH YOU.
RUFFL

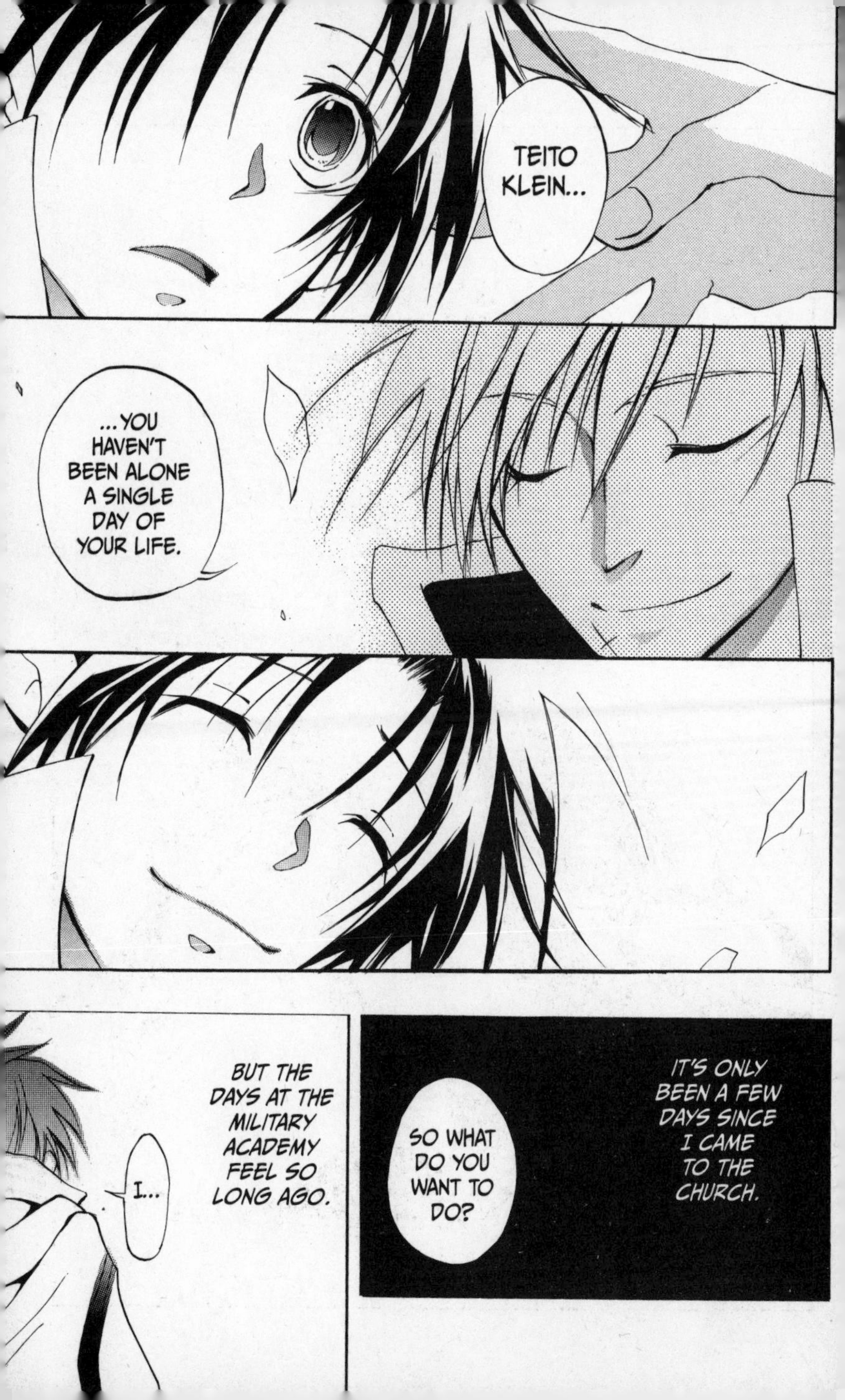
TEITO KLEIN...
...YOU HAVEN'T BEEN ALONE A SINGLE DAY OF YOUR LIFE.
IT'S ONLY BEEN A FEW DAYS SINCE I CAME TO THE CHURCH.
SO WHAT DO YOU WANT TO DO?
BUT THE DAYS AT THE MILITARY ACADEMY FEEL SO LONG AGO.
I...

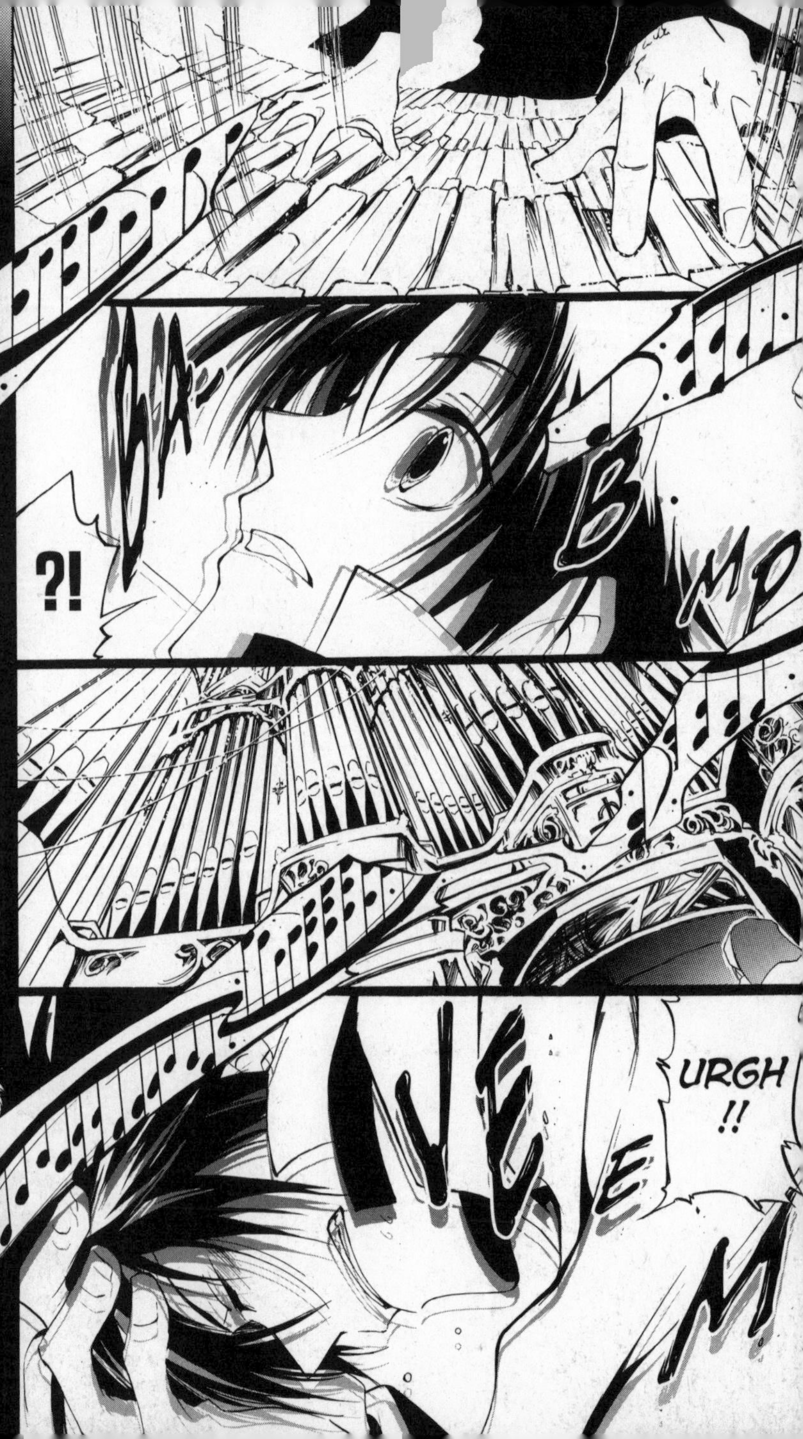
?!
URGH !!

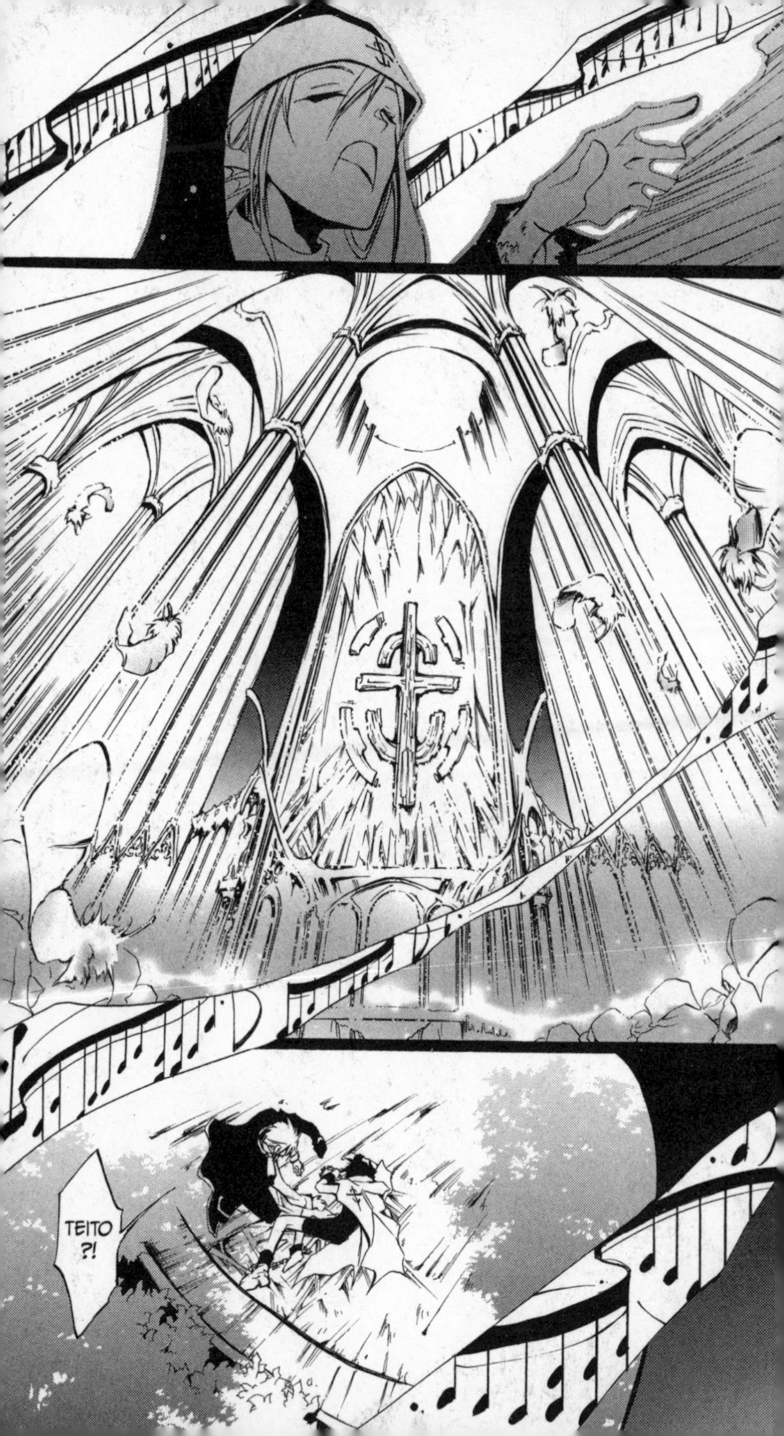
TEITO ?!

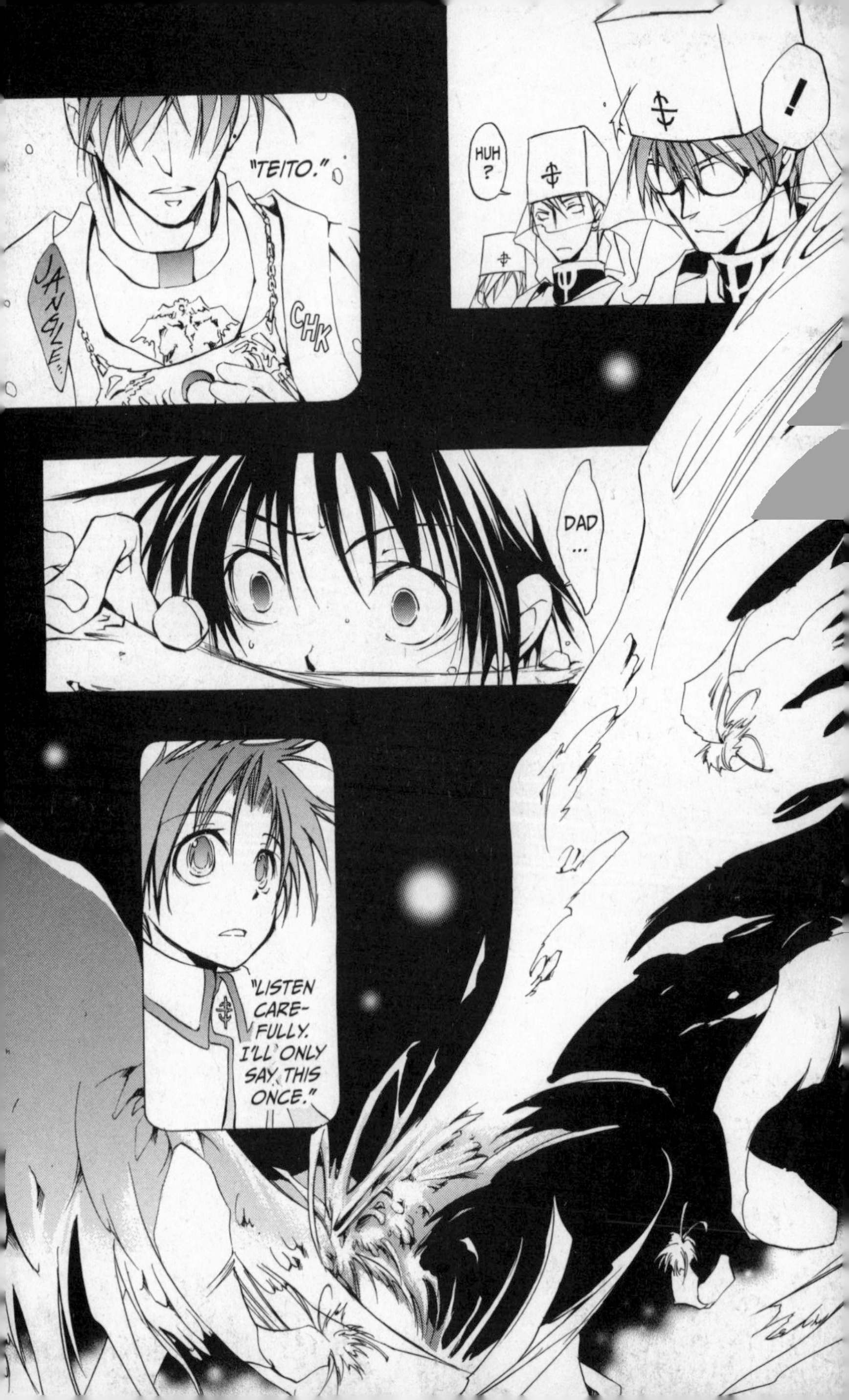
!
HUH?
"TEITO."
JANGLE...
CHK
DAD...
"LISTEN CARE-FULLY. I'LL ONLY SAY THIS ONCE."

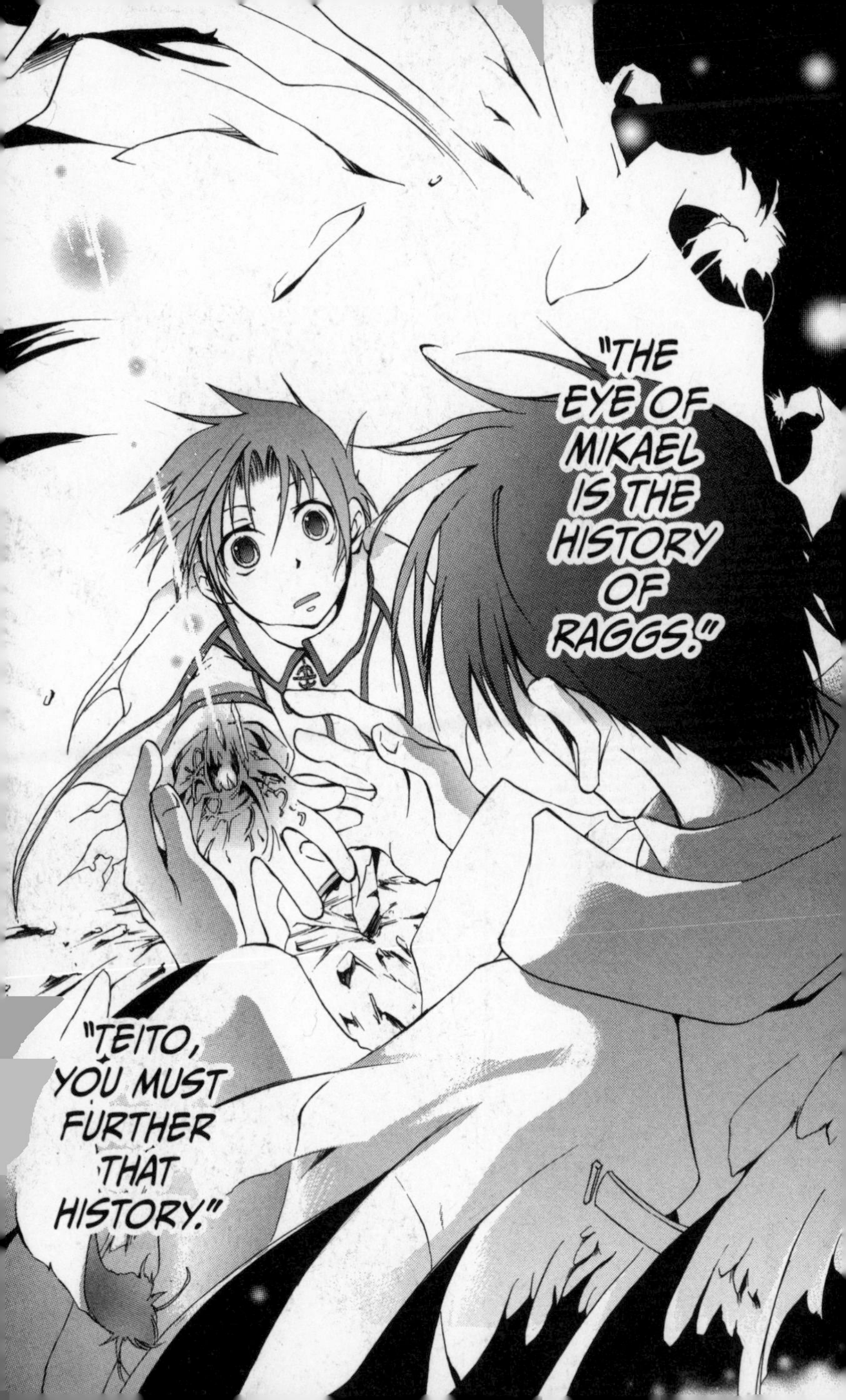
"THE EYE OF MIKAEL IS THE HISTORY OF RAGGS."
"TEITO, YOU MUST FURTHER THAT HISTORY."

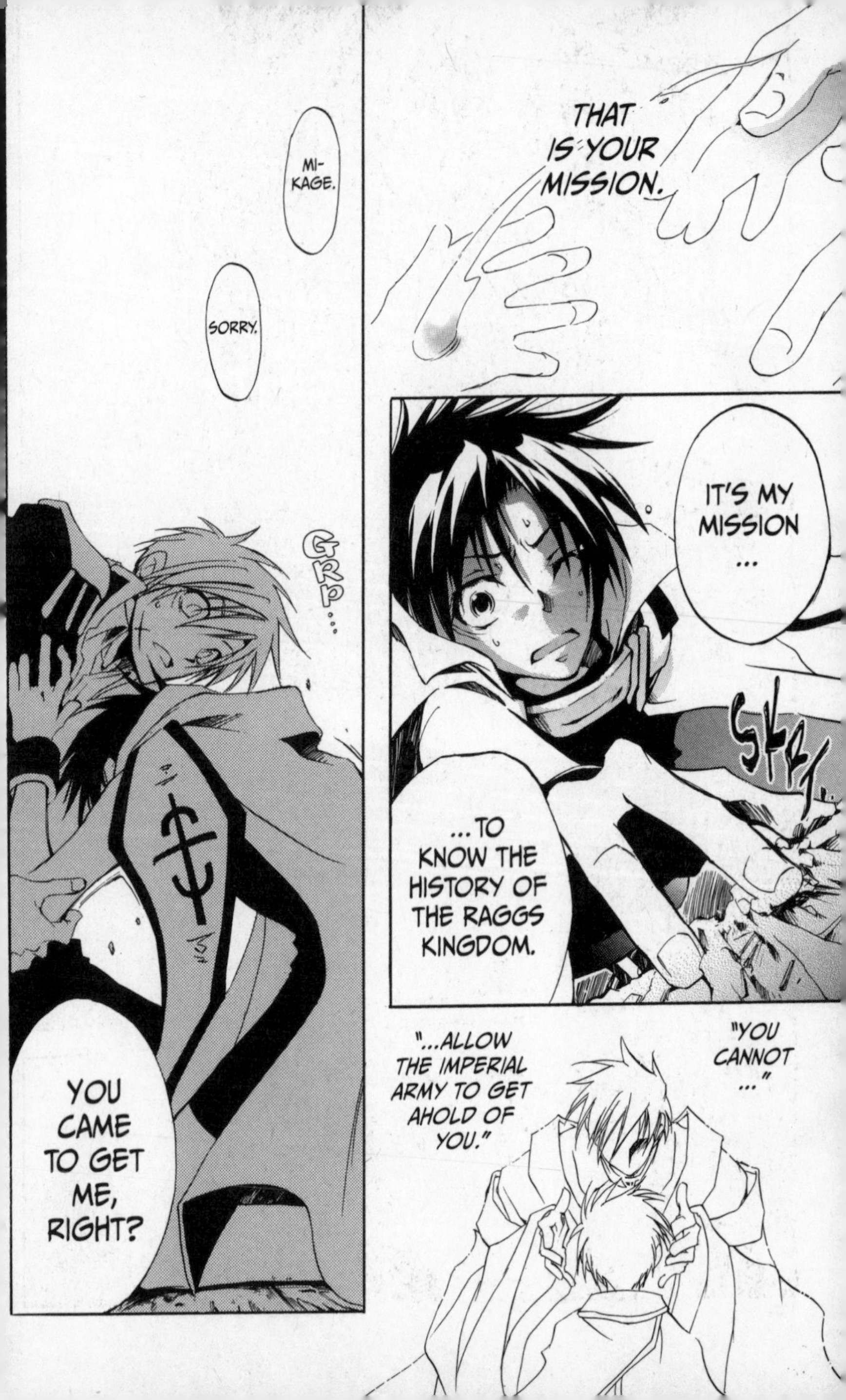

THAT IS YOUR MISSION.
IT'S MY MISSION ...
...TO KNOW THE HISTORY OF THE RAGGS KINGDOM.
"YOU CANNOT ..."
"...ALLOW THE IMPERIAL ARMY TO GET AHOLD OF YOU."
MI-KAGE.
SORRY.
GRP...
YOU CAME TO GET ME, RIGHT?

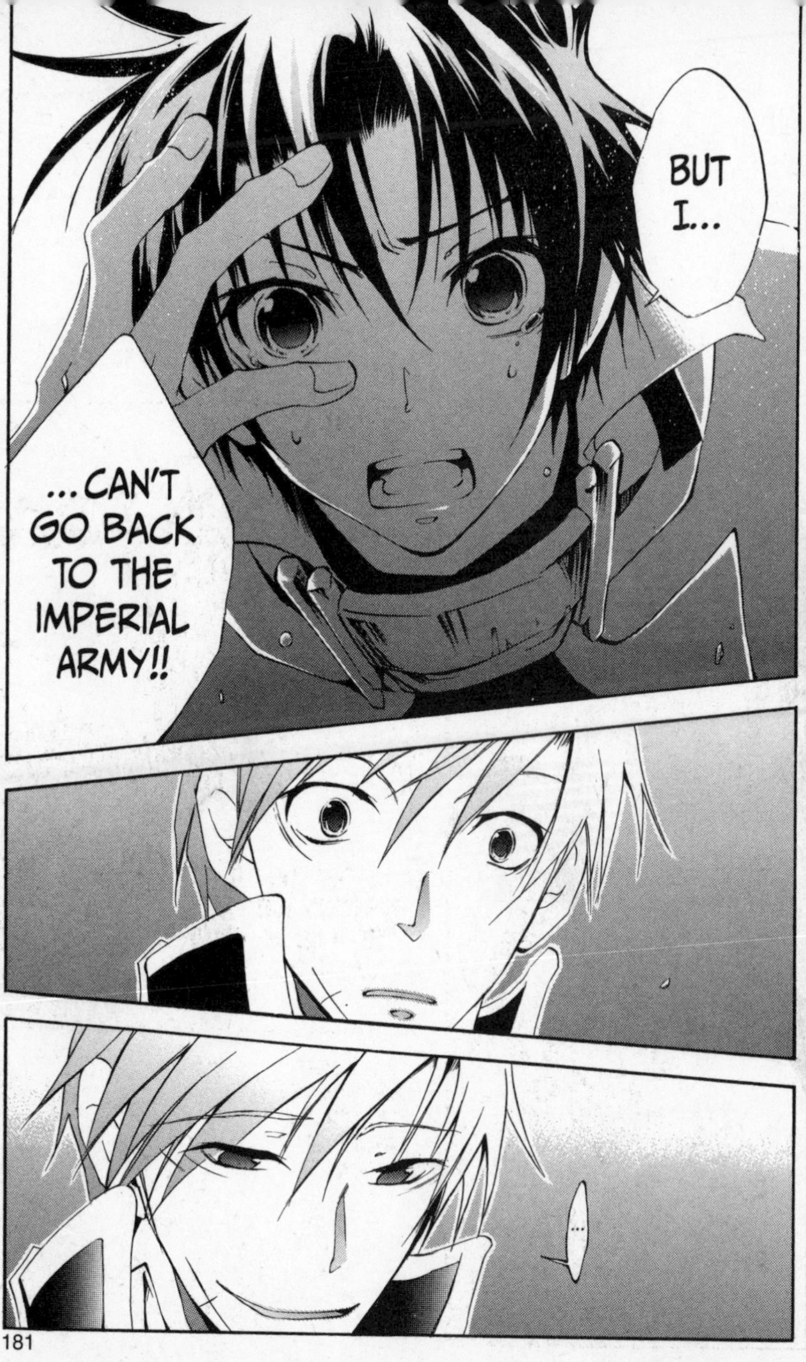
BUT I...
...CAN'T GO BACK TO THE IMPERIAL ARMY!!
...

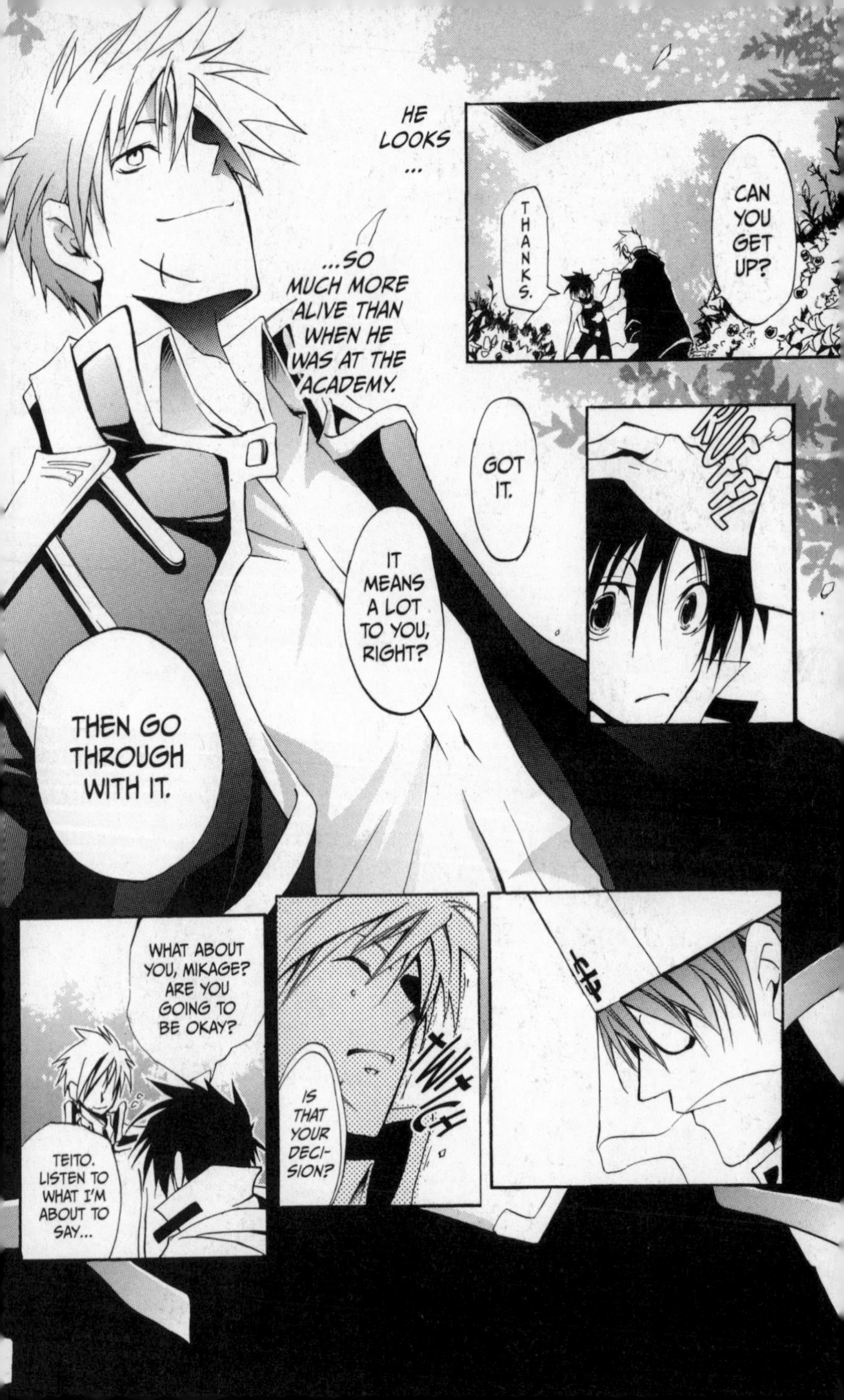
CAN YOU GET UP?
THANKS.
HE LOOKS...
...SO MUCH MORE ALIVE THAN WHEN HE WAS AT THE ACADEMY.
GOT IT.
IT MEANS A LOT TO YOU, RIGHT?
THEN GO THROUGH WITH IT.
TWITCH
IS THAT YOUR DECISION?
WHAT ABOUT YOU, MIKAGE? ARE YOU GOING TO BE OKAY?
TEITO. LISTEN TO WHAT I'M ABOUT TO SAY...

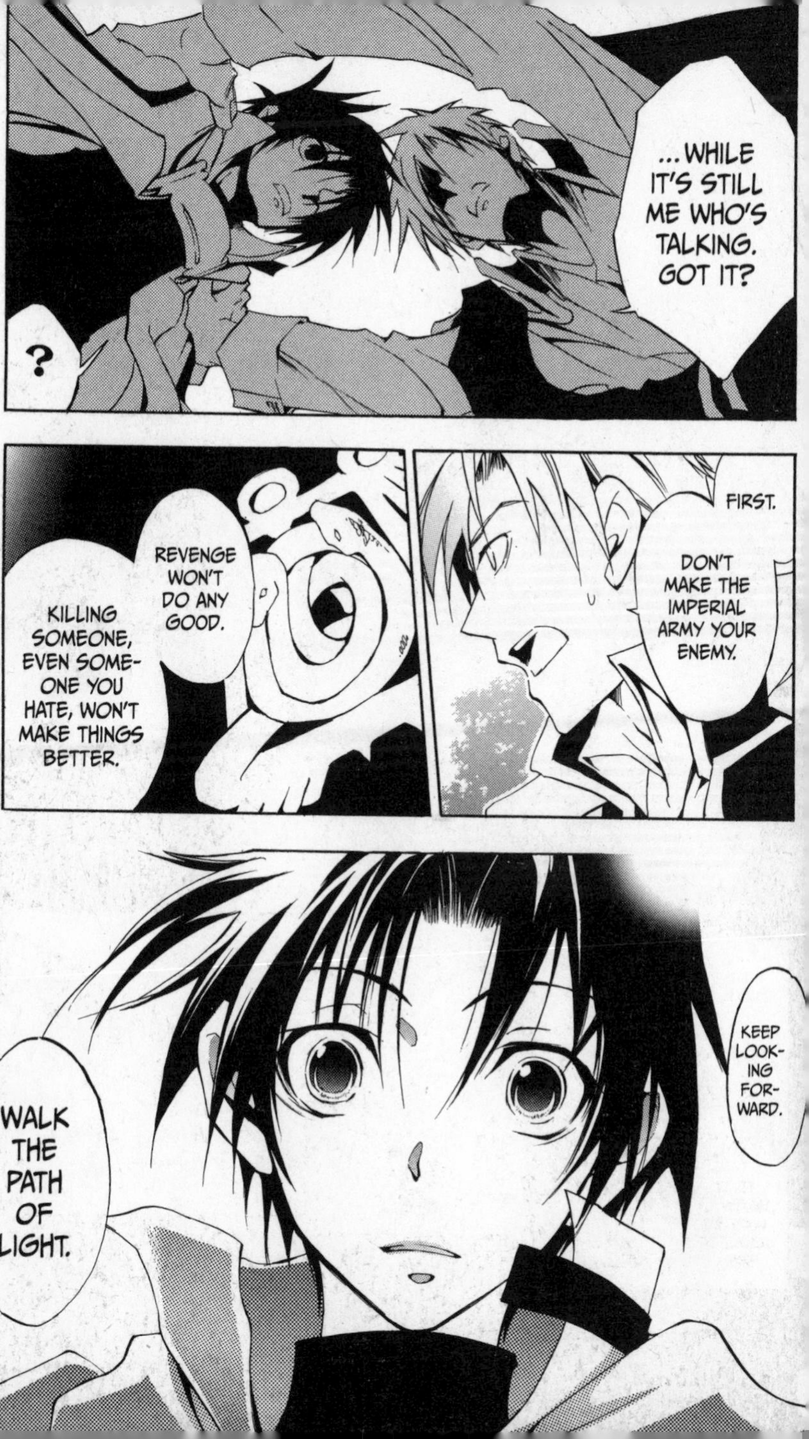
...WHILE IT'S STILL ME WHO'S TALKING. GOT IT?
?
FIRST.
DON'T MAKE THE IMPERIAL ARMY YOUR ENEMY.
REVENGE WON'T DO ANY GOOD.
KILLING SOMEONE, EVEN SOME-ONE YOU HATE, WON'T MAKE THINGS BETTER.
KEEP LOOK-ING FOR-WARD.
WALK THE PATH OF LIGHT.

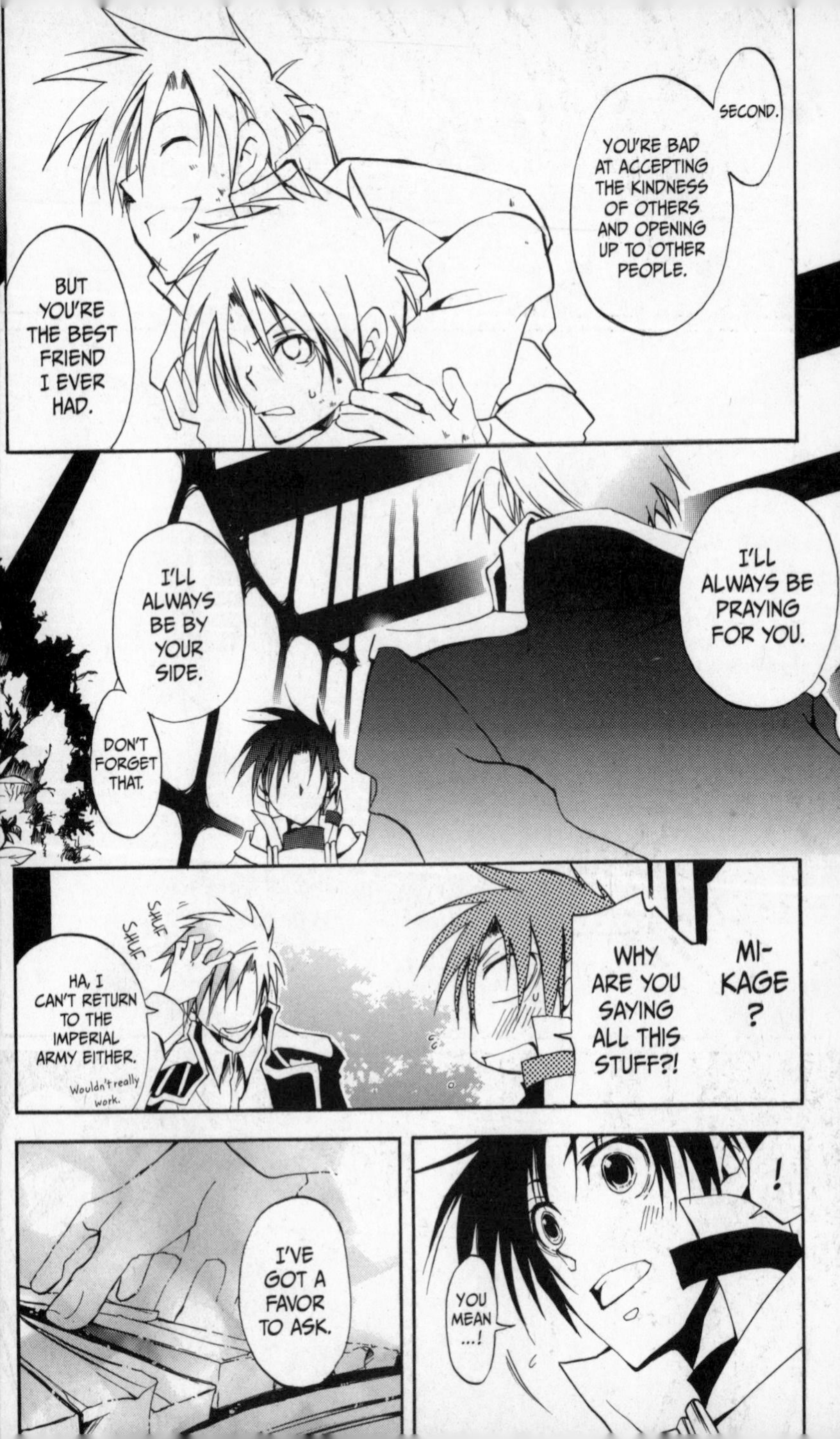
SECOND.
YOU'RE BAD AT ACCEPTING THE KINDNESS OF OTHERS AND OPENING UP TO OTHER PEOPLE.
BUT YOU'RE THE BEST FRIEND I EVER HAD.
I'LL ALWAYS BE PRAYING FOR YOU.
I'LL ALWAYS BE BY YOUR SIDE.
DON'T FORGET THAT.
MI-KAGE?
WHY ARE YOU SAYING ALL THIS STUFF?!
SHUF SHUF
HA, I CAN'T RETURN TO THE IMPERIAL ARMY EITHER.
Wouldn't really work.
!
YOU MEAN...!
I'VE GOT A FAVOR TO ASK.

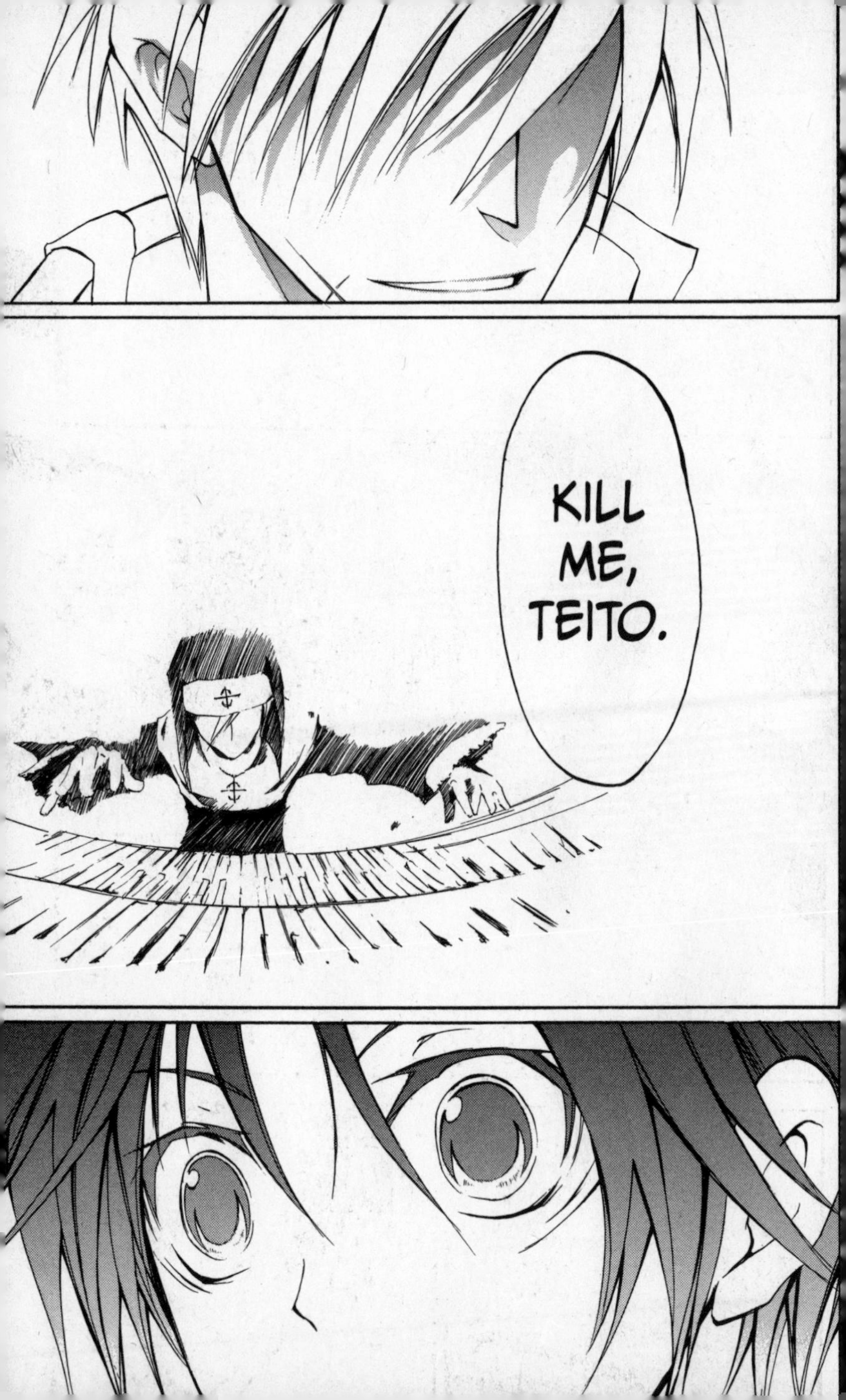
KILL ME, TEITO.

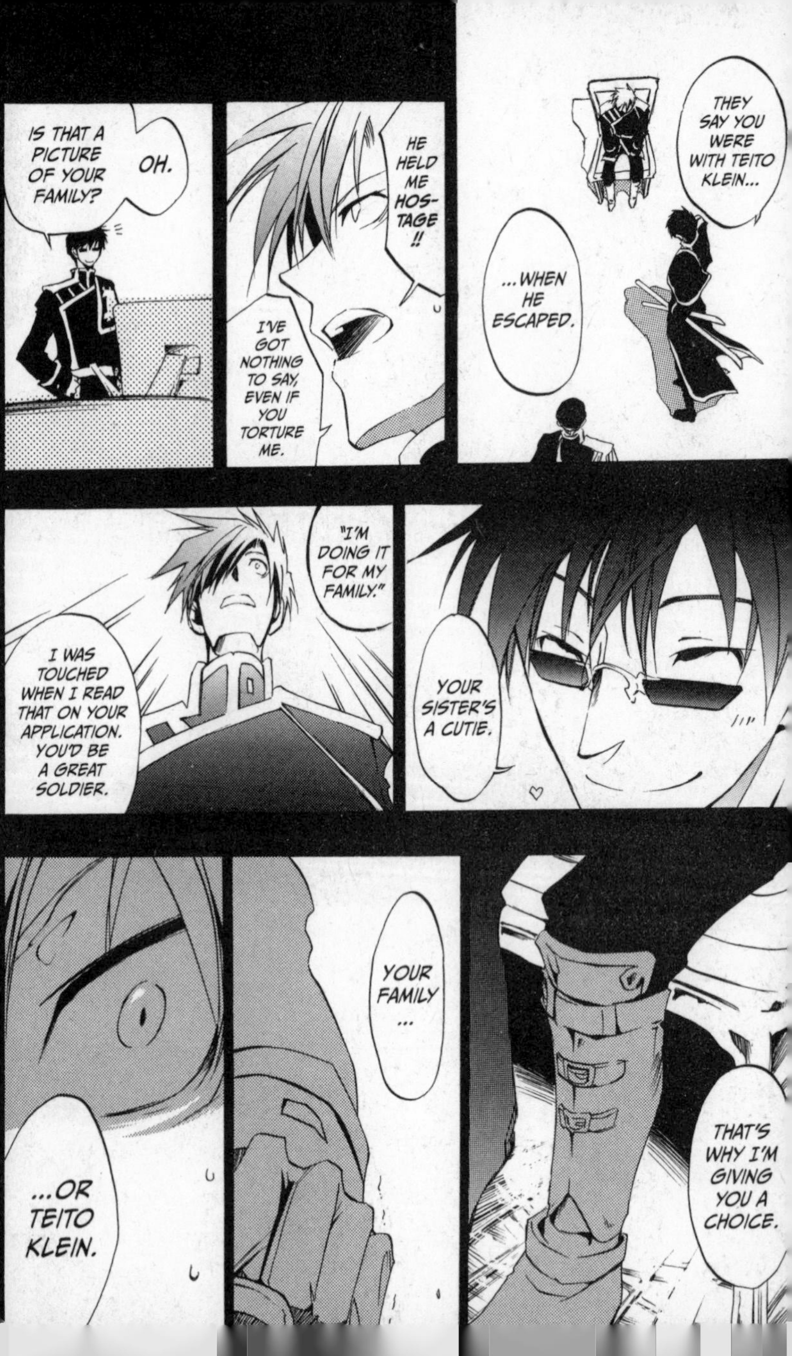
THEY SAY YOU WERE WITH TEITO KLEIN...
...WHEN HE ESCAPED.
HE HELD ME HOSTAGE!!
I'VE GOT NOTHING TO SAY, EVEN IF YOU TORTURE ME.
OH.
IS THAT A PICTURE OF YOUR FAMILY?
YOUR SISTER'S A CUTIE.
"I'M DOING IT FOR MY FAMILY."
I WAS TOUCHED WHEN I READ THAT ON YOUR APPLICATION. YOU'D BE A GREAT SOLDIER.
THAT'S WHY I'M GIVING YOU A CHOICE.
YOUR FAMILY ...
...OR TEITO KLEIN.

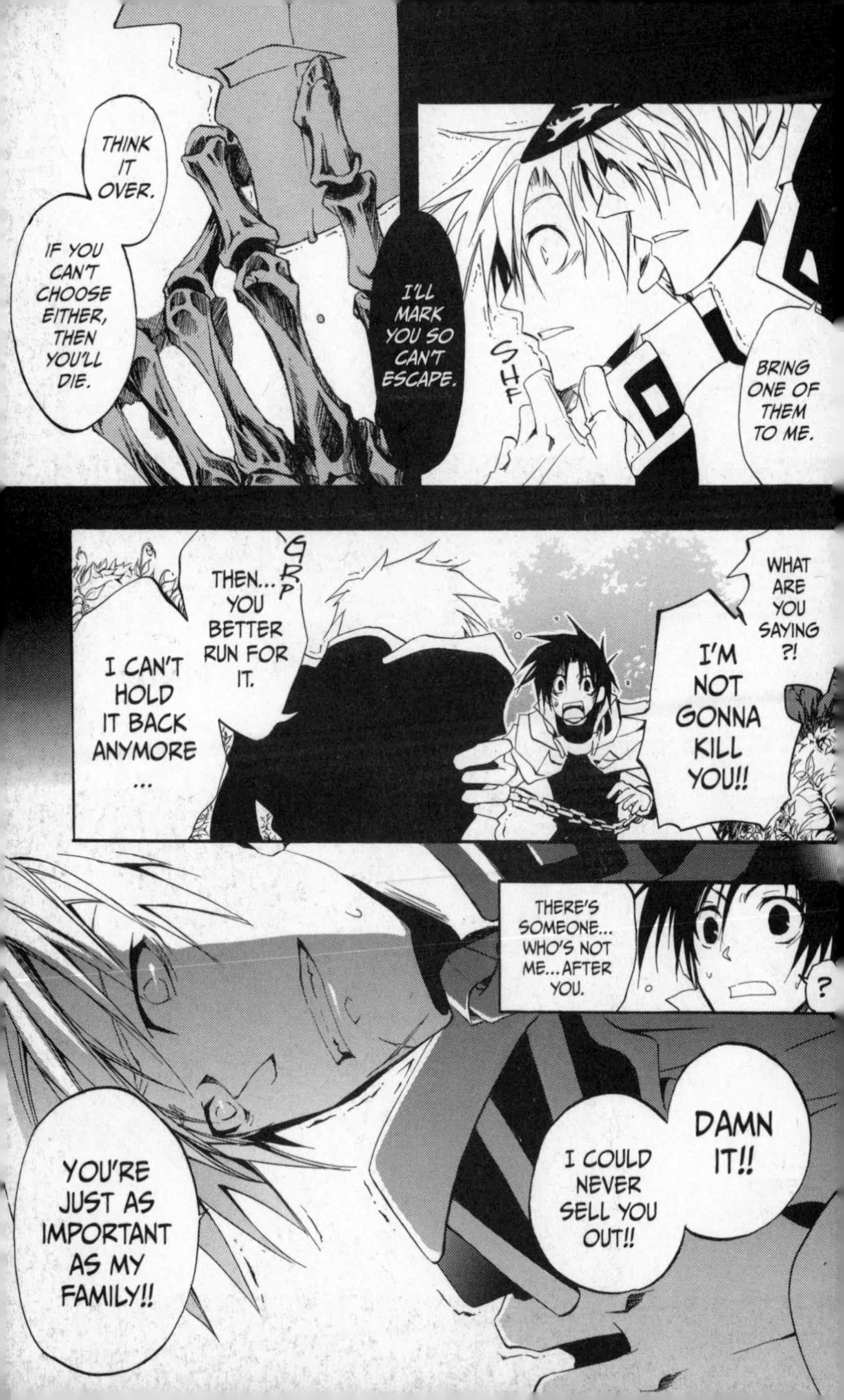
BRING ONE OF THEM TO ME.
SHF
I'LL MARK YOU SO CAN'T ESCAPE.
THINK IT OVER.
IF YOU CAN'T CHOOSE EITHER, THEN YOU'LL DIE.
WHAT ARE YOU SAYING?!
I'M NOT GONNA KILL YOU!!
THEN... YOU BETTER RUN FOR IT.
GRP
I CAN'T HOLD IT BACK ANYMORE ...
?
THERE'S SOMEONE... WHO'S NOT ME... AFTER YOU.
DAMN IT!!
I COULD NEVER SELL YOU OUT!!
YOU'RE JUST AS IMPORTANT AS MY FAMILY!!

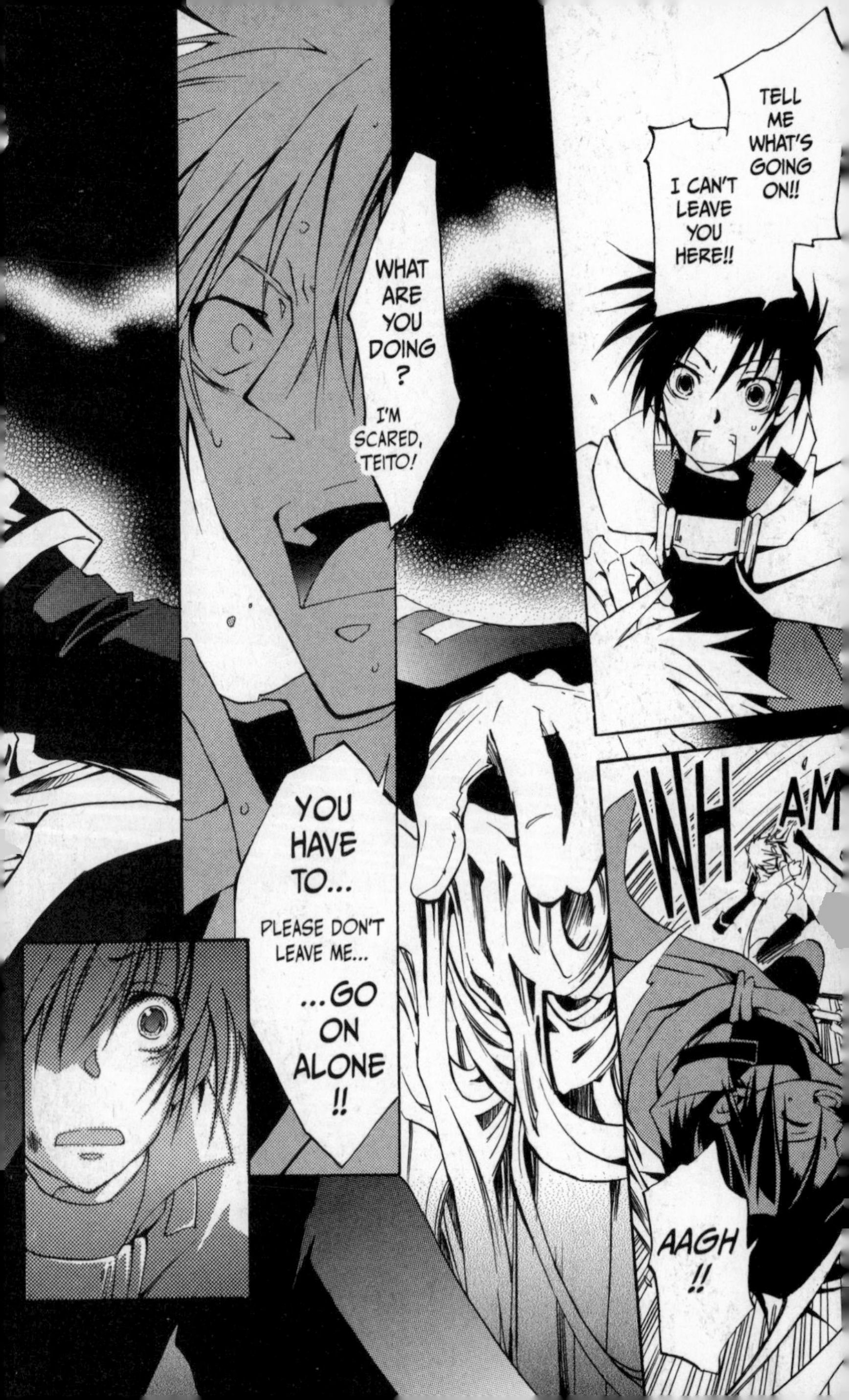
TELL ME WHAT'S GOING ON!!
I CAN'T LEAVE YOU HERE!!
WHAM
AAGH!!
WHAT ARE YOU DOING?
I'M SCARED, TEITO!
YOU HAVE TO...
PLEASE DON'T LEAVE ME...
...GO ON ALONE!!

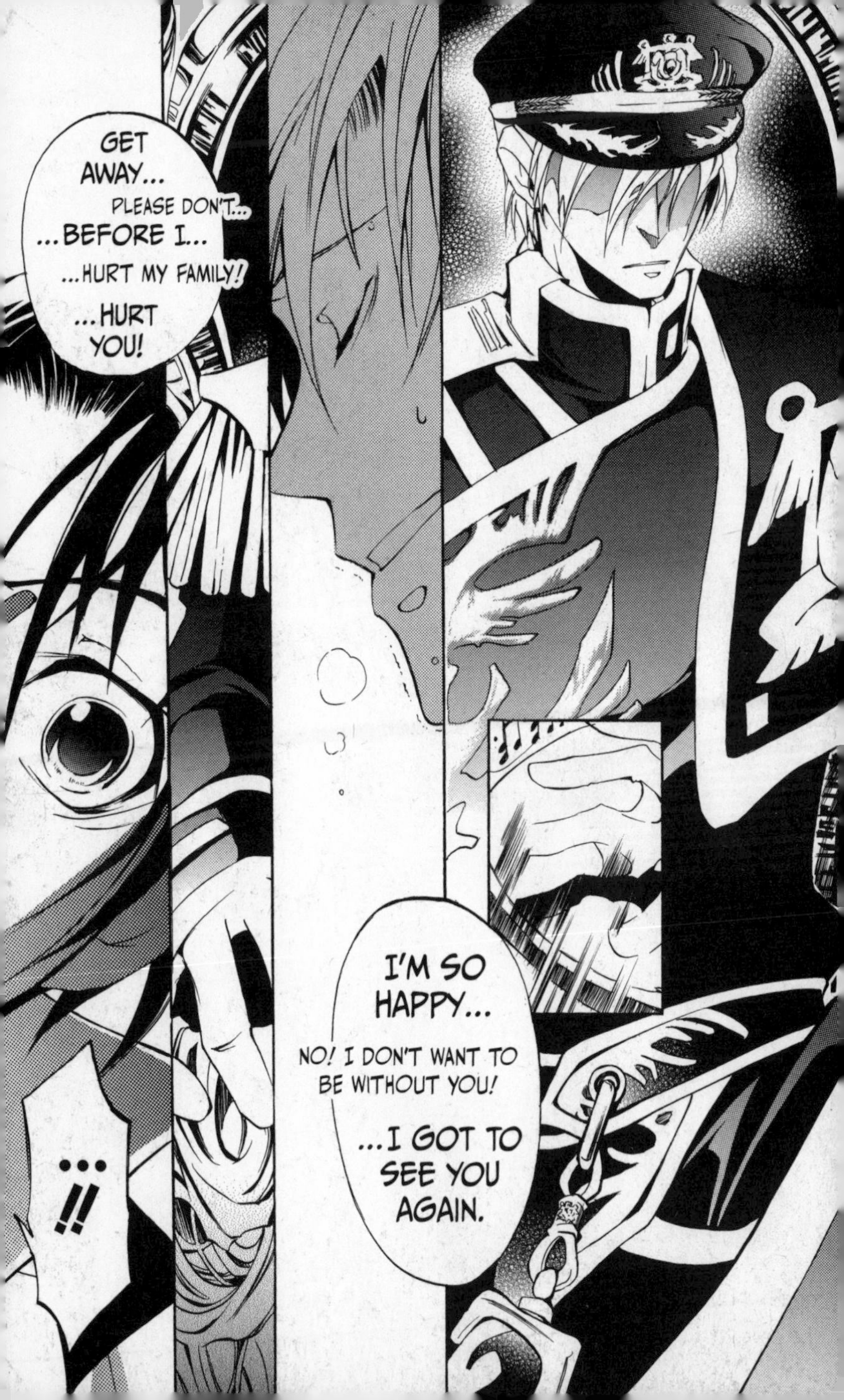
I'M SO HAPPY...
NO! I DON'T WANT TO BE WITHOUT YOU!
...I GOT TO SEE YOU AGAIN.
GET AWAY...
PLEASE DON'T...
...BEFORE I...
...HURT MY FAMILY!
...HURT YOU!
...!!

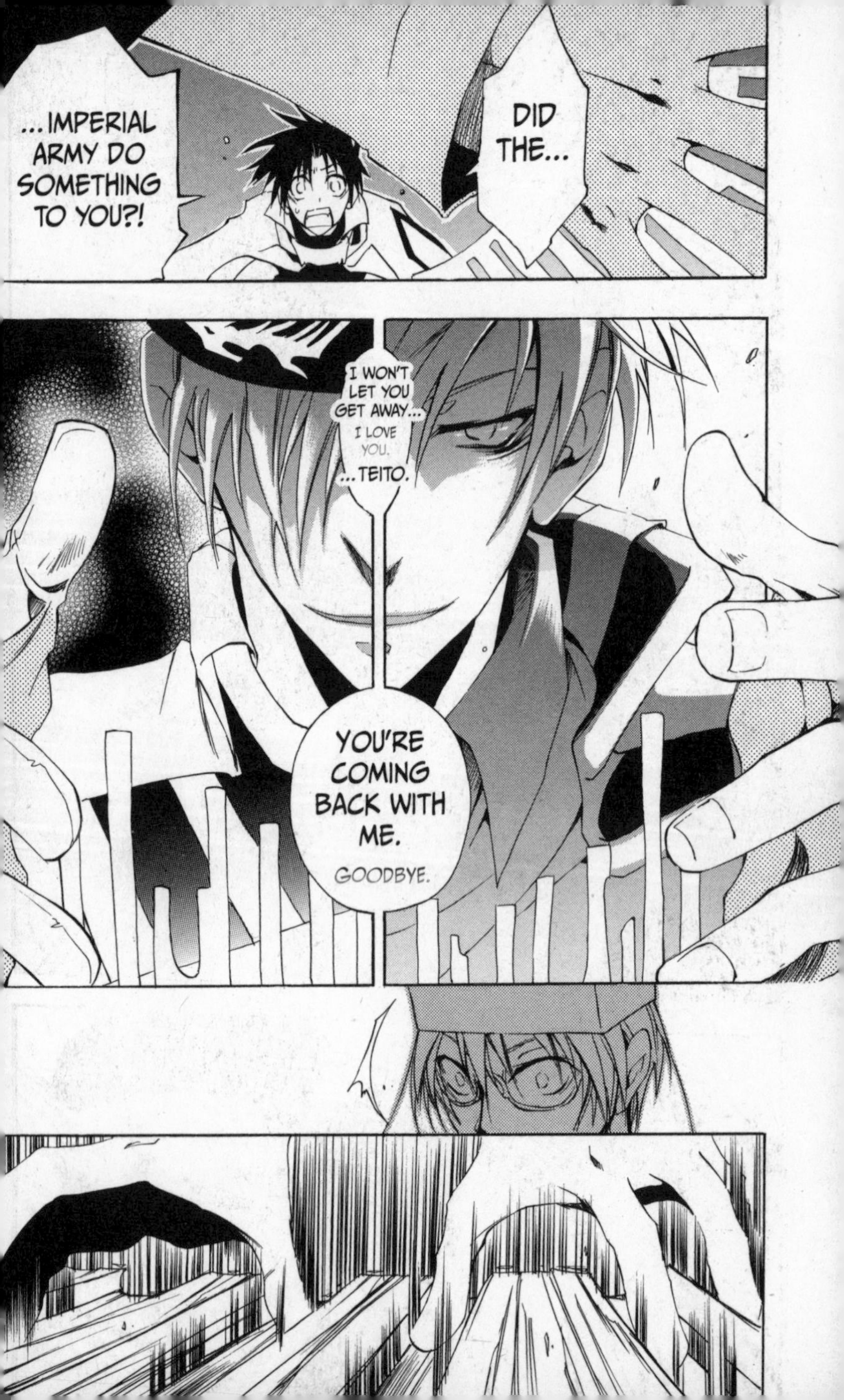
DID THE...
...IMPERIAL ARMY DO SOMETHING TO YOU?!
I WON'T LET YOU GET AWAY... I LOVE YOU. ...TEITO.
YOU'RE COMING BACK WITH ME.
GOODBYE.

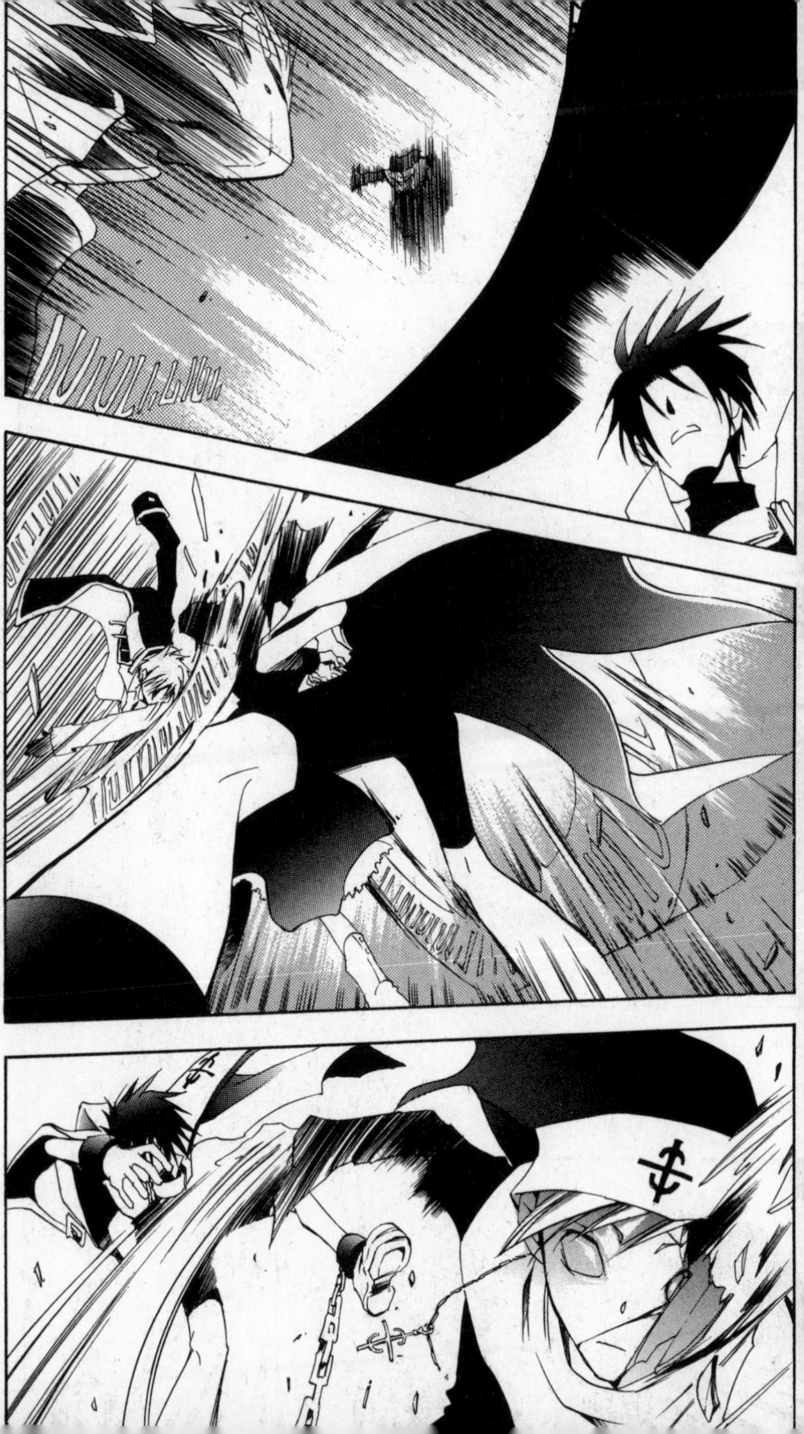

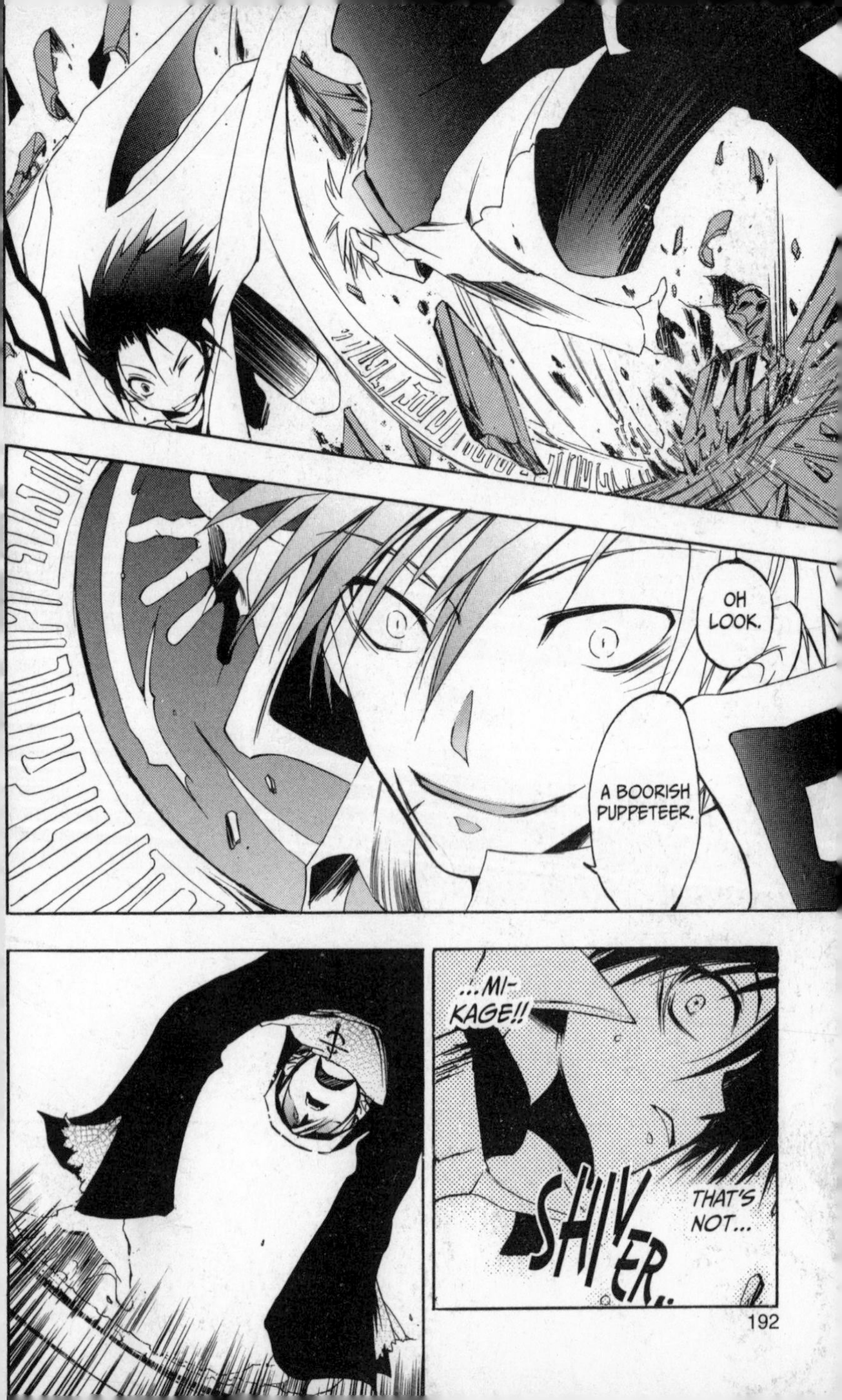
OH LOOK.
A BOORISH PUPPETEER.
...MI-KAGE!!
THAT'S NOT...
SHIVER..

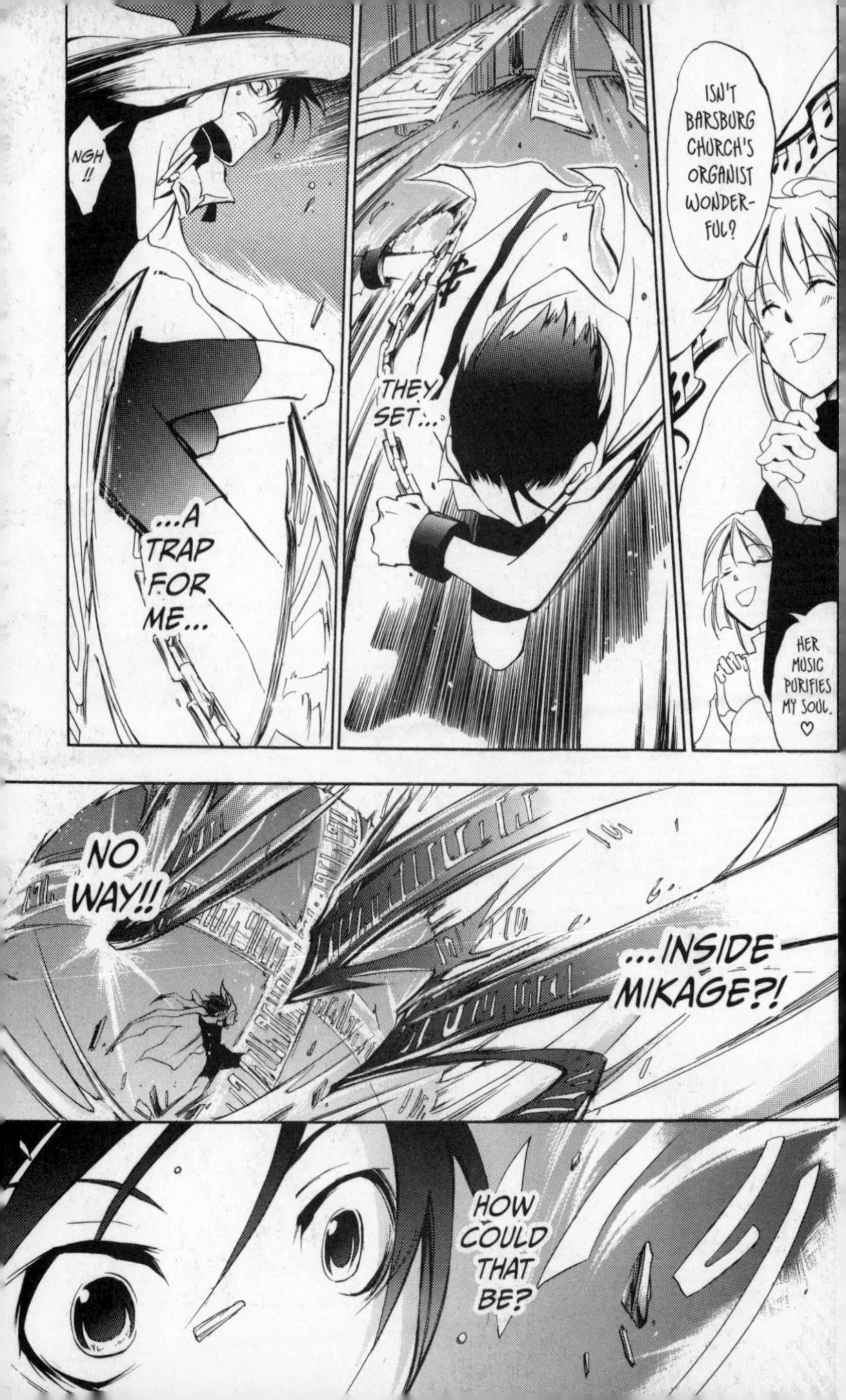
ISN'T BARSBURG CHURCH'S ORGANIST WONDERFUL?
HER MUSIC PURIFIES MY SOUL. ♡
THEY SET...
NGH!!
...A TRAP FOR ME...
NO WAY!!
...INSIDE MIKAGE?!
HOW COULD THAT BE?

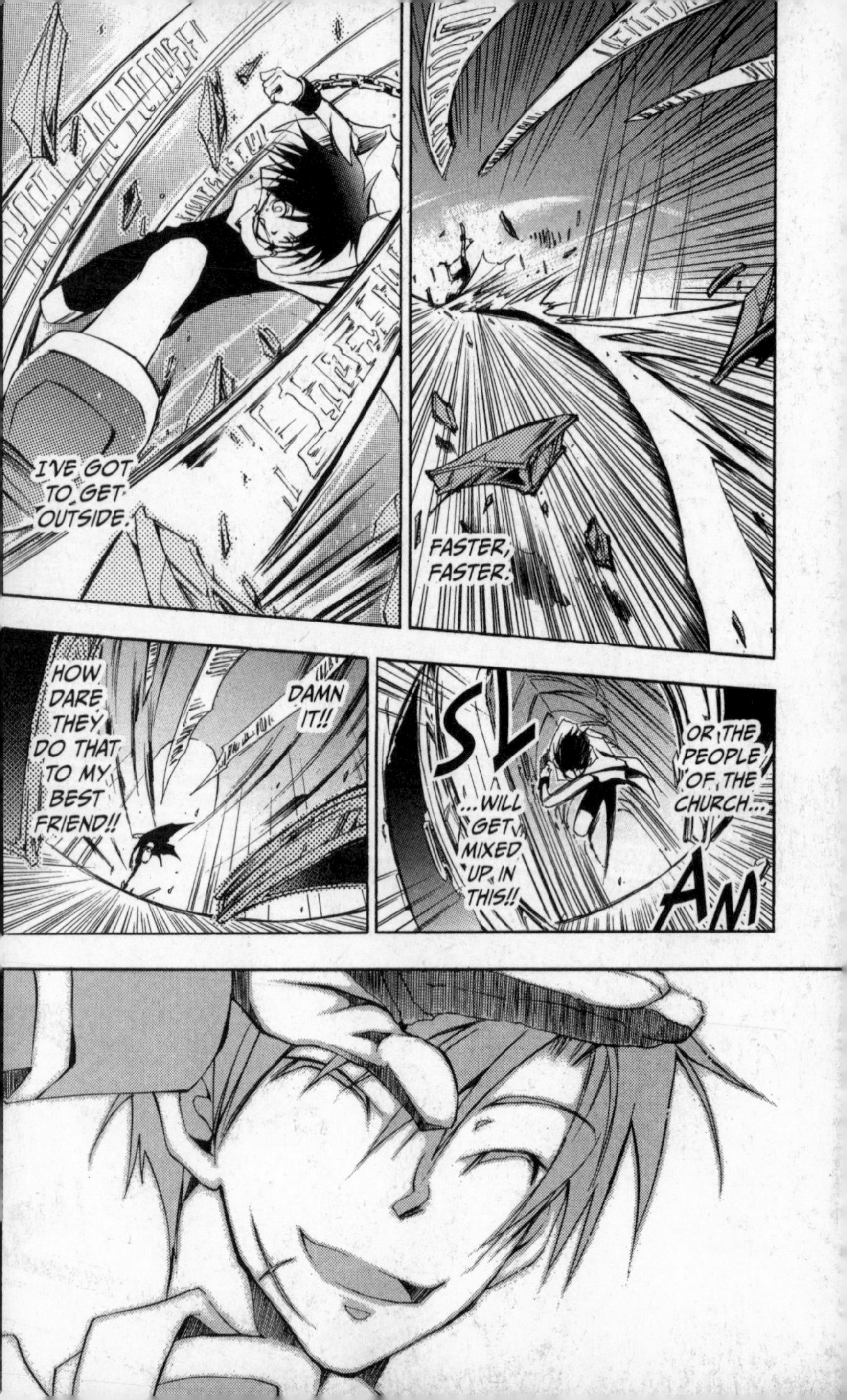
FASTER, FASTER.
I'VE GOT TO GET OUTSIDE.
OR THE PEOPLE OF THE CHURCH...
...WILL GET MIXED UP IN THIS!!
SLAM
DAMN IT!!
HOW DARE THEY DO THAT TO MY BEST FRIEND!!

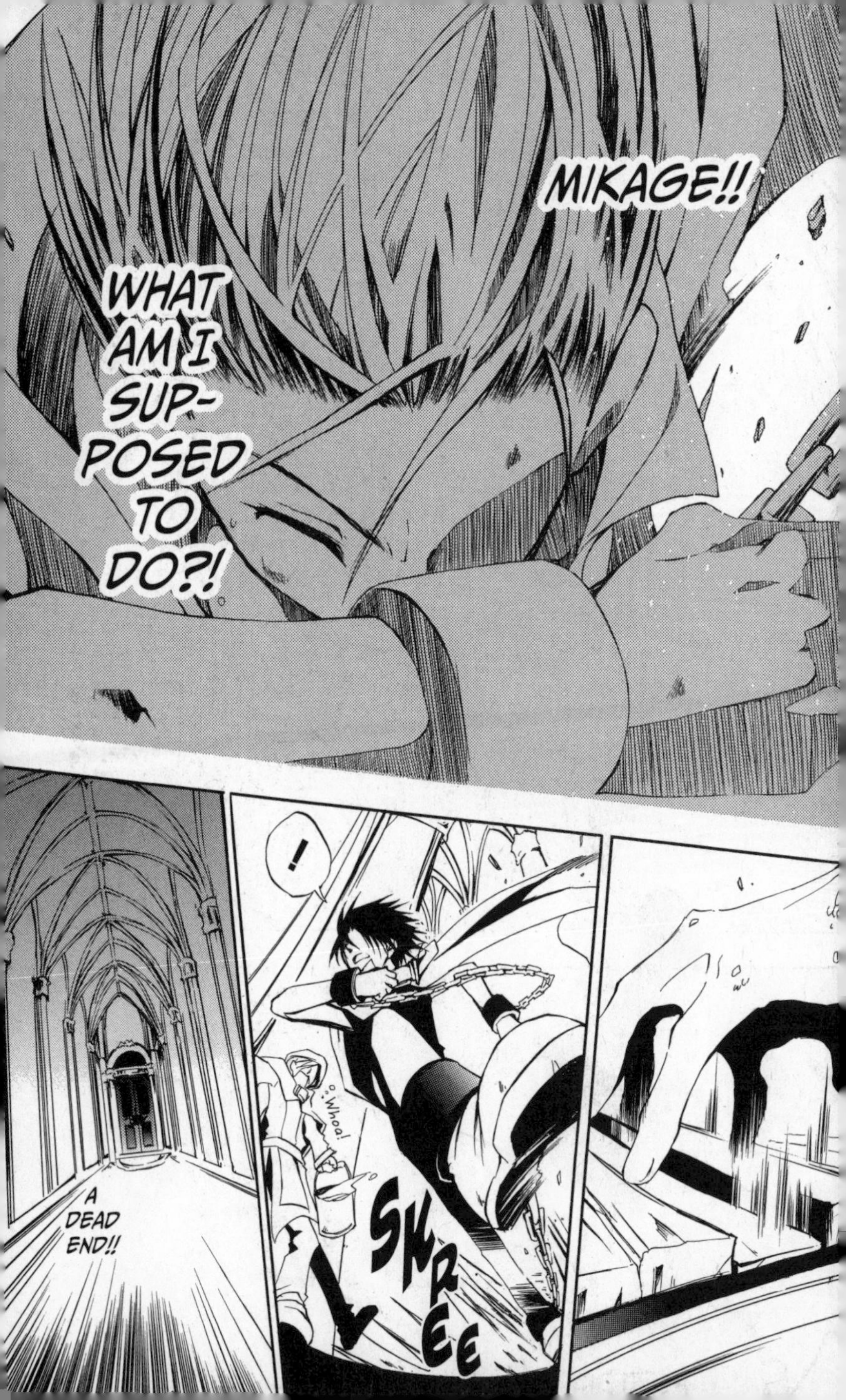
MIKAGE!!
WHAT AM I SUP-POSED TO DO?!
!
...Whoa!
SKREE
A DEAD END!!

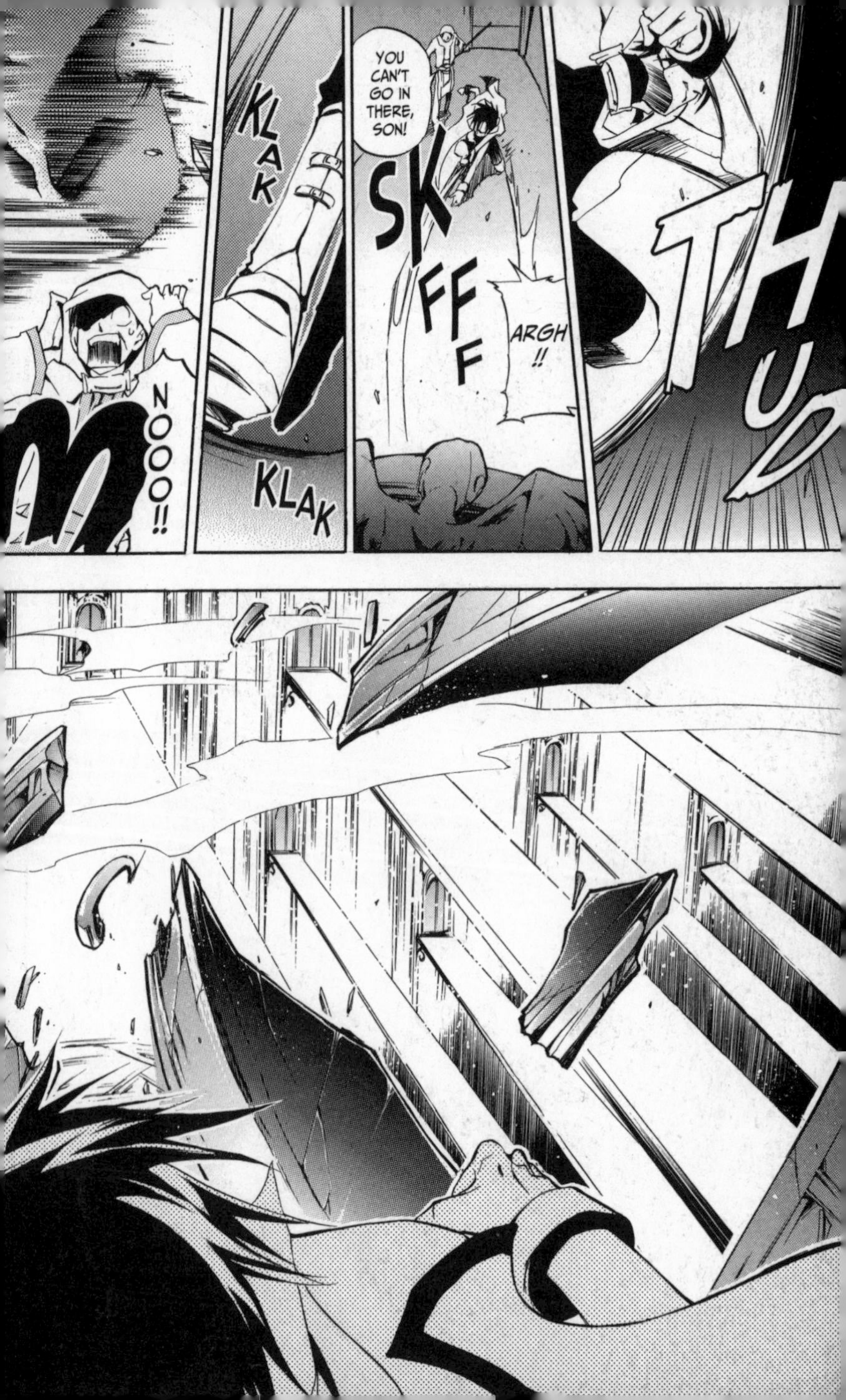
THUD
YOU CAN'T GO IN THERE, SON!
SKFFF
ARGH!!
KLAK
KLAK
NOOOO!!

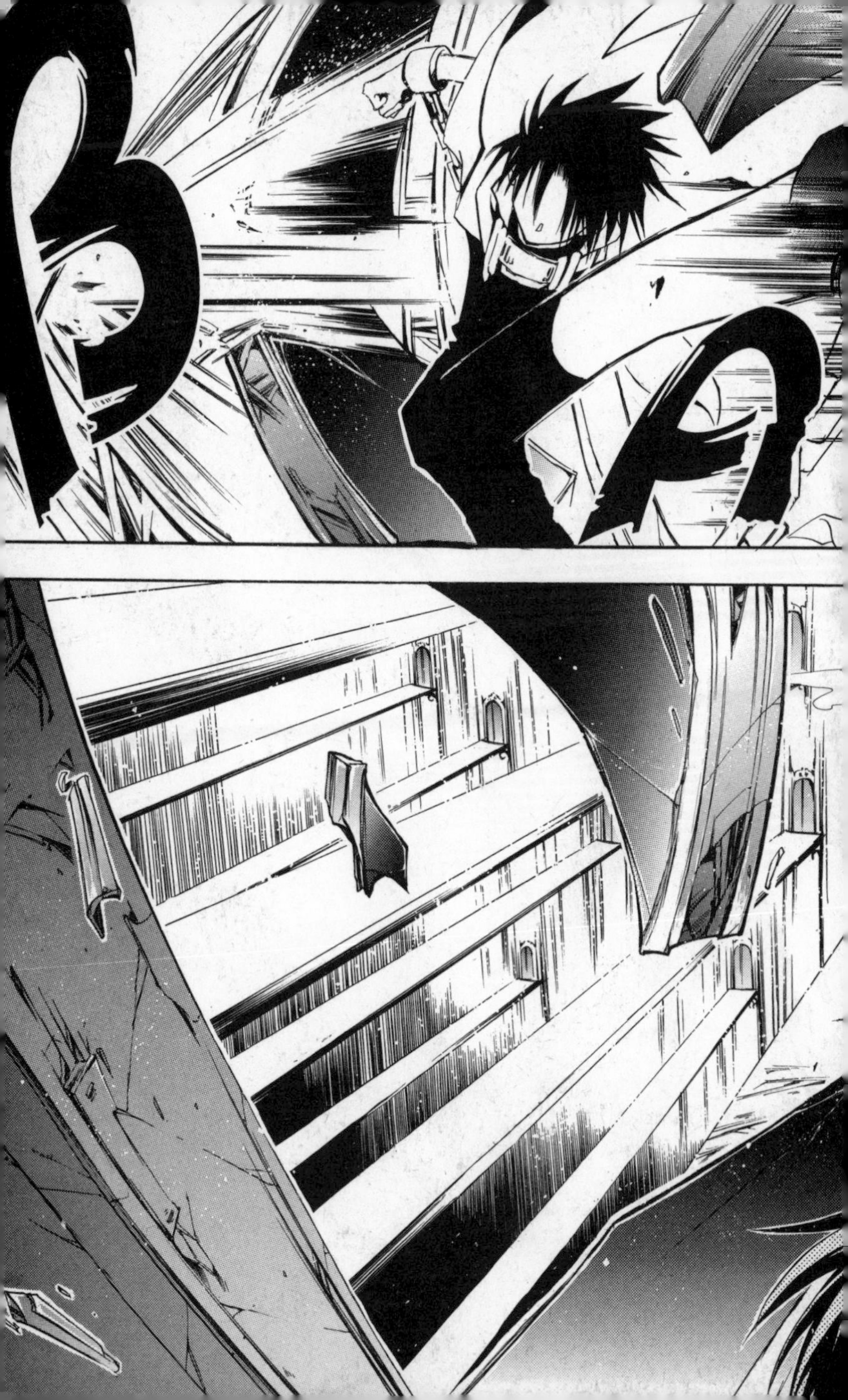

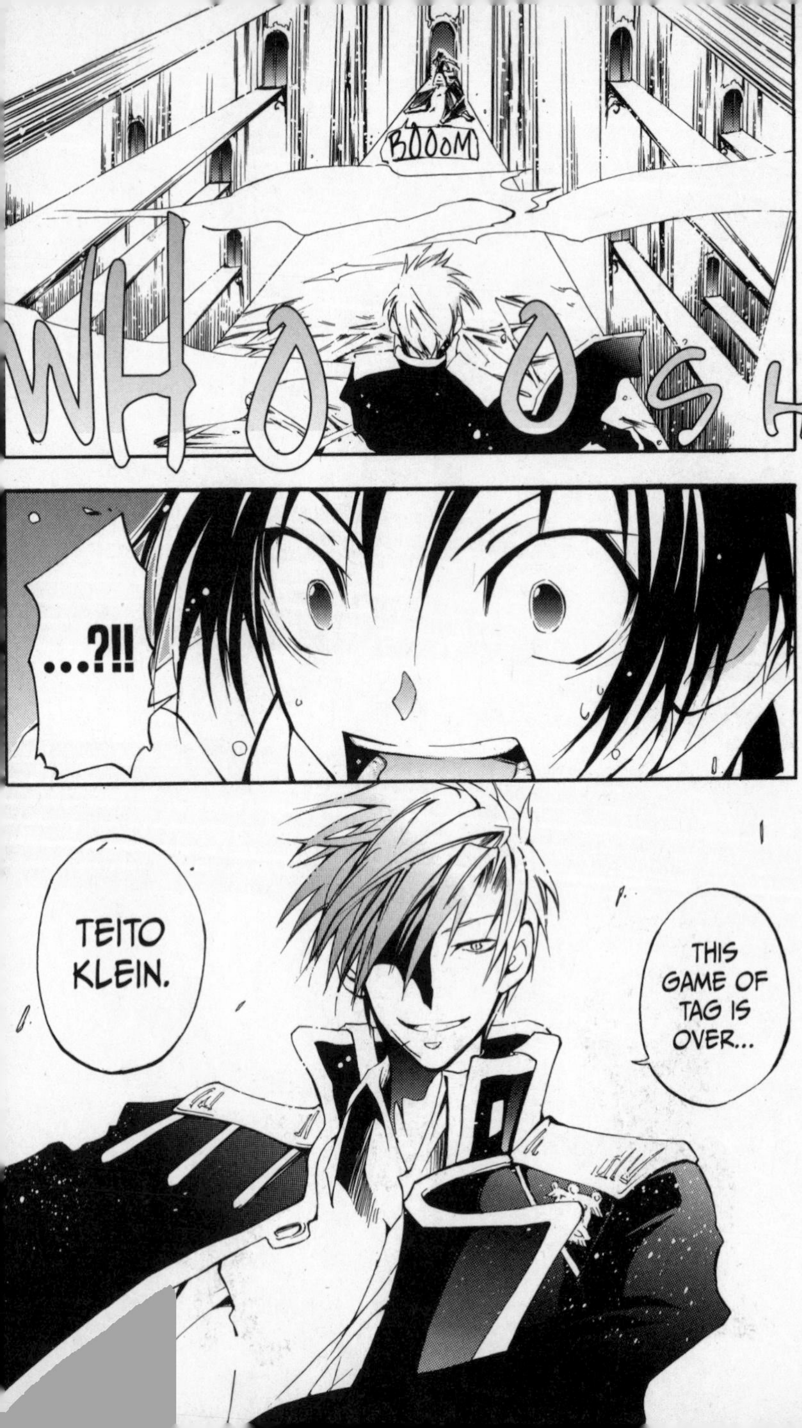
BOOOM
WHOOSH
...?!!
THIS GAME OF TAG IS OVER...
TEITO KLEIN.

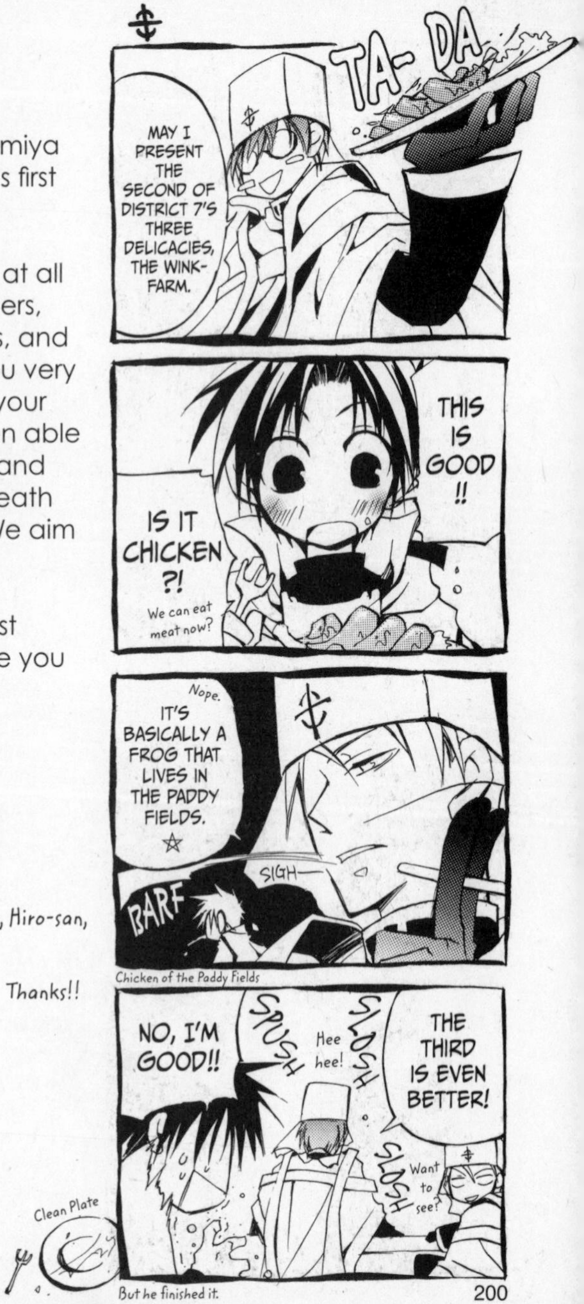
TA-DA
MAY I PRESENT THE SECOND OF DISTRICT 7'S THREE DELICACIES, THE WINK-FARM.
THIS IS GOOD!!
IS IT CHICKEN?!
We can eat meat now?
Nope.
IT'S BASICALLY A FROG THAT LIVES IN THE PADDY FIELDS. ☆
SIGH
BARF
Chicken of the Paddy Fields
THE THIRD IS EVEN BETTER!
SLOSH
Hee hee!
SPUSH
NO, I'M GOOD!!
SLOSH
Want to see?
Clean Plate
But he finished it.

07-Ghost is Yuki Amemiya and Yukino Ichihara's first book.

The fact that it exists at all is thanks to you readers, our awesome friends, and the editors. Thank you very much! It's thanks to your help that we've been able to draw this manga and survive some near-death experiences (*sob*). We aim to keep improving.

Teito's journey has just begun, and we hope you follow it till the end!

Special Thanks ♥

AD, Zenko, A-bou, Ranmaru, Hiro-san, Kiyo, Ouchi.

And our families. ♥ Thanks!!

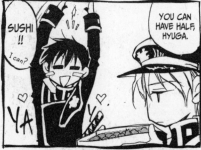

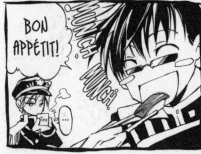

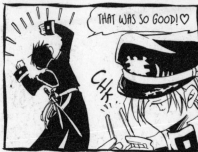

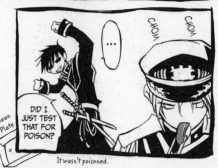

Afterword

YOU CAN HAVE HALF, HYUGA.
SUSHI !!
I can?
YA
Y
MUNCH
MUNCH
BON APPÉTIT!
Tea
...
THAT WAS SO GOOD! ♡
CHK
CHOM
CHOM
...
DID I JUST TEST THAT FOR POISON?
Clean Plate
It wasn't poisoned.

Thank you so much ♥♥ October 2005

Amemiya Ichihara

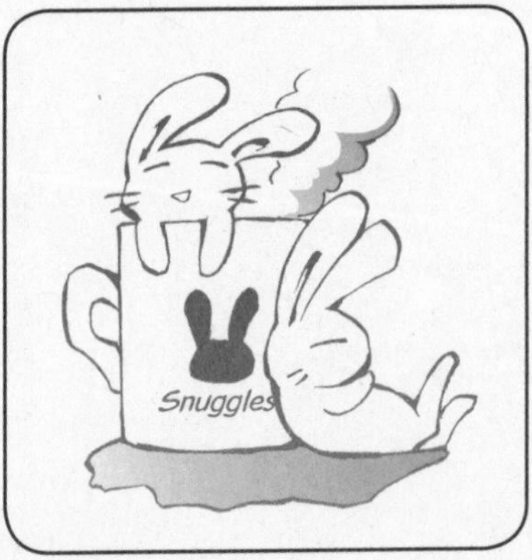
Snuggles

Hi, nice to meet you! This is our first published book. Ever. It's such an awesome experience that we can barely keep from fainting. More people than we can count have helped us along the way... (*cries*). Thank you so, so much. We hope you enjoyed the book.

—Yuki Amemiya & Yukino Ichihara, 2005

Yuki Amemiya was born in Miyagi, Japan, on March 25. Yukino Ichihara was born in Fukushima, Japan, on November 24. Together they write and illustrate *07-Ghost*, the duo's first series. Since its debut in 2005, *07-Ghost* has been translated into a dozen languages, and in 2009 it was adapted into a TV anime series.

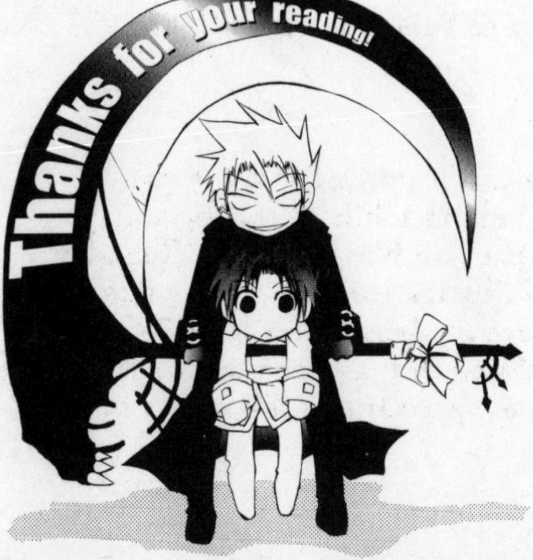
Thanks for your reading!

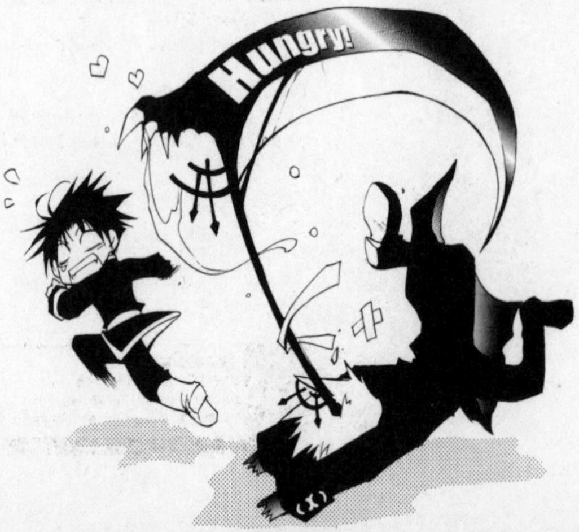
Hungry!

07-GHOST

Volume 1

STORY AND ART BY
**YUKI AMEMIYA and
YUKINO ICHIHARA**

Translation/Satsuki Yamashita
Touch-up Art & Lettering/Vanessa Satone
Design/Yukiko Whitley
Editor/Hope Donovan

07-GHOST © 2005
by Yuki Amemiya/Yukino Ichihara
All rights reserved.
Original Japanese edition published by
ICHIJINSHA, INC., Tokyo.
English translation rights arranged with
ICHIJINSHA, INC.

The stories, characters and incidents
mentioned in this publication are entirely
fictional.

No portion of this book may be reproduced
or transmitted in any form or by any
means without written permission from the
copyright holders.

Printed in Canada

Published by VIZ Media, LLC
P.O. Box 77010
San Francisco, CA 94107

10 9 8 7 6 5 4 3 2
First printing, November 2012
Second printing, March 2015

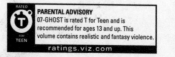

PARENTAL ADVISORY
07-GHOST is rated T for Teen and is
recommended for ages 13 and up. This
volume contains realistic and fantasy violence.
ratings.viz.com

www.viz.com

Seraph of the End

— VAMPIRE REIGN —

STORY BY **Takaya Kagami** ART BY **Yamato Yamamoto**

STORYBOARDS BY **Daisuke Furuya**

Vampires reign— humans revolt!

Yuichiro's dream of killing every vampire is near-impossible, given that vampires are seven times stronger than humans, and the only way to kill them is by mastering Cursed Gear, advanced demon-possessed weaponry. Not to mention that humanity's most elite Vampire Extermination Unit, the Moon Demon Company, wants nothing to do with Yuichiro unless he can prove he's willing to work in a team—which is the last thing he wants!

THE LATEST CHAPTERS SERIALIZED IN WEEKLY SHONEN JUMP

www.shonenjump.com   www.viz.com

OWARI NO SERAPH © 2012 by Takaya Kagami, Yamato Yamamoto, Daisuke Furuya /SHUEISHA Inc.

BLUE EXORCIST

STORY AND ART BY
KAZUE KATO

⬡ THE ORIGINAL MANGA BEHIND THE HIT ANIME! ⬡

Raised by Father Fujimoto, a famous exorcist, Rin Okumura never knew his real father. One day a fateful argument with Father Fujimoto forces Rin to face a terrible truth — the blood of the demon lord Satan runs in Rin's veins! Rin swears to defeat Satan, but doing that means entering the mysterious True Cross Academy and becoming an exorcist himself.

Available wherever manga is sold.

VIZ media
www.viz.com

SHONEN JUMP
ADVANCED
www.shonenjump.com

RATED
T+
FOR OLDER TEEN
ratings.viz.com

AO NO EXORCIST © 2009 by Kazue Kato/SHUEISHA Inc.

Hey! You're Reading in the Wrong Direction!

This is the end of this graphic novel!

To properly enjoy this VIZ graphic novel, please turn it around and begin reading from right to left. Unlike English, Japanese is read right to left, so Japanese comics are read in reverse order from the way English comics are typically read.

This book has been printed in the original Japanese format in order to preserve the orientation of the original artwork. Have fun with it!

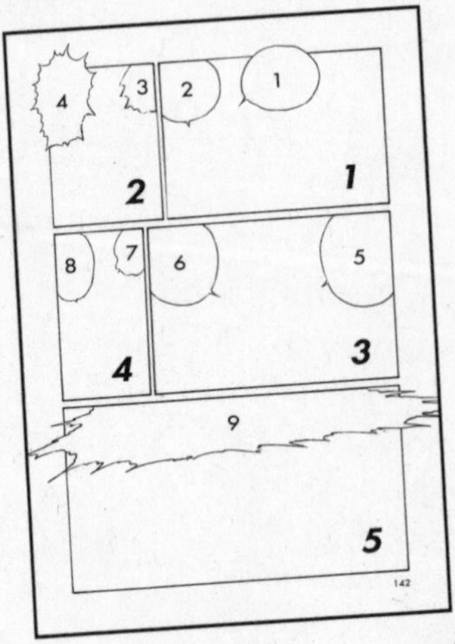

1
2
1
3
4
2
5
6
3
7
8
4
9
5
142

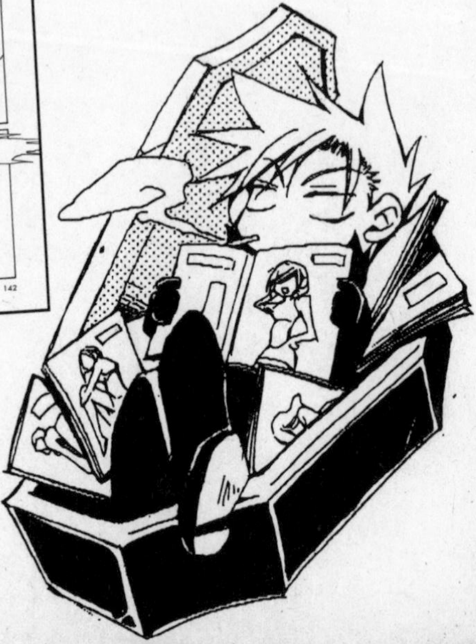